HOMELESSNESS AMONG OLDER ADULTS IN PRAGUE

CAUSES, CONTEXTS AND PROSPECTS

MARIE VÁGNEROVÁ
JAKUB MAREK
LADISLAV CSÉMY

CHARLES UNIVERSITY
KAROLINUM PRESS 2020

Peer-reviewed by:
doc. Mgr. Pavlína Janošová, Ph.D.
doc. PaedDr. Eva Šotolová, Ph.D.

Originally published in Czech under the title
Bezdomovectví ve středním věku. Příčiny, souvislosti a perspektivy
by Karolinum Press in 2018.

This text was supported by a grant from the Czech Science Foundation
GAČR P407/16/11776S: A psychosocial analysis of middle-aged homeless people
in Prague and an evaluation of the possibility of their resocialisation.

Cataloguing-in-Publication Data is available from the National Library
of the Czech Republic

ISBN 978-80-246-4525-4
ISBN 978-80-246-4526-1 (pdf)

CONTENTS

FOREWORD

The object of our research was to ascertain the circumstances that led older people, especially those in middle age, to find themselves on the street. We also wanted to find out why some of them remained there for so long. The situation of middle-aged people is different to that of young people, the subject of our previous study. Middle-aged people grew up under the communist regime, in which an obligation to work was enshrined in law and anyone living on the street could be sent to prison. Many of them gained professional qualifications and found work. And yet, as time passed, they found themselves down and out, often due to the lack of a stable family environment, inadequate socialisation, and/or an ability to comply with rules. We were interested in how long these people had been living on the street, why they had become chronically home-less, and in which phase of their downward trajectory it would still be possible to mount an effective intervention. Generally speaking, young people have not spent as long on the street and therefore have a better chance of returning to society. This is not so in the case of middle-aged people, because over time they have lost the necessary habits and become accustomed to street life. They would therefore find any fundamental change of lifestyle far more demanding. A problem that afflicts both age categories is an addiction to psychoactive substances (substance use disorder). Middle-aged people tend to be addicted to alcohol, younger people to drugs. Similar findings have been reached in other countries. We also examined how effective the assistance provided by state and non-profit organisations is. The aim was to discover how the service users themselves rated it, to what extent they availed themselves of it, and whether they believed it had helped them.

We also followed up on our research into young people by monitoring developments in their lives subsequent to our study. We wanted to discover whether the people we had interviewed were still living on the street or whether they had managed to escape, i.e. whether and how they had coped with such a fundamental change of lifestyle. It would appear that an important element of any return to mainstream society is having close relationships with people who are not homeless and can assist in the process of resocialisation. Older homeless people do not have such relationships because they have been living rough for far longer. Another point of crucial importance was that younger people had not yet found themselves lumbered with such levels of debt that the sheer amounts involved and the threat of execution proceedings rendered any return to society and employment impossible. Another significant barrier to resocialisation is a criminal past, which can contribute both to a person finding themselves homeless and remaining so. This was more frequent in our older cohort.

People in both age groups had experienced big problems coping with the demands of adulthood and had been unable to accept responsibility for their own lives. Their unresolved problems escalated over time and led to further social disaffiliation and chronic homelessness. Our analysis of this process may lead to the creation of a more effective system of support and assistance that could prevent such a downward spiral.

The authors

I. INTRODUCTION

1. SPECIFICATION OF THE PROBLEM

To be homeless is to lack any kind of private space, with its formal and emotional demarcations, i.e. to lack a concept of "home". Being homeless also tends to involve a lack of stable relationships and the safety and security that a home provides. A person's home forms a stable environment. It is a central feature of the life of every individual. It can both define them and be defined by them, and offers a sense of rootedness and belonging. (The need for a home is evident in the way that many homeless people construct their lean-tos so that they resemble houses.) A permanent place of abode serves as the physical foundation of a home, offering a person the privacy that permits them to create more stable social bonds. The loss of a home leads to reduced feelings of security and safety (Mallett et al., 2010; Nemiroff, 2010; Ravenhill, 2014).

Homelessness is one manifestation of **extreme social exclusion**. It reduces a person's sense of security and the material resources available to them. The loss of a home and the breakdown of stable social bonds is associated with more general feelings of disorientation and a lack of belonging to a particular social group and society at large. This space is then filled by the homeless community (Mallett et al., 2010). Homelessness is a manifestation of dysfunctional behaviour and problem solving, as well as **complex social failure syndrome**, i.e. an unwillingness or inability to respect societal norms and act accordingly. Opting for a life on the street liberates a person from the pressure to meet all the demands placed on them by society, while at the same time depriving them of the protection that social inclusion provides (Vágnerová, Csémy, Marek, 2012, 2013). Homeless people do not normally suffer mental illness as such, though their social failure indicates that they are not completely psychologically balanced. At the very least, the executive functions[1] on which the regulation of all conduct depends are subnormal. Whatever the proximate cause, such people are unable to exploit fully their potential, deal with ordinary life situations and the stresses arising therefrom, and occupy different social roles (often as a consequence of substance use disorder) (Mohr, 2016).

---

1 Executive functions are a set of cognitive processes that are necessary for the cognitive control of behaviour.

The concept of homelessness includes many variants of a non-standard existence that is unstable and can change depending on circumstances. The European Typology on Homelessness and Housing Exclusion (ETHOS) takes due consideration of the variability of circumstances such people find themselves in: being homeless is not a life sentence, though by the same token a return to society is not necessarily permanent (Hradecký, 2015). **Homelessness must be viewed more as a process** than a fixed state. It is a reaction to unmanageable problems and represents a last-ditch attempt to resolve them. There are many paths to homelessness and they possess a multidimensional character, i.e. there is always a combination of different factors in operation. People find themselves without a roof over their head for many different reasons. As a consequence, their subjective experience may differ, along with their willingness to strive to change their lives.

In terms of the way that people on the street choose to survive, **two basic forms of homelessness** can be distinguished (Hradecký, 2015):

- **Manifest homelessness** refers to people sleeping rough in public places, e.g. beneath bridges or in drainage canals, railway carriages or illegally occupied buildings (squats). There are fewer people living in full view on the street or in places that are not intended for human abode than there are hidden homeless people.
- **Hidden homelessness** refers to people without accommodation living in dormitories or shelters and/or crashing with friends and relatives. (Low-threshold reception centres or the Hermes vessel [originally a cargo vessel converted into a reception centre and moored on the River Vltava in Prague] do not offer 24-hour accommodation or any personal space, and therefore fall into the first category.) Hidden homelessness can be a transitional phase in the movement from street to society or vice versa.

We can further differentiate between short-term homelessness, which might involve merely a temporary episode lasting months, and chronic homelessness lasting years. The latter has more serious consequences and involves more significant changes to habits, ways of thinking and conduct, and even to an individual's entire personality. Short-term homelessness is deemed sleeping rough for a period of up to one year (Johnson and Chamberlain, 2008). According to the social adaptation hypothesis, the longer a person lives on the street, the more they adapt to this lifestyle. They strike up relationships with other homeless people and begin to adopt their patterns of behaviour. As a consequence, a return to mainstream society becomes more and more difficult. Homelessness can trigger devastating life changes often including alcohol and drug abuse and **gradual desocialisation and/or nonstandard resocialisation** within the homeless community. This decoupling from former values, norms and customs is intensified by the social stigmatisation of homeless people and their rejection by mainstream society. Changes in personality amongst the homeless then continue (Marek, Strnad and Hotovcová, 2012; Vágnerová, Csémy, Marek, 2013; Ravenhill, 2014).

Older homeless people differ from their younger counterparts both in respect of the reasons they find themselves on the street and the period of time they remain there. Middle-aged people may also possess a wider range of experiences than those on offer on the street. Many of them had previously lived a normal lifestyle. They had a family, with all the stability that implies, and a job, by means of which they were able to support themselves and which helped determine their social status and identity. For various reasons they then lost all of this. **Their descent into homelessness is accompanied by a sense of loss** that is not balanced by any significant gain (leaving aside the relative freedom and lack of obligation). People who have lived on the street from their youth and have no other experience to draw on find it easier to adapt to their social exclusion and unusual lifestyle. They did not lose a relationship or career, because they had none to begin with. A separate category comprises people who brought an alcohol or drug addiction with them onto the street. A person may find themselves in such a downward spiral at any time in life.

The **age composition of Czech homeless people is changing**. This is because thirty years ago (i.e. before the Velvet Revolution in 1989 that brought down the communist regime) nobody slept rough. Homelessness is a phenomenon that only appeared later. Over the last twenty-five years the numbers have been rising. Some people have been living on the street for several years, whereas others, especially young people, are only just arriving. (According to the employees of Naděje, an organisation working with people in need, the numbers of young homeless are rising, and this is confirmed by people who work with drug addicts.) It is therefore difficult to compare the research outputs of foreign studies with our own. Foreign studies are based on completely different assumptions, though they also occasionally note a rise in the number of homeless people in their country. This was the conclusion, for instance, of the American study by Culhane et al. (2013), which found that the age at which people were at risk of homelessness was rising. In 2010 the group most at risk in the USA was aged 49 to 51. In the Czech Republic the increase in the number of older people sleeping rough is more the result of long-term homelessness.

If we stand back and look at homelessness within a broader context, we find it is influenced by a **range of factors that can be both its cause and the reason it becomes chronic**. The greater the number of risk factors in an individual's life, the higher the likelihood that they will end up on the street or follow another downward trajectory and, for instance, end up in prison. An individual's experience of childhood can contribute to this increase in risk factors. The relationships between individual members and the overall functioning of the family unit are important factors, and can be either stressors or sources of support (Ravenhill, 2014). Their experience of childhood will affect the entire trajectory of an individual's life and will impact on the level of education and professional qualifications acquired and their lifestyle choices, including criminal activity and alcohol or drug abuse (Mabhala et al., 2016). The family serves as a nurturing environment, while its members function as models of the behaviour of adult people. If the family is in some way dysfunctional, this can in turn lead to other problems. Coping with adulthood requires the acceptance of responsibility and the restrictions ensuing therefrom, whether this involve a career or a relationship. In both these spheres the conditions for success are already formed during childhood and adolescence, and many current homeless people lack the necessary positive experience.

A person finds themselves sleeping rough usually as a consequence of the accumulation of multiple risk factors (an atypical childhood, lack of education, problems finding work, and a tendency to escape into undesirable activities such as alcohol abuse or criminality). However, a certain trajectory in life, including homelessness, can be triggered by **personality traits** that can be genetic in origin or related to poor upbringing (Robert et al., 2005; Kidd and Shahar, 2008). Social skills are also important (Holton, 2011). Bassuk et al. (1997) confirmed that disadvantageous personality traits can increase the risk of homelessness, and the same conclusion was reached by Wong and Pilliavin (1997, 2001). Fertig and Reingold (2008) point out that, while the influence of social factors is significant, personality is more important because it determines how an individual will deal with pressure. However, there is no cast-iron personality profile of a homeless person, and many different kinds of people can find themselves on the street.

Both young and middle-aged homeless people have a higher **propensity for negative emotional experiences**. This can refer to depression, as well as irritability and a tendency to respond disproportionately to minimal stimuli with anger or rage. Such people have little control over their feelings. Similar conclusions were reached by Pěnkava (2010). Social adaptability is an important trait, or in this case its opposite, namely an **inability to adapt to society's demands**. This involves a complex of qualities manifest in relations with other people and the surrounding world and refers above all to an individual's ability to accept responsibility, respect valid rules, and not be driven solely by their own selfish needs. Without this ability a person is more reckless and prone to conflict. This then leads to **problems with interpersonal relationships**. These result from low empathy and an inability to put oneself in another's shoes, and a tendency to resolve common conflicts through radical solutions without regard for others. Poor social adaptability is usually manifest in behavioural problems during childhood and an inability or unwillingness to meet the demands of adults. Individuals with poor social adaptability cannot maintain close relationships with people and therefore lack the necessary social support in adulthood (Levinson, 2004). Undesirable personality traits are evident in work relationships and are one of the reasons why these people lose their jobs (Pěnkava, 2015).

Young homeless people admit they are indifferent to conventions, ignore social norms, are irresponsible and undisciplined, and have no desire to be subordinate to anything or anyone (Vágnerová, Csémy, Marek, 2012). Their middle-aged counterparts have a similar attitude towards rules. They too are irresponsible and undisciplined. This can be congenital in origin but also the consequence of emotional deprivation caused by a childhood spent in a dysfunctional family or an institution. It is likely that **sleeping rough intensifies and expands the undesirable personality traits** that these people already possessed (Štěchová et al., 2008). These traits are so advanced in some homeless people that they can be deemed personality disorders. The prolonged abuse of drugs and alcohol merely serves to exacerbate the situation.

A life on the street **leads to the disruption of relationships with members of mainstream society** (Davies, 2010). The homeless are a disadvantaged and vulnerable group, whose members are routinely ostracised and even on occasion subject to physical assault by the public. Their feelings of insecurity are not alleviated by the fact that their social networks comprise other homeless people, who for the most part do not represent a stable, nurturing environment. Life on the street involves many traumatic experiences that impact negatively in the form of the stress caused by social stigmatisation, low self-esteem, and a lack of support ensuing from the depletion and distortion of interpersonal relations (Renedo and Jovchelovitch, 2007. Davies, 2010). Homeless people live in relative social isolation, without the standard protection commonly available to members of mainstream society. Homelessness liberates a person from the pressure of society's duties and demands. However, this is a freedom that functions as a vacuum. Homeless people are aware of their low social status and react to their social exclusion by isolating themselves still further and engaging in minor infractions such as harassment.

The habits and lifestyle of a homeless person usually take several years to become entrenched. This process is accompanied by a transformation in self-image. Homeless people gradually lose all control over their lives, and a meaningful return to mainstream society becomes more and more difficult. Generally speaking, the longer a person is on the street, the more they change. Their values and competencies change and the negative consequences of risky activities (e.g. drug addiction and alcoholism) are compounded. Sometimes their health deteriorates or further social disaffiliation occurs (e.g. time spent in prison). An awareness of their downward trajectory, their rejection by mainstream society, and the lack of a supportive environment complicate the process of rejoining society. They are now part of the homeless community and have no other friends or acquaintances. By this time they usually identify with this community. They are aware that they have changed for the worse and that they are deemed unacceptable by the public, but they are no longer willing or even capable of seeking to change. In the chronically homeless a feeling of resignation and a reluctance to deal with problems that appear to them to be irresolvable (repaying a debt or abstaining from alcohol or drugs) prevails. These people reject any course of action that would require effort from them, and their desocialisation and personality disintegration continues, especially if they are long-term drug users or alcoholics.

1.1 OUR OBJECTIVES

Above all we wanted to **learn how middle-aged homeless people view the course of their lives** and the situation they now find themselves in.

- To what extent they believe their family and their experience of childhood played a role; how they lived as adults prior to becoming homeless; what kind of education they had and whether they were able to find and hold onto work, live with a long-term partner, and look after their children; and what milestones of their lives they consider important and why.
- We were also interested in how they explain their descent into homelessness, how they rate themselves and their life on the street, and to what extent they believe they contributed to their own downfall. It is clear that any evaluation of previous phases of life will be influenced by the current situation, which in turn could impact their view of the future.

We hope that the life stories of the people we interviewed will contribute to a general understanding of the paths that can lead to homelessness. This in turn will provide a data set that could assist in the selection of an appropriate strategy for working with people at risk.

We also set out to discover **whether, and if so how, chronic or long-term homelessness differs from short-term homelessness**, i.e. whether people sleeping rough for longer than 10 years differ in any way from **those who have been homeless for a shorter time**. It has been shown that middle-aged people take longer to adapt to life on the street than young people. In the case of older people the critical period is four to five years, whereas in the case of young people it is only two years. Between both groups there can be a difference in terms of personality (personality traits, ingrained experiences and habits, and level of education or professional qualifications), but also in terms of risk-related activities, especially alcohol and drug abuse and criminal conduct, and ultimately in terms of the severity of personality disorder and mental health. Identifying the potential differences will make it easier to define more precisely the risk of chronic homelessness and enable outreach workers to focus more on what might prevent people from remaining indefinitely on the street.

1.2 METHODOLOGY

Our research was based on a qualitative analysis of detailed interviews that took place from June 2016 to May 2017. We conducted a semi-structured interview, i.e. one with a predetermined range of topics. The interview focused on the life story of individuals, their childhood and adolescence, the education they had received and their social adaptability as children and teenagers, their entry into adulthood, and their experience of employment, relationships and parenthood. In short, we examined the period prior to our respondents becoming homeless, but also looked at their lives as homeless people and how they felt about the future. During the course of the interview, the people interviewed were given sufficient space to say anything and everything they wanted, and most of them responded to this positively. Generally speaking, they were happy with the interest being displayed in their life story, possibly because this was not something they had often encountered. Each interview lasted an average of two hours and was recorded with the permission of the participants and then transcribed verbatim.

Recurring themes were identified and the transcripts then divided into certain spheres. These spheres were then further broken down into subcategories offering the opinions and experiences of the respondents. The analytical induction method was used to determine these subcategories, which is based on a search for similarities allowing for a consistent strategy of comparison (Osborn and Smith, 2008). We compared the resulting subcategories with those of other studies and discovered that other researchers, e.g. Mabhala et al. (2016), examined the determinants leading to homelessness in a similar way. The narrative of homelessness can be seen in relation to the past, present and future. Our approach to the present and our future expectations derives from our interpretation of the past. Over time, some people have a tendency to "amend" their life story and interpret it in a different way so as to bring it in line with their current self-image.

It is clear that the life stories as recounted by our respondents may not be accurate. Distortions may appear depending on the significance of individual events and the gradual disappearance of recollections, especially regarding events stretching back further back in time. There are inaccuracies regarding the timing of events, and the stories are sometimes self-contradictory. People sleeping rough have a tendency to "polish" their life story so as to appear in a more favourable light. The positive correction of a story helps boost their self-esteem, which has been damaged in all sorts of ways by their awareness of their own social disaffiliation. Certain inaccuracies and lacunae can be attributed to the long-term use of drugs that affect the functioning of memory, and/or the effects of a homeless lifestyle that makes no demands on cognitive activity. The stories recounted by young people were shorter. Our younger respondents felt no need to defend their homeless status and often understood it as a process of finding themselves. We did not encounter this approach in older people.

In order to supplement the information acquired we used a questionnaire intended to track several key areas of life on a far larger cohort. The questionnaire focused on identifying demographic data, the process that led to people finding themselves on the street, which life events had influenced them, what their current sources of income were, and where they lived. Using the questionnaire we explored the frequency of chronic somatic diseases and mental disorders, individual psychiatric symptoms of addictive behaviour, and the degree of social alienation.

1.3 A DESCRIPTION OF THE GROUP UNDER EXAMINATION

Our cohort comprised 90 homeless people aged between 37 and 54, of whom 70 were men and 20 women. The ratio of men to women was 78/22, which corresponds to the ratio of men and women in the homeless community as a whole. For instance, McDonagh (2011) found that 84% percent of homeless people are men and 16% women, Panadero et al. (2015) found the figures to be 83% and 17% respectively, while Ciapessoni (2016) studied a cohort comprising 77% men and 23% women. We sought respondents by means of various charities for the homeless (a Salvation Army shelter, the low-threshold drop-in centre run by the organisation Naděje as part of its outreach programme, and the dispensary of the Mobile Social Services), the *Nový Prostor* magazine sold by homeless vendors [the Czech equivalent of *The Big Issue*: trans.], in the waiting room of a probation officer, and out on the streets (in Malešice and at the Vltavská metro station). All the people we met were contacted and all agreed to be interviewed. A small remittance of CZK 200 [USD 8.7] was paid.

Tab. 1. The group under examination

	no.	average age	SD	average duration of homelessness	SD	average age upon becoming homeless	SD
men	70	45.6	5.3	9.5	7.0	36.3	7.2
women	20	43.5	4.2	8.4	6.1	33.1	8.2

The average age of homeless women is somewhat lower than that of their male counterparts. Women also found themselves sleeping rough at a younger age than men, though the difference is not statistically important ($t = 1.68$).

The age a person became homeless is important. People currently aged 47–55 began sleeping rough on average aged 38.4 (SD = 7.98), while people aged 37–46 became homeless aged 32.9 (SD = 8.04). The difference between both groups is significant: $t = 3.19$, df = 88, $p = 0.01$. What this means is that **the age at which people are becoming homeless is dropping**. The reason is clear: older people were young adults under the former communist regime, when it was impossible to stop working and when a person could not become homeless because they would find themselves in prison for what was called "parasitism".

The length of time these people have spent on the street is important. People aged 47–55 (N = 39) have been homeless for an average of 11.5 years (SD = 4.06), people aged 37–46 (N = 51) for an average of 7.9 (SD = 5.83). This is an important difference statistically: $t = 3.25$, df = 88, $p = 0.01$. What this means is that **older homeless people have been living on the street for a longer period of time**. This may be because, after several years of sleeping rough, they are no longer able to change their lifestyle.

Those of our cohort who have been on the street for 10 years and more comprise 38 individuals. Their average age is 46.3 (SD = 5.3) and they have been homeless since the age of 30.3 on average (SD = 6.6). Those of our cohort who have been on the street for four years or less comprise 24 individuals. Their average age is 42.6 (SD = 9.7) and they have been homeless since the age of 42.5 on average (SD = 5.5). The groups do not differ significantly in respect of current age (t = 1.9, df = 60), but more in respect of the age they became homeless (t = 7.4, df = 60, p = 0.001). Middle-aged people who have been sleeping rough for a short period of time only became homeless later in life. We may assume that these groups will differ in respect of other aspects (see below).

The cohort for the questionnaire comprised 342 homeless people, of whom 271 were men (79%) and 71 women (21%). The average age was 48 (SD = 14). The time spent homeless differed, with 51% of the group having lived on the street for three years or more. We sought respondents in shelters (27%), low-threshold drop-in centres (70%) and on the street (3%) at locations in Prague (39%), Brno (28%), Ostrava (21%), Mladá Boleslav (7%) and Beroun (5%).

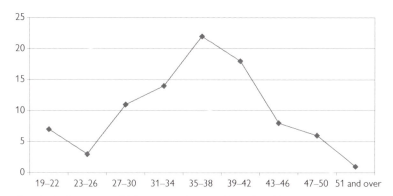

Graph 1. The age at which a person became homeless (the graph shows absolute figures).

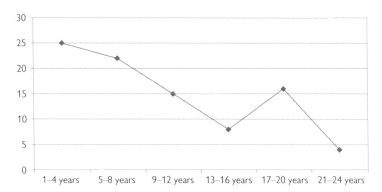

Graph 2. Length of time middle-aged people have been homeless (the graph shows absolute figures).

II. LIFE PRIOR TO BECOMING HOMELESS

1. HOMELESS PEOPLE RATE THEIR CHILDHOOD AND FAMILY OF ORIGIN

There are many different risk factors that increase vulnerability to homelessness, with these individual factors then accumulating (Coward-Bucher, 2008). One such factor is a person's **negative experience with their parents, i.e. with the way they spent their childhood and adolescence**. These early experiences are important for the rest of life and the direction an individual takes in adulthood. The relationships a person has later in life derive from their experience with their parents. If the parents neglected, mistreated or even abused them, they have no idea how such relationships should function and end up acting towards other people as inconsiderately as their parents behaved to them or to each other. People who had no satisfactory relationship in childhood often cannot trust anyone and cannot respond appropriately in ordinary situations. They have never learned to take responsibility and to reach decisions with a view to their possible consequences. They have not learned to take other people into account. If the family of origin of people who are currently homeless did not provide a stable, functional environment and suitable models of conduct and problem solving, our respondents lacked support and were unable to acquire the requisite experiences. The absence of positive experiences is manifest in repeated failure at school and subsequently in their employment and interpersonal relationships.

The influence of a problematic family environment on the subsequent lives of homeless people has been confirmed primarily by studies of young people living on the street (Cauce et al., 2000; Votta and Manion, 2003; Tyler, 2006; Bearsley-Smith et al., 2008; Coward-Bucher, 2008; Ferguson, 2009). According to these researchers, people who have lived on the streets from a young age are far more likely to come from families that did not provide a stable and nurturing environment. Their parents drank to excess and were often in prison. They sometimes suffered mental health problems or personality defects and were unable to manage their own lives. They probably also possessed less favourable genetic predispositions, which they may have passed on to their children. This might involve a tendency to be impulsive, non-empathetic, irresponsible, or to display negative affectivity and aggressive responses. Though most of these studies were concerned with the families of young homeless people, the burden ensuing from a lack of the security and safety of a functional family environment has been shown to affect the lives of people who are now middle-aged (Caton et al., 2005; Ravenhill, 2014; Hradecký, 2015; Mabhala et al., 2016). Caton et al. (2005) report that 21% of middle-aged people sleeping rough grew up outside their own family, and 24% of them had experienced a very troubled family environment. Brown et al. (2016) found that 38% of people sleeping rough had not spent their childhood in their natal family and lacked a nurturing environment.

A third of the young homeless people we questioned felt they had had an unsatisfactory childhood. Many of them were raised in a children's home or by foster parents (Vágnerová, Csémy, Marek, 2013). A similar experience was reported by some of our middle-aged cohort, with **37% describing their family of origin as problematic**. Some of them (16%) spent their childhood in institutional care or with a foster family. Almost half (47%) rated their natal family as having functioned satisfactorily at least up until the age of 12. In the group of young homeless people, 45% rated their family positively. Middle-aged people who found themselves on the street while still young (by the time they were 28) made up 18% of the entire group. In the majority of cases (75%) they came from dysfunctional families or spent their childhood elsewhere, either in foster care or a children's home. It is likely that people with negative family experiences find themselves on the street at a younger age because they lack the basic requirements to deal with the demands of adulthood.

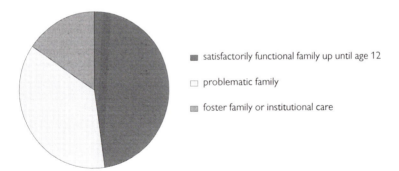

satisfactorily functional family up until age 12

problematic family

foster family or institutional care

Graph 3. How middle-aged homeless people rate their childhood (shown in absolute figures)

Thirty-two percent of our middle-aged respondents believed that the problems in their dysfunctional families were caused by the **father** (whom they described as an alcoholic, gambler, repeat offender, or suffering mental health issues). Only 14% of those questioned cited the **mother** as problematic (for reasons of alcoholism, criminality or mental health issues). In the group of young homeless people, 31% cited their father as the source of problems and 20% the mother (Vágnerová, Csémy, Marek, 2013).

The parents of our middle-aged respondents often drank to excess. Foreign studies report problems with drugs, though this did not feature large in

Czech families. According to Fergusson (2009), 42% of the parents of young homeless people took drugs or drank. Mallett et al. (2005) found that 26% of the parents of young homeless people had problems with alcohol, and if the family split up, the mother's new partner would be similarly inclined. Thompson et al. (2007) found that at least one of the parents drank to excess in half of the families of young homeless people, with both drinking to excess in 20% of cases. The excessive consumption of alcohol by either parent will negatively impact on the life of the entire family. The children who grow up in such families will lack self-confidence and trust in other people, and will find it difficult to establish close relationships. They do not learn how to handle stressful situations in an acceptable fashion because such situations represented the rule rather than the exception in their families. Instead, they react impulsively, and this then creates further difficulties. Such is their experience of family life that they often opt to leave home in favour of life on the street (Ravenhilll, 2014).

The source of problems is usually the father, who is an alcoholic and behaves aggressively. (The adult children of such men often drink to excess, either due to genetic predisposition, their childhood experiences, or simply in an attempt to resolve their own problems).

- S (52, male, homeless for 17 years): "***Dad was an alcoholic*** *and ended up drinking himself to death. He moved out and I never saw him again. I don't even know when he died. I had a bad relationship with him because he was always yelling at my mum or trying to hit her. When I was 15 years old he started to shout at her and made as though to hit her, so I grabbed his hand and slapped him. Mum was fine about it. She wasn't strict, she was nice, and in fact it was me who sometimes screamed at her, though then I would apologise. I picked that up from my dad, who used to scream at her.*" S is an alcoholic, single and childless. He is aware that he treated his mother as badly as did his father.

- P (50, m, homeless for 12 years): "*I don't like thinking about my father, because he was a **real alcoholic**. He could be nice, but when he drank things got bad and **he used to beat us all, including mum**. One time when I was 15 I came home and he was beating my mum. So I punched him and after that it was never again like father and son. Dad was sometimes pleasant, but when he was drunk he was fucking horrible. Mum was lovely.*" P is also an alcoholic, single and childless.

- J (51, m, homeless for seven years): "*Mum and dad were together until I was 10. **Dad was basically an alcoholic** and mum drank occasionally. But then dad walked out on us and mum wasn't strong enough to cope on her own. **She had a few boyfriends**, four maybe, who were kind of uncles to us. And she had two more children, each with a different bloke. I didn't see my father for a few years and then one day I saw him in the pub.*" J is also an alcoholic. He has served repeated jail sentences and does not look after his children. The fact his mother had several boyfriends might represent a further source of insecurity.

E (43, female, homeless for 11 years) also grew up in a problematic family with an aggressive father and stepfather: "*When I was little my **dad used to beat me**. My mum loved me, and that helped. But my real father, who died, he used to hit me all the time when I was little. Then my parents got divorced when I was still little and mum got married to another bloke, so I have a stepfather and I can't stand him. **He also hit me**.*" E drinks to excess and takes drugs. She has one daughter but does not look after her. Her current partner is also homeless.

Tensions and conflicts in a family can be related to the father's mental health problems. This was so in the case of H (40, f, homeless for nine years): "*My parents got divorced when I was little. My dad used to go bonkers at home. He didn't hit my mum, but he used to break things and threaten to jump out of the window. He smashed a whole table to pieces during one argument. He was always arguing. **He had mental health issues, schizophrenia**. Under his influence my mum ended up seeing a psychiatrist.*" H has herself received psychiatric treatment and has a disability pension. For a while she was an alcoholic. She surrendered her children immediately after birth for adoption.

A non-functioning mother, either for mental health reasons or alcoholism, can also leave her mark on a child.

- Z (42, f, homeless for 11 years): "*At the age of seven I ended up in a children's home because **mum became schizophrenic**. I grew up outside the family. My childhood was shitty, and being in a children's home wasn't exactly a bundle of laughs either.*" Z is an alcoholic. She has neither a stable partner nor children.

- L (38, f, homeless for 21 years) tells a similar story: "*My dad brought me up, he raised me from a young age. I wasn't in contact with my mum at the time. But when I started school, I went looking for her and eventually I found her and then remained with her. Dad didn't like the arrangement, because my **mum was ill**, and was useless with money. They took my brother away because **she simply wasn't able to take care of him**, and put him in a children's home. I moved between my dad and my mum, but mostly I was with my dad.*" L drinks to excess and has served repeated jail sentences. She does not have custody of her children. She did not complete her junior school education and attended a school for children with special needs.

If the mother drinks to excess, this can be an even worse problem than an alcoholic father, since it means there is no one in the family to create a calm and stable environment for the children.

- D (48, m, homeless for five years) is a case in point: "*Grandma looked after me until I was six, and then **mum took over. She was an alcoholic**. Between the ages of 6 and 11 I lived with my mother and then she found another partner, with whom she had my brother. Her partner used to beat me. Well, most of the time my mother beat me while my stepfather held me down. Then **she attempted suicide** and was placed in Bohnice* [a psychiatric hospital in Prague] *and I returned to my grandmother's.*

Grandma had also spent time in Bohnice. She was a manic-depressive, so all in all it was kind of out of the frying pan..." D is an alcoholic. He does not have any children. As an adult he did not have much contact with his mother: *"We didn't see much of each other. I visited her a few times and we would drink together, but then she died in Bohnice of cirrhosis of the liver."* His brothers suffered similar problems: *"The youngest had problems with drugs. I've a feeling he's in prison. I've never met the middle one, though I know he's also homeless."*

- K (37, m, homeless for nine years): *"Mum lived with dad but **she had different interests. She used to like partying in the pub**. When I was born she was already an alcoholic and didn't want to look after us. So I ended up in a children's home at the age of two. Dad split up with mum and found himself another woman. But I remained in the children's home, where I stayed until I was 19."* K is an alcoholic and has no partner or children.

If neither of the parents are capable of taking care of their children, they are looked after by their grandparents or other relatives.

- M (48, m, homeless for 20 years): *"I grew up with my grandma on my father's side, because my father handed me over to **grandma** when he was sent to prison. He had already split up with my mother. **He received a prison sentence for burglary.** He was a real alcoholic, so grandma looked after me until I was 11. I used to skip school and just loiter. School did nothing for me, I learned nothing. **Grandma was also addicted to alcohol**. When I was 11 I was sent to a youth detention centre and then to a children's home, because granny couldn't cope."* M is a drug addict and has repeatedly spent time in prison. He has no children.

- V (48, m, homeless for seven years) was cared for by relatives because his parents were in prison: *"**They banged up both mum and dad**. Dad got 15 years and mum got 3.5 for child neglect. Mum left me with my granddad, returned to Prague and washed her hands of me. I don't know why. Maybe she had no money or just couldn't be bothered. She was young. So I was raised by my aunt and uncle."* V's relationship with his mother did not improve and he refused to meet her: *"When I learned that mum had simply washed her hands of me and abandoned me I didn't want any contact with her whatsoever. My aunt and uncle rejected me when I was sent to prison."* V is an alcoholic who has repeatedly spent time in prison. He does not have custody of his children.

A significant number (16%) of middle-aged homeless people **spent their childhood in a children's home or foster family**. This figure was 20% in the case of young people (Vágnerová, Csémy, Marek, 2013) and is far higher than the national average, where it is at most one percent.

- S (46, f, homeless for four years): *"I lived with my mum when I was little, and I never met my father. **But then mum simply stopped looking after me** and I was sent to an adoptive mother. I only saw my mum on visits, because **she wasn't interested in me**. I was with my adoptive parents in Australia until I was 15. Then* *my real mum found me via the Red Cross. I made a mistake and I returned to her. I would have been far better off remaining where I was. But even though what she had done to me was bad, firstly it was my mum, and secondly, she really helped me with my children. So when I was working at the post office, she took care of my kids. In Australia it was beautiful. To this day **I regret not having returned there**. There is a wonderful life to be had there. But there you go, my bad. In the end it's what I wanted, except that you never anticipate it's going to end up like this."* S ended up sleeping rough after she and her husband split up and he threw her out of their apartment. In this particular case a certain naivety around relationships plays a role, which was manifest in the way she returned to the biological mother who had abandoned her when she was a young girl. S does not look after her children. She does not consume alcohol or drugs.

- O (53, m, homeless for 20 years) spent his childhood in institutional care: *"When I was little mum and dad would argue every day. **We children were in a children's home**. Between the ages of three and eight I was in a children's home, then a young offenders' institution, and then when I was 18 I returned home. When I came out of the institution, I returned to dad. I have a kind of on-off relationship with dad, because he used to beat me when I was naughty."* O drinks to excess and takes drugs, and has repeatedly spent time in prison. He was unable to deal with a relationship and does not look after his children.

- J (45, f, homeless for twenty years): *"I lived with my mum until I was 10, **after which they sent me to a children's home**. I remained there until I was 15, then I fucked things up so they transferred me to a young offenders' institution. At the age of 18 I returned to my mum and I got married at 19… I always had a really good relationship with my mum. I don't know my father. I've looked for him and asked mum. He was a drinker too, but he held down a job. I only know this from what mum has told me, I didn't know him at all. I'm the youngest of the girls. The oldest boy died of an overdose."* J is an alcoholic and drug addict and does not look after her children.

Not all the parents of people who are currently homeless neglected their children. Sometimes **there was a simple lack of understanding, or the child felt their parents preferred the other children**. Whether this was actually the case is neither here nor there: the effect was the same. Feelings of being unwanted and unaccepted, either by their parents or stepparents, often featured in the stories recounted by young homeless people (Vágnerová, Csémy, Marek, 2013), and the same is true of the cohort examined by Ferguson (2009). It is clear that for many homeless people home does not represent the stable environment it is supposed to. It is also possible that these individuals were not completely standard personality types and therefore felt uncomfortable, even though the family was functioning in an acceptable fashion.

- L (52, m, homeless for two years) is not addicted to alcohol or drugs: *"**My parents were decent enough, but I didn't get on with them,** and that feeling persisted throughout my life. They raised me in accordance with their principles, but* *didn't understand me at all. I loved my mum in a way, but when they died, it was a relief, if I can put it like that.*" L had similar difficulties in his own relationships and does not have children. Mental health issues very likely account in part for his being homeless.

- P (52, m, homeless for about two years) was not happy in his family, though he has a more balanced overview of his feelings at that time: "*When I was 13, I ran away from home. **I had the feeling of having been pushed to the sidelines**. My parents seemed fully occupied with my younger sister, although looking back I realise that wasn't true. My parents lived together. Sometimes things were difficult between them, but you can't get away from the fact that they remained married until they died.*" P had a university education. He became homeless in part because of an internal conflict over his homosexuality, and in addition he drinks to excess and has mental health issues. He suffers bipolar disorder and is being treated by a psychiatrist.

- D (39, m, homeless for four years) also suffered feelings of rejection in childhood, and had problems accepting his stepfather: "*Up until the age of six things were ok and I had both my parents. Then my brother was born and the problems began. **Being the youngest he was the favourite**. When I was seven mum and dad split up. When I realised that only me, my brother and mum would be left I started to play up. I stopped attending school, that kind of thing. Mum took my brother everywhere and I began to feel sidelined. Mum didn't want me to be in contact with my aunt on my father's side and after six months she got married again. I didn't like her new partner from the moment he entered our home... then I was sent to a children's home after being found on the street by the police. That was when I was eight. But in fact I'm grateful I was sent to children's home because otherwise I don't know what would have happened. I remained there until I was 18.*" D does not have a relationship or children. He is not addicted to alcohol or drugs. He probably suffers personality disorder.

Our respondents' problems may well have been exacerbated by the breakup of the family and the subsequent departure of one parent or the **arrival of a new partner**, whom they were unable to accept. Many young homeless people had problems accepting a stepfather (Vágnerová, Csémy, Marek, 2013). The need to accept either their mother's or their father's new partner, a person they do not know, is deemed a stress factor by Ravenhill (2014) too.

- L (38, m, homeless since the age of 18) had a problem accepting his father's new partner when his own mother died: "*I had had a good relationship with my dad. But dad didn't want to live alone, so **he found himself a woman with whom I didn't see eye to eye**. I really went for her and told her no way was she my mum. I was pleased when she died because I really didn't like her.*" L has problems with alcohol and criminality. His current girlfriend is also homeless and does not have children. He became homeless because he drank to excess, something his stepmother was unwilling to accept.

- D (40, m, homeless for 19 years) had a conflictual relationship with his mother's new partner: "*We lived as a family up until I was eight years old, when my parents got divorced. My dad was an alcoholic and used to beat my mum. Then mum found herself another bloke, a taxi driver here in Prague, and **we didn't get along**. One time I beat my stepfather up for cheating on my mum.*" D is an alcoholic and drug addict. He has repeatedly spent time in prison and does not look after his children.
- V (48, f, homeless for five years) had a poor relationship with her stepfather: "*I lived with my mum and stepfather from the age of five. Basically I felt that it was only my grandma that gave me what I needed. Granny was really strict but fair. I don't remember my father and never knew him. I have no idea how things were between us. Then my sister was born and from about the age of six I was regularly beaten until I was 16. My stepfather even hit me when I was pregnant. It continued right up to the last minute and has remained with me all my life. **My stepfather was really strict with me**. When I was older I started to have rows with my mother. We were never your model family. So basically my childhood was pretty shit.*" V has serious problems with alcohol. Her daughter is a drug addict who is also homeless. Her granddaughter has been placed in a children's home.

SUMMARY

More than half of our respondents grew up in a family that was problematic in some way or were not looked after by their parents and spent their childhood elsewhere. The most frequent cause of family breakup was the excessive consumption of alcohol, particularly on the part of the father, though many mothers drank to excess too. Alcoholic fathers were often aggressive and battered their wives and children. As a consequence the family did not provide a nurturing environment and became instead a source of threat. Some of these parents spent time in prison for various crimes and their children were looked after by relatives or ended up in a children's home. Parental failure, aggression and neglect are not desirable modes of conduct and yet this was often the only model our respondents encountered as children. Several of our respondents were unable to cope with the breakup of the family and the arrival of a new partner, be this on the side of their mother or father, and this led to a deterioration of their relationships with those close to them and to increased behavioural problems. In these cases the child's own personality traits may also be a cause of their subsequent disaffiliation. A feeling of having been rejected and misunderstood (which may have been one of the reasons they ran away from home) sometimes persists to the present day, and as a result the people we spoke to are unable to request their parents for assistance even at times of crisis. Most of them are not even in contact with their parents.

There is no doubt that problematic parents can impact negatively on the development of their children. This may be the result of undesirable character traits being passed on or because of neglect, emotional rejection, poor up-bringing, and the parents' embodiment of an undesirable model of conduct. However, we also wanted to find out to what extent a deprived childhood might influence how long a person remains homeless, i.e. whether the stress experienced and the inadequate satisfaction of basic psychological needs dur-ing childhood might be manifest in the form of such a steep downward spiral (chronic homelessness and a complete inability to resolve matters). The opin-ions held by people who have been sleeping rough for less than four years and those who have been homeless for ten years regarding their childhood and family differ to a statistically significant extent (chi square distribution = 9.71, df = 2, p = 0.001). We may therefore conclude that **a dysfunctional family en-vironment does not only increase the risk of homelessness, but increases the risk of chronic homelessness** (whether homelessness is caused by an inability to adapt to the requirements of an adult life, lack of support, criminal activity, or drug abuse).

1.1 CURRENT RELATIONSHIPS BETWEEN OUR RESPONDENTS AND THEIR PARENTS

The relationships between the people we spoke to and their parents are many and varied. In the case of the oldest of our cohort it is difficult to evaluate these relationships since their parents are for the most part no longer alive. Younger

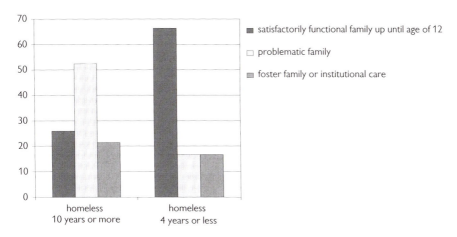

Graph 4. What our middle-aged respondents thought about their childhood by duration of homelessness (the graph shows relative frequencies).

people exhibit a variety of feelings towards their parents and are in contact with them to varying degrees. If they are not in contact, there are many different reasons. Maintaining or resuming a relationship with parents can be a source of support and help the homeless in their endeavour to return to mainstream society. This assumes, of course, that the parents themselves are not so problematic as to complicate matters still further.

Only 60% of our middle-aged respondents have at least one parent, and only 20% of these have an acceptable relationship with either one or both of their parents. However, **those who say they have a good relationship with their parents are not always in contact with them**.

- K (42, m, homeless for two years): "*I'm in touch with mum regularly, **I have a good relationship with her**.*" Both K and his mother were the victims of K's aggressive father, with whom K is not in touch: "*I don't see my father. I can't stand him.*" K does not have a problem with alcohol or drugs. He is in contact with his own children and helps with their upkeep as far as he is able.
- M (43, f, homeless for eight years): "***I have a fantastic relationship with my mum**. I lost everything and only my mum and sister remained. I had to communicate with them. I got hold of a telephone, which I then promptly sold. I got hold of another one and the same thing happened. I taught my mum and sister to ring me back when I rang from a kiosk. I didn't want to insert the twenty crowns, because that was for booze.*" M's mother and sister have tried to help her, though thus far without success. She is addicted to alcohol and drugs and does not look after her own children.

Some of the people we spoke to are not in contact with their parents because they are ashamed of where they have ended up. They say that if they had a normal life, they would be happy to meet up. This is especially the case if the family, particularly the mother, provided a nurturing environment during childhood.

- H (50, m, homeless for 20 years) enjoyed a good relationship with his mother and father. His main problem was drug addiction: "*I would like to see my mum.*

an acceptable relationship with at least one parent

not in contact

the parents are no longer alive

Graph 5. Current relationships between middle-aged homeless people and their parents (the graph shows absolute figures).

If I was married with kids and an apartment or if I lived a normal live, then I'd pop round. But that's not how things are. She was right when she said that things were going nowhere. I haven't seen her in 12 years. I haven't seen my father either. Or my brother. **I don't want them to see me like this.**" H does not have a partner or children.

- M (38, m, homeless for two years) is a drug addict: "*I haven't been in touch with my parents because* **I know I've disappointed them**. *Just imagine what the neighbours would say: their son takes pervitin* [methamphetamine]. *Once or twice a year I used to visit my family, but it wasn't like it had been at the start.*" M's drug addiction disrupted his relationship with his parents. He is single and has little to do with his daughter.

The parents are often unaware that their child is living on the streets.
- J (51, m, homeless for seven years) is an alcoholic: "*Mum died. We hadn't been close over the last few years, we might only see each other once every five years. I didn't have a bad relationship with her, we got on ok, but* **I didn't want to tell her I was homeless**. *I was in prison when she died.*" J's father was also an alcoholic who abandoned his family. J is divorced and does not look after his children.
- M (40, m, homeless for seven years) is an alcoholic whose parents still have no clue that he is homeless: "*We communicate together and I get on absolutely fine with both mum and dad. Mum thinks I have a job, dad too.* **They don't know that I live on the streets**. *I suspect that my father* [stepfather] *would come for me immediately and wouldn't leave me on the streets. Mum would have a heart attack, she wouldn't be able to cope, no way would she leave me on the streets. I'm ashamed to go home without money.*" M is divorced and does not look after his children. His own (biological) father was also an alcoholic, which is why M's mother divorced him.
- T (39, m, homeless for six years): "**My parents don't know that I'm sleeping rough**. *I hide it from them. We speak on the phone from time to time and visit each other. But it's complex. I see my mum more often.*" T does not want to admit to his failure, though he has no other problems (he is not an alcoholic or drug addict).

One reason a homeless person might restrict contact with their parents is because of a reluctance to burden them in any way, e.g. with their debt.
- R (46, m, homeless for four years) grew up in a trouble-free family and has a good relationship with his mother: "*I could return home, but* **I don't because I've got debts**. *I don't want the bailiffs to take my mum's apartment away from her.*" R is an alcoholic and is one of very few homeless people who looked after his own children.
- J (40, m, homeless for four years) does not want to upset his mother: "*I'm in contact with my mum, but* **I've never told her that I'm homeless**. *We spoke to each other yesterday, but* **if I said anything it would break her heart** *and she would*

tell me to come home. But without money you know how it is." J is not dependent on either alcohol or drugs, does not have a partner, and does not look after children.

Some of our respondents believe there is no reason to contact their parents since the latter displayed no interest in them when they were children..

- V (48, m, homeless for seven years): *"I didn't want any contact with mum **after I learned that she didn't give a fuck about me and had abandoned me**."* V is also not in contact with his aunt and uncle, who raised him, because *"they rejected me when I was sent to prison."* V is an alcoholic. He does not look after his own children, just as his parents failed to look after him.
- D (37, m, homeless for nine years) refuses to contact his mother, who did not look after him when he was a child: *"After a while I didn't bother getting in touch with my family. I didn't want to go home **because I didn't any longer feel any love towards my mother**. She still drinks, she can't keep her mitts off the beer, she's always in the pub."* D is also an alcoholic and does not look after his own children.

Sometimes an ongoing conflict or sense of grievance is the reason for breaking off contact with parents, as well as the feeling that assistance was not provided when the respondent really needed it.

- A poor relationship **may be related to drug addiction or alcoholism**. The parents find it difficult to accept the conduct of their adult offspring, which they fear could have a knock-on effect on the entire family. K (40, m, homeless for 19 years) is a case in point: *"I haven't seen my mum for ages. I never visit. **Mum slipped me a tenner so that I would leave Prague**, and that was what pissed me off the most..."* K's biological father was an alcoholic and he had problems with his stepfather, i.e. his mother's new partner, who was unwilling to accept him.
- P (45, f, homeless for eight years) is a drug addict: *"**Me and my mum had a really ambivalent relationship**. We still do. She's the only person who could infuriate me in just a matter of seconds with a few words... She doesn't know where I am. I last visited her a year ago when I was sleeping rough in some cellar or other and it occurred to me that she was 70. So I got myself together and went round to her place thinking she'd be pleased. Instead **she told me I smelled** and asked if I'd spent time in a drugs unit and that **I should come back when I was cured**."* P looked after her daughter for several years, but then became addicted to drugs again.
- D (39, m, homeless for four years) resented the greater interest shown by his mother in his younger brother. He also rejected his stepfather: *"I don't know whether mum is still alive. **I've heard nothing about her for eight years and have no interest in seeing her**. I don't for the life of me know why she married that guy. From the moment I set eyes on him I couldn't stand him."* D is not an alcoholic or a drug addict. He spent his childhood years in institutional care. He does not have a regular partner or children. He most likely suffers a personality defect.

SUMMARY

The kind of relationship our respondents have with their parents is highly influenced by their experience of childhood. If their parents neglected them or caused them suffering, these relationships continue to be bad into adulthood. Such people often say there is no reason to be in touch with their parents since they were not looked after when they were young. Cutting off contact with parents, especially with the mother, can also be the result of the parents rejecting the lifestyle of their adult offspring, especially if it involves problems with drugs or alcohol. A fifth of people who are homeless at present (20%) have a good relationship with their parents (particularly their mother) and communicate with them, but are unwilling to admit that they ended up on the street. They do not wish to burden their parents with their problems and are ashamed of how they live. These are usually individuals who spent their childhood in a functioning family and who found themselves homeless for other reasons (e.g. an addiction to alcohol that developed later in life).

A third of our younger cohort were in contact with at least one of their parents, usually their mother (Vágnerová, Csémy, Mark, 2013). Noom et al. (2008) found this figure to be 47%. Contact with someone from the family of origin was maintained by 41% of variously aged shelter users, which is far higher than in the case of people sleeping rough over the long term (Marek, 2017).

2. SIBLING RELATIONSHIPS

The relationships that our middle-aged respondents have with their siblings are many and varied. An important factor is whether they have shared childhood experiences or whether they are linked by a similar trajectory in life. If their siblings are not living on the street and do not share the same problems, they can represent a source of support. However, many homeless people reject the help of their siblings because they are ashamed or because the support offered is conditional (usually upon abstinence and finding a job). Some homeless people are in touch with their siblings and have a good relationship with them, while others reject them and are convinced that they have been somehow hurt by them.

Some of our respondents told us they have a good relationship with their siblings and value their support. M (43, f, homeless for eight years) is a case in point: "*I love my older sister. **She helps me with everything**. We ring each other a lot and she really looks after me. She has a pub and I go there every two weeks to cook. I have great respect for her and I make sure not to drink there... Six years ago I met up with her and she offered her support. She said that they were all behind me and that it didn't matter if I disappointed them, I wouldn't be punished. I simply somehow had to function... I would definitely be boozing were it not for her support.*" M has had behavioural problems since childhood. She has experienced drug and alcohol addiction, and her son is cared for by his father.

Others are in contact with their siblings but **spurn their assistance**, even when it is offered.

- M (38, m, homeless for two years): "*My family looks at me askance. My sister knows I'm on the street and has **urged me to come home** many times. **But I don't want to**.*" M is a drug addict. He does not have a regular partner and does not look after his daughter.
- P (45, f, homeless for eight years) does not want her sister's help: "*I have a sister who is troubled by how I've ended up, or at least that's what my mother says… We're not in contact because I didn't want to exploit her. **I felt I was a burden on her**. I've met her a few times and she always tries to help. She makes the effort, but I don't want to drag her down when she has three kids of her own*." P used to take drugs. Her partners have also been addicts. She only looked after her own daughter for a short period of time.
- F (43, m, homeless for five years) is in a very similar situation: "*I have a sister. She's got three kids, a house, the whole bit. I could live there if I wanted to but **I don't want to bother her**. In any case I wouldn't live there because they'd want me to find a job*." F refuses help because does not want to be put under pressure to change his lifestyle. He is an alcoholic. He does not have a regular partner or children.

Some of our respondents **are not and do not plan to be in contact with their siblings**, because they feel no great affinity with them and don't see the point. They accept that they live differently. Sometimes their siblings are not even aware that they are living on the street.

- O (53, m, homeless for 20 years) is one such case: "*I had two sisters and six brothers… I know nothing of them save that they are married. I'm not in contact with them. **They have their lives and I have mine**.*" O is addicted to drugs and alcohol and has repeatedly served time in prison. He does not look after his children.
- J (51, m, homeless for seven years) is another: "*I'm not in contact and I don't want to be. **They have their own lives. What would I say to them? That I'm home-**less and that I sleep at the refuge run by Naděje?*" J does not have a regular partner and is not in contact with his own children.

Other respondents **accuse their siblings of letting them down in various ways** (though it is impossible to say whether these accusations are justified or fabricated). This mostly involves men living and sleeping outside who expected greater support from their siblings and, when this was not forthcoming, are vitriolic when speaking of them.

- G (50, m, homeless for ten years) is very much a case in point: "***My sister**, who has received money from me, **didn't even let me sleep in the toilet** in the corridor* *on a carpet. I had to sleep outside on a bench. I made the effort to travel here and she wouldn't even let me sleep on the stairs. **My brother's a complete fucking jerk**. I hope I'm still alive when he dies so I can piss on his grave... I said to him: I'll just stretch my legs and in the morning I'll be off, no problem... Listen, I live like I live, like a wolf among wolves. Why would I complicate anyone's life? Why would I do it?"* G had problems adapting as an adolescent and spent time in a youth detention centre. He is a drug addict and alcoholic. He does not have a regular partner and does not look after his children. He is not in contact with his mother. It is possible that he has been rejected by his siblings for placing too much of a burden on them.

- M (50, m, homeless for 20 years) is of a similar opinion: *"**I have two brothers. I used to visit them and say: listen, I need work for a month**. I'll find something no problem. Could you accommodate and feed me until I receive my first pay check? I won't bother you. **And they refused**. The middle one said: listen, you can spend one night here. Then he gave me a hundred crowns for a ticket to K and came with me to the station to make sure I left the city. It was because of what my two brothers said that my mother disinherited me two years ago."* M is not a drug addict or alcoholic. He does not have a stable relationship or children. It is very likely he suffers from personality disorder.

- V (51, m, homeless for ten years): *"**My sister** is a right old bitch. **She has stolen so much money from me**. She robbed me of my share [of their inheritance]. It's true that when I was in prison she sent me some money."* V is a repeat offender but is not a drug addict or alcoholic. He does not have a regular relationship and does not look after his children.

A homeless person's relationship with their siblings is often negatively influenced by an addiction to drugs or alcohol. Some of our respondents are aware that their relationships deteriorated as a consequence of alcohol or drug abuse. Their siblings can find contact with such an individual trying, and may shy away from such contact either because of the individual's behaviour to them or because they are ashamed of them.

- H (40, f, homeless for nine years) experienced such problems with her brother: *"At present I'm in contact with my brother. He's a shop assistant in a bookshop. While I was drinking **he didn't want anything to do with me**. I don't think he liked the fact I was sleeping rough. **He was ashamed of me for living on the street**. He told me that as long as I was homeless, he didn't want anything to do with me."* H is now living in sheltered accommodation and has cut down on her consumption of alcohol. Her children have been adopted and she does not have a partner.

- P (37, m, homeless for four years) has similar problems with his siblings: *"All my brothers and sisters are sorted out. They are older and have families. They always behaved normally when we were together. But I always sensed I was a disruptive element and that **they were looking at me suspiciously**."* P has neither children nor a partner.

Some of our respondents have siblings, usually brothers, who are also home-less, have spent time in prison, or are addicted to drugs or alcohol.

- J (45, m), a repeat offender, has similar problems to his brothers: "*I have a pretty normal relationship with my brothers. They know I'm out. **Only my youngest brother has never been in prison, the rest of us have.***" J reports nothing out of the ordinary about his parents.
- D (48, m) is in a similar situation: "*The youngest **had problems with drugs**. I have a feeling he's locked up. I met the middle one the other day, **he's also sleeping rough**.*" All the brothers grew up in a dysfunctional family. Their mother was an alcoholic.

SUMMARY

It is clear that homeless people learn not to rely on assistance from their sib-lings, either because they do not wish to be a burden, or they are aware that they would in any case meet with rejection. These sibling relationships can be very intense, and our respondents often accused their siblings of behaving badly towards them, deceiving them, and even robbing them. At other times they are indifferent, and it is this mutual lack of interest that leads to a break-down in contact. The siblings of our middle-aged respondents usually lead a fairly normal lifestyle, with families, an apartment or house, and a job. It is rare that they are also homeless. Only 12% of our respondents were in contact with one or more of their siblings. The situation was similar in the case of our younger cohort, of which only 15% maintained a relationship with their sib-lings (Vágnerová, Csémy, Marek, 2013).

3. PARTNERSHIPS PRIOR TO BECOMING HOMELESS

The existence of close, stable relationships limits the risk of a person becoming homeless, and if such should take place, can support a person in their attempts to return to normal life. Many homeless people either lack such relationships al-together, or those that they have function more as a source of trauma rather than support (Votta and Manion, 2003, Bearsley-Smith et al., 2008, Coward-Bucher, 2008, Ferguson, 2009, Caton et al., 2005). The homeless community is unable to provide these people the support they need, since their members are linked more by a common destiny than close personal relationships. It has been shown that membership of such a group, combined with the breakdown of earlier re-lationships, can prevent homeless people from returning to mainstream society (Vágnerová, Marek, Csémy, 2016).

The ability to live in a stable partnership is an important sign of social adaptability. We may assume that if a person is able to establish a relationship and, above all, maintain it, this is evidence of maturity and a balanced outlook on life. On the one hand, a stable relationship offers a supportive environment. On the other, it demands thoughtfulness, consideration and the acceptance of certain limits. As a consequence, a person must be prepared to give something up for the sake of the relationship. Maintaining a long-term relationship is simply too restrictive for certain individuals and thus unacceptable. Immaturity and an inability to deal with the daily routines and burdens ensuing from a relationship intensify the need to break free. Pěnkava (2010) shows that homeless people, as socially inadaptable individuals, lack a sense of orientation, not only as regards their own feelings, but the emotions of others too. Their lack of empathy often means they have unsatisfactory relations with other people, which is then manifest in the collapse of partnerships, failure as parents, and a lack of friends.

If an adult person is unable to have a stable relationship, this may be the consequence of disadvantageous personality traits combined with undesirable habits that are unacceptable to their partners. This might involve drug use or drinking to excess, as well as a tendency to be work shy and to seek out money in some other, often antisocial, way. In addition, negative experiences from the family of origin, which did not provide a calm and stable environment, can influence their personal development. The model of conduct inherited from their fathers, and sometimes their mothers, leads finally to the breakup of their own family of procreation. In the case of our respondents, the ability to maintain a stable relationship correlated closely with the quality of their parents' relationship: $r = 0.372$, $p = 0.001$. In other words, **people who grew up in a problematic family are usually unable to create a nurturing environment**. The deterioration of partnerships can also be the result of a poor choice of partner, who may also be problematic (especially in respect of drug addiction or alcohol abuse).

We were interested in the relationships people currently homeless had prior to becoming homeless, how they approached these partnerships, and how they would evaluate them in hindsight. We wanted to know whether it made sense to our respondents to have a stable relationship, and, if so, whether they had sought one out, or whether they regarded such relationships as pointless. On the basis of the interviews we conducted it seems that longer-term relationships (i.e. of at least five years), whether this involve marriage or cohabitation, feature less frequently in the homeless community than in the population at large. Only 41% of our respondents had experienced such a long-term relationship at least once in their lives. Other studies yield similar results. Goering et al. (2002) found that only 29% of homeless people had lived in a longer-term partnership prior to becoming homeless.

The marriages or partnerships of people who are currently homeless have largely failed, in many cases because they were unable to adapt to a new situation and accept the duties associated with such relationships. After their marriages broke down, many of our respondents found themselves sleeping rough or in a transitional phase in a hostel. As one said: "*I couldn't cope, I couldn't hold*

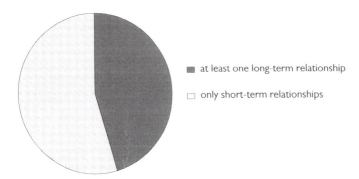

at least one long-term relationship

only short-term relationships

Graph 6. The relationships people had before becoming homeless (in absolute figures).

on any longer, it just wasn't worth it." In the case of women, the most frequent cause of marital breakdown was the abusive conduct of their partner, though sometimes the women themselves shared some of the blame, usually as a consequence of alcohol or drug abuse.

There were many reasons why marriages and partnerships failed. Some of our respondents did not even know why their relationships fell apart, for instance K (42, m, homeless for two years): *"She just gave up on me without saying why. She upped and left. She never said why. We don't talk much. I don't know what snapped in her, it was a bolt from the blue. Right now I don't have a long-term relationships. All of my relationships have been short and it was always me that was given the boot."* K does not drink to excess, nor does he abuse drugs. He has spent time in prison, but is not a repeat offender. It is likely that his partner had a reason for leaving him, but that K was unwilling or unable to sense her dissatisfaction.

Many marriages fell apart because one party found another partner.
- This was what happened to S (51, m, homeless for 14 years), who voluntarily became homeless and began drinking more than he had previously. Of his marriage S says: *"We hadn't been getting on for a while. Money, money, money, she was always after money, and in any case it simply didn't work. If there was work, then things were ok. But she always wanted more and more and I don't mean that in a horrible way. **I've been on the street since we separated**. She was 18 when I met her. She was a stunner. We split up because she could never get enough dosh. Then one day we had a terrible row and **she fled into the arms of some guy she had on the side**. Of course, she continued living in the apartment. Why would she have to leave? No, it was me that left... We had been together for 15 years."*
- M (50, f) saw her marriage end because of infidelity: *"After completing school I started seeing someone. Then I got pregnant and had a baby boy. But I simply couldn't live with my mother-in-law, she made life hell. I lived for around ten years with my husband and then we got divorced. I was about 28 at the time. I was his first*

*girlfriend and he wanted to sow his wild oats, so you could say that **infidelity was basically the reason for our divorce**. I had forgiven him on many occasions, but I'd had enough. I was exhausted by these affairs. I had a nervous breakdown and ended up in Bohnice.*" M's second marriage also broke down, and it is possible that her mental health issues played a part. She suffers anxiety disorder and has been hospitalised on many occasions.

- S (46, f, homeless for four years) is submissive by nature: "*We got married, we had two children, and after 17 years together we got divorced. **My ex-husband already had someone on the side**. Psychologically it was an awful time. It took a huge toll on me, I was on the verge of cracking up. I even started seeing a psychiatrist. I really loved my husband. I'm that kind of person. I'm not someone who would just start something with anyone... I always hoped we could save the marriage if only because of the kids.*" The divorce and the loss of accommodation were the reasons S found herself sleeping rough.

On occasion infidelity triggered an aggressive reaction that ended a relationship for good. E (46, f, homeless for eleven years): "*I got married at 18. I knew virtually nothing about life. I had lived up until then in a village. I gave birth to a son. But then we separated because he cheated on me. **I ended up stabbing the girl.** There I am pregnant and **he's screwing some fucking tart**. I slashed my wrists and the police locked me up in a drunk tank.... I received a conditional sentence.*" E's subsequent relationships were no more stable. She is an alcoholic.

In the case of women who are at present homeless, a frequent cause of marital or partnership breakdown was aggression on the part of their partner or husband. Half of our respondents stated that they had suffered intimate partner violence. Sometimes mutual assault was involved. Zugazaga (2004) found that domestic violence was the cause of homelessness in the case of 67% of women. Our questionnaire shows that 32% of women who are sleeping rough at present have been subject to domestic violence.

- J (45, f, homeless for 20 years): "*I got married when I was 19 and gave birth to Kath. I had Michael when I was 22. Things started to go downhill with my husband and **he started to hit me**. He hit Kath too and started ranting on about how useless I was... **I occasionally smacked him in the mouth**.*" J is an alcoholic and drug addict.

- D (48, f, homeless for five years) tells a similar story: "*When I was 18, I met someone who was much older than me. I married him when I was 20... To begin with he was nice and he gave me what I had never had from my family, apart from granny. But the moment I told him I was pregnant he slapped me. That carried on for 10 years. **One time he beat me up so badly I went to the police**. I was used to being beaten from when I was a child, and it didn't hurt as long as I was boozing. But you can probably guess the rest... I became an alcoholic.*" D has experienced alcohol addiction and has had psychological problems.

- M (43, f, homeless for less than a year) experienced domestic violence at the hands of her mentally ill partner: "*I had been living with my boyfriend for 20 years. He found himself a younger girlfriend, though we still get on in terms of communicating together. I started seeing someone else and lived with him for four years. After two years* **he began to tyrannise me physically and psychologically**. *I fled from him in just a t-shirt and jacket. Right now he's under investigation. You can be so naive and be convinced that things will change. I don't know… he's a schizophrenic.*" M is not an alcoholic or drug addict and it is not expected that she will remain homeless.

Divorce or separation can also result if **one partner is sent to prison**, and this in turn can lead to homelessness.
- O (53, m, homeless for 20 years) is a repeat offender, alcoholic and drug user: "*When I got out of prison I got together with a girl in T. We got married, had a kid, but then* **I was sent to prison again and she divorced me**.*"
- Z (51, m, homeless for ten years), a repeat offender and alcoholic, has been through many relationships: "*I got married young and* **when I came out of prison I found I was single again**. *I have a son with one woman, but I lost her the last time I was sent to prison.*"
- Z (49, f, homeless for 15 years) saw her marriage break down when she was sent to prison: "**I split up with my husband when they locked me up**. *Both marriages weren't worth a flying fig. Both men drank. I don't.*" Z does not drink or take drugs.

Alcoholism or drug abuse as the cause of marital breakdown

Excessive consumption of alcohol will always impinge on relationships, especially if it applies to only one partner. Many of our male respondents were alcoholics (50%), while another 13% said that they drank frequently but were not addicted. Many women also drank to excess (50%), and this was usually the case even prior to their becoming homeless.
- M (55, m, homeless for 17 years) admits to excessive drinking and irresponsible behaviour: "*I fell in with a bunch of people, about two years previously, and I started to act strange. My wife asked for a divorce.* **It was basically because of alcohol** *and the fact that I no longer paid any attention to the kids.* **I used to arrive home late** *and it was impossible to have a conversation with me.*" M's subsequent relationships were even more problematic and most likely simply fall-back measures: "*For 12 years I lived in Votice. Some woman came up to me at a concert of country music and took me home. My permanent residence had ended so she registered me there. To begin with it was like a proper relationship, but soon it was just because I had nowhere else to go.*"
- V (48, m, homeless for seven years): "*We got divorced because* **I acted like a prick and was drinking heavily**. *She was really nice. She wasn't from the city, she had grown up in a village with a decent family. In their eyes I was a criminal and*

they constantly reminded me of the fact. It was doomed to failure." V remains an alcoholic.

- M (40, m, homeless for seven years): "*I had a girlfriend I lived with for eight years when I was in Slovakia. She was a really good woman, but I treated her badly and she hated my drinking. I haven't had a partner here.* **Who would want me given that I'm still drinking?**" M is an alcoholic. He is aware that most women find this unacceptable.

In the case of J (51, m, homeless for seven years), a gradual increase in alcohol consumption led to the collapse of several relationships and finally to home-lessness: "*Two years after completing my military service I got married, and just as I completed the construction of our home we split up…* **Then I got married a second time and that was when the alcohol began**. *It took its toll on the relationship, and after four years we split up. I knew no limits. It wasn't just alcohol.* **My wife had a friend I started flirting with**, *and then something just snapped inside me and I moved in with the friend. I split up with her too, again because of alcohol. I was starting to become cruel.* **And then I got married for a third time**. *That was some time later, I was 45, and I had a son with her. She was still a young girl when we started… I lived in her place and it was at this point that things began to get serious with the alcohol, it was impossible to carry on.*" J has moderated his drinking but does not have a partner.

A drug addiction is an even more serious obstacle to maintaining a relationship. As it develops faster than an alcohol dependency, longer-term relationships become virtually impossible. If a person begins such a relationship, it very soon ends.

- M (38, m, homeless for two years): "*I found a partner and she was a great help. I stopped taking drugs. For five years things were ok, but then we began to drift apart because her parents started talking…* **She didn't take drugs. Only I took drugs** *and she tolerated it, in inverted commas. Her parents were always getting between us, telling her I was the wrong guy and that she had no future with me. It all got to me and I started doing drugs again. Nobody minded a bit of grass, but pervitin* [meth-amphetamine]*, now that was a different matter.*" M is still an addict.

- K (37, f, homeless for ten years) tells a similar story: "*When I was 18 I started going out with a cool guy. He had his own apartment and I was with him for over eight years. We had two children together. He was really nice. He looked after his grandfather, he had a job and everything…* **I had begun to do a lot of drugs** *at that time and the worst thing was he found out. He said that as long as I was bringing in money it didn't matter. But then I lost my job and we started rowing and I stabbed him. The reason I don't have any teeth is because of the fights we used to have. I lost the children because I had stabbed him with a knife, and I ended up on the street.*" K is a drug addict and alcoholic. Her subsequent partners have all been homeless.

- P (37, m, homeless for four years) had no desire for a stable relationship: "*I haven't really had such relationships, I didn't feel inclined. My relationships are* more one-night stands. I've never had a long-term partner. **When you're on drugs it's not something you want** because you know there's no future in it." P has neither a partner nor children.

The wrong choice of partner often led to the breakdown of a relationship. In several cases our respondents' partners were more problematic than they were, and the downward spiral continued. The breakup of a relationship was **often associated with a partner's dependency on alcohol or drugs**.

- V (51, m, homeless for ten years), who is not dependent on either alcohol or drugs, though likes the occasional drink, had a habit of choosing the wrong partner: "*I was never married. I lived with one girl for seven years. While I was in prison, she found someone else, **some dickhead who taught her to drink and take drugs**. Our son ended up in an institution. When I came out of prison I took up with a woman who had four kids. She was divorced and her husband was a confirmed alcoholic. The fact is I saved her life, because he threw a knife at her. So we got together, I got my son back, but things didn't go well. I was with her for eight years or so, but things fell apart when **they released her former boyfriend from psychiatric hospital** and she got back together with him and threw me out*." V's relationships always came to an end, even though he looked after his partners. His family of origin was problematic.

People who drink to excess often have partners who also have problems with alcohol.

- P (50, m, homeless for 12 years) is a repeat offender and alcoholic: "*I used to have a girlfriend but everything went wrong. Alcohol unfortunately. **She used to get absolutely fucking bladdered**. It's just my bad luck in life to always end up with alcoholics. I've never yet met a normal woman. It was the same when I came out of prison, my girlfriend had found some other bloke. She threw out all my stuff and so I ended up where I am now, with only the clothes on my back*." P's problems with women are very probably linked to his personality. It is difficult to imagine him being attractive to women. P also grew up in a dysfunctional family.

- J (52, m, homeless for five years), a repeat offender and alcoholic, also had relationships with women who drank: "*While in R [in prison] I met a woman and we wrote letters to each other for two and a half years. She used to visit me and wanted me to move in with her on my release... so that's what happened. She was a really nice person **but she drank like a fish**. I hadn't known that. I was with her for about a year and then I fled. Then I met another girl and we started seeing each other and then moved in together. We were together for about five years. One day at work I got together with a Polish girl. I split up with Z and began going out with the Polish girl. She was really nice, worked hard, and suddenly had this idea that we could travel to Poland, because she had an apartment there. So there I was in Poland, for fuck's sake. I had some money, a job, **but after a year she began to drink heavily**. The next thing they got rid of her from work because of her drinking and we split* *up. Ever since then I've been on the street. I often say to myself that I should have remained with Z. She was a nice girl, didn't drink, didn't smoke.*" J has limited his alcohol consumption but does not have a partner.

- R (40, m, homeless for six years) is an alcoholic and was unable to hold down a relationship: "*I only ever had short-term relationships, six months max. I don't know why... **somehow things always went wrong** and we grew apart. **I choose the wrong girls**, that's how I see it.*"

Homeless people who are drug addicts often have partners who take drugs.
- F (40, m, homeless for ten years): "*I guess I've never really had a long-term relationship. We were together three, maybe four years. **She was also homeless and a junkie**. She still is, but unlike me she lives in an apartment and looks after her children. We drifted apart.*" At present F has limited his drug use. He has no partner.
- P (45, f, homeless for eight years) takes drugs and has had drug addicts as partners in the past: "*Me and my boyfriend used to live with a friend of mine, but then my boyfriend was sent to prison. **I found someone else**, but it was more a case of out of the frying pan into the fire. **He was also an addict**. The next boyfriend borrowed the company car I had while working for the Chinese* [a lazy but common designation of the Vietnamese community in the CZ – tr.], *he stole it basically and then I had the Chinese on my back. So I lost my job and in addition I had a rap sheet with embezzlement on it.*" F has had many problems linked with her drug addiction. At present she is trying to resolve her drug problem.
- Z (51, m, homeless for ten years) does not take drugs but drinks to excess: "*My longest relationship was with a woman from L. I was with her for four years. The problem was **she was addicted to drugs**, she used to like pervitin.*"

An inability to have a relationship or sheer indifference. Some of our respondents **were unable to hold down a relationship** even prior to becoming homeless. In addition, many of them are not interested in a genuine partnership, which in their minds is associated with responsibility and the need to adapt to another. This reluctance is often the consequence of psychological problems or personality disorder.
- L (52, m, homeless for two years), who is not dependent on either alcohol or drugs, though does have psychological problems, has never had a stable relationship: "*I have always lived with my parents because I'm single. However, I have had girlfriends. I've always had someone on the go, but then we've split up. Plus I like my privacy and **I wanted to retain my freedom**. Two years is the longest I've lived with anyone. I had a such a relationship ten years ago, but it ended badly. Twice in my life I've raised my hand against a women. We were both violent towards the other. It simply didn't work out.*" L does not even get on with his parents and does not have any real friends.
- H (40, f, homeless for nine years) has never had a long-term relationship, though in her case this is caused by mental health issues: "*I've been with*

*blokes, sure. **But it's never worked out. They've tended to be short-term flings**.*"
H receives invalidity benefit for reasons connected with mental health.

An inability or unwillingness to enter into a stable relationship is sometimes associated with the consequences of emotional deprivation suffered by **people who spent their childhood in an institution**.

- C (47, m, homeless for 23 years) was abandoned as a baby and grew up in a children's home: "*I never felt the need for a stable relationship as such. It's just not my cup of tea. There's always some kind of relationship on the go.*" C is not dependent on either alcohol or drugs. He does not have children.
- Z (42, m, homeless for eleven years) spent his childhood in an institution after his mother was diagnosed as having schizophrenia: "*A couple of relationships looked like they might lead somewhere, but **I didn't want to become dependent**. I reckon my official marital status is single.*"

J (50, m, homeless for two years) has had many short-term relationships and is a repeat offender. This is probably linked to his personality disorder and could also be the consequence of negative experiences from childhood, which he spent partly in a dysfunctional family with illiterate parents and partly in a children's home : "*When I came out of prison, I found myself a girlfriend and started a family. We were living in the apartment left to her by her parents. We had three children in quick succession, though we never got married. Whenever I was released from prison, I always went back to her. **Then I left her**. The worst thing is she was a really great girl, she had everything. The problem was **I was simply unable to live a normal life with a woman**, I couldn't do the whole mommy-daddy-me thing. I lived with her, but that meant kind of being with her for six months and then taking off somewhere else. I was constantly trying to end the relationship during the five years we were together. If I could go back in time and have those years all over, then I would, because she deserved better from me. I don't hit women or nag them. But I have to break free, I can't stick around. A girl's only got to put a foot wrong and I've already grown tired of her.*" J spent a large part of his adult life in prison.

SUMMARY

The relationships that homeless men had even prior to finding themselves on the street were not stable. These relationships failed because the man was uninterested in family life, drank to excess, and paid insufficient attention to his partner and children. Men with a drug dependency tended not to have longer-term partnerships. Many of our respondents expressed indifference regarding stable relationships, probably because they would have to adapt their behaviour to their partner and are unused to displaying self-control. Others were married, but later divorced because of infidelity or some other major life change. Often a poor choice of partner led to divorce, with many girlfriends or wives being addicted to alcohol or drugs.

Many middle-aged homeless women spent their adult lives in a long-term relationship that ended later. However, not even their marriages were successful and it was often clear that they had made a poor choice of partner. The breakup of a relationship was most often caused by infidelity or violence on the part of their partner, and sometimes by their own tendency to resolve problems by means of alcohol or drugs. Women who became homeless as young adults tended to be addicted to alcohol or drugs, and this impacted on their relationships. Many of them had spent their childhood in a problematic family and were unaware of what a conventional relationship between and man and a woman looked like.

Our questionnaire revealed similar results, with 53% of homeless people single, and 34.5% divorced. Only 7.5% were married or cohabiting. Many other researchers have reached similar conclusions, though they unfortunately do not distinguish between the partnerships of men and women. Caton et al. (2005) found that 91% of people sleeping rough were single or divorced, i.e. that their marriage had ended or they had never been married. Muňoz et al. (1999) arrived at similar conclusions, namely that 93% of people sleeping rough were single or divorced. The same was true of Rhoades et al. (2011), who discovered that 94% of homeless people were divorced or single. According to Garibaldi et al. (2005), 95% of homeless people were divorced or single. Zugazaga (2004) distinguished between men and women: men living on the street were usually single (89%), while women were less often single (65%).

4. PARENTHOOD

Many of our respondents grew up in a problematic family or children's home and did not have the opportunity to acquire the necessary life experience. They then went on to fail as parents or not to have children at all. **Half of the men we questioned do not have children** and do not want any (this figure is 10% in the case of the women). (Holton (2011) found that 73% of homeless people are childless.) Some of our respondents have children, but do not look after them, do not or did not pay child maintenance, and are not even in contact with them. The children remained either in the care of their partners or are in foster care or with an adoptive family. A third of the women and a tenth of the men looked after their children for a certain period of time, and paid alimony. It is clear from the interviews we conducted that **most middle-aged homeless people were unable to cope with parenthood, just as they were unable to deal with long-term relationships.**

The role of parent is more demanding than that of partner. It requires a far greater sense of responsibility and the ability to put aside the satisfaction of

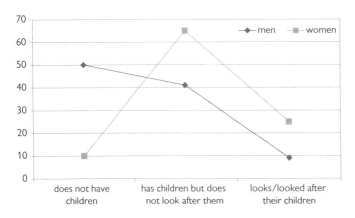

Graph 7. Middle-aged homeless people as parents (in percentages)

one's own needs to the benefit of the child, which is completely dependent on its parents for a long time. People who are unable to have a stable relationship and have not managed to accept responsibility even for themselves, usually fail as parents. If an adult is to provide for their children, they must work. Most homeless people are unable to meet this condition. Sometimes it is even difficult for them to establish an emotional relationship with the child, often because they themselves did not enjoy such a bond with their own parents. The importance of the experience acquired as a child in dealing with the role of parent is confirmed by the extent to which the approach of our respondents to their children conforms to the behaviour of their parents when they themselves were children: $r = 0.545$ ($p = 0.001$). In general, **the level of care a homeless person is capable of offering their own child corresponds to the level of care they were provided in their own childhood**. People who grew up in a functioning family are more able to look after their own children (chi-square = 7.93, df = 2, p = 0.02).

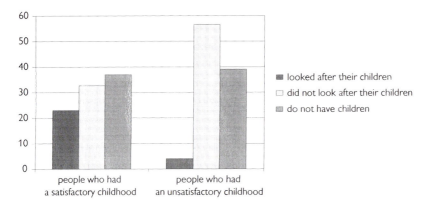

Graph 8. The influence of experiences from childhood on ability to deal with parenthood

Those of our respondents who had only recently become homeless had looked after their children for a certain period of time. In the case of men, they had lived with their wife or partner and children in a joint household up until their divorce. A third of homeless women had looked after their children. The fact that they later lost custody of them was often because they were subsequently abandoned by their partner and had nowhere to live.

- S (43, f, homeless for four years) had a husband who left her for another woman: "*I lost custody of the children because I found myself on the street. I had nowhere to lay my head, and so I pay my husband child maintenance. I have to because the girls are still underage. At present **I give him a thousand crowns** [USD 43], because I find myself in extremis. But I have a problem, because he doesn't want me to see the children. I miss the children most of all.*" S has been sleeping rough since the time of the divorce. She is not an alcoholic or drug addict.

- M (43, f, homeless for eight years) lost her son after her marriage split up as a consequence of her actions: "*I knew that if we split up I would have nowhere to live, and so I agreed that it would be better if he remained with my husband. My husband was clean, had a job, everything. We were together for nine years... We got divorced because I was always escaping.*" M pays maintenance for her son, but is not in contact with him: "***I pay two hundred crowns** [USD 8.6] **in child maintenance** and a hundred for the debt ensuing from alimony.... I just sent him two hundred crowns for Christmas. **In court my son told me he does not want to see me**. It saddens me, but what can I do? My own son doesn't want to communicate with me. He says he sees no reason after six years.*" M was unable to deal with marriage or parenthood because of her addiction to alcohol and drugs. She has spent time in prison.

It is clear from the graph that people who have been sleeping rough for a long time did not discharge their duties as parents even prior to becoming homeless. We can assume that this is the consequence of certain personality traits or

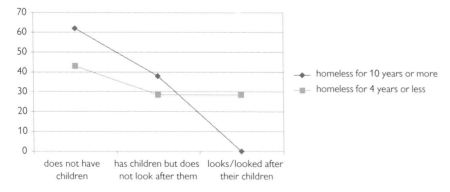

Graph 9. Parenthood amongst middle-aged homeless people according to time spent on the street (shown in percentages)

a deprived childhood, because many of them did not even want children. Childlessness is one of the factors that can weaken links to society and to any close friend who is part of it. **The period of time a person has been sleeping rough impacts on their approach to parenthood** (chi-square = 8.41, df = 2, p = 0.001). Those that have been homeless for the shortest period of time are more often parents who look after their children in some way. They have retained at least certain socially important abilities that allow them to live a standard lifestyle, including the creation of a family, for a certain period of time.

Some of our respondents, especially those who lived with their children for a significant period of time, **are interested in them and contribute to their upkeep**.

- M (45, m, homeless for five years) still sees his own children and those of his partner too: "*I travel there a lot. I take care of the younger girl* [not his biological daughter]. *The courts ruled that her grandparents should have custody, because they were full of shit about me being an alcoholic and her mother undergoing psychiatric treatment and our home being a mess, blah blah. Everyone says I'm a complete asshole to look after her. But I have never differentiated between the children and* **they looked on me as their dad**, *because they didn't have their own dad.*" M grew up in a functioning family, which is perhaps the reason for his willingness to look after both his own children and those of his partner. However, he drinks to excess and so the grandparents' reservations were not without justification.
- R (46, m, homeless for four years): "*I get on fine with my sons.* **We chat over the internet**. *They know that I am living rough and don't make a big deal of it.* **I pay alimony** *of CZK 1,000* [USD 43]. *I earn the money by doing casual work because no way am I going to prison.*" R also grew up in a functioning family and only found himself on the street later in life as a consequence of his drinking.
- I (40, m, homeless for one year): "**I'm in contact with my daughters**, *though they don't know that I'm sleeping rough right now. I pay alimony of CZK 1,000. I agreed with my ex that* **I'd send her at least something**." I was also raised by caring parents.

Sometimes it is adult children, especially daughters, who are interested in contact.

- L (50, m, homeless for one year) was tracked down by his adult daughter: "*I'm in contact with my daughter by telephone. She knows I'm homeless. In fact,* **it was she who tracked me down in Naděje** [see above]. *It's a weird feeling.*" L was married for many years and took care of his children after a fashion. Alcohol abuse is a big problem.
- E (53, m, homeless for one year) is in a similar position: "*My daughter lives here in Č.M. She has two children and is contact with me.* **She comes to check me out occasionally** *and brings me food.*" E is recovering from a stroke, the consequences of which restrict him considerably.

- M (50, f, homeless for eight years) has a son who wants to see his mother: "*My son is wonderful, a lovely child. He's 29. **He visits me once every week or so** and says he will help me find my way back into normal live.*" M is an alcoholic.

Many of our respondents are not interested in their children and know nothing about them. (82% are not interested in their children, and only 18% display some degree of interest.) There are many reasons. Sometimes they are too ashamed or do not want to leave their comfort zones. Other times their lack of interest is the consequence of a severely damaged personality. For instance, L (38, m, homeless for 21 years) has no interest in and knows nothing about his children: "*I have a boy and a girl. **Both are in foster care**. I couldn't tell you exactly when they were born, though I know the girl was born in May 2000. I was with my ex-wife. I regret the fact they took my boy away from me. They waited for me to make yet another mistake and then swept him directly into foster care.*" The children were taken by the Office for the Protection of the Social Rights of Children (OSPOD) from the family at a time when L was in prison. L grew up without a mother and with a very problematic father.

The **excessive consumption of alcohol or drugs** is often involved in these cases, and the individuals involved tend to have been sleeping rough for some time.
- D (40, m, homeless for nine years) uses drugs and alcohol, is not interested in his children and knows nothing of them: "*I have three kids in all. Two with one woman, they're now 18 and 16… **I have no idea where they are** and the police don't want to tell me.*"
- O (53, m, homeless for 20 years), an alcoholic and drug addict, is in a similar position: "*I know the boy is still alive, but **that's all I do know**. **I'm just not interested**. I was supposed to pay alimony. He always received something from prison.*" O comes from a problematic family and spent some of his childhood in a children's home. He is incapable of sustaining a relationship.
- M (40, m, homeless for seven years) is an alcoholic and has no interest in his daughter, though the daughter has expressed an interest in seeing her father: "*I had one daughter who's probably about 20. She wrote to me via Mr Pěnkava* [director of the Department of Social Prevention, Prague] *asking me to get in contact and saying she would like to see me. But **I'm so lazy, I can't even be bothered**. It makes me sad.*" M spent his childhood in a normal family. His later relationships were no doubt negatively impacted by his excessive drinking.

Women who drink heavily can also lose interest in parenthood.
- M (37, f, homeless for five years): "***I left my children with my parents** because I had nowhere to go… The younger one, the daughter, is with her father and my son is with my mum. **I don't pay alimony** because he* [the former partner] *forbade me from being in contact with the children. So I told him he wouldn't receive a single cent from me. And I don't pay for my son because I let my mum have my share of my dad's*

*inheritance if she looked after the kids. I last saw my daughter two years ago when I rang her. **I don't know where she lives,** she's not allowed to tell me.*" M has been dependent on both drugs and alcohol. She herself grew up in a functioning family.

- V (46, f, homeless for seven years) lost one of her children in a car accident and blames the trauma induced for her inability to cope with parenthood and her excessive alcohol consumption: "*I wasn't on maternity leave for long the second time around, because my daughter was killed in a car accident. In 2001 I gave birth to Patrick, but it was too soon after the accident and I hadn't yet got over it, and so in 2003 I lost my boy because I was getting drunk. Psychologically I simply wasn't ready. I left my daughter with my parents, but **my son is in foster care**. I fucked it up basically, and I know it's my fault… In the end my parents brought up my little girl. She's an adult now, and **I have no idea where she lives**.*" V drinks alcohol frequently but is not addicted. She spent her own childhood in a functioning family.

Drug addiction, especially when combined with alcohol abuse, negatively impacts the fulfilment of all obligations, including those of parent. Drugs undermine human relationships to an even greater extent than alcohol. In these cases, it no longer matters what kind of childhood a person might have had, since the drug addiction is so dominant that it overwhelms all positive experiences.

- M (38, m, homeless for two years) is a drug addict and has no interest in his daughter: "*I have a daughter, the result of me being careless with a girlfriend when I was 21. **I left her** because I simply wasn't up to the job. **I send them some money** whenever I find some casual work.*"
- J (39, homeless for five years) is a drug addict, has no interest in his children, and does not make any contribution to their upkeep: "*I don't pay alimony because my ex wrote that she is a single parent and didn't want to place a burden on me. **I'm not in touch with the children** because that was what the courts ordered. **But because of that they don't want alimony from me**.*"
- J (45, f, homeless for 20 years): "***I lost my children because I took drugs and drank**. There was no contact with Katka, the elder, and then after seven years she came to visit me at work. **I have no contact whatsoever** with Michael* [her son]. *He doesn't even remember me. He was three years old when I left home.*" J's daughter wants nothing to do with her. She blames J for abandoning the family and displaying no interest in her children. Speaking of the situation, the daughter told us: "*She abandoned me and my brother when he was only one year old and I was four. She told the court she had no intention of looking after two brats and upped and left… I don't know whether she is still alive or not and frankly I don't give a damn.*" J's daughter grew up in a children's home and ended up on the street. At present she lives with her young son in a refuge. She does not drink or take drugs.

A lack of support, the accumulation of personal problems, and an unreliable partner leads some women **to relinquish their child**. They explain why they gave up their child for adoption by saying they wanted it to have a better life.

- H (40, f, homeless for nine years): "*I gave birth to twins, both girls, and I gave them up for adoption. I think it was the right decision. It was my fault for bringing them into the world.* **I wanted them to have at least a normal life**. *I was already half living on the street at that time.*" H is an alcoholic and is at present receiving invalidity benefit for psychiatric indications.

- J (50, f, homeless for most of her adult life): "*I gave up my son for adoption because we had absolutely nowhere to live and apartments are expensive. My step-mother took care of things.* **It's best not to have the kind of mother I had**, *don't you think? I didn't really take much care of him.*" J spent her childhood with an adoptive family. She is not an alcoholic or drug addict.

- P (37, f, homeless for 15 years) has given birth to eight children and does not look after any of them. She gave her consent to adoption in the case of one of them. She was unable to cope with the duties of motherhood: "*I looked after the little girl until she was two, and the little boy until he was about six months. But there were arguments and I wasn't up to it psychologically and I left for Prague.*" Since 2001 she has alternated between being homeless and living in different shelters. She did not look after her next daughter, who was born in 2005: "*I had no idea that shelters existed, and so I put my daughter up for adoption. A friend agreed to take the girl when she was born, because I knew that with her she would have everything she needed… I knew I would have to go to prison and I couldn't be bothered to find a shelter, so I carried the child to term with the thought that she'd end up with her cousin or be adopted.*" This was what happened and the child lives in foster care with her cousin. At present P is again pregnant, for the twelfth time: "*If it's born and survives, it'll be my ninth child. The father of my oldest daughter is dead, the father of my younger son has him living with him. I have a daughter from an affair and the rest I have with my husband.* **These are in foster care** *with my cousin in Karlovy Vary… They took my children away from me because I couldn't provide a stable environment, and in the case of the last one it was because I was living in shelters.*" P communicates with her children via Facebook, but does not look after them: "*I miss them. On the one hand I have greater freedom without them, but on the other it's a strain, especially when you're serving time.*" P grew up with only her father. Her parents divorced when she was three and her mother left the family. She was quickly pregnant with her first and then her second boyfriend. She drinks heavily and has been in and out of prison. Her husband is also homeless.

Several of our respondents now regret not having taken care of their children and not being in contact with them today. They console themselves by saying that it would make no sense. They are convinced that their children would have a low opinion of them for not having coped with parenthood.

- S (51, m, homeless for 14 years) had no interest in his son: "*I have a 20-year old. He knows I am homeless.* **He thinks it's my fault.** *'You left and we often had nothing to eat on a Saturday and Sunday.' So when he was 15 he said, 'Listen, I'm not going to go on about things. I'll go for a beer with you if you want, but I'm not going to ring you.'* **It's true I could have done more.**"
- G (50, m, homeless for ten years) drinks to excess and takes drugs and is not in contact with his daughter: "*We have a daughter. I had her when I was 27. No,* **I'm not in contact with her.** *She has her own life.* **I don't want to complicate her life.** *It's quite enough to have fucked up my own shitty life. We haven't been in contact for ten years, maybe longer.*" G has never had a long-term relationship and does not have a partner at present. He has not been in contact with anyone from his family for a long time.
- V (48, m, homeless for seven years), a repeat offender and alcoholic, has the same approach to parenthood: "*Yeah, I had two children with her.* **I never see them.** *I paid alimony mainly from prison. I haven't seen them for almost 15 years. They have their own lives and there'd be no point whatsoever in interfering. God knows how they're doing.* **It might hinder them more** *than it would help them.*"

Some of our respondents would like to be in contact with their adult offspring but **not so long as they are homeless**. Z (51, m, homeless for ten years) is an alcoholic: "*I'd like to meet them, but* **I have to get my life in order first.** *They barely know me. I saw both of them when they were small. I'll travel there and check things out as soon as I get my shit together and have a place to live.*" This will probably not happen, though his procrastination means that Z has not resigned himself to never renewing the relationships with his children. Inasmuch as work is ongoing on reuniting our respondents with their children, the process takes place within the framework of a motivational interview spread over several stages. First off, the individual admits that they don't know the whereabouts of their children. They then claim that the children are better off without them. The third stage is characterised by shame at the thought of their children seeing them as homeless people, and at this point the respondent expresses the desire "to get his shit together". Then, and only then, is there an attempt made at establishing contact.

SUMMARY

Many of the people we spoke to grew up in a problematic family in which they were unable to acquire any experience of standard parental behaviour. As a consequence, many of them have themselves failed as parents or have no children of their own. The individuals who have been sleeping rough for a longer period of time especially tend to be those who coped least well with parenthood. There is also a greater likelihood of personality disorder in these people. They often do not know the whereabouts of their children or what they are doing. Many of them refuse to re-establish contact because they think they might have a bad influence. People who have been sleeping rough for a shorter period of time or only became homeless in middle age usually looked after their children successfully for a certain period of time. Many of them pay for their children's upkeep, albeit the minimum amount, and despite living on the street have not broken off contact altogether. Alcohol or drug addiction is often the reason they lose interest in their children and terminate their relationship. Drug addiction especially can destroy any and all relationships.

Most homeless people (80%) who have children did not look after them. At present only a quarter of them are in contact with their children. Only 13% of people living in shelters maintain contact with their children (Marek, 2017). In our younger cohort only 10% of men and 50% of women had children, but they too did not look after them. The children of such parents end up being looked after by relatives, living in a children's home or being adopted. Some of our respondents gave up their children for adoption immediately upon giving birth, while others took care of them for a period of time before realising that they were incapable of dealing with such a fundamental change of lifestyle (Vágnerová, Csémy, Marek, 2013).

A lack of interest in their own children and the alienation that comes from not being in contact with them eliminates one of the possible supports that might help our respondents find their way back to mainstream society. Loss of contact with the next generation consolidates a person's links to the homeless community and contributes to their homelessness becoming chronic. Their social disaffiliation leads to generational links being severed and their exclusion from the broader family community, which could otherwise represent a nurturing environment.

5. EMPLOYMENT AND ACCOMMODATION PRIOR TO BECOMING HOMELESS

For the most part, homeless people have neither work nor accommodation, and it is not important which of these basic requirements of a normal life they lost first. In order to understand their life stories what is important is to know whether and how long they worked and how they supported themselves. Given that our respondents became homeless between the ages of 30 and 40, up until then they usually had some kind of job. However, right from the start many of them were restricted by a lack of education and professional qualifications. Similar conclusions were reached by Kuchařová and Janurová (2016), who found that 37% of homeless people who had been clients of the Naděje centre only had a basic school education, sometimes uncompleted. Education and professional qualifications are an important prerequisite for finding a job. The ability to hold down a job, however, depends on other factors, e.g. personality traits

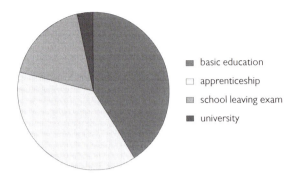

basic education

apprenticeship

school leaving exam

university

Graph 10. Level of education among middle-aged homeless people (shown in absolute figures)

(conscientiousness, a sense of responsibility, a balanced outlook, etc.), the level of work habits acquired, an ability to resist alcohol and drugs, and the possibility of acquiring funds through illegal means.

It is clear from graph 10 that homeless people often have only a basic education (41%). This figure is far higher than in the population as a whole: in 2011, 22.6% had only a basic education (Czech Statistical Office, 2014). Our questionnaire revealed similar results, with 37% of respondents having received only a basic education, 44% an apprenticeship, 16% having passed their school-leaving exam [equivalent to a baccalaureate], and 3% having graduated from college or university. The level of education can impact on the risk of becoming homeless. As is clear from the following graph (11), people who have been sleeping rough for a long time are more likely to have received only a basic education. The difference between chronic and short-term homeless people is statistically significant, chi-square = 14.67 (df = 2, p = 0.001). It is clear that **a lack of education increases not only the risk of ending up on the street, but also the**

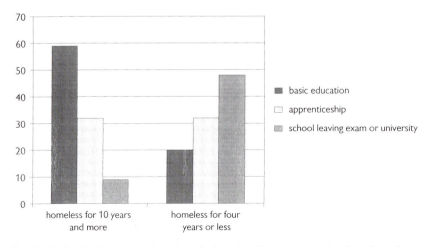

basic education

apprenticeship

school leaving exam or university

Graph 11. Level of education based on the length of time a person has been homeless (the graph shows relative frequencies)

likelihood of becoming chronically homelessness. (A low level of education may have many different causes. It may be associated with neglect within the family or with unfavourable personality traits.) People who have been sleeping rough for ten years and more often lack professional qualifications and it is therefore more difficult for them to find a job. More complex factors may also be involved. Social disaffiliation may be caused by personality traits and a reluctance to observe and discharge duties, first of all within an educational context, and later on in employment. It is not only more difficult for such people to find work, but also to hold down a job. Another significant factor is a lack of productive work habits, which many homeless people never had the chance to acquire since not even their parents had them.

Most young homeless people (81%) had difficulties in fulfilling their duties even as children and, as a consequence, did poorly at school (Vágnerová, Csémy and Marek, 2013). Failure at school and hence a lack of qualifications was a significant risk factor contributing to their later social disaffiliation. The same conclusion was reached by, amongst others, C. Bearsley-Smith et al. (2008) and M. van den Bree et al. (2009). The most frequent cause of poor school results in young homeless people was a combination of disadvantageous personality traits and underdeveloped self-regulatory functions. These traits are manifest in a lax approach to work and an employer's requirements, and even failure to respect and abide by the rules of a hostel or shelter (Votta and Manion, 2003).

5.1 MEANS OF LIVELIHOOD PRIOR TO BECOMING HOMELESS

A factor that plays an important role in a person both becoming and remaining homeless is an **inability or unwillingness to work systematically**. This may be caused by a lack of work habits, irresponsibility, and an unwillingness to accept the various restrictions and discomfort that any job occasionally involves. Some of our respondents sponge off their relatives and acquaintances, and when the patience of these people has run out, they end up on the streets. They have problems managing their lives and are unwilling to adapt. Their lives centre around loitering and merely surviving, something that requires no effort. As Pěnkava (2015) reminds us, it is difficult for them both to find work and to retain it, because there is no interest in unqualified and unreliable workers. The path to homelessness very often begins with an unfavourable starting position with zero social, economic and educational capital (Prudký, 2015).

Work is an important prerequisite for the existence of an adult person in society. A person without work is at greater threat of becoming homeless. Many of the same reasons people lose their jobs or are not hired can also be risk factors as far as homelessness is concerned (e.g. alcoholism or drug addiction). Given the importance of work as a source of both economic security and self-fulfilment, one of the goals of our research was to discover whether and how long people who are currently homeless worked when younger, whether they held down a job for any significant period of time or moved from job to job, and why they eventually lost their job.

The difference between people who have been homeless for varying periods of time is significant (chi-square = 18.70, df = 2, p = 0,001). **People who have been sleeping rough for a long time were unwilling or unable to work from the very start**. Their professional career is often interrupted by a stretch in prison. These are often individuals with only a basic education and no professional qualifications. The relationship between education and employment is shown in the following graph.

Educational level and employment history are related (chi square = 18.37, df = 2, p = 0.001). People **who have some kind of professional qualification will find better jobs and last longer in them**. The level of education usually has a positive influence on motivation to work, though it is true that even qualified people are sometimes unwilling to work. In these cases the fault lies elsewhere (alcoholism, drug addiction, or criminality).

If we divide up our group of middle-aged respondents on the basis of whether and for how long they worked prior to becoming homeless, several subgroups are created. One of these comprises **people who have no professional qualifications, are unwilling to work and lack work habits**. Laziness and an unwillingness to observe and discharge duties was often the cause of failure to complete any professional training, and the resulting lack of qualifications led to difficulties in finding work. Such people experienced problems right from the start. They found it difficult to find work, always supposing they wanted to. They ended up on the street earlier. Some of them, e.g. C (47, m, homeless since the age of 23), have never officially worked in their lives: "*I've never had a paid job,*

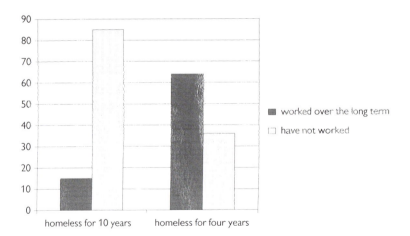

Graph 12. Ability to work prior to becoming homeless according to duration of homelessness (in percentages).

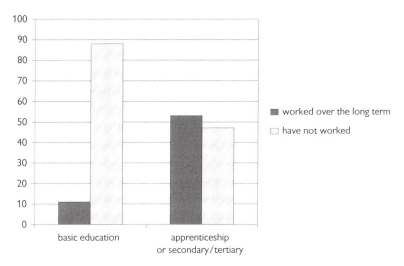

Graph 13. Relationship between level of education and ability to work (in percentages). NB: Long-term employment refers to being in a job for five years at least.

never in my life... I made a living by busking." C grew up in a children's home and only has a basic education.

Some of our respondents found work but were unable to hold down a job.

- R (40, m, homeless for five years): "*I didn't finish school. I didn't give a damn.* ***I mucked about a bit, I was on the dole****, and then a friend told me about some casual work building scaffolding. So I became a scaffolder.*"[2]
- M (54, m, homeless for 20 years) has only a basic education: "*I was banged up for vagrancy when I was twenty. Then I went to work for Liaz* [a manufacturer of trucks], *where I worked for two years,* ***after which I got the sack for not turning up to work****.*"
- O (53, m, homeless for 20 years) tells a similar story: "*I was in and out of prison and otherwise I did bugger all. I'd work for two or three months, that's all.* ***I'd work the first month then wait for the second and leave****. For as long as a paycheck lasted. One time I only lasted 16 hours.*"
- P (37, f, homeless for 15 years) has only a basic education and was unwilling to work for any lengthier period of time: "*I worked as a street cleaner, then in the food industry in a kitchen. I'd stick it out for maybe two to three months, but then I'd get bored and leave. My problem has been sticking around in one place...* ***I've never managed to hold down a job for long****.*"

---

2 People who are unemployed can receive unemployment benefit for a certain period of time. However, they must fulfil certain duties, e.g. they must regularly visit the employment office. If they fail to meet these conditions, they lose their benefit.

Most people who are currently sleeping rough were at least employed to begin with. Some were able to hold down a job, while others simply moved from one job to another. V (51, m, homeless for ten years) remained in his first job for some time, but then decided to quit: "*After leaving school I found a job... I remained there for twenty years, by which time I was about forty. **I was bored out of my skull**. The money was good, and if I hadn't spent everything on women I'd have saved something. Then I was unemployed, after which I found work at a glassworks. The work was hard and we did shifts, and my pay was far lower. I lasted about three or four years there and **then I quit and became unemployed*** [at the age of 43]." In V's case problems with relationships and the loss of his home led to his becoming unemployed.

A turning point in the lives of many of our respondents was losing their job, whether because the company they were working for went bankrupt or because of redundancy. An inability to cope with the loss of employment increases the risk of a person becoming homeless, especially if they have no social support to fall back on or money saved. Š (46, f, homeless for four years) was made redundant: "*I always had a job. The Post Office basically kept me alive. But **they made me redundant** and offered me severance pay of three months' wages. I found myself jobless and I was on the dole for six months.*" A contributing factor in Š becoming homeless was her divorce and the subsequent loss of accommodation. She has been unable to find other work even though she does possess professional training.

An individual **may possess qualifications** but be unlucky enough to work in a sphere **for which there is no longer demand**. Mass layoffs mean they are forced to look for work in another area, often without success.
- M (55, m, homeless for 17 years) received professional training but was part of a mass layoff: "*I worked in a mine on one of the huge machines they have. I worked there for fifteen years. **But then we were laid off and I found it difficult to find work**. I moved from job to job.*"
- R (49, m, homeless for ten years) tells a similar story: "*After completing my military service I returned to agriculture. I drove a tractor and got married. Then I found casual work on a silo and remained there for a year or so. **But they needed to reduce headcount so I was laid off** and joined a travelling fair... I worked on the carousels for around two years, and then bolted.*"

The loss of a person's livelihood may be related to **failure in business** and the debts arising therefrom.
- L (52, m, homeless for two years) completed his secondary-school education but was unsuccessful as an entrepreneur: "*I used to work for a travel agency. Then I set up my own brokerage agency and that closed down in 2006. The agency **simply wasn't bringing in enough for me to survive** and the **big agencies were walking all over me**.*"

- M (50, m, homeless for twenty years) is another unsuccessful entrepreneur: "*I worked for a year at Mercedes. Then I handed in my notice and ended up unemployed.* **I started to do business in the advertising industry and that was a total cock-up**." M has a university education. He has qualifications and is not dependent on either alcohol or drugs. His disaffiliation was probably caused more by personality disorders that impacted not only his career but his relationships too.

Self-employed work on the basis of a Trade Licence can be risky, as L (50, m, homeless for one year) discovered to his cost: "*I was a construction engineer at the same firm until I was 45. Then I sorted out the paperwork and went self-employed.* **However, things didn't go as I'd planned**. *At the age of 45 I lost my job and since then I've had no work. Before becoming homeless I tried to find work, but to no avail.*" L has a secondary school education. He has not helped by his heavy drinking.

Some of our respondents had **many jobs in the past but never held any of them down for any period of time**. There may be many reasons for this. Either **they were unable to do the work, they did not like it, or they were laid off**. If they do not have a family, they are more inclined to move from job to job, often because they do not enjoy the work and see no point to it.
- Z (42, m, homeless for eleven years) is a good example: "*My first job involved excavation. I was a kind of auxiliary worker. Then I worked for a goldsmith, but only for a short time. To be honest I was pretty crap at the job. Then I worked for Gastro, a kitchen facility.*" Z has received training. His situation is complicated by his drinking problem.
- F (43, m, homeless for five years) tells a similar story: "*I had a driving licence, everything. I was a truck driver for eight years. Then one day I simply stopped enjoying it.* **I got drunk with a few of my buddies and decided that was it, to hell with it**... *Then I went to Šumava* [the Bohemian Forest, a mountain range in Central Europe] *to plant trees, and then to Krkonoše* [a mountain range on the border of the Czech Republic and Poland], *where I worked at a sawmill. Then I worked for Baťa* [a shoe shop], *but* **I didn't enjoy that either**. *Since then I've had loads of different jobs.*" F has received training in the past. He too has problems with alcohol.

A person can be laid off or quit their job because of **workplace conflict**, especially with managers. This is often related to reduced social adaptability.
- S (52, m, homeless for 17 years): "*I had a job even before doing my military service. I worked in a DM warehouse, you know, the drugstore. After military service I returned, but not for long because they sacked me. Then I became a hospital porter and then I was a security guard for a year. After that I started moving between casual jobs because I'd end up quarrelling with my boss and have to leave.*" S has only a basic education and only limited job opportunities.

- G (50, m, homeless for ten years) is a repeat offender who had problems with his superiors: "*I've been a locksmith, fitter, binder, whatever. When they released me from prison I worked down a mine in Ostrava. I was a locksmith for about three years, but then **I punched the foreman**, who was stealing from the company, and had to leave.*" G has received training in the past.
- P (52, m, homeless for two years): "*I taught for fifteen years and then worked for a juvenile detention centre. But I felt the financial conditions weren't ideal and **I had a row with the director**. I handed in my notice on the spot and left.*" P has a university education. His situation is not helped by his mental health issues and he has been diagnosed with bipolar disorder.

Quitting a job is sometimes linked with a loss of accommodation, whether this be the consequence of divorce or failure to pay rent. Many people discover that they have misjudged a situation and have unrealistic expectations. When these are not met, they find themselves on the street because they have neither work nor accommodation.

- B (51, m, homeless for 20 years) simply upped and left his job: "*I was trained and after military service I worked in Vlašim, where they make hunting rifles. I was there for nine years. I was a tool setter on the ball bearings. The money was good, but I can't say I enjoyed the work. So me and my father decided we'd sell our apartment and I'd travel to Prague. And so **I left my job just when the apartment was being sold**. I was sure I'd find work.*" In the end, B spent all of his money, found no work and ended up homeless.
- S (51, m, homeless for 17 years): "*I used to work in Poldovka as a carpenter. After three years I moved to Prague and began to work digging drains. I did that for two or three years. **After my divorce I stayed in a hostel**, but it was temporary accommodation and it always came to an end in winter. **When there's no work or you're not paid, that's where you end up**. On Friday I couldn't pay the rent. Nobody was interested in why, they simply chucked me out and locked the door.*" S had received training, but his employment prospects were not helped by his alcoholism.
- J (52, m, homeless for five years) had the same problem: "*For a year I worked on demolition. Everything was going fine and I was living in a hostel in Palmovka. And then **suddenly he** [the company owner] **stopped paying us and we had to move out** because we couldn't afford the rent.*" J had received professional training and has been on the street for five years. In his case, too, the situation was made more complicated by his heavy drinking.

Our respondents most often lost their job because of drinking to excess. This led to their neglecting their work, absenteeism, and sometimes workplace conflict. In these cases education and professional qualifications did not play such an important role, since alcohol had already had a devastating effect on everything.

- V (48, m, homeless for seven years): "*I used to work for Mitas* [a tyre manufacturer in Prague]*, but **they got rid of me because I got drunk and didn't turn up to work for three days**.*"
- M (40, m, homeless for seven years) tells a similar story: "*I used to work in Baník as a miner. I was there for about two years. But then they made us redundant because there was no work for us. So I started work for Škoda, but **they chucked me out, because of alcohol it goes without saying**.*"
- R (46, m, homeless for four years) lost several jobs because of alcohol: "*After senior school I became a soldier in a division based in Kleč. In 2000 they discharged me from the army because **I had begun to have problems with alcohol**. After that we moved to S, and I began working for Penny Market. I remained there for about four years and then started drinking again. **I failed to turn up for work three or four times and they got rid of me**.*"
- M (37, f, homeless for five years) also had problems with alcohol: "*I was a waitress in the Hotel Evropa, but then I was sent to prison… Then I worked in a factory and that came to an end because of my boozing. I slit my wrists and they locked me up in a lunatic asylum.*" M is not only an alcoholic, but has problems with drugs.

Drug use, with the increased risk of dependency, leads even more quickly to **loss of employment**. In addition, the economic situation of drug addicts is exacerbated by the accumulation of debt and often also by property crime. After completing a stretch in prison, people often find themselves without accommodation or work and end up on the street.

- H (50, m, homeless for 20 years) lost his job because of drug use: "*I worked for about four years for a company called Hand Tables. But when **I began to take pervitin they got rid of me**. That was it, suddenly I found myself in debt.*"
- Some drug addicts have never had a stable job, such as P (37, m, homeless for four years): "***I've never had a job**. I don't have one now. I do casual work but I can't find a proper job. It's the same problem everywhere, i.e. my criminal record.*" P has repeatedly spent time in prison for property crime. Like other addicts, he resorted to crime in order to fund his addiction.

A prison sentence will bring a swift end to a promising career. This usually involves property crime, which is related to a poor attitude to work. Some people find it easier to steal money than to earn it.

- J (50, m, homeless for two years) is a repeat offender. He was unable to hold down a job because of a poor attitude to work and has spent a considerable part of his life in prison: "*I worked for about a year in a factory, **but then I started to get bored**. I left the job and started wondering about how to earn a bit of cash without having to work. **I started to steal** and once more found myself in prison, this time for a year. When I came out I couldn't find work. So I started stealing again and they locked me up. After that I gave up the idea of work.*" J has only a basic education.

- M (49, m, homeless for twenty years) has no desire to work: "**Work is a necessary evil**. *It's something you have to do when you need money. Because you have to work, I found lodgings and a job, but* **I simply didn't have the right habits**. *I didn't give a shit about anything.* **If anything, I wanted to return to prison**, *because at least there I had some security. I didn't have to worry about a thing. Outside, in a hostel, you have to worry about food. I have never known how to cook or do the laundry or whatever, so I just wandered around and basically just survived until they locked me up again.*" M is another who has only a basic education.
- J (45, m, homeless for six years) tells a similar story: "*I trained as a carpenter. Then I did military service and after that I began to steal.* **That was the first time I went to prison**. *When they released me because I had received a conditional sentence, I went to work for the Vietnamese. The whole time I worked for the Vietnamese I was on the dole.* **I had no desire to work whatsoever. I was incredibly lazy** *when working for the Vietnamese. It was far easier work, but above all I had money in my pocket.*" The client had received professional training in the past.

A person may sometimes lose their job and have difficulties in finding another due to a deterioration in their state of health. Several of our respondents found it difficult to find and hold onto work due to mental health issues.
- I (41, m) has schizophrenia: "*After passing my school leaving exams I joined a building company and worked there for two years... After these attacks* [involving psychological problems] **it became difficult to find work** *and I ended up just taking casual work.*"
- H (40, f) quit her job due to mental health issues: "*I was a teacher in a music school...* **but I lost the confidence to contact the schools** *and ended up accepting casual work in a bakery in Ostrava. For two years or so I distributed the newspaper Metro.*" H was diagnosed with acute psychotic disorder, which prevented her from continuing in her profession of music teacher. This situation was made more complicated by her heavy drinking. At present she is receiving invalidity benefit because of psychiatric indications.

Our respondents' ability to work is sometimes affected by **more serious somatic symptom disorder or post-injury pain**.
- M (51, m, homeless for one year) suffered kidney disease: "*I used to be a travelling rigger, but that became impossible when I went down sick.* **I have been sick for the last ten years. I need dialysis** *because my kidneys don't work.*" M has a secondary school education. He lives in a shelter.
- J (51, m, homeless for seven years) lost his job and found himself living on the street as the result of an injury: "**Ten years ago I had an accident**. *It was the last time I had a secure job and I fell off a roof... I basically found myself without a home and without a job.*" J has received professional training in the past. Problems with alcohol contributed to both his injury and his homelessness.

SUMMARY

It is clear from our interviews that our respondents often behaved irresponsibly and failed to consider the consequences of their decisions. They were inclined to react impulsively, and were unwilling to accept any restriction on the satisfaction of an immediate need. This may have been due to laziness, an unwillingness to subordinate themselves to the whims of a manager, or their consumption of drugs or alcohol. They were unable to weigh up situations, and it is possible that they were not even interested in the potential risk of their ill-considered decisions. They were unwilling to fulfil their duties at work, and if they were not enjoying themselves or the behaviour of their superior was not to their liking, they quit their job. If they lost their job, they often gave up hope of finding another. They were unwilling to make any effort or to accept any compromise, and always followed what for them was the path of least resistance, i.e. they remained unemployed. Their inability or unwillingness to give any thought to the future was reflected in the reckless way they spent money (on the rare occasion they had any), and they lacked any financial reserves to help them through periods without work.

Excessive drinking or drug use destroyed their motivation and their work habits, and accelerated their decline. An unwillingness to work systematically, coupled with the need to make money, saw them give priority to casual work without an official contract, a policy that carries its own risks. They would often not be paid for such work, and in the meantime their back payments for health and social insurance would mount up. Later this would become a serious problem. Repeated stretches in prison made it more difficult to find work upon their release. In addition to skills atrophy, they would acquire a criminal record, which would often be the reason they were turned down by other potential employers.

As regards the career they were pursuing prior to becoming homeless, our respondents can be divided into three subgroups.

- Some individuals had **problems finding work right from the start**. They lacked not only an education, but also the motivation to work and constructive habits. Sometimes they would acquire funds through illegal practices and would then spend time in prison. This group includes individuals who began drinking alcohol or taking drugs when they were still young.
- Some of our respondents had **gained professional qualifications and begun work**. However, they were unable to hold down a job, were often absent from work and involved in workplace conflicts. The career trajectory of several was severely disrupted by an increasing problem with alcohol or drug use.
- The career path of some of our respondents was not disrupted by an inability or unwillingness to work. These individuals **lost their jobs as a**

consequence of mass redundancies or bankruptcy, after which they were unable to find a new job. Their career was in some cases derailed by an ill-considered decision to leave home or an overly optimistic view of the possibility of finding work and accommodation elsewhere. In several cases either physical or mental health issues led to their losing their job.

III. LIFE ON THE STREET

1. CAUSES OF HOMELESSNESS

The descent into homelessness may take place over several stages. It often takes the form of a downward spiral symbolising gradual disaffiliation (Hutson and Liddiard, 1994). There may be many different causes and a variety of triggers that immediately precede it. These may sometimes seem banal. Nevertheless they represent the culmination of longer-term problems that have gradually accumulated. A domino effect ensues in which one problem triggers another, and this process can be very difficult to deal with for the individual concerned. If a person only becomes homeless in middle age, this will be a process that manifests itself in a gradual deterioration of their status. Such people display an unwillingness to accept unpleasant duties or to resolve and adapt to ordinary situations. The situation is then compounded by a tendency to resort to alcohol. This in turn results in the breakdown of a relationship, after which the individual concerned leaves home. They then may stay temporarily with friends or in hostels and move from job to job. The final stage of this downward trajectory involves the loss of work and accommodation.

An accumulation of stressful events contributes to a person becoming homeless. Muňoz et al. (1999) found that people currently on the street had experienced most of these events prior to becoming homeless (45% prior to, and 39% concurrently with, the descent into homelessness, which means these events can be deemed triggers). Our respondents stated that, as soon as they found themselves living on the street, the frequency of these stressful events decreased to around 19%. The following were regarded as serious matters: financial problems (80%), a breakdown in close relationships (48%), imprisonment (40%), and alcohol or drug-related problems (53%). These results may have been influenced by the way people evaluate their experiences and what they consider a seriously stressful situation.

During the period when the problems that eventually lead to a person becoming homeless are intensifying, a family member or friend could be of assistance. However, the relationships of people who subsequently find themselves on the street tend already to have been negatively affected by their often unacceptable conduct, and so these family members and friends are reluctant to help out their problematic relatives, who themselves often spurn such assistance. This is especially so if an offer of help is made conditional in some way, e.g. on a reduction in alcohol consumption or a willingness to work. In certain instances, individuals can only rely on help from their family for a temporary period of time until the necessary funds run out. On other occasions an individual may not have been in contact with their family for some time and is therefore reluctant to ask for help and burden the family with their problems. In addition, people who grew up in a dysfunctional family are more used to mutual exploitation rather than support. Very often our respondents, especially those with only a basic education, knew nothing of possible institutional assistance, and did not know where and how to apply for it.

I. A frequent cause of homelessness is divorce, during which a person leaves or is thrown out of their home. Walking out of the door may be an impulsive reaction to an escalating situation. It is not a rational decision, but a knee-jerk response that may be influenced by personality factors and heavy drinking. It tends to lead to problems with accommodation and, sometimes, with finding work. To understand the situation it is important to know both the underlying and proximate causes of the conflict and how it developed over time. As we see below, people offer various reasons as to why they abandoned their family. All of the following cases involve men who are addicted to alcohol, and we may therefore assume that their departure was the result of an accumulation of problems, the primary cause of which was excessive drinking and an unwillingness to confront this problem. As time passes, such men begin to realise that their decision was not the right one.

- S (51, m, homeless for 14 years): "*We were forever rowing at home. It was Becherovka* [a rather tasty herbal bitters – tr.] *that divorced us. The next day I grabbed a sleeping bag and headed for Prokop Valley and that was that, I was on the street. I spent the night there and then went to Masaryk Station. I still had some money on me.*"
- A (47, m, homeless for 20 years) reacted in the same way: "*There was no real problem. I simply upped sticks and left, and since then I've been on the street. It was my fault I left.*"
- R (49, m, homeless for 20 years) tells a similar story: "*I quarrelled with my mother-in-law and my father-in-law and then I left the family. It was probably the biggest mistake I've made in my life.*"

The most frequent reason women left home was the violent behaviour of their partner (MacKenzie and Chamberlain, 2005, Johnson, Gronda and Coults, 2008, Tually et al., 2008). Women who are physically and mentally abused leave home in order to obtain greater safety. Domestic violence can affect women of any age in any relationship and regardless of financial conditions. It most often affects women aged between 25 and 44. Many of our female respondents left home because they were being physically abused by their partner.

- J (45, f, homeless for 20 years) left her aggressive husband, though bears some of the blame for the breakup for the family (she is dependent on alcohol and drugs): "*I left home because **my husband began beating me**.*"
- M (43, f, homeless for less than a year) also left home due to domestic violence: "***I fled because my boyfriend was beating me**. For three days I slept in my car. It was a catastrophe, really horrible, and it had a bad psychological effect. I wasn't on the street, I was in my car. I couldn't even bring myself to go round to my ex's. He offered to let me sleep there, but I just couldn't bear to be a burden.*" This case involves a single, uncontrolled crisis situation. M has all the necessary qualities to allow her to return to normal life. This is her first year on the street.

There are many reasons why a relationship breaks down and one partner leaves home. What is more significant is that the parties involved are unable to deal with the situation, but instead react in a way that serves only to complicate matters.

A dissatisfied girlfriend may initiate the break, as in the case of V (48, m, homeless for seven years): "*I found myself on the street **after an argument with my girlfriend**. We'd been living together for about nine months and it wasn't working out. Work wasn't heading anywhere, so I started taking casual jobs. **They paid very little and we didn't have enough for the rent**. She had a one-year-old child to look after, **so she kicked me out**.*" V's life prior to the situation described had not been stable, both in terms of work and relationships.

- M (45, m, homeless for five years) decided to leave home when his girlfriend became pregnant with another man: "*She did the dirty on me and had a third child with someone else… When I found out she was pregnant I decided to bugger off, because otherwise she wouldn't have anywhere to live. So **I actually moved out for my daughter's sake**. I moved in with a friend, but it didn't work out, and so I fetched up on the street.*" M is one of the few men who continues to look after his children.
- Š (46, f, homeless for four years) is at present is living in a shelter. She became homeless after she got divorced and was thrown out of her partner's apartment: "***Our marriage collapsed and he told me to find my own place**. I asked him where I was supposed to go. I had a friend and I stayed with her. But she hadn't told me that there was a debt of CZK 80,000* [USD 3,500] *on the apartment, and one day it was simply locked and that was that, I was fucked.*"

The breakup of a marriage or partnership led in the cases above to problems that the individuals concerned were unable to manage in an effective way. They moved in with a friend, and which this did not work out, they ended up on the street.

Walking out recklessly of accommodation or employment is sometimes followed by yet more disproportionate behaviour ensuing from **unrealistic ideas**

regarding how easy it will be to find a new job and accommodation in Prague. People who arrive in the city without some form of employment and accommodation already arranged are not very likely to succeed. They do not know anyone, they do not know how to look for employment and accommodation, and many of them have nothing to offer potential employers.

- B (51, m, homeless for 20 years) found himself sleeping rough after poorly assessing his situation. Money management is not his strong point: "*I left for Prague with money to rent an apartment and I was convinced that I'd find something immediately. To begin with I was in a hostel.* **But I frittered away my money, and suddenly I found myself on the street**. *This was after only two or three months, it all happened pretty quickly.* **I was convinced there would be work** *and suddenly nothing turned up. I didn't want to return home.*" B has received professional training and is not dependent on alcohol or drugs. However, he has no network of contacts.

- J (40, f, episodically homeless) misjudged her possibilities: "*There were disagreements between me and my mum, so I left home.* **I thought I'd find work, but I didn't**. *The disagreements grew worse between my mum and me and my brother and we began quarrelling. It was mainly to do with work and how I should find some. I remained in Prague and resorted to the Salvation Army.*" J has only a basic education.

- M (55, m, homeless for 17 years) was also unsuccessful when it came to finding work and accommodation: "*After I got divorced, I packed a bag and came to Prague. I arrived in Velká Chuchle* [in the southwest of the city] *and lived there for two years with Mrs K in her summer house. I never thought I'd end up like that. I was always convinced I'd find something, that I'd fall on my feet in Prague.* **Well I didn't. Instead, I sat here chatting with other homeless people and had no interest in finding a job**. *So I sat with them and chatted to them, I had some crappy cash-in-hand work. Things seemed ok, so I put off reaching a decision to autumn, then winter… Everyone thinks that Prague will save them, but it's not true.*" M is an alcoholic, which was probably the cause of his decline.

II. A sudden transition into homelessness tends to be the consequence of a combination of a loss of employment and accommodation, not necessarily in that order. It is clear from the examples below that the cause of the speaker's situation was their inability to predict the consequences of their behaviour and to resolve their problems in good time.

- R (48, m, homeless for seven years) lost first his job and then his accommodation as a result of his problematic behaviour: "*I was a security guard for E. There was some kind of fuck-up and the manager called me into her office. She was a young woman, so I told her she was a cow and that I had a daughter the same age, and she sacked me on the spot for conduct unbecoming. And* **because I'd been fired I had no right to anything**, *no unemployment benefit or social security. So* **I had to leave the dormitory** *I'd been staying in and I began to walk the streets of Prague.*"

- R (40, m, homeless for five years) ended up on the street after his employer stopped paying him and he was unable to deal with the situation. "*I had a job and then* **they didn't pay me for three months. I had no money for the rent**, *I had no money full stop. I had nowhere to go, and* **so I ended up sleeping rough.** *I didn't look for anything, either I was too lazy or I just couldn't be bothered.*"

Sometimes the primary cause of a person's social disaffiliation is **a deterioration in their state of health to such a degree that they are unable to work and so lack the money to pay for their accommodation**. People who live on their own and have no one who might help them are especially subject to such a risk. In these cases too there is an inability to give thought as to what might happen in the event of future difficulties.

- J (51, m, homeless for less than a year): "*I was a bricklayer until last year, and then* **suddenly my muscles atrophied**. *It happened so quickly that I ended up on the street because* **I didn't have the money to pay the hostel**. *I basically became homeless overnight.*" J has received professional training and is not dependent on alcohol or drugs. At present he is living in a shelter.
- K (51, m, homeless for seven years): "*I had an accident and became homeless virtually the next day.* **I am officially an invalid, but without the right to any benefits.**" Both these men were working on the black economy. They did not pay health or social insurance and so had no right to benefits.

Several of our respondents lost their apartment because they did not pay the rent, either because they did not have any money or out of sheer carelessness. This was especially so in the case of men with only a basic education and a small income insufficient to pay rent and energy bills. As long as they lived with another family member, they were able to cope, but alone they were not.

- E (53, m, homeless for one year) failed to keep up with his rent payments. He has had a stroke and in the past has suffered depression and been treated by a psychiatrist. It is therefore perfectly possible that he is unable to deal with his situation for health reasons: "*I was married for 18 years, after which we were divorced. My mother died and I remained with my father.* **I wasn't able to pay the rent and so we lost the apartment.** *After that it was downhill all the way… I had nowhere to go, so I wandered the streets until I found help and lived in shelters.*"
- D (39, m, homeless for four years) lost his apartment because he failed to pay the rent: "*I was living with grandma and doing bits and pieces of work. When grandma died,* **I managed to hold onto the apartment for another two years or so, but then I lost it because I had no money.** *There was no way I could pay rent of CZK 8,000* [USD 350], *even with benefits and income from the cash-in-hand jobs I was doing.*" D is not dependent on alcohol or drugs, but has only a basic education and thus finds it difficult to find work. When he does, his income is low. A market rent is too high for him.

- M (45, f, homeless for one year) lost her apartment because she was unable to pay the rent. Her partner was a foreigner who had no work and was unable to contribute to the shared expenses: "***We were simply unable to manage the rent***, *so we lost the apartment. We stayed together, but the debt continued to rise. And then we were taken to court by the bailiffs and chucked out. We lived for about six months with a friend, then hopped from one friend's to another.* ***We ended up in the Atlas hostel***, *but that costs an arm and a leg. We got into debt and we were borrowing from everyone. I returned all the money to my boss, but one day he turned round and said he no longer needed me. When I saw that we had no means of getting by whatsoever and that they would throw us out of any hostel and that we would be on the street, I couldn't cope and I tried to commit suicide. I swallowed an entire packet of Neurol and chased it down with vodka. Then I rang a friend and she rang the police...* ***It was a waste of time, but it all arose on the back of the accommodation***." M now lives in a shelter and her partner has found a job, and so there is a real chance they will return to normal life.
- R (40, m, homeless for three years) found himself in a difficult situation **as a consequence of overestimating his ability to pay off debt**: "*I was duped by a fraudster. We needed more money, I wanted to look for work abroad and so I took out a loan. We bought a large plasma television and with the rest of the money I paid the fees for work abroad. But then* **the collection agency had my account blocked and the owner of the apartment told us we had to leave**. *If we'd returned to my wife's family, the executor would have begun confiscating my mother-in-law's property, and so my wife found a place in a refuge in K. I live on the street and do cash-in-hand jobs. Every crown I earn I put in the account so as to get the collection agency off my back.*" R has yet to find a more effective solution. He is not dependent on alcohol or drugs.

It is clear from the stories they tell that **many homeless people recognise that their situation was caused by their own irresponsibility**, a focus on the present, and a lack of any plans for the future. These are traits we often find in homeless people.

- Z (51, m, homeless for ten years): "*I actually lost two apartments. The first I should have got after my mum died. It was all set forth in writing, but at that time I didn't need it. I had lots of girlfriends where I could spend the night.* ***The turning point came when I learned that I wasn't going to have that apartment.*** *I could really do with it now. That was a huge mistake I made. At that time I didn't have a home and I simply didn't put my name down.* ***I didn't even give it a thought, and now I realise what a massive mistake that was***. *Right from the start I didn't take things seriously. When I needed somewhere to stay, I simply unrolled my sleeping bag and lay down. I didn't have a bad life and I was managing to make money. At that time in my life I didn't give any thought to such things. Life in hostels suited me. But then I fell from some scaffolding and they put a screw in my leg that is not healing well.*" Even if Z had not had the occupational accident, he would probably have found himself in a similar situation upon reaching retirement age.

- M (54, m, homeless for nine years) was naive: "*I lost my job. I was living with my grandmother and she died. So I decided to move to Prague, and here I am, nine years on.* **I'm on the street because I signed a form for a Ukrainian**. *I received CZK 4,000* [USD 175] *for my signature. There was something written there, but I didn't read it. It turned out that I had apparently created my own company. When I went to the job centre, the woman behind the counter told me I was an entrepreneur and* **so I wasn't entitled to the dole or housing benefit**. *Since then I've been living on the street and I can't find work. I'm basically here because I'm a dickhead.*" M has only a basic education and was the victim of a conman. However, his own naivety in not reading the document he signed played an important role. He has been on the street for nine years.

III. The loss of a job and accommodation and a subsequent descent into homelessness is often the consequence of excessive drinking. Alcohol abuse first impacts on relationships, and then on employment, with the drinker quitting their job or being fired. Finally they lose their accommodation. Half of all homeless men are or have been dependent on alcohol, and it is a very common cause of homelessness.

- D (48, m, homeless for five years): "*When my grandmother died, I started drinking. I was making pretty good money at the time, but within two years I had spent everything she had left me and stopped working. I spent everything, and when it was all gone, I was forced back to work.* **I had no money to buy booze so I had to work**... *I found a job as a courier. The problem was that my boss stopped paying us. He was forever promising to. On top of that my mother died, and since she left me some money, I decided there was no point in going back to the job and I quit.* **Then I really fucked up by drinking and losing my driving licence**. *Without that I had no work and I gave up even looking. And that's how I found myself on the street. To begin with I lived in the apartment my grandmother had lived.* **But I didn't pay the rent, so they chucked me out**."

- M (43, f, homeless for eight years): "*I was forever escaping. I began to drink, I admit. We were living with my mother-in-law and it was shit. There were arguments over the baby and I tried to block it out through drink. My partner found someone else. So I moved in with my parents and stopped drinking. The problem was that one day I couldn't help myself. I bought a litre of cheap wine in a carton and within 20 minutes it was gone. I went home and* **trashed the place and my parents laid into me**. *I moved in with a Ukrainian who would occasionally boot me out, and it was during those two years that I got to know some homeless people. I used to take friends from the street back to his apartment, and when that ended I went and lived with them in a squat.*" M drinks and takes drugs.

- R (46, m, homeless for four years) had work, accommodation and a girlfriend. And then...: "*Alcohol has always played a big role in my life. I once spent* *three months in rehab in Dobřany. After that I didn't drink for maybe 13 months. I lived with my girlfriend, the relationship was good. Except that **suddenly I started drinking again** and she left me and things started to deteriorate. When she left me I held out for a time. I had a job and I lived in another hostel. I found some casual work stocking shelves. But then along comes the alcohol again and that was that. **They fired me from my job and chucked me out of the hostel**, because I had no money to pay the rent. And that was the start of my life on the street. I lost my job, then I was mugged, I lost my ID pass and I simply walked the streets."* R has a secondary school education and had no problems except for an inability to control his alcohol consumption.

Several of our respondents found themselves on the street because their **families refused to accept their alcohol consumption and threw them out of the family dwelling**.

- R (40, m, homeless for six years): *"I had a job for a year and then I went slightly off the rails. **I began to drink and play fruit machines**... I don't even know why, just stupidity. When I started on the gambling machines, **my father threw me out**. I found a different job, which I did for two and a half years. And then I started drinking again, youthful imprudence. I found myself on the street out of sheer stupidity. Every cent I had I would spend on drink."* R has neither a partner nor children.
- Z (42, m, homeless for 11 years) tells a similar story: *"**I had a row with my stepmother** because I was drinking... yeah, **I was drinking and I'm still drinking**. My stepbrother said it might be for the best if I left. I lived with a friend for a year and then I found myself on the street."* Z blames his family for not helping him. He does not acknowledge his own culpability. He has a partner who is also homeless, and does not have any children.
- Z (47, m, homeless for 20 years) began drinking when he was very young and lost his job and accommodation as a result: *"I was friends with the older boys, who taught me things... at the age of 12 I was getting drunk and since then I drink regularly. When I was 27 I went to a charity because I'd spent all my money on drugs and booze. However, I still had a job. I was living in a tent and going to work every day. But what I was earning was all spent on alcohol, drugs and gambling, and soon I had nothing left for food. **I overdid it with the booze and they fired me at work. My job came with accommodation provided, so I ended up losing both**."* Z does not have a partner or children.

A decline into homelessness is sometimes linked with drug use, especially in the case of younger people.

- H (50, m, homeless for 20 years): *"I moved to Prague, and because I didn't have a girlfriend I started going out a lot. **I started taking pervitin, and because of that they fired me from work**. That was that, I got myself into debt. My mother told me that was the last straw. Then **they took away my apartment** and now I'll never return."* H does not have any children.

- M (38, m, homeless for two years): "*I began taking drugs at secondary school. First it was grass, then* **when I was 18 I tried pervitin, and after that it was downhill all the way**. *I moved to Prague and found some casual work. Things were up and down, but the sole constant was pervitin. I spent five years in prison and for a while I was clean. But then I started again. I fell in with a bad crowd and once again it was pervitin, grass, and on top of that alcohol...* **I lost my job and shortly after I was on the street**." M does not have a partner and does not look after his daughter.
- Drugs often give rise to criminality, which in turn can lead to homelessness. Take V (38, m, homeless for 13 years): "*When I come out of prison* [where he had been for drug-related offences], *my mum took me in. I held out for about a year and stayed relatively clean, but then* **I got into drugs again**. *I didn't want to have to own up to my mum, so I moved out of her apartment and into a hostel. Then I served another sentence in prison, after which* **I went straight into rehab**. *I was there for a few months, but then I started taking drugs again and ended up on the street*." V does not have a partner or children. His criminal activity (theft) is drug-related.

An ex-convict will often find themselves on the street, since they have nowhere else to go. It is especially difficult for repeat offenders to return to society. People with no network of any kind are at increased risk of becoming and remaining homeless.
- C (47, m, homeless for 23 years): "**After that amnesty, I found myself on the street**, *because I didn't even have a family or anywhere I could live.*"[3] C is not an alcoholic or drug addict. He does not have a long-term relationship or children.
- P (47, m, homeless for seven years) is a repeat offender: "*In 2005 things were looking bad. I had my first prison sentence, for non-payment of alimony, fraud, and unlawful possession of a firearm.* **I was inside for three years and seven months, and when I came out I found myself on the street**. *I lived on the Hermes shelter and in a squat.*" P is divorced and does not look after his child. He is not an alcoholic or drug addict.
- V (48, m, homeless for seven years) made mistakes when attempting to resolve matters upon being released from prison: "*You're not really aware of it. You come out of prison, you've got a bit of money, you go to the pub, to the club.* **It's only later when you sober up and you've nowhere to go that you realise**. *And now you've got no money. And so the day begins normally. You buy something to eat,*

---

3 This is a man who grew up in a children's home because his mother had mental health issues. He is aware of how easy it is to become homeless upon leaving a children's home: "*When it comes to young people it's simple. Every other kid comes out of an orphanage, and that means that, at the moment they leave the home there are three things open to them: drugs, crime and prostitution... I know most of these homeless people and they're here because they took drugs.*"

you know there's nowhere to go so you decide to go to the pub. You sit there and think maybe I'll find something… but you don't, that's obvious." V is divorced and does not look after his children.

IV. A person may find themselves homeless because of psychological problems and an inability to deal satisfactorily with an ongoing situation. In the case of L (52, m, homeless for two years) the decline was slow, but he failed to take control: "*It was a sort of slow decline. The big change was that I could no longer work in the field I knew something about. So at the age of 40 you find yourself working on a production line with a bunch of weirdoes. I was used to a slightly different class of person…* [L has a secondary school education]. *After my father died my mum looked after me.* **I did casual work or just mooched around**. *I had some savings, so I survived as best I could. The last relationship was the reason I found myself on the street. I met a divorced woman. We fell in love, or rather I fell in love and she had nowhere to live. I had inherited an apartment from my parents.* **I'd already had one execution order slapped on me, so I transferred ownership over to her**. *She claimed we'd draw up a contract establishing 50-50 percent ownership. In the end I moved out. I was psychologically exhausted, so I moved onto the street.*" There is a question mark over what actually happened. L has the somewhat unrealistic expectation that his partner will look after him as his mother used to. It is possible that a worsening depression was the cause of his becoming homeless. He is not an alcoholic or drug addict and has been on the street for two years.

Psychological problems combined with heavy drinking and the reluctance of her family to help her was the reason D (48, f, homeless for five years) found herself on the street: "*My suicide attempt was the last straw. They took me to a psychiatric ward. Mum came to visit me and told me they had thrown half of my stuff out of the apartment. The landlady had seen me in a pretty bad state and decided I was no longer welcome in the apartment. When I came out of hospital I went round to my parents to ask if they would lend me the money for a hostel. I rang the door bell. Mum came down carrying my duvet and pillow. It was raining, I'd just come out of hospital and was carrying my bags. She threw the duvet down the stairs into the rain and **told me to fuck off and die somewhere else**. So I left.*" D receives invalidity benefit for psychiatric indications.

SUMMARY

As is clear from the above, the process of becoming homeless takes many different forms. Many people act rashly and their impulsive decisions lead to further complications. Unresolved family conflicts and the loss of a nurturing environment increase the risk of a person becoming homeless. Relationship problems are often bound up with the personality and lifestyle of both partners, and it can often be more a case of when, rather than if, such a relationship will break up. The next stage in the process involves the loss of employment and accommodation. An irresponsible approach to family life and work is often associated with heavy drinking or drug taking. The same is true of absentee-ism, laziness and workplace conflict. Non-payment of rent may be down to a lack of money, but may also be the consequence of a person's unwillingness or inability to resolve their situation. This is manifest in our respondents' focus on the present and reluctance to think about the future. When problems arise, they react with passive resistance and the hope or expectation that the problems will somehow go away of their own accord or that someone else will resolve them.

Whatever the final impulse that causes someone to walk out of their home and find themselves on the street, it is always related in some way to their inability or unwillingness to consider the possible consequences of their conduct and to take measures to remedy the situation. Our respondents offered many different reasons as to why they found themselves sleeping rough. Many conceded that it had been their own fault, that they had been unable to get on top of the situation and had not given thought to the future until the problems were upon them, at which point it was too late. However, not all of them were so self-critical. Several blame other people, namely their parents, partners or relatives.

The age a person finds themselves on the street also plays a certain role. The earlier it happens in life, the more serious are its causes and effects. **People who have been homeless from young adulthood have more problems and are less able to deal with them**. As a consequence there is less likelihood of their returning to normal life. The average age at which a person finds themselves on

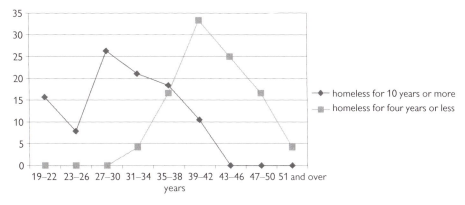

Graph 14. The age a person becomes homeless as against the length of time they have been on the street (shown in absolute figures)

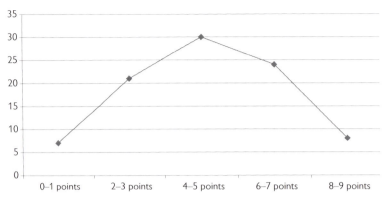

Graph 15. Frequency distribution of manifestations of maladaptation in middle-aged homeless people (in absolute figures).

the street in the case of people who have been homeless for 10 and more years is 29.9 (SD = 6.76): this figure is 42.5 (SD = 5.48) in the case of those who have been homeless for four years or less. The difference between these two groups is significant: t = 7.55, df = 60, p = 0.001. We may conclude that the earlier a person finds themselves on the street, the greater the risk of chronic homelessness. This is probably because of an accumulation of serious problems that represent a barrier to life in mainstream society.

Many different factors contribute to a person becoming and remaining homeless. These include a problematic childhood, a lack of education (only basic education or attendance at a school for special needs), an inability to work systematically, an inability to establish and maintain long-term relationships and a family environment, failure to look after their offspring, excessive consumption of alcohol or drugs, criminality (especially property crime), and mental health

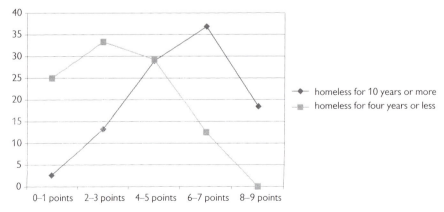

Graph 16. Frequency of maladaptative manifestations according to length of time spent homeless (in percentages).

issues or personality disorder. Certain factors may contribute to a person becoming homeless, while others may develop or intensify as a consequence of a homeless lifestyle. Taking into account all the factors referred to above that contribute to problems with adaptation, we obtain a maladaptation coefficient ranging from 0–10 points.

The difference between both groups is significant: t = 5.71, df = 60, p = 0.001. **People who have been living on the street for ten years and more have more adaptation problems** (x = 5.71, SD = 1.86) than those who have been on the street for four years or less (x = 2.92, SD = 1.82). They drink to excess, take drugs, are unwilling to work, and commit crime. This result confirms our assumption that people who find themselves on the street earlier in life and remain there for a longer period of time tend to have greater problems managing the demands of everyday life.

2. FIRST DAYS ON THE STREET

Finding oneself homeless is a culture shock. The fundamental change of environment, the inability to control the situation, and the social disaffiliation provoke fear and undermine the very foundations of a person's existence. From the results of Davies's analysis (2010) of the life stories of eight homeless people we may deduce how these people experienced the process of becoming homeless. They suffered feelings of despair at being unable to influence the situation, a loss of self-esteem, and the feeling of a "broken life". They were keenly aware that they were now on the very margins of society and that most people rejected them. They felt a sense of loss, of their past lives and the environment to which they had previously belonged, as well as a concomitant loss of identity. The negative feelings of shock, depression and helplessness reflect their awareness of having fallen into the trap of homelessness and their inability to come to terms with it. As part of a defence mechanism, they attempt to suppress negative emotions, often by increasing their consumption of alcohol and drugs. Their recognition of the rejection and even hostility of other people, and the resulting feelings of isolation, create feelings of loneliness, inferiority and shame (Rowland, 2011). Sometimes there are feelings of dehumanisation that might be summed up in the phrase "*I am no longer human, I am simply a rat*" (Davies, 2010). Our respondents reacted similarly.

I. Inexperience and ignorance of the ways of the street were significant problems. To begin with most people did not know how to deal with the situation and where they might obtain food or shelter. They did not know who might help them or that there exist various charities to which they might turn.

- J (50, m, homeless for two years) was utterly lost: "*The first day, when I was at Main Station, **I had no idea what I should do**. I ended up telling myself that, having screwed up so badly, I now had to deal with it.*"

- As was L (52, m, homeless for two years): "*The first year was catastrophic. I was all over the place,* **I simply had no experience of this**. *So I slept in the airport. And then they let me sleep at the school of economics…* **I had no idea what to do** *and I simply hung around doing nothing. I sought out my friends and some of them put me up for a night, but during the day it was a problem. I found myself in this street and spent the night in Hostivař Nature Park.*"
- R (40, m, homeless for three years) was completely disorientated: "**It was horrible. I had no idea what to do***, where to find food, who to turn to and how to contact them. In time certain possibilities open up as to what you should do and how you might set about doing it.*"

Many of our respondents **were unaware that there were charities** they could turn to. Our work shows that information on charitable organisations and what they offer should be available in the places where the people who might need it gather (stations, prisons, etc.), but this is not always the case.

- V (51, m, homeless for ten years): "**I didn't know that an organisation like Naděje existed***. Nobody told me. And so I went kind of crazy, I didn't know what to do, I didn't know anyone, I had nowhere to go. I was sleeping in Main Station without a cent and without documents.*" It is worth pointing out that the headquarters of Naděje are situated not far from Main Station.
- D (37, m, homeless for nine years): "**I had no idea where to go for food***, where I could wash, or that* **there exist charities** *and shelters. It was quite a while before I started using their services.*"
- V (48, m, homeless for seven years): "**I knew of the existence of Naděje and the Salvation Army, but I didn't know where they were based***, because there were no leaflets in prison.*"

II. Becoming homeless is a traumatic and psychologically draining experience for most people, who feel very insecure and do not know how to deal with the new situation.

- P (40, m, homeless for 20 years) found the first few days highly stressful: "**It's difficult to describe the feelings involved. I guess you could say it was scary**."
- Š (46, f, homeless for four years) didn't feel good: "**It was horrible**. *I didn't know where to turn. I was used to leading a decent life and suddenly I found myself hitting rock bottom. It was awful.*"
- R (49, m, homeless for 20 years) had similar feelings: "**It was brutal**. *I knew nothing, I had nothing except the clothes on my back.*"
- M (37, f, homeless for 5 years): "*I didn't receive my paycheck and found myself on the street, under the hot-air ventilator at Main Station.* **The first day** *beneath the ventilator* **was terrible**, *though at least it was warm.*"

R (40, m, homeless for five years) describes his first days on the street in more detail: "*At the very start, when I started sleeping rough, I felt depressed. But that* *disappeared. I felt that way for six months maybe. **The first few days I felt terrible. Psychologically I had hit rock bottom**. I drank simply in order to sleep. I slept on various different benches. I had a carrymat and sleeping bag in my bag, and near the mansion in Libeň I found a bench and lay my head down. I tried to be as inconspicuous as possible. It's a huge life change when suddenly all you eat is what you can find. You can't go to a supermarket and pick and choose."*

Some of our respondents felt so scared that they could not sleep for the first few nights.

- Z (41, m, homeless for six years): *"I couldn't sleep. **I wandered around like a madman the whole night**. I just couldn't get used to the idea of not having a roof over my head."*
- H (40, female, homeless for nine years) felt the same way: *"**When I first hit the street, for night after night I couldn't sleep**. I simply wandered around town."*
- As did P (52, m, homeless for two years): *"The first night on the street I was in a bus shelter near the railway station in Kladno and trembling in fear. On the one hand I desperately wanted to sleep, and on the other **I simply couldn't**. Luckily it was a warm night. Some of the townsfolk checked me out but couldn't believe I was really homeless. They told me to take care of myself and not let anyone mug me. **I've still not fully come to terms with the fact that I'm living on the street**."*

III. More experienced homeless people tend to help out new arrivals by offering advice. In this way the newcomers are slowly integrated into the society of street dwellers.

- R (49, m, homeless for 20 years) was advised by old hands: *"When I arrived at Main Station, **a number of people tried to advise me as to where to find food and where to sleep**. They took me to the* [Salvation] *Army and to Mother Theresa* [a charity providing assistance to people in a crisis situation], *they showed me where I could get bread. And then I met other people who told me I shouldn't rely on the charities, that it was possible to find food by other means, i.e. by scavenging in containers."*
- P (50, m, homeless for 12 years) received help from homeless people at Main Station: *"In Prague I had a friend I'd been in prison with. I tried to find him but without success. I was basically completely on my own here in Prague and headed straight for Main Station. **I met a few decent people who helped me out**. We used to sleep in the station toilets. I stuck it out for a year. We used to give the toilet attendant CZK 50* [USD 2.2] *if she let us sleep there."*
- P (47, m, homeless for seven years): *"It was winter and they released me* [from prison] *in January in a light sweater. It was the first time I'd ever found myself in this situation and for two or three weeks I travelled around by tram. And then **someone told me about** a charity above Náměstí Míru, and the workers there directed me to Pernerova Street* [the headquarters of the Salvation Army, Naděje and Charita], *and from that point on I learned how to live on the street."*

- Z (49, f, homeless for fifteen years) learned how to live on the street from other street dwellers: *"Put yourself in a situation in which suddenly you're completely fucked and have no idea what, where or why things are as they are. You have to learn everything. I cried and cried. **To begin with I had no idea where to go, and then some of the lads took me in hand and taught me**. They had to teach me how to scavenge and collect returnables. You had to learn how to survive, you had no other choice."*

Some of our respondents recall how **a specific individual helped them**, with whom they remained in contact.
- V (42, m, homeless for 21 years): *"How can I put this? I was desperate, I couldn't return home. I had come to Letná Plain and **the only person to help me was D, who showed me the ropes**. He woke me up while I was sleeping on a bench. Underneath me I had lit candles in an effort to keep warm and I was in a sleeping bag. D woke me up and asked if this was my first time on the street. I told him it was, and he told me to stick with him and he'd show me the ropes."*
- E (46, f, homeless for eleven years): *"After coming out of prison for the first time I went to Petřín Hill. It's full of bushes and cliffs, so I thought I'd lie down and no one would see me. **But instead I met a friend who really helped me**."* Sadly, E was eventually attacked by this friend, who had mental health issues.
- Š (46, f, homeless for four years) received help from the man who is now her partner: *"**My partner helped me out**. He helped me at a time when I simply didn't know how to operate, to live on the street. So he said, listen, we have to do something, so we slept in V in a shelter. He basically dragged me out of the depths of despair and changed the way I thought. **He showed me a place we could sleep**, because I'd told him I wasn't going to sleep outside. He found us food or we visited a charity."* Š still lives with the same man, though he is sometimes aggressive towards her. Women who become homeless are often targeted for a relationship by homeless men.

Initial contact with the homeless community can be stressful. Someone new to the street has to get on with the people they are now surrounded by and learn how to behave in their presence, because the centres they will be attending will be full of the homeless.
- M (51, m, homeless for less than a year) had problems adapting: *"One day I slept at the airport and whenever I had money I'd find a hostel. And then I went to U Bulhara Street [where there is a branch of Naděje]. **Madness. I couldn't believe what kind of people were there**. I'd never seen such people before in my life and it **had a really bad effect on me**. I was depressed, because up until then I'd been convinced I would escape this life. And now I was like, what the fuck has happened to you? Everyone was asleep, snoring, and the smell… I wondered what I'd done to deserve this. **But then you find your bearings**, you realise no one's going to bite you, they're just normal blokes – well, most of them – and so you find yourselves*

getting on." M is still in his first year on the street. People who have been living on the street for a short time find it difficult to come to terms with the way that homeless people sometimes act.

- M (43, f, homeless for less than a year) tells a similar story: "*When I arrived* (at the refuge) *I sat down and cried for two hours. **I couldn't believe what the people were like**. Everyone was interested only in themselves, they went round spreading gossip, they were vulgar, there were loads of recovering alcoholics, ex-cons... I couldn't deal with such people. The way they have to bellow, the language they use... That was the worst Christmas of my life.*" M has what it takes to return to a normal life. She originally became homeless having made a poor choice of partner.
- I (40, m, homeless for one year): "*To begin with I used to sleep in shelters, places like Naděje, the Salvation Army... yeah, **it's a shock of course, that's logical, until you get used to it**. But it's better than nothing.*"

IV. The initial stages of homelessness are difficult for most people, especially during the winter months. **However, they usually acclimatise and learn the necessary survival techniques**.

- R (48, m, homeless for seven years) found himself on the street over Christmas: "*The first year was fucking horrible, I didn't know a thing. And **it was Christmas, freezing cold. The first year was the pits**. On Christmas Eve I sat on the tram looking out of the window and saw all the Christmas trees and fairy lights... I basically lived the first year on the tram. It's not like I cried, but there were tears in my eyes. I told myself what an idiot I'd been and I looked at the flats where all the Christmas lights were and people eating dinner and I said, my god, you've fucked things up. **Slowly I got used to things**. I decided I had to find some fixed point I could go to and eat.*"
- B (51, m, homeless for 20 years): "***It was a shock to begin with**. The beginning is definitely the worst, when you still don't know what you're supposed to do and where you should go. **It was difficult, but after a while I began to get used to it** and these days it kind of suits me.*"
- J (51, m, homeless for seven years) spent his first few days on a tram: "*It was difficult at the start. I sat on the tram for the warmth, because it was winter and freezing cold. **You're assailed by nasty thoughts, like, do I smell or am I filthy? It was about a month before I got used to life on the street**.*"

SUMMARY

For most people finding themselves on the street is stressful, not least because they do not know what they are supposed to do and where they might find food and shelter. During the first days of homelessness they catnap in a park or train station, walk the streets or wile away the hours on a tram. For the most part they are unaware of the existence of charities, and so more experienced homeless people become a valuable source of information. Over time the old hands teach the novices how to survive. On the other hand, initial contact with the homeless community is another source of stress. Their appearance, rowdiness and method of communication can be unpleasant for new arrivals, not least because it brings home to them what fate might well have in store for them. After the initial insecurity and fear, a newcomer gradually gets used to their new life. The homeless community becomes their new environment and they are forced to adapt if they wish to become part of it. They learn how to survive, overcome their feelings of insecurity and create new defence mechanisms. The knowledge and skills thus acquired are only rarely of a prosocial character (Rowland, 2011).

3. LIFE ON THE STREET

Life on the street requires different knowledge and skills to those of life in mainstream society. In one sense it is simpler: the priority is the simple satisfaction of basic needs. However, it also involves insecurity, frustration and stress. Homeless people are at threat, not only of material deprivation, but social exclusion or aggression on the part of other homeless people. Different rules and values apply on the street (Ravenhill, 2014). The ongoing process of social disaffiliation creates stress. There is a conflict between a person's earlier identity and their new homeless existence, and to begin with denial is the response. Homelessness activates strategies necessary for survival that are not always acceptable within broader contexts and can serve as confirmation of a person's inferior status (e.g. begging or scavenging). Homeless people have to come to terms with their own social disaffiliation, isolation and the judgements of other people. Members of mainstream society are ambivalent, to say the least, towards them. A homeless lifestyle is deemed a forlorn existence that lacks any meaning. As a consequence, the stigma of homelessness is frustrating and a person's self-esteem declines. Moreover, many of these people have had to come to terms with being cold-shouldered even before becoming homeless.

Individuals deal with this in different ways. They may exhibit signs of denial by pretending that they are not homeless and do not belong to that community. They may distance themselves from other homeless people. Several of them attempt to maintain a basic level of hygiene and take care over their attire, so that people do not regard them as homeless. The need to distance themselves from other people on the street sees them reject the offer of food and shelter from charities. For the same reason they may refuse to use methods typical of the homeless community to support themselves, e.g. scavenging or begging, because they do not want to present as victims of their own life situation. The need to retain their self-esteem is sometimes visible in an emphasis on their earlier status and an attempt to place a distance between themselves and other homeless people who cannot boast of such achievements. Many people new to the street prefer to maintain a distance from people who are drunk, foul-mouthed and filthy. Their rejection of people whose degeneration is clear upon first sight may be the sign of a nervous recognition that this is the fate that awaits them at some point in the future (Ravenhill, 2014).

During their time on the street, most people undergo gradual resocialisation, i.e. the acceptance of those rules that, though fluid and inconspicuous, apply on the street and nowhere else. As we discovered, **most homeless people think that life on the street is tough but that a person has to adapt**, since no other possibility exists.

- G (50, m, homeless for ten years) regards adaptation to be an important attribute of a homeless person: "*Listen, we're incredibly adaptable. We're like rats. If I don't have something, I have to get hold of it* by hook or by crook."
- A new arrival must learn to survive on the street and cope with the unpleasantness that complicates the lives of homeless people in different ways. J (50, f, homeless for twenty years) has this to say: "*So sometimes the police will chuck you out of a place. Someone who has lived a normal life can't imagine what that's like. You have nowhere to do the laundry, nowhere to eat, maybe one of the charities... you have nowhere to sleep, nowhere to pick up essential supplies. You have nothing.*"

One of the fundamental aspects of life on the street is the lack of a network and insecurity in all areas. A homeless person has to think differently and focus on the here and now. They do not have either the strength or motivation to worry about the future. Z (42, f, homeless for eleven years) confirms this: "*On the street you take each day as it comes.*" Adaptation to such a lifestyle eliminates those very habits and ways of thinking necessary if a person is to return to mainstream society, creating a feedback loop that leads to chronic homelessness. Material hardship can intensify feelings of loneliness, anxiety and despair. Adaptation leads to a change in the way one thinks, solves problems and experiences life. Rokach (2005) found that people living on the street are overwhelmed by feelings of distress, hopelessness and emptiness, and social alienation, including interpersonal isolation caused by a dearth of deeper relationships. It is therefore not surprising that people who are socially excluded or at threat of being so tend to behave as though they belong somewhere and are accepted. They try and establish relationships at least with those people who do not reject them, and adapt their opinions and habits accordingly (DeWall, Maner and Rouby, 2009). Pickett et al. (2004) showed that the threat of social exclusion can intensify sensitivity to social signals and induce a desire to differentiate between them accurately, be they positive or negative, since both may be useful under any given circumstances. The behaviour of socially excluded people is influenced by the tension between their desire for acceptance and the need to avoid condemnation or worse. People living on the street have had many negative experiences and take any signals of a possible threat more seriously. More experienced homeless people tend to be cautious to the point of paranoia when establishing new social contacts.

DeWall and Baumeister (2006) confirmed that the social exclusion associated with long-term stress can gradually lead to **reduced emotional sensitivity, including a loss of empathy, and to a decrease in sensitivity to physical pain**. This can be seen as a defence mechanism that allows an individual to deal with stressful and sometimes traumatic situations. As a result, people who are homeless for a long time are often detached and emotionally desensitised. This is manifest not only in the suppression of immediate feelings, but in an indifference to the thought of future experiences, be they positive or negative, i.e. by a drop in the intensity of anticipated joy or sadness. This emotional numbness is also manifest in an inability to empathise with other people and the suffering they too may be experiencing on the street. A lack of empathy and sensitivity will influence the way a person is viewed by people around them and lead to their rejection, which in turn reinforces their scepticism, etc. This renders the process of course correction through experience highly problematic.

Twenge et al. (2007) found that social exclusion, coupled with repeated rejection and condemnation, leads to a reduction in prosocial behaviour. People who are accepted by others more often act prosocially. Social exclusion can exacerbate feelings of irritability, mistrust, a lack of concern for others, aggression, and other asocial manifestations. People who have more negative experiences and have experienced repeated disappointment tend to be cautious and mistrustful because they are afraid of being hurt again. They would be happy to be accepted by other people, but since they are not, then they themselves will not be accommodating. Negative experience leads to egocentrism and an attempt to prevent further harm by blocking out closer relationships. Exclusion and the negative feelings ensuing therefrom reinforce caution and mistrust. Individuals who do not trust other people are more likely to behave in a way that comes across as inconsiderate or hostile. If social exclusion and the negative experiences associated with it last too long, apathy and disinterest in any relationships whatsoever will come to prevail.

Someone living on the street **must adapt to the homeless community and its customs and routines**. This is not always easy, because people sleeping rough are not in the habit of displaying extra levels of consideration.

- J (39, m, homeless for five years): *"**You have to find some way of adapting to the collective**. You have to come to terms with it because life has dealt you a shitty hand. On the street it's **the crafty that survive**, the people who steal from you that survive."*
- L (38, m, homeless for 21 years) agrees: *"There is only one law on the street, i.e. that **the strongest wins**, as in the jungle."* Although relationships between

homeless people are often problematic, it is better to have a problematic relationship than none whatsoever. Someone who is completely and utterly isolated is at greater threat.

People who have only been on the street for a short time do not want to adapt to the customs and practices of the homeless community. On the contrary, they are convinced that **it would be a bad idea to become accustomed to this way of life**, because it would make a return to mainstream society more difficult. I (40, m, homeless for only one year) is of this opinion: "*It is a shock to find myself living on the street. But **I mustn't become used to it**, that would be the worst thing I could do. People get used to it, adapt to it, and then find it's impossible to do anything about it. **They begin to think differently**. All they are concerned about is where to find food, where to earn a few bob, where to wash, etc.*" People get used to considerable freedom on the street and no longer wish to accept the responsibilities that would ensue from a return to work. They adapt to the homeless community and lose contact with people who do not live on the street. This then intensifies their social isolation.

3.1 A TYPICAL DAY

Life on the street takes the form of a **monotonous routine that includes the search for food and other basic requirements**. These activities take longer than they do in ordinary life. A person must wait in line for food or search through trashcans. Otherwise, idleness prevails in the life of a homeless person. Nevertheless, some homeless people believe they are active, e.g. J (52, m, homeless for 20 years): "*It's certainly not boring on the street, no way. You are constantly walking, **constantly on the lookout**.*" A person spends most of their time looking for food, cigarettes, or money with which to buy alcohol.

- B (51, m, homeless for 20 years) provides a good example of the daily life of a homeless person: "*In the morning I'll walk for two or three hours. If I find some food, all the better, I'll buy some lemonade. Once in a while, if it's possible, then I'll buy some wine. I find a seat in the park, read the newspaper. I'm a kind of laid-back guy. In the morning I walk or travel by tram. I go to the centre, **collect a few bottles, a few cigarette butts if there's no money**, so that I have something to smoke. I find a newspaper and if it happens to be the sports page, then so much the better. If I have any money, then I'll buy something to eat. **If the weather's nice, I sit in the park**, read and do crosswords. In the afternoon I might buy a carton of wine for CZK 25 [USD 1], sit drinking until around seven, and then slowly return home to my lair.*" For the most part B sleeps rough. Occasionally he will use the services of a shelter.
- V (46, m, homeless for three years) leads a similar life: "*I sleep in a shelter, and if it's not raining they I'll head into town. I'll find somewhere to sit. A lot of us head to the library, because you can spend all day there. **If the weather's good I'll sit outside**, places like Old Town Square where other homeless people meet, sometimes*

on *Square of the Republic. I walk around **collecting cigarette butts** and then I head back to the shelter. If it's not raining, I prefer to sit in the park. There is a little park behind the stalls on Old Town Square, so **I take a seat, have a cigarette, chat with the lads** if there is someone else there, and then head back.*"

- J (50, f, homeless for 13 years) tells a similar story: "*In the morning I'll wash and then go for a smoke. I call it my breakfast. **Then I head off, walk around for a while**, and then head for Palmovka, say. I walk around it a couple of times and then come here* [to the charity for lunch]." As is clear from the stories our respondents tell, their activities are based around finding money for alcohol, food and cigarettes.

The daily programme of many of our respondents is centred on the offer of charitable institutions and other possibilities of finding food. When they learn that there will be something to eat at a certain time in a certain place, they make their way there.

- M (54, m, homeless for nine years) lives according to this routine: "*I'm used to getting up at six because people are going to work. So I pack up and head for Main Station. At seven I go upstairs to a platform, because **a nun gets off there every day carrying food**, so I help her, and during winter she'd have something hot to drink… **then at half past nine I head over to Naděje**. I receive breakfast there, and then at 10.45 I head over to the Salvation Army. I might remain there until midday and take a bath, put on some clean clothes and shave. **At one o'clock I return to Naděje, because that's when they serve lunch** and then back to Main Station.*"

Illus. 1. A day on the street can take many forms. Some homeless people play cards (photo: Martin Pokora).

- P (42, m, homeless for one year) is a repeat offender: "*I walk the streets and collect cigarette butts. Then I head somewhere to relax, **over to Naděje for lunch**, to the Salvation Army where they give me soup, then I take a bath and that's my day. **I might go for a pizza**.*" P manages to salvage food rejected by restaurants, especially pizzerias.
- R (48, m, homeless for seven years): "***In the morning we go scavenging round the back of Albert**, after which we smoke some cigarette butts. We are there before five and at seven we're back at Na Příkopě. We've gone through the ciggy butts **before the Sally Army opens** and have some tobacco ready, so now it's time for a shower, some food, and then whatever takes your fancy.*"

If they are not so dependent on the support of charities, our respondents may have a different routine or **may be more active at night**. This is true of R (40, m, homeless for five years), who survives by begging and scrounging: "*It's worse in winter, but it's still possible. It's better at night. **I arrive at nine in the evening and beg till three**. Then I go to the pub, a nonstop, and have a cup of tea or some beer or grog* [made with rum and water] *to warm up. I remain there until eight or nine in the morning and then I sleep during the day.*" Many of our respondents regard such activities as work and a source of livelihood.

Someone living on the street loses track of time, since they have no duties to perform by a certain time. Apart from finding food, alcohol and cigarettes, they have nothing to do, and this is reflected in their daily programme. They become

Illus. 2. Homeless people are mostly to be seen sitting on benches (photo: Martin Pokora)

Illus. 3. Drinking is a regular activity (photo: Martin Pokora).

listless and unable to meet any basic requirements, e.g. to respect the opening hours of the job centre. They will tend to postpone any activity arranged in advance. O (53, f, homeless for twenty years): "***When you live on the street, your brain switches off and you don't give a damn about having to do something****. Basically, you know two or three things. You know you have to eat at half past ten, eat lunch, take a bath at four, and collect your stuff. Then you go to your shelter and endure the night and do the same thing the next day, and the day after that...*" During the time a person spends on the street their self-regulatory abilities dwindle. They are **no longer able to plan and manage their activities**, especially if this requires some special effort. It gradually becomes an increasingly bigger problem for them to react flexibly to any demands whatsoever. The long-term abuse of alcohol or drugs simply exacerbates this tendency.

Some of our respondents are aware of their inability to organise their own lives. They know that they have a tendency to postpone things and are unable to adapt to current requirements.

- R (46, m, homeless for four years): "*I used to say to myself, ok, next month, then the next month, and so on, and suddenly it had been two years and the time had passed so quickly. **You completely lose track of time**, you lose so much as a concept of time.*"

- R (48, m, homeless for seven years) has a different explanation: "*When you live on the street, **you can only do what's possible**. The Salvation Army opens at ten and if I am going to the job centre, I want to have a shower first. When I was looking for work, I had to arrange all my meetings for the afternoon as a consequence.*" Moreover, adherence to anything, including some notional timetable, is not of huge importance to our respondents. While living on the street, they become unused to respecting ordinary rules and performing duties. They spend a considerable part of their time simply passively surviving and idly waiting for nothing in particular.

Life on the street is heavily influenced by alcohol and drugs. Alcoholics and drug addicts are either looking for their next fix or under its influence.
- Č (42, m, homeless for five years): "*You get up in the morning and resolve to take a walk before your first wine. But then it actually becomes immaterial.*"
- D (37, m, homeless for nine years) spends his day drinking: "*I stick around the street and drink. **If I find twenty crowns** [just under a dollar] **I buy a carton of wine**. I'm on the street because I don't want to do anything else. **I just want to drink**. All I want to do is eat, wash, and buy booze.*"
- V (38, m, homeless for thirteen years) tells a similar story: "*I get up in the morning and **steal something so that there's money to buy smack**. You shoot up, steal something else, and then sleep in the evening.*"

SUMMARY

The daily programme of a homeless person involves a simple routine based around the satisfaction of the most basic needs. It is centred around the offer of charitable institutions or other sources of livelihood, e.g. begging. There is no activity that has any other objective. When not looking for the wherewithal to buy alcohol or drugs, our respondents are unlikely to be doing anything. They walk the same route and then sit on a bench with other homeless people. Since they have no other duties, they lose track of time and no longer organise their lives around it. If they were asked to abide by a daily routine or respect time limits, most would be unable to. They don't care whether they arrive early or late. However, in terms of their possible return to society, this indifference to the passage of time is a considerable handicap. If they wanted to be successful, they would have to abide by a certain timetable. Attempts at finding a job often come to naught since they are unable so much as to arrive at work on time. They often lose their benefits for exactly the same reason, even though they have no other source of income and benefits could be of considerable assistance to them.

3.2 HOW OUR RESPONDENTS FEEL ABOUT THEIR LIVES ON THE STREET

Homelessness is subject to social stigmatisation. For mainstream society, a homeless existence is undeniable evidence of social disaffiliation, incompetence and ignorance, and therefore deserving of condemnation and rejection. Homeless people are the most vulnerable and disadvantaged group, especially if their stigmatisation covers other areas of their lives, e.g. alcohol or drug abuse or mental health issues. Mainstream society often has an ambivalent attitude towards the homeless, a combination of antipathy, contempt and compassion provoked by its confrontation with human wretchedness (Rowland, 2011; Ravenhill, 2014; Vágnerová, 2014). Sometimes a negative opinion prevails and people regard homeless people as parasites who are to blame for their own tribulations. Rejection and contempt is reinforced by the unkempt appearance of the homeless, their dirtiness, smell, signs of alcohol, and vexatious behaviour (Štěchová, 2009). Some people even feel justified in attacking homeless people, as though their social status is so low that this is barely to be considered a crime. It is striking how many attacks upon homeless people appear to be random and motiveless. Coates (1990) explains the negative approach of mainstream society to the homeless in terms of Jung's theory of the personality, using the archetype of the shadow, the dark, averted side of life, with which the majority do not wish to be confronted. In short, homeless people do not create a favourable impression, and are themselves aware of this fact (unless they are by now completely lost causes).

A few (albeit not many) **of our respondents do not regard life on the street to be quite as bad as it is made out to be**. They do not regard their lives as involving only unpleasant experiences, even though on the whole this is the case. Sometimes this represents an attempt to rationalise their lives, though not always. Very often people who have been in prison repeatedly are relatively satisfied and feel that life on the street is acceptable compared to life in prison. Or

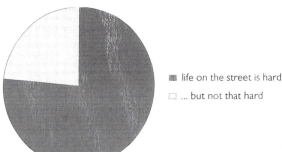

■ life on the street is hard
□ ... but not that hard

Graph 17. Evaluation of the negative aspects of homelessness they might be dependent on alcohol or drugs and simply glad that there is no one to impede their consumption on the street.

- M (48, m, homeless for 20 years): "*On the street **I have experienced pleasant moments** because I've met loads of people with whom I've got on well. **I don't only have negative memories**.*"
- P (42, m, homeless for only one year) was a repeat offender before becoming homeless: "***I feel completely fine on the street***. *I take things as they come.*"
- D (37 when interviewed, m, homeless for ten years), who drank and took drugs, was not wholly damning of his lifestyle: "*Right now, when I'm not in prison, **I don't particularly care that I'm on the street. I'm simply trying to get on with life***." D recently died.

As is clear from the graph, **most homeless people give life on the street a negative rating**. Many would like to live differently, but are unable to change their lifestyle even though they sometimes think about returning to mainstream society.

- J (52, m, homeless for 15 years): "***I don't feel good on the street***. *But what can I do? I have no other options.*"
- J (44, m, homeless for nine years) feels similarly: "***I can't say life on the street suits me*** *and I'm wondering about what I could do to change things.*"
- S (51, m, homeless for fourteen years): "***There's nothing to like about living on the street***. *I mean, that's obvious, right? The mere fact of being on the street is bad.*"

I. Social conditions of life on the street

When our respondents were asked to say **what bothered them most about life on the street**, the most frequent answer was the **behaviour of other homeless people**. People who have been homeless for a short period of time, have a secondary school or university education, and have retained at least certain basic social customs, are the most critical. They do not belong to the group of hardened homeless people who have lost their social attributes over the course of a long period of time spent on the street, coupled very probably with the influence of alcohol or drug abuse.

- J (52, m, homeless for five years) has this to say on the topic: "***The worst people on the street are the homeless***. *I don't like homeless people, even though I am one myself. When I see how they behave around the van dispensing soup. They **arrive drunk, they start shouting** that the soup isn't salty enough, and they pour it away or make a complete mess. They're the worst.*"
- P (52, m, homeless for two years) feels similarly: "*What really bothers me on the street is that the filthier I am, the smellier I am, **the more of a racket I make and the more drunk I get, the more likely it is that I'll survive**. It's insane.*"
- R (46, m, homeless for four years) also has reservations: "*Spend 24 hours here and you'd see **how these people treat each other**, how they scream and shout at*

*each other. **It's pure selfishness**, me me wanna wanna more more. And then if something goes wrong they will start shouting that the Salvation Army should be renamed the Salvation Barmy, that kind of crap."*

Most of our respondents agree that the streets are dangerous and rate this fact negatively. They know that they are exposed to an increased risk of theft or injury. The people they meet are not just unpleasant, but sometimes downright dangerous. Most of our respondents have been on the receiving end of aggressive behaviour or been mugged. They might well encounter disturbed people, people with mental health issues, repeat offenders, as well as drug addicts and alcoholics, and can easily be the victim of criminality. Of our group of middle-aged homeless people, 45.5% had been mugged or attacked. The figures were roughly the same in McDonagh's group (2011), with 43% having been victims of criminal activities. People on the street are aware that they are more vulnerable than members of mainstream society. According to Z (51, m): "***On the street**, especially in Prague at night, **it isn't safe** and it isn't a good idea to walk around on your own.*" Some were only harassed, but others suffered worse treatment, for instance E (43, f): "*One time I was sitting on a bench and a gypsy came up behind me and urinated all over my jacket.*"

Many homeless people have been mugged and know of other people with similar experiences:
- Z (42, m, homeless for eleven years): "***I've been mugged I don't know how many times**. I've given up counting.*"
- H (40, f, homeless for nine years): "*I used to sleep in a park, the one at Arbes Square. One morning I saw **my handbag had been cut open**, all the things had spilled out, and the bag was gone. And as for losing my ID documents, that's a regular occurrence.*"
- J (39, f, homeless for nine years): "***I've had stuff stolen from me about a hundred times**. It sounds incredible, but it's true.*"
- R (40, m, homeless for three years): "***Last week I was mugged on the night bus**. My documents, telephone, everything was gone. I had been on my way to the airport to sleep and fallen asleep on the bus.*"

Some people had not only been mugged, but beaten up badly:
- P (50, m, homeless for twelve years): "*I've been mugged two or three times and **sometimes I've been beaten up**... That's life on the street for you.*"
- J (49, m, homeless for four years): "***They stole my telephone and kicked me**. I had a black eye and I lost all of my money and my telephone.*"
- Z (51, m, homeless 10 years): "*It happened to me right in the centre of town. **They attacked me with a club** and nearly took my eye out. They left me lying on the street.*"
- P (52, m, homeless for two years): "*I basically found myself sleeping rough last year. **Three ex pupils mugged me and beat me up. They left me with a broken***

arm, concussion and robbed me of what I had. The worst thing was, I recognised them and they recognised me, they knew who they were beating up... It damaged me psychologically, I felt really bad about it."

Their negative experiences have left these people feeling fearful of further robbery or assault.
- S (52, m, homeless for 17 years): *"The worst thing is the **fear of being mugged**, of having everything taken from me. The fear is always greatest at night. You really have to be on your guard, you can't even sleep... You never know whether you'll survive or not. The street taught me that it's best to be on the lookout. Most of all **I'm afraid of aggression, of someone physically assaulting me**."*
- Z (44, m, homeless for fifteen years): *"I'm afraid that **someone will attack me when I'm sleeping outdoors** and I'll have no way of protecting myself."*
- C (40, m, homeless for nineteen years) is convinced that things are becoming more dangerous: *"**There's more aggression on the streets than there used to be** and you yourself have to be aggressive. You have to take control... either you take the piss or you smack someone hard in the mouth. The worst of the lot are the new homeless."*
- Some of our respondents no longer wonder whether they will or will not be attacked, but only about the seriousness of an attack. P (20, m, homeless for 12 years) has this to say: *"If someone stabbed me with a knife, that wouldn't bother me too much. I've already been stabbed three times. But **if someone poured petrol over me and set me alight**, that would be far worse."*

Many homeless people do what they can to reduce the risk of assault.
- V (46, m, homeless for three years) takes precautions: *"If I see a drunken bum behaving like a fucking twat, then I turn around and walk away. **I do my best to avoid the aggressive types altogether**."*
- R (40, m, homeless for six years) prefers to avoid possible threats: *"**I'm not looking for a quarrel**. If I hear someone arguing, I'm off... I'm afraid of dying in a stupid way."*

II. Social exclusion and the behaviour of members of mainstream society

Although most homeless people are fully cognisant of the fact that they do not leave a good impression, **this awareness of their own social exclusion is both unpleasant and stressful.** The way that members of mainstream society ignore or reject them bothers them. Many feel they have fallen into a trap from which there is no escape (Kidd and Davidson, 2007). People condemn them for being drunk, noisy, filthy and smelly, and this hostility in turn makes a person resort even more to drugs and alcohol in an effort to block out these unpleasant feelings and ease their discomfort for at least a short time (Hodgetts et al., 2006). Newburn and Rock (2005) say that homeless people are often scared not only by other people living on the street, but by members of mainstream society.

The distance maintained by members of mainstream society from homeless people matters most to those of our respondents who are better educated and on the street for two years or less.

- P (52, m, homeless for two years) finds the situation difficult to deal with: "**The worst thing is the shame you feel**. *Hunger is one thing, and during the cold you can always find somewhere. But the worst thing is when people see you and immediately look away.*"
- K (46, m, homeless for two years) feels similarly: "**The worst thing is other people, how other people behave to you**. *Some of them are polite and others aren't.*"
- L (41, m, homeless for only one year) is finding it difficult to come to terms with people being judgemental: "*The most difficult thing is **not rising to the bait**. You've not had enough sleep, you've nowhere to lay your head, and life on the street is something of a shock.*"
- L (52, m, homeless for two years) finds the way that people behave unpleasant: "***Most people treat you like garbage***, *so I do my best not to look like that. Most people don't like the homeless, so it's a really unpleasant feeling.*" These comments are atypical. For the most part our respondents have become resigned to the way they look and how they behave and are indifferent to how others see them.

V (38, m, homeless for seventeen years) is aware of the disapproval homeless people face and the reasons for it. "*I think the worst thing is the **way you lose your dignity as a human being, the way that people look at you as simply some filthy, smelly, hairy thing**. You get pissed off, but you can't do anything about it.*" After some time living on the street, many homeless people, especially those dependent on alcohol or drugs, become resigned to public opinion.

III. Loss of a stable environment and meaning in life

Life on the street evokes feelings of **insecurity, loneliness, helplessness and hopelessness** that intensify feelings of depression and fear. People become defensive and resort to strategies that permit at least a temporary escape from stressful situations, e.g. they consume alcohol (Rokach, 2005). They are aware that they are in a situation from which there is no escape and over which they have no control, often because in order to change their lives they would have to make a huge effort and relinquish their attitude of passive resistance, often associated with excessive drinking or drug taking. They are unwilling even to look for help. When asked what bothers them the most, hopelessness and a feeling of powerlessness are the commonest responses.

- M (38, m, homeless for two years): "*You carry on though you have no idea where you are heading. **The insecurity**. You have no roof over your head, that's the worst thing, and you lose your friends.*"

- V (51, m, homeless for ten years): "*As far as I'm concerned the real damage is psychological. The **feeling of hopelessness, emptiness, the feeling I have nothing and that there's no structure**... Ten years ago I saw it all differently and didn't really give it any thought.*"
- D (37, m, homeless for nine years): "*For me the worst thing is the **feeling of powerlessness that comes with living on the street**. I'm constantly **scared by the feeling of insecurity**, because I work on the black market, I never have any security, and that's the same, month after month.*"
- J (39, m, homeless for five years): "***The feeling of sadness you get when you realise you have nothing in life**. What pleasure are you supposed to get out of life when you have nowhere to live, no one to love... I mean, these are the basics, aren't they?*"

Some people lack the security of a home, be this simply a place they can call their own or somewhere they are surrounded by loved ones. People who have been on the street for a long time feel this lack the most.
- R (48, m, homeless for seven years): "*The worst thing is **not having somewhere to return to**. Other people, when they finish work around five or six, they've got somewhere to return to. Whereas I haven't.*"
- P (45, f, homeless for eight years): "*That's the worst thing, **not having anywhere to go**. You need people around you who love you, but instead you've no one you can turn to.*"
- J (50, f, homeless for 23 years): "*The worst thing is **not having anywhere to rest your head**.*"

Boredom and a feeling of emptiness represent a problem for certain of our respondents. Though someone living on the street has no duties to perform, they do not have sufficient funds to ensure a decent livelihood and **their lives lack any content and meaning**. Survival on the street is monotonous and lacks any deeper meaning. It is about finding something to eat and feeding an addiction.
- G (50, m, homeless for ten years): "***Boredom is the worst**. The boredom is deathly. I wake up, I come here, we always find some wine, drink, have another drink, after which I need to lie down again. I wake up at one and repeat the same routine. Boring, boring. **In the morning I have nothing to get up for**.*"
- I (40, m, homeless for one year) reports similar feelings: "*You're just killing time, that's all you're doing. **The problem is all the free time you have**, it's never-ending.*"

IV. Material conditions of life on the street

Homeless people often have a problem with hygiene. Many of them are aware of this and it does not make them happy. It bothers them that they are dirty, neglect their appearance and smell. **The approach they take to dirt can be an**

indicator of the extent of their social disaffiliation. Some of our respondents attempt to observe at least basic hygiene and dress in clean clothes.

- R (40, m, homeless for three years): "*The whole issue of hygiene bothers me. I do my best to buy clothes and look normal.*"
- Several of our respondents felt it was impossible to maintain the same standards of hygiene on the street. V (38, m, homeless for 13 years): "*The street changed me. **It's impossible to remain clean** and I'll quite often wear clothes for a week at a time.*"
- J (45, m, homeless for six years) deals with the problem by become reclusive: "***I hate being filthy***. *I'd prefer to go off somewhere and be on my own. I could have my laundry done except I'd need money for that and somewhere to go.*" J is lacking as much in motivation as money, since many charities provide washing facilities and even clean clothes.

Many of our respondents are aware that homeless people are often dirty and neglectful of their appearance, **but do not include themselves in this group**. This applies to other people, they claim, usually people who drink to excess.

- J (51, m, homeless for one year): "*The people here could take a bath if they wanted to, but they don't. They're not bothered. They get on a tram and the smell is overpowering. But they don't give a damn.*"
- M (54, m, homeless for nine years) is not an alcoholic: "*Some of them have a real problem. They don't observe the basic rules of hygiene. **They're filthy and stink**.*"

Several of our respondents said that **drinking to excess was one reason for giving up on personal hygiene**.

- R (40, m, homeless for three years) is convinced of this: "*I have a friend who drinks. He'll announce he's off to Naděje for a bath. But in the meantime he buys a bottle of wine, and then another, and soon he's forgotten about his bath. **He forgets about personal hygiene** because he's feeling good.*"
- P (47, m, homeless for seven years) agrees: "*I have seen people who have been destroyed by alcohol, **people who have given up on hygiene altogether**. The people who are sitting here on these benches drink wine. They're filthy and smell. As far as I'm concerned, it's a line in the sand beyond which I don't want to step.*"
- J (52, m, homeless for five years): "*I see these homeless people every day with their cartons of wine. The next day they have been beaten up and they're a mess. **They sleep on benches, they smell of piss**, and there's a lot of them.*" Such people are indifferent to anything and everything and the extent of their precipitous decline is clear on first glance. T (39, m): "*We call them zombies. **They're the filthiest of all, the people who have simply given up completely**.*"

All our respondents hate bad weather, the cold and rain, especially older people.

- Z (51, m, homeless for ten years): "*The worst thing is when you're sleeping out of doors at night and it's minus 15. Weather is a bummer, especially **rain**. There's* *simply nothing you can do. And then **imagine it's cold on top of that**. And though Prague may be large, there are not many places where you can go at night if you have no money."*

- J (45, m, homeless for six years): *"**The weather is important without a doubt**. Otherwise things are bearable, you can get round most things, but not bad weather."*
- P (37, f, homeless for 15 years): *"It's worst **when it's cold and rainy** and the charities are closed. You have nowhere to go and maybe you desperately need the toilet."*

Most of our respondents (77%) rated life on the street negatively. Many would like to live a different life but are not yet able to. (The situation was similar in the case of our group of young homeless people, 80% of whom rated life on the street negatively.) They are aware that the street is not safe and that one can meet all kinds of people who may represent a threat. Many of them have been attacked and mugged and know that this could happen again at some point in the future. Our questionnaire revealed the same results, with 23% of men and 31% of women being the victims of criminal activities. Most homeless people find the rejection and condemnation of people from mainstream society unpleasant, since it reminds them of their social disaffiliation. The complications of life on the street create feelings of insecurity, helplessness and hopelessness. Many of our respondents, especially the older ones, lack the security of a home. They suffer boredom and a feeling of emptiness brought on by the dull routine of mere survival without any meaning to life. Dirt is another problem and symbolises the extent of their social disaffiliation. Smelly, drunk and filthy homeless people serve as a reminder to newcomers of what might await them in the future. Bad weather, the cold and the wet are another burden that has to be dealt with, especially by those sleeping rough.

People living on the street tend not to be very happy with their lives, a fact that should come as no surprise. Only a third of our respondents believe it has brought something constructive into their lives. Panadero et al. (2015) arrived at

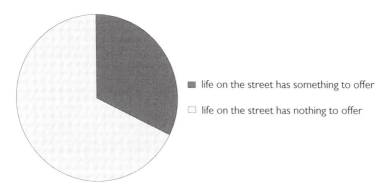

■ life on the street has something to offer

□ life on the street has nothing to offer

Graph 18. Evaluation of the positive aspects of life on the street.

slightly different conclusions: almost half (46.7%) of homeless people in Madrid feel happy overall, and only 21.8% were unhappy. The rest were neither one nor the other. One of the possible explanations for this discrepancy is the weather, since Spanish people living on the street do not have to deal with the cold to anything like the same extent. A lack of secure relationships with those around them impacted negatively on their feelings of happiness.

Most middle-aged homeless people in Prague feel that life on the street offers nothing good. **If coaxed into identifying a positive aspect, they cite the freedom of the street**. They are not obliged to do anything and are not responsible for anything. The flight from commitments and duties is one of the most frequent reasons a person finds themselves on the street. A life without duties is valued by a third of homeless people, most of them young. People aged 50 and over do not rate freedom as highly because they know that they are also losing something in the process. They have begun to experience health problems and are aware their chances of a better life are minimal.

- R (40, m, homeless for five years) values his freedom: "*It's great that **you're free in a certain sense**. You can be yourself, you can decide to do this or go there and you're not restricted by what time you have to be at work, what time you have to get up, all of that.*"
- L (38, m, homeless for 21 years) is of a similar opinion: "***It's great that you're free** and you can do what you want. **You don't have to listen to the bullshit** and you're not chained to a desk.*"
- V (42, m, homeless for 21 years): "*Perhaps I'm not expressing myself well... it's the freedom, **the fact that you can do what you want and you're not at anyone's beck and call**. You simply live, lie down, wake up whenever you want, get out of bed, scrounge a bit of cash, get drunk, and then take a rest. Nothing more, nothing less.*"

Some people like the fact that **they are not limited by any commitments or responsibilities**.

- R (46, m, homeless for four years): "*The peace and calm... Everyone will tell you the same thing, that **you don't have to take responsibility for anything**. You kneel down in the street, beg for money, visit the Salvation Army for a meal, a shower and some clothes, and that's it. You get through the night or you find a berth on the Hermes or at the Salvation Army and away you go.*"
- D (48, m, homeless for five years) feels the same way: "***It's a way of escaping from all your commitments and problems** and enjoying a sense of freedom.*"
- V (51, m, homeless for ten years): "*On a purely rational basis it's incomprehensible, but that's the way it is. You can be incredibly free, you can come and go as you please, do what you want. **You don't have any duties** or even problems, as long as you have the right mentality and it's not minus ten outside.*"

All of this may have some truth to it. However, the freedom of the streets is problematic. When our respondents were asked about the advantages of the freedom they enjoyed, doubts were expressed as whether it was an especially good lifestyle. The limited freedom of a homeless person is recognised by people who are not dependent on alcohol or drugs and for whom a life on the street does not meet their needs or has ceased to meet them over time.

- I (40, m, homeless for one year): "*The positive aspects of life on the street? You can't really claim it's extra special in some way.* **Agreed, you're freer**. *You can do what you want, that's true.*"
- Many of our respondents realise their freedom comes with conditions attached. Z (42, male, homeless for 11 years) is of this opinion: "*I don't really believe there's anything positive to living on the street. The freedom possibly.* **But it's a relative freedom, it's the freedom to live a shitty life**. *The police harass you and move you on, and it's not just the police.*"
- M (51, m, homeless for one year) agrees: "**I think freedom is a different thing**. *It's what you feel when you've got some cash in your pocket and you don't have to go searching for a piece of paper or bottles. That's a completely false idea of freedom.*"

Life on the street offers nothing positive. Two thirds of our respondents believe there is nothing good about this lifestyle. In their opinion it is a tough life.

- M (50, m, homeless for 20 years): "**There's no upside to living on the street**. *If you've got money, you buy freedom. When you've got no money, then you don't have any freedom.*"
- P (50, m, homeless for 12 years) agrees: "*I don't see anything positive about being homeless whatsoever.* **It's a really tough life**."
- B (50, male, homeless for 20 years): "*I guess I'm reconciled to it, but* **I don't see anything positive** *in it.*"

Though life on the street has nothing positive to offer, a person can learn things, and the experience acquired can contribute to their further development. Many of our respondents are proud of how they have dealt with homelessness, and view such an episode as an opportunity to acquire self-knowledge and act in accordance with the people they really are. A period of time spent on the street will inevitably affect the way they view the world and themselves (Kidd and Davidson, 2007).

- M (45, m, homeless for five years): "*The only good thing to come of this whole experience is* **how often you have to reach inside yourself and find the strength to carry on**."
- D (48, f, homeless for five years): "*I don't know... maybe you learn something... I guess* **I learned how to survive**, *how to find food and that kind of thing.*"
- J (39, f, homeless for nine years) agrees: "*I think what's good is that* **you learn to be independent in any situation**. *The other thing is that you lose some of your pride, though that's not necessarily a pleasant thing.*"

Some of our respondents felt life on the street had been a useful experience, though they would be happy to see it come to an end.

- P (52, m, homeless for two years): "*It's been an interesting experience, **but I now know that I will have to do everything in my power to ensure I don't end up on the street ever again**.*"
- M (55, m, homeless for 17 years): "*I tell myself it was a good experience. I've hit rock bottom, so I know what it's like. But **right now I'd like to head upwards**.*"

SUMMARY

Most of our respondents felt that life on the street brought nothing positive, but that if pressed they would cite freedom as a plus. They have no duties, they can do what they want and are not responsible for anything, not even themselves, a situation not many adults expect in life. One is justified in arguing that these people have not been successful in the transition into adulthood. They exist in a state of hiatus that they are incapable of breaking out of. Though many appreciate this freedom, others question it and are aware that they are simply surviving on the margins of a society that rejects them. They believe that life on the street has only one benefit, namely that they acquire experience and confirm their ability to survive under arduous conditions.

4. RELATIONSHIPS BETWEEN HOMELESS PEOPLE

Everyone needs to belong somewhere and to someone in order to feel secure. This clearly applies to homeless people, even though relationships in this community differ in many respects from those in mainstream society (Ravenhill, 2014). Homeless people's experience of social exclusion affects their interpersonal relationships, the character of those relationships, and the way they are established and maintained. These are not traditional friendships or partnerships, but more about commonalities of lifestyle. Homeless people are a marginalised group with reduced social capital, and for the most part interact exclusively with others in their situation. Neal and Brown (2016) confirm that the social networks of people on the street is relatively small. Their research reveals that a third of homeless people have no friends and some of them do not even care. Such people are highly mistrustful of those around them and prefer to live a solitary life. Two thirds have friends, though these relationships are complicated. On the one hand they are linked by the bonds of solidarity. But on the other, they exist within a hierarchy and compliance with street norms is often imposed, sometimes by force. A hierarchy is created in the homeless community that is the inverse of that in mainstream society. The result is that individuals who are stronger and more ruthless often attain an important status they would be unable to under different circumstances. (The situation is similar in prison.) Violence is a common, daily occurrence on the street and a part of homeless culture (Ravenhill, 2014).

Relationships between homeless people feature exploitation and parasitism. They are very variable, because the people involved often do not remain in one place, but come and go, whether to prison or elsewhere. The circle of people living on the street who are linked by relationships is limited and dependent on ongoing contact and shared experiences. Such people spend most of their time together and participate in the same activities. These include drinking and drug taking, as well as non-standard means of livelihood.

Relationships with other homeless people are important. People on the street often have no other social contacts and are dependent on those of their own community. They cannot isolate themselves completely, because they often share a common space where there is no privacy. Relationships with other homeless people may be affected by a decline in emotional sensitivity and empathy caused by social exclusion and the stresses of life on the street (DeWall and Baumeister, 2006). This attenuation of emotional experience can be seen as a defensive reaction that allows people to restrict the intensity of unpleasant feelings of insecurity and threat. Emotional apathy and reduced empathy are manifest in inconsiderate conduct towards other people and a greater focus on the satisfaction of immediate needs. As a result, deeper and more lasting relationships are not often created. Though a lack of empathy and the deployment of less common ways of reacting to people may serve as a defence mechanism, it also reduces the chance of a person being accepted by those around them and creating more stable friendships. Emotional apathy is not necessarily a momentary reaction to stress, but can become fixed and restrict a person's ability to function in society. This in turn will impede their reintegration into mainstream society.

Relationships with other homeless people take many different forms, most of them negative. However, there are **people who are convinced that it is possible to find genuine friendship on the street**. For the most part these are people who drink to excess and take drugs, though do not have other problems.

- R (40, m, homeless for five years): "*I met a friend here and he told me to follow him and not simply to walk the streets. So I did and **the people I met were friendly to me from the off** and I became part of their group. We look after each other and it works, though obviously from time to time we're pissed off with each other.*"
- Some people view the people around them as replacement for a family they don't have, as in the case of Z (47, m, homeless for 20 years): "***I lived in a group for a long time. They were my friends.** I think we kind of made up for the people each of us had lost and we formed a kind of family. And in the time we've known each other we've helped each other out.*"
- M (54, m, homeless for nine years): "*I was sleeping at Main Station on a bench. I got to know loads of people **some good, some bad. But there were only a few of the good ones** and loads of the bad ones.*"

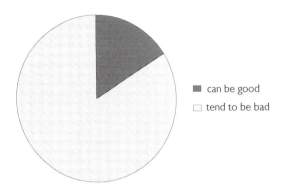

Graph 19. Evaluation of relationships between homeless people

- can be good
- tend to be bad

Our interviews showed that, **though our middle-aged respondents have friends on the street, they do not number many**, usually only two or three. In this respect they differ from their younger counterparts, who usually live in groups.

- J (52, m, homeless for five years): "*I have one or two friends. They can be found, though it's not easy amongst homeless people.*"
- Č (42, m, homeless for five years): "*There's definitely two or three people I trust. After a while you begin to recognise what a person is like and what you can expect of them.*"
- The impression given by our respondents is that a friend is someone with whom they spend their free time, drink, and can trust not to steal from them. J (42, m, homeless for nine years) has such friends: "*The people I hang out with I can trust. There's not many, three at most. We walk around and have a drink together. Sometimes we'll find somewhere to sit and relax.*"
- F (43, m, homeless for ten years) has a similar understanding of friendship: "*I have two friends, and the understanding is we don't steal from each other.*"

People who have been living on the street for several years have lost their former friends and often no longer exhibit any interest in forming new friendships.

- Z (42, m, homeless for eleven years): "*You can find good people here, but I unfortunately no longer have many because they're dropping like flies. I have no desire to join one of the large groups. I'm quite happy with two or three friends that I can chat or a smoke or a drink with.*"
- Z (44, m, homeless for 15 years) has no new friends: "*I have a few friends. Some of them are old school friends, but I don't have many new friends. The older I get, the less I can be bothered.*" Z might be increasingly mistrustful, but might also find it more and more difficult to find things in common with people who have a very different experience of life. In the homeless community, too, there exist different subcultures associated with age or other commonalities, e.g. drinking.

Most of our respondents do not place much trust in friendships that arose on the street. This is very likely due to both negative experiences and the

Illus. 4. The coexistence of two or three homeless people is the most frequent variant (photo Martin Pokora).

Illus. 5. The coexistence of homeless people usually includes sharing a sleeping space (photo Martin Pokora).

problematic behaviour of certain homeless people whose actions can be unpredictable depending on the situation.

- H (50, m, homeless for 20 years) places little faith in friendship: "*You tend to have **acquaintances rather than friends** on the street.*"

- S (51, m, homeless for 14 years) is of the same opinion: "*Friends amongst the homeless? Not really... I mean,* **I talk to people and so on, but you can't really call them friends.**"
- L (50, m, homeless for a year): "**I don't have any friends** *and I live alone. Of course I had to establish some kind of status and respect in order to survive.*"
- Women feel similarly in this respect. H (40, f, homeless for nine years): "*I think there's loads of contacts on the street, plenty of opportunities to have a chat. Maybe someone will take you back to their lean-to whatever.* **But it's not friendship.** *Relationships on the street are different to normal relationships. One moment they're sharing stuff, the next moment they're robbing each other blind.*"
- D (46, f, homeless for 11 years): "**You can't find friends on the street.** *Some will help each other out when they can, but if it came to it they'd kill each other too.*"

Other research backs up our findings. Crane and Warnes (2005) observed greater aggression displayed by young homeless people to their older counterparts. Newburn and Rock (2005) and Huey (2012) also found higher levels of aggression on the part of men toward women living on the street.

Many of our respondents are of the opinion that **what links people on the street is more a sense of being socially excluded and sharing the same lifestyle.** Contact with other homeless people is dependent on the situation. People meet and spend a great deal of time together simply because they have no contact with other people. However, often it is only force of circumstance that links them.
- D (37, m, homeless for nine years). "*We saw it purely as a way of passing the time, having a drink and chilling. We didn't think in terms of relationships or anything like that.* **It's the street that brings us together.**"
- D (48, m, homeless for five years) is emphatic that it is not friendship that brings people together on the street: "**People on the street are linked more by alcohol or the same fate.**"
- P (37, f, homeless for 15 years) is of the same opinion: "*It's not easy to find friends on the street.* **People mostly get together because of booze or drugs.** *They're forever scamming you, although sometimes they help you too.*"

Mutual trust is fragile and easily destroyed. **A lot of people are unnerved by the ease with which homeless people concoct mistruths.** This may reflect the need for a certain self-stylisation, an attempt to improve the way they appear to others and even perhaps to themselves. Such confabulation may be caused or exacerbated by alcohol and impeded reality correction. Telling fictional stories that improve a person's own past and present serves as a defence mechanism against a drop in self-esteem (Levinson, 2004).
- S (51, m, homeless for 14 years): "*Most people on the street* **live in their own fantasy worlds.** *I know people who claim they own four buildings and have millions in their bank account. And they're homeless.* **A lot of people living on the street lie.**"

- P (52, m, homeless for two years): "*There's a lot of duplicity on the street, a lot of deceit. If you were to believe some of these people, they were multimillionaires in the past. And yet now they have trouble finding the few crowns they need to book a berth on the Hermes. I don't know if it's a defence mechanism or just being a pathological liar.*"

Many of our respondents believe that relationships between people on the street are worse than they used to be. This applies especially to older people who have lived on the street for ten years or more. There are many explanations offered. Some people believe it is because the number of homeless people is constantly rising and life is becoming more difficult on the street. In the past the homeless would stick together and try not to draw attention to themselves. Ch (47, m, homeless for 23 years) believes the **deterioration in relations between homeless people is down to the availability of charitable services**. This, he believes, encourages over-reliance on someone else: "*I think it was because these organisations were set up that offer everything, and **that caused these people to change**. The system looks after them and **solidarity dwindles**. It didn't used to be like that and people had to scavenge or beg. And they all stuck together. It's not like that now. They steal from each other and even take each other's place.*" There are many reasons why relationships between homeless people might be worse than in the past. It is certainly significant that there are now fewer sources of sustenance (garbage cans are locked and begging is banned or deemed a misdemeanour), and this leads to greater competition for those resources that are available.

Our respondents believe the main reason for the breakdown in relationships is a **rise in selfishness and inconsiderateness**, as well as the loss of barriers that results from excessive consumption of alcohol or drugs.
- M (40, f, homeless for 25 years): "*Homeless people used to help each other out, but **now they simply steal from and cheat on each other**.*"
- J (39, m, homeless for five years): "*I have met some truly awful people who are fake and dishonest. They behave like animals. **These days no one helps anyone else**, everyone is out for themselves.*"
- Z (47, m, homeless for 20 years) has no doubts things have got worse between homeless people: "*There used to be a sense of solidarity between people on the street. They would **help each other out and remain united**. If someone found something, they would share it out between the rest. These days everyone swoops down on it. They're altogether more selfish.*"
- R (49, m, homeless for 20 years) agrees: "*It used to be one for all and all for one* [in a squat]. *Nobody would do the rounds of containers on their own just for themselves. We used to go in a collective. We all had something in common and it was fun. **These days everyone is out for themselves**.*"
- V (51, m, homeless for 10 years): "*These days everyone's more predatory in the sense of wanting to grab whatever they can find. **Everyone is looking out for them-***

selves… there's more selfishness around the bins and homeless people are nearly coming to blows whenever someone finds a profitable spot."

It is possible that our older respondents are simply idealising the period of their youth, which always appears better in hindsight than it was in reality. It may also be the case that young people are more willing than their elders to operate in a group and support each other, though the truth is that younger people on the street also reported problematic and conflictual relationships (Vágnerová, Csémy, Marek, 2013).

Our interviews reveal that a **degree of expedience is in operation in relationships between homeless people**. People are doing their best to survive, sometimes at the expense of others. A crisis situation increases the tendency to exploit those who have something. As soon as someone has nothing of interest to anyone else, interest in them wanes.

- O (53, m, homeless for 20 years) is aware that people act in a friendly way only if they expect something in return, and it concerns him: *"There are bad people amongst us. As long as you have some food and money then you're popular. **If you don't have anything, nobody is going to help you**."*
- M (50, m, homeless for 20 years) has the same experience: *"**If you have no money**, you sink to the bottom. If you've no clothes on your back, **then forget friendship**."*
- Z (42, m, homeless for 11 years) rejects such relationships: *"**Some people are your friends as long as you have something to drink**. I don't give a toss about such people."*

Egocentrism and parasitism feature in the lives of homeless people. A state of ongoing crisis reinforces selfishness. This is a strategy that can be effective on the street. The obviousness of this parasitism bothers many people, especially those whose disaffiliation is not so pronounced.

- Z (44, m, homeless for 15 years) sees this going on around him and is bothered by it: *"The idea is that if you have a two-litre carton of wine, everyone has to have a swig. You have to offer it around and nobody cares whether you had to earn the money or save up for it. **It gets on my nerves, this idea that you have to share everything** whether or not you earned it. I hate it because I know that the moment I start talking to them, they'll come running up and it'll be, hey mate, you haven't got a cigarette to spare or a joint?"* This is the behaviour of people who are dependent on alcohol or drugs.
- K (42, m, homeless for 11 years) is also unwilling to accept such parasitism: *"Recently I've hardly had any friends at all. They're just a bunch of chancers and bastards. How am I meant to chat to them when **all they want to know is what there is to stick their snouts into?**"*

- J (50, m, homeless for two years) feels the same: "*I was surprised by the behaviour of these people. They simply wanted whatever they could get for free. **Ninety-nine percent of the people here are freeloading off someone**, basically abusing someone who has done nothing to deserve it.*"
- J (39, f, homeless for nine years) also has experience of being exploited by other people: "*You have to be strong in order not to be caught up in it, because everybody's doing it. **They arrive, have a drink, sleep**, it's like they want you to wash their socks **before they steal from you**. It's a real bundle of laughs.*"

Many of our respondents feel there are no rules on the street, and inasmuch as the community recognises any, they are different to those applied in mainstream society. An example would be survival of the fittest. Since these are maladjusted individuals, it cannot be expected that they will respect rules that would restrict them. Furthermore, their behaviour is often erratic and unpredictable.

- M (49, m, homeless for 20 years): "*It works both ways on the street. **The same guy will help you one moment then fuck you over the next**. When he himself is in the shit, that's simply the way it operates.*"
- I (40, m, homeless for two years) is convinced that no rules apply: "***I have never seen any sign of rules between homeless people**. Basically, everyone argues over where they're going to beg.*"
- M (50, m, homeless for 20 years) agrees: "***They simply don't know when to stop**.*"
- R (40, m, homeless for six years), blames alcohol: "*It's the result of alcohol... ok, they used to argue, but it had to over something serious if someone attacked another person during the night. **These days there are simply no rules**.*"

Most of our respondents believe that you cannot trust anyone on the street and that deception and theft is an everyday occurrence. Many people have been robbed by other homeless people and know that this could happen at any point in the future.

- J (51, m, homeless for one year): "*I thought that homeless people stuck together. But that's not the case at all. It's a nightmare. **They're forever stealing from each other**.*"
- M (55, m, homeless for 17 years): "*I have to keep my backpack on me the whole time. Otherwise, **anything that isn't fastened in some way they will steal**.*"
- M (37, f, homeless for five years): "*They are as two-faced as you can believe on the street. They're always gossiping about each other and shafting each other at the drop of a hat. **They no longer even know what to steal from you, simply that they have to steal**.*"
- P (45, f, homeless for eight years): "*I have found out an awful lot. You have to keep them at arm's length. Your so-called friends will sell you down the river. **You can't trust anyone here**. You think you have a best friend and then one day you wake up and your pockets have been sliced open and your money and telephone are gone*

with the guy you thought was your friend. These people have nothing, and so out of desperation they behave in this way."

Z (51, m, homeless for ten years) believes there is a knock-on effect taking place: *"They're capable of stealing from each other. Mind you, some of them are ok. It's about people, it's acquired behaviour. Someone robs them a couple of times and they say, right,* ***if they're going to steal from me I'm going to do the same back.****"* It would not be a huge exaggeration to claim that mutual theft has become the rule in the homeless community. Themselves victims of theft, people find themselves sucked into stealing from others.

People living on the street are threatened by the aggressive behaviour of other homeless people (usually caused by alcohol or drug abuse).

- L (52, m, homeless for two years) believes levels of aggression are increasing: *"It depends on the circumstances. For instance, last month I was in a hostel and* ***most of the homeless people there were aggressive.*** *There were moments I was genuinely worried that something would explode, because they were completely uncontrollable. The relationships there were awful, you could feel the hate between people."*
- Increased aggression is reason why some of our more experienced respondents maintain a distance between themselves and others. M (55, m, homeless for 17 years): *"It's best to be on your own on the street and not to be dependent on anyone. It sometimes drives you mad, because you just want to talk to someone. But they're all getting drunk,* ***they're fighting amongst themselves, sometimes even with knives.****"*
- Z (49, f, homeless for 15 years) believes caution is essential: *"When you go to prison for the first time, what everyone tells you is not to speak confidentially with anyone and not to trust anyone. The same is true of the street. Don't speak confidentially and don't trust anyone. There are people who will strike up a conversation, offer you some cheap plonk. So you have a drink with them and the* ***next moment you've got a knife in your back.*** *I'm sorry, but that's just the way it is."*

Women are more often the victims of aggression than men. The violence is not always from their partners.

- D (48, f, homeless for five years) was physically abused by her roommate, a drug addict: *"Things went on there that scared the fuck out of me.* ***I shared a squat with a young bloke*** *who used to get completely out of it.* ***He'd be really aggressive.*** *I got this black eye from him and one time he hit me so hard I lost my hearing. Then there was the time that he dragged me outside into the snow at night and poured a barrel of freezing water all over me. If something wasn't quite right, say he didn't have any grass or a cigarette lighter, he would take it all out on me. He'd fly into a complete frenzy."*
- M (40, f, homeless for 25 years) was attacked by a drug addict: *"In February 2014, when I came out of prison, some guy broke my jaw. He was a friend from the*

*street and had long been a junkie. **He punched me and broke my jaw**. I still have the scar on my throat."*

- E (46, f, homeless for 11 years) was attacked by a psychotic: "*I had made a friend who had really helped me. He was Slovak and later he hanged himself because **he had schizophrenia**. At that time he was still ok, but then it all kicked off. When he drank he became convinced he was being followed by the FBI and that I was in cahoots with them. **Twice he set fire to my stuff**.*"

Drinking to excess has a negative impact on the behaviour of homeless people. Alcohol is a frequent cause of problems in relationships between people on the street. It inflates the ego and intensifies aggression. Someone who is dependent on alcohol will do anything to get their hands on it.

- M (54, m, homeless for nine years) is convinced that alcohol destroys relationships: "*They can be getting on fine, and then **they get their filthy paws on some wine and that's the end**. They all start stealing from each other.*"
- Z (51, m, homeless for ten years): "*It's a really sad thing that someone who might be far worse off than you can rob you. The main reason is always that they have no money to buy drink. **They're so out of it they can't think straight**. That's the main reason they act as they do. Whenever there's a group of them, they booze and fight.*"
- Ch (47, m, homeless for 23 years): "*A lot of these homeless people are really nasty and **are capable of killing each other over drink**. These days everyone has their own plan. Say they decide to sleep in a tent. One will get so drunk he'll fall asleep and the other one will steal everything he owns.*"

The non-standard behaviour of people on the street can have many different causes. Often these are individuals with mental health issues and dependent on alcohol or drugs. They may also be experiencing trauma. One or more of these factors may apply at any one moment. Some of our respondents are aware of this. G (50, m, homeless for 10 years) believes this problematic behaviour is the result of issues from the past: "***These are people who have had bad experiences that have scarred them**. Each of them has a story to tell and it's not for me to judge.*"

SUMMARY

The relationships that people living on the street have with other homeless people are important. They spend a lot of time together and have no other social contacts. Some make friends, though most do not. Interpersonal relationships on the street are not like those of mainstream society, and friendship arises under different circumstances. The friendships of homeless people are rarely capable of offering a source of security. They are established quickly but are unstable and end easily. Bad experiences have led most of our respondents not to trust other homeless people, whom they regard more as acquaintances sharing a similar destiny. Loneliness is a frequent problem. More than half the people that completed our questionnaire experienced loneliness. Certain individuals, especially those who have been homeless for a long time, are convinced that relationships between homeless people are worse than they used to be. They believe that solidarity is no more and has been replaced by selfishness, inconsiderateness and parasitism. Freeloading off others without offering reciprocal assistance is more widespread. Our respondents believe that relationships between people on the street are marked by expediency and that many form friendships only if there is something to be gained. They say that there are basically no rules in operation on the street, the main principle being survival of the fittest.

The behaviour of people on the street is greatly influenced by excessive consumption of alcohol or drugs. This leads to the breakdown of both personalities and relationships. It contributes to the creation of conflict and may often lie behind bouts of aggression and physical abuse. Most of our respondents believe that no one on the street is trustworthy. Theft and exploitation is common and the perpetrators are often known by the victims. Someone may well be robbed by a person they deemed a friend. This often takes place under the influence of alcohol or drugs or as a consequence of mental health issues. Whatever the cause of problematic behaviour, there is the risk that such models of behaviour will become fixed, after which it is difficult to change them. This then creates another barrier to a return to mainstream society, especially in the case of the long-term homeless (Leufgen and Snow, 2004).

A comparison of the opinions of young and older homeless people reveals that people aged 40–50 are far more pessimistic regarding interpersonal relationships. Almost half of young people (45%) give a positive rating to relationships between homeless people: in the case of middle-aged people this figure is 15%. It would appear that, in addition to reflecting the greater length of time spent on the street, this is the result of a tendency to reduce the number of friends one has as one gets older. Generally speaking, middle-aged people are not as open to new relationships, and the same is true on the street. If a necessity arises for someone to be in constant contact with people they have not chosen and who are in some way problematic, they will tend to be more critical in their assessment (Vágnerová, Csémy, Marek, 2013).

Inasmuch as young people rated their relationships with others poorly, this was for similar reasons to older people. It became clear from our interviews with young people that they too reject behaviour that does not respect any boundaries. Most of them resented being exposed to the inconsiderateness of others, who robbed them and sometimes injured them. However, young people on the street more often stated that homeless people were capable of providing assistance to others and sharing. They believed that assistance could operate on a reciprocal basis and that if a person helped someone else, then this favour would be returned at some point in the future. They acknowledged a law of reciprocity that might be summed up as "do not thank, but do not forget", applied both positively and negatively. On the other hand, they were aware that people on the street were not to be trusted and that many of them were ruthless and parasitical. Younger homeless people also admitted that the principle of survival of the fittest applied on the street in the sense of "first come, first served", regardless of whether there would be anything left for others (Vágnerová, Csémy, Marek, 2013).

Middle-aged homeless people are more pessimistic. They are convinced that people on the street are not willing to return a favour and that they are interested only in themselves. It is interesting that several young people also believe that life on the street used to be better and that people helped each other more, even though this opinion was not as common as amongst our middle-aged respondents. Some young people think that they themselves provide more assistance than others, whereas this opinion is not widespread among middle-aged people. Both young and old think that friendship does not survive on the street and that relationships fall apart quickly. Both young and old are also convinced that interpersonal relationships are negatively impacted by drugs and alcohol, and members of both cohorts have extensive experience with this problem.

4.1 SEXUAL PARTNERSHIPS BETWEEN HOMELESS PEOPLE

The partnerships enjoyed by people on the street are of a different character to those they had before becoming homeless. Men do not usually have a stable female partner, and if they do, then she will be homeless too. For women life on the street is more difficult, and as a consequence most will have a male partner. These partners are usually homeless too, and many are dependent on alcohol or drugs and are repeat offenders who behave badly towards their female partners.

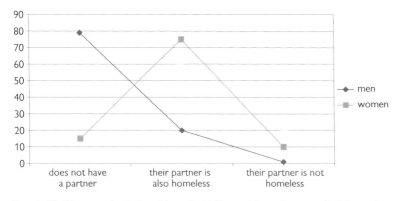

Graph 20. The sexual relationships of middle-aged homeless people (shown in percentages).

I. The sexual partnerships of homeless men

Most men living on the street do not have or want a stable partner. They have occasional and short-term relationships that do not place them under any obligation. This is not only because of the limitations of their lifestyle, but because of a focus on their own problems and a reluctance to address the complications that would ensue from a long-term partnership.

- H (50, m, homeless for 20 years) has been a drug addict for all of his time on the street: "*I've hooked up with loads of women, but just for the weekend whatever. I've kind of weaned myself off all of that. **Nobody would want to meet someone in the state I'm in**.*" H is aware of the devastating effects his lifestyle has had on his attractiveness: "***I feel really ugly** and I can't even bring myself to chat to girls. Pervitin will give you those sorts of hang-ups. I didn't look quite as bad while I still had my front teeth, but now I look like a fucking monster. I didn't used to look this bad. It's the drugs, I guess, that make me look like an imbecile.*"
- Z (51, m, homeless for 10 years) is a repeat offender and alcoholic: "*Yeah, I had a homeless woman not that long ago. The last time was a year ago. I was with her for about 14 days. **I think you have to be really careful**. I don't just want to jump into something.*"
- J (45, m, homeless for six years): "*I'm not looking for a woman. **It makes no sense**. I don't own anything and **I'm alone on the street**.*"
- R (48, m, homeless for seven years) is an alcoholic: "*I haven't had any long-term relationships on the street. I've liked women, but I've always thought, no, fuck it, right now **it's me I have to look after**. I no longer even play the field. How could I provide for a partner? I'd simply end up feeling guilty.*"

Another reason often cited for not wanting a stable partnership is an **unwillingness to be restricted and to have to take another into account**.

- G (50, m, homeless for 10 years), who drinks and takes drugs, did not have a stable relationships even before becoming homeless: "*While on the street I've had one woman. Unfortunately I can't get rid of her and she still calls me all the time. Just because I slept with her a couple of times doesn't mean I'm going to marry her. She's got her own apartment, but she can shove that up her arse. **That would mean me losing my freedom. I'm not about to start eating the crumbs that fall from the table**.*"
- D (40, m, homeless for 19 years): "*I go to the minimarket to beg. There's a bird there that buys me food costing CZK 300* [USD 13]*... But I'm not interested. She's got three kids and **I'd have to get a job** and shit.*" It is by no means clear whether D's benefactor sees him as a potential partner or is simply being generous. D drinks to excess and takes drugs.

Some men are convinced that **longer-term partnerships cannot work on the street**.

- S (51, m, homeless for 17 years): "*There's been nothing serious. It's not that I've turned my back on women per se. But these days if you don't own anything, then what do you tell the woman? I don't want anything stable.* **I don't believe it works on the street**."
- O (53, m, homeless for 20 years): "*From time to time I've copped off with some slag.* **But on the street it means nothing**, *it's basically about drugs.*" Most of these men we spoke to had had girlfriends or wives prior to becoming homeless, but these relationships had ended, usually through their own fault.

Most homeless men do not want their partners to be homeless too. They tend to be more critical of homeless women than homeless men. They don't like the fact that such women drink to excess, take drugs, engage in prostitution, and steal from their partners. They are convinced that life on the street is more difficult for women and that they are exposed to greater risks than men, and that therefore their disaffiliation is greater, or perhaps more visible.

- S (51, m, homeless for 14 years): "*When I see these women on the street, I can't help thinking* **they're worse than the men**. *A drunk man is ugly: a pissed woman is a fucking catastrophe on legs.*"
- T (39, m, homeless for six years): "*The older women tend to be hardened alcoholics.* **The younger girls are junkies, and I have no desire to be with a junkie**."
- J (52, m, homeless for five years): "**I'd be afraid of having a relationship on the street**. *I mean, I'd love to have someone close. But I couldn't be with a girl from the street.* **They drink and they're junkies** *and I can do without that. It's not a good look for a woman. I was at Anděl today and a woman I know by sight suddenly appeared. She was wearing no shoes, she was filthy dirty and she smelt of piss.*" Despite his judgemental approach, J himself consumes alcohol.
- B (51, m, homeless for 20 years): "*I'm not looking for a relationship on the street.* **Some of these women look so fucking awful I wouldn't lean my bike against them**."
- V (42, m, homeless for 21 years) is wary even of just sex: "*You sleep with her and then* **she robs you of everything**."

Some of our respondents felt sorry for these women but were still not keen on the idea of a girlfriend from the street. Z (47, m, homeless for 20 years) on the topic: "*I have always felt sorry for the women on the street, because* **they have it far worse in all respects**, *although there are times when it's easier for them. Because I know what they've been through,* **I feel sorry for them**. *There's one I know, she used to be a prostitute. Later I saw her and she looked so slatternly. There's no way I'd dip my wick in them, you don't know what you'd catch. Sex with homeless women is a bit of a no-no, firstly because most of them are pig-shit ugly, and secondly the passable ones always have a bloke in tow.*"

The opposite stance towards homeless women and probably women in general is taken by L (38, m, homeless for 21 years), a repeat offender: "*I meet a girl on the street, invite her to dinner and then say,* **right you fucking cow, you think this dinner comes free of charge?** *Well it comes with strings attached. Now it's time to spread your legs darling, because that just set me back five hundred crowns* [USD 22] *and I'm not interested in hearing you whine. And if you make a big deal of it I'll beat the shit out of you.*" L admits to having beaten even his longer-term partners, whether or not they were homeless or prostitutes.

Inasmuch as our respondents believe that a longer-term relationship might be possible in their situation, **they stipulate conditions both on their own side and on the side of their potential partner**.

- **Quitting the street is a condition for the acceptance of a stable relationship**. This is at any rate what T (39, m, homeless for six years) believes: "*Right now I have the odd friend-with-benefits. But* **a long-term relationship will only be possible when I am no longer homeless** *and I don't have any debts.*" M (55, m, homeless for 17 years) feels the same: "*I wouldn't want a relationship with someone on the street. Having said that I'm not god's gift to women, so it's not for me to choose,* **unless I was able to re-enter society and leave the street.**"
- Only a woman who does not live on the street and who accepts them as they are would be an acceptable partner for our respondents. This is how S (51, m, homeless for 14 years) feels: "*Definitely not from the street.* **She must be a completely normal woman.**"
- R (48, m, homeless for seven years) feels similarly: "*No way can you be with someone from the street.* **Only a normal girl**, *a shop assistant, for instance.*"
- D (39, m, homeless for 10 years): "*I don't want to be a drag on someone. I don't want them to have to look after me.* **If I found a really intelligent girl**, *I mean really sensible, who just accepted me for the way I am, then* **I wouldn't be against it.**" Just how attractive D would be to such women remains a moot point.

Some of our male respondents have in fact established partnerships on the street. However, **these relationships tend to be unstable and tempestuous**. Take L (38, m, homeless for 21 years), an alcoholic and repeat offender: "*I met her when I came out of prison. She was 18 years old and already pregnant. We were both squatting in the same cabin. We split up because without my permission she gave the boy up to Klokánek* [an organisation caring for children at threat]. *I was in trouble with the law at that time, and when I came out of prison, we had a massive row that graduated to violence.* **I hit her for having taken the boy from me and put him in an institution.** *Of course I hit her, she got what she deserved, because she gave my boy away without my permission.* **I was fond of her.**" L appears satisfied in his most recent relationship, though he remains incapable of self-control: "*I met her at Naděje one time after I had come out of prison. I thought she was homeless but in fact she wasn't, she worked at the post office. But she'd blown all her wages. She had nothing to eat, so she went to Naděje and we got together. Then she joined me on the street.* **I ended up hitting her too**, *though inadvertently. Somehow we got into a fight and I completely lost it and my hand just kind* *of flew out… **We get on well the two of us**. It's not because she's older than me, but she does have a lot of experience of life and that's important. **She keeps my head above water** and if I can just keep things this way then I'll never have to go back to prison."* L most probably suffers a personality disorder and has limited intellectual ability. He grew up in a dysfunctional family where there was no role model. His current relationship persists simply because his girlfriend is extremely submissive and is convinced that she would not be able to survive on the street on her own. As a consequence she is prepared to tolerate a lot.

The consumption of alcohol or drugs features in many relationships between homeless people. Such relationships will not provide the necessary support for a return into mainstream society.

- V (42, m, homeless for 21 years) **found a partner dependent on alcohol** who is now dependent on him too: *"I've found a woman and I wouldn't want to lose her. **She used to drink a lot and has cirrhosis of the liver**, but her sister has taken her under her wing and she no longer drinks a drop. She used to drink because of her boss and because she hated her work. We've been together five years."*
- M (54, m, homeless for 21 years), who drinks to excess, has a partner who is an alcoholic: *"I've been with a woman for 15 years. Right now she's in hospital. We used to live in that tent. I met her in Hostivař. She was living with a boyfriend and he used to beat her. **She used to drink** and smoke a lot."*
- P (47, m, homeless for seven years) has a partner who drinks to excess: *"When I came out of prison I met Mrs O. It's a kind of street relationship. We've been together two years. She has a good relationship with alcohol. I've tried to help her a bit."* P is a repeat offender and it can be assumed that he was not attractive for women leading a standard lifestyle.

When they do find partners, **male drug addicts tend to have relationships with female drug addicts**. V (38, m, homeless for 13 years): *"I've had a few girlfriends, but they never lasted more than six months, maybe a year. **They were also drug addicts**. My second or third relationship lasted almost three years and we were on Subutex* [a brand name for Buprenorphine, an opioid used to treat opioid addiction, acute pain, and chronic pain]. *I don't know exactly why, but **things didn't work out between us**. I can't even say why we split up. We both had jobs, so it wasn't a relationship built purely on drugs. Right now I have a girlfriend and the two of us are on methadone, not for long, two months…"*

Homeless partners usually share the same addiction, and when this is not so, the relationship quickly ends. It is clear that these are not standard partnerships but more based around the shared use of drugs or alcohol.

- V (48, m, homeless for seven years) is aware of this: *"I've had a girlfriend who's also homeless. Yeah, people get it together on the street and stay together, I don't know,* *six months? It can last, but **you have to be on the same track, it won't work if one's an alcoholic and the other a junkie**. That's bad.*"

- P (50, m, homeless for 12 years) drinks and had a partner who was a drug addict: "*I found one girl, or rather she found me… I haven't seen her for four years. **She left me because of the drugs**. I really liked her. She lived with me for a while in the tent, but I didn't have time to look after her.*" This case would tend to confirm the idea that relationships between people with different addictions will not last long.

Even though the girlfriends of homeless men tend to be as problematic as their partners, their **relationships do not immediately break down, especially if both share similar values** and are accustomed to living the same lifestyle. D (37, m, homeless for nine years) is an alcoholic and repeat offender who is in a stable relationship with someone he met on the street: "*I met my current girlfriend in a refuge in Brno. We have two kids. Previously I just used to have one-night stands, that kind of thing. I fancied them, but it wasn't serious. I'd prefer being down the pub having fun rather than having to look after someone else. But this one, even though she was homeless, **she's clever, she thinks ahead**. She knows what to do to make things ok. She used to be married and I have met her ex. She had two kids before meeting me, but her mum looks after them.*" D is very dependent on his partner and it is thanks to her that he began working, albeit on a cash-in-hand basis. The fact that his partner no longer cares for her children from an earlier relationships does not surprise him, very probably because it corresponds to his experience with his own parents.

II. The sexual partnerships of homeless women

Unlike their male counterparts, homeless women usually have partners, also homeless. These relationships tend to be conflictual and problematic. However, because many women believe they would not survive on the streets on their own, they tolerate relatively unacceptable behaviour.

- M (43, f, homeless for eight years): "***A woman on the street can't afford to be without a man**. Look at me. I wouldn't be on the street alone. You have to have someone by your side, at the very least another woman.*"
- J (50, f, homeless since she was young). "*I've always had a partner. **They more or less looked after me**.*"
- Š (46, f, homeless for four years): "***I'm really happy I've got him**, because on my own I'd go mad, I wouldn't dream of setting foot outside at night.*" Š's partner does not always treat her with consideration. However, the situation as it stands is clearly more acceptable to her than if she were to remain alone.

Women have a greater need for a relationship than men, and this is sometimes reflected in an inability to gauge how their partner conceives of the relationship and a willingness to tolerate violence and insensitive behaviour.

- J (50, f, homeless for 20 years): "*I was with one bloke for eight years, and then he found a newer model. He simply upped and left. I called him and returned to the places he used to hang out, and then I learned that he was married and living with his wife in a cottage. Then I got together with J, who was also homeless. But he went off with some young girl, younger than me. But what I have with V I've never had before with anyone. We've been together two years, he's my latest partner. What makes me sad is that we're forever arguing over nothing. **Several times he's behaved strangely to me**. Just when I feel we're getting close, he insinuates it's just a sympathy fuck. **No way could I split up with him**. When I love someone I love them completely, **whatever they do, whatever they say**.*" In fact, J's current partner, 51-year old V, has no interest in her, as he told us: "*I've got a girl from a shelter. I feel sorry for her. I don't love her, I feel more fatherly towards her.*" J has been homeless since she was young. She grew up in a foster family. She suffers from low self-esteem and is used to being rejected.

- J (45, f, homeless for 20 years) has had many partners while on the street, though is not as dependent on them: "*I was single for years before I found someone suitable. I had male friends, but I didn't need a permanent companion. I was quite capable of looking after myself. I used to go begging or I visited a charity, picked out some clothes at Naděje and had a shower. I lived on the street with D, but **I split up with him because he was jealous and drank like me**. But it was mainly because of his jealousy. Right now I'm with R. He helps me with the dog, because otherwise I wouldn't be able to go to work. This kind of dog can't spend all day there. **R is a nice guy. He doesn't drink**, though sometimes he does pervitin, though not when I'm around. He also receives emergency financial support.*" J has drunk alcohol and taken drugs the entire time she has been living on the street.

- P (37, f, homeless for 15 years) has a stable relationship with a man who is now her husband and is also homeless. As she says, **they are linked by the same experiences and lifestyle**: "*I've been with the same guy since November 2005, more than eleven years. We got married after eight years. We have similar experiences. **He was in prison, and so was I**, so he understands me and I understand him… We're together the whole time and sometimes we get on each other's nerves. But it's ok. When the rows get too much, sometimes it's best just to bugger off somewhere.*" Her husband sometimes disappears. He was once gone for three months, but then returned: "*He was in England, where he went for work. I didn't know. He went to Naděje on Friday to take a bath and returned three months later.*" P has eight children, five of which are with her current husband. However, neither P nor her husband look after the children.

Sexual relationships on the street often feature insensitivity, violence and the exploitation of one partner by the other. The stories told by our female respondents display marked similarities and are basically bleak in character. Insensitivity and violence are often related to an addiction, be this to alcohol or drugs.

- E (46, f, homeless for 11 years) has encountered exploitation and insensitivity in her partners: "*When I came out of prison, I hooked up with another jerk. He's now left me. I waited for him to come out of prison for non-payment of alimony and then he left me. Right now I'm single and I don't want a guy. He was ten years younger than me, except* **he took advantage of me**. *I gave him some money, and when he returned he said he'd bought a few items. I asked where they were, but he'd taken them elsewhere. That's why I don't want a man. I have my animals.*"
- M (43, f, homeless for eight years) has been exploited by her partner: "*I lived in Řepy with Lugy.* **He was nice, but when he drank he turned nasty.** *I ran away from him and into the arms of R, with whom I've been since then. I've tried living with him. He was also in a shelter and* **I gave him some money** *so that he could pay for accommodation.* **But he drank it all**, *so they chucked him out. I'll don't mind giving him a few crowns here and there, but I can't live with him.*" For a time M was addicted to alcohol and drugs. At present she lives in a refuge.
- P (45, f, homeless for eight years) has been on the receiving end of violence from her partners, who are mostly drug addicts also living on the street: "*I used to be in a long-term relationship. I had CZK 200,000* [USD 8,900] *saved in an account and I spent it all on drugs. Naturally, as soon as I had no money the next thing I know the boyfriend is out of the door. Another guy moved in, except that the whole time I suspected he was simply sponging off me.* **I was forever looking after him** *while he was dreaming up different plans.* **I started to feel used** *and then I started to feel he was losing interest. We started being violent with each other, and before long it was an on-off relationship. He was forever in and out of prison. As a friend he was ok. But the moment you wanted to be his lover, then he started to act despotically.* **He even started hitting me.**" P is a drug addict, a fact that lies behind all of her problems, including those related to partners.

Many of our respondents have had to cope with violence on the part of their partners, which has sometimes had serious consequences.
- K (27, f, homeless for 10 years): "*I found a new boyfriend and he ended up* **breaking my ribs seven times**, *one time five ribs after a fall.* **I'd already had a boyfriend who beat me up, but this was far worse**... *I started to have panic attacks and after we'd been together seven years I ended it. In the end they locked the bastard up.*"
- J (39, f, homeless for nine years) has repeatedly been the target of violence from her partners, who are also homeless: "*I met him at* Nový prostor *[a street newspaper sold by homeless people equivalent to* The Big Issue *in Britain]. I invited him for a mulled wine. We spent some time getting to know one another and then we began to go out together. But it didn't work out and I lost everything. In the end I had to escape to a hostel.* **He treated me badly**... *it's difficult to talk about, but, yeah,* **domestic violence**. *In the end I was a complete wreck because of him. I was shaking and I couldn't go to work. We lived together for two years. Then I escaped. I told him I'd had enough and that I was going to live somewhere else and that I wasn't going to tell him where. In fact I moved into a hostel, which is where I met V. Mind you,*

he wasn't much better and slapped me around even more. **To say he hit me barely does justice** to what he did to me. He punched me twice when he was drunk and for a month I couldn't set foot outside. Then he cut all my hair off, then he burnt my backside, and so on and so on." J drinks and takes drugs. After a series of bad experiences, she eventually decided she would rather not have a partner: "I don't need a boyfriend on the street. I can deal with things on my own. There are other people where I live so I'm not on my own, even though things can be difficult for a single woman."

- M (40, f, homeless for ten years) also had problematic partners: "*The guy I was with before I went to prison is now serving time. It was the first time I had ever left a bloke in my life. In the past a guy could do anything to me and I'd stick around if I still had feelings for him. Then there were guys I met on the street. I only felt something for three of them. One of them taught me how to steal from shops, the second taught me how to steal from apartments and cars. The third didn't teach me anything, although it was because of him that I was in prison the last time. I had stolen some chocolate for him so he could take it to his grandmother in Most and ask for money.*" M has been addicted to alcohol and drugs during her time on the street.

III. The sexual partnerships of older homeless people

The more stable relationships of older homeless people often involve an element of **caring** on the part of one or other partner due to increasing health problems. This is often more a case of making a virtue out of necessity.

Illus. 6. A homeless couple in a tent (photo Martin Pokora).

- J (50, m, homeless for four years) looked after his partner, whom he met on the street: "*I found the perfect woman here. I had pitched my tent and she would do the laundry and cook. She was homeless and had been a fairground worker. We were together for three years. She had grown up in a children's home.* **I enjoyed looking**

Illus. 7. A homeless couple in the wild (photo Martin Pokora).

Illus. 8. A homeless couple in an abandoned building (photo Martin Pokora).

after her *and I knew that she needed it. But she died. At the age of 46 she had a heart attack. She used to drink.*" J had a normal childhood. Before becoming homeless he was married for seven years. He does not look after his children. He is not addicted to alcohol or drugs.

- V (51, m, homeless for ten years) also acts as carer. One of his girlfriends was a homeless drug addict: "*I met her here in Prague. She was a friend, if you can call a friend someone you've known for two days who spreads her legs for you. I fell in love with her.* **I used to visit her in Bohnice.** *Every day I would travel there in order to support her. She was there for 15 months and then she left.* **I looked after her** *after she was released. She remained with me for another four or five months and then she left me and got back together with the bloke she'd been with before. I didn't feel good about it. She no longer takes drugs, but she drinks.*" V is something of a carer in his current relationship: "*My current girlfriend is from a refuge.* **I feel sorry for her.** *I'm not in love, but we've been together about one year.*" During his childhood V was looked after by his mother and grandmother, and so he knows about parental behaviour. However, he has no interest in his own children. He is not addicted to alcohol or drugs.

- R (49, m, homeless for twenty years) also looks after his partner, who lives on the street: "*My girlfriend is from Slovakia and we've been together for ten years. I had others before her, but I'm glad they left because* **all they thought about was booze.** *She's been in a wheelchair since last year. There's something wrong with her heart and lungs. At a guess she's 53, 54. She has no right to benefits because she's Slovak, so* **I basically keep her head above water.**" R's marriage came to an end more than twenty years ago and he does not look after his children. Looking after a sick partner who is dependent on him satisfies some need he has and gives his life some meaning.

Some older homeless men are grateful to be cared for by their girlfriends. O (53, m, homeless for twenty years) is happy to receive help from his current partner, who also lives on the street: "*At present I'm going out with crazy E. I would give my life for her, I'm mad about her. We've been together six months. The truth is that* **she found me in the street near Main Station and looks after me** *in a fabulous way. She visits me every day and brings me food. I'm so happy to have her. I listen to her and do whatever she says. When we got together, I stopped smoking within a month, I stopped drinking and doing drugs. I haven't taken anything for six months and have given up alcohol altogether.*" O was no doubt prompted to give up risky behaviour due to a deterioration in his state of health as well as by his partner, who is happy to look after him. Previously he had had only one-off sexual relationships and no interest in a more stable relationship.

SUMMARY

Our interviews reveal that most homeless men do not have a stable relationship and often do not want one. They believe they already have enough on their plate and do not need further complications. They also believe that relationships between homeless people do not work. They do not regard women living on the street as potential partners. They are very critical and judgemental, though some of them express sympathy. An acceptable partner for them is a woman who is not living on the street.

Homeless women on the other hand usually have partners, who are almost always on the street. They believe this is necessary for survival. Women feel a greater need for a relationships than men. Women who became homeless while still young often had several problematic relationships with men who treated them insensitively, physically abused them, and exploited them. Their partners often drink and take drugs and have repeatedly served time in prison. The greater tolerance shown by women to their partners reflects both a desire not to be on their own and the different standards of people living on the street. They only became able to reject unsatisfactory relationships later in life. It is clear from their stories that life on the street is far more difficult for women.

The personality traits of those we interviewed are reflected in their relationships, especially reduced empathy and an inability to perceive and respect anyone else's needs. Personality and experience are also reflected in a person's choice of partner, i.e. the acceptance of individuals who, one might anticipate, will be risky partners. The relationships of people living on the street are not stable or harmonious. Often one party will exploit and abuse the other, and such relationships usually end dramatically. Many of these relationships arise on the basis of a shared propensity for drink or drugs. The relationships of older people are of a different character to those they had when they were young, and often feature one partner caring for the other. No doubt such partners need greater security and support as their state of health deteriorates.

5. WHERE OLDER HOMELESS PEOPLE LIVE

Homelessness involves limited privacy and lots of time spent in public spaces. The lack of privacy is especially significant at night, when a person wishes to feel they are in a safe place surrounded by their personal effects (i.e. at home). During the day this lack of privacy is less stressful because it applies to most people. Homeless people tend not to have a permanent safe place to sleep and so must either live in a space that is public and therefore unsafe, or must adapt to the presence of other, sometimes unpleasant, people. Deciding between spending the night in a reception centre and sleeping rough is the choice between relative comfort combined with social stress, and an uncomfortable freedom that also has its downsides. The decision that each individual reaches may be guided by the risk of being burgled or suffering other harm. The place where a homeless person sleeps and to which they return offers information regarding the current situation, i.e. the degree of desocialisation of the individual in question (Marek, Strnad and Hotovcová, 2012).

Homeless people can spend their time outdoors, in non-residential or public places, or in emergency or temporary accommodation, i.e. in a reception centre, shelter or hostel. **Most people alternate between these options**. Their preferences change depending on the season, the length of time they have spent on the street, and their age. Most alternate time in reception centres and shelters with sleeping rough or in non-residential premises. Cohabitation can be stressful, and some therefore prefer to sleep rough, where they choose whether they wish to be with someone, and if so with whom.

- F (43, m, homeless for five years) spends time in different places: "*Right now I sleep in a tent, outside, on the tram, or in a squat at Bílá Hora. I have even slept in an elevator in an apartment block going up and down. What am I supposed to do? I'm not like some who complain that they live under a bridge. If I want, I have somewhere to live.*"
- D (48, f, homeless for five years) tells a similar story: "*This is my third year in a refuge. I spent six months in a squat after my last attempt at suicide. The advantage was that I didn't drink. I knew that I had to be vigilant because I was alone. I slept in a reception centre once... or rather I didn't sleep because I was afraid that someone would rob me.*"
- V (38, m, homeless for 13 years): "*Depending on money I might spend time on the street or in hostels. I only began using shelters last year. When I had some money I went to a hostel. But that only lasted a month and then I slept basically everywhere, from a squat to a tent to a park bench. Sometimes I'd simply enter the first door I opened, or if it was warm I'd lie down in the first place that occurred to me.*" Alternating the places they sleep is typical of individuals who want to be alone.

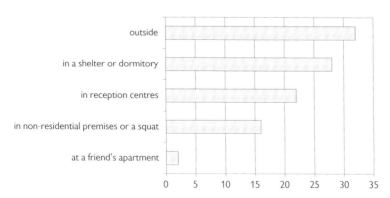

Graph 21. Where older homeless people live or sleep (shown in relative figures)

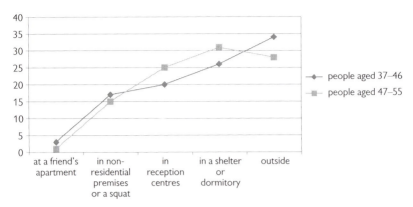

Graph 22. Where older homeless people live or sleep (shown in relative figures).

The graph clearly shows that preference depends on age. Young people prefer to sleep rough (chi-square = 3.98, df = 1, p = 0.005), whereas older people prefer to sleep in a shelter or reception centre (the difference between young and old is not significant as regards this latter category).

Homeless people choose where to sleep depending on the options open to them at any given moment in time. However, their choice also depends on how long they have been living on the street. The graph shows that people who have been homeless ten years and longer often sleep rough or in non-residential premises, while those who have been on the street for four years or less prefer hostels, shelters and reception centres. The difference between these groups is significant only in the case of reception centres, which are more often unacceptable to someone suffering chronic homelessness (chi-square = 3.57, df = 1, p = 0.05).

5.1 SLEEPING ROUGH

Sleeping rough[4] outside assigned places is an option often chosen by homeless people, especially younger people. There are approximately 4,000 people in Prague sleeping rough, according to Hradecký et al. (2012). Kuchařová et al. (2015) claim that these are mainly single men with a basic education. As regards middle-aged people, at least 32% occasionally opt to sleep rough. (Our questionnaire indicates that 28% of people sleep rough.) There are also disparities in the results of foreign studies. According to Muňoz et al. (1999), only one fifth of homeless people sleep rough. McDonagh (2011), on the other hand, found that up to 77% of people slept rough, and similar findings were reported by Johnson and Chamberlain (2008), with 74% of their cohort sleeping rough. These variations might reflect the offer and availability of social services in individual countries.

---

4 A person may sleep in the street, beneath a bridge, at a station, in a culvert, a cave, a train wagon, an old car, a tent, a garage, or in the laundry room, cellar or loft of a building.

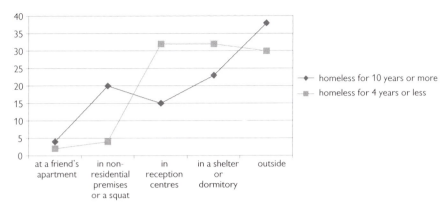

Graph 23. Where older homeless people live or sleep depending on the length of time they have spent on the street (shown in relative figures).

There are many reasons why a person opts to sleep rough. When a person first finds themselves on the street they may have no other option. Several years on and their decision reflects a disinclination to abide by the rules of reception centres and shelters and a rejection of the company of other homeless people because they are dirty, smell, have lice or behave inappropriately. There is also a fear of being robbed or harmed in some other way. However, sleeping rough is also unsafe, and so a person opts to sleep during the day and thus suffers sleep deficit. Notwithstanding all this, some people are only able to sleep rough.

- C (47, m, homeless for 23 years): "***I don't think I could any longer manage to live in a building****. I tried it and after three days I had to return to nature.*"
- A (47, m, homeless for 20 years) tells a similar story: "***Summer and winter I sleep outside****. Here at Masaryk Station. I prefer to have fresh air and I feel fine about where I sleep. I sleep here. It's called ramp no. 2.*"
- J (52, m, homeless for 15 years): "***I've been outside when the temperature has been minus 20****. For many years I slept under a bridge.*"
- Sleeping rough is something that several women do too. J (45, f, homeless for 20 years) is a case in point: "*We live in a tent. **If I can, I live outside***. *I used to sleep under Libeň Bridge. I had a friend living there and she recommended it right from the start.*"
- J (39, f, homeless for nine years): "***I live in a tent with cats****. At present V and P also live there. We had to be strict about who could because there were people who wouldn't clean up and made a huge mess. There are wild boars where I have my tent. I'm not afraid of them. We feed them and they recognise us by smell. We live collectively.*"

Our respondents sleep in various locations (under a bridge, in a park or even in a tree). Some are happier on their own, while **others sleep in public places** to which anyone has access (e.g. by the entry doors of a building or on a bench). Nevertheless, most of them try to ensure that the place is safe and at least symbolically separated from human traffic. Though they may be in public places, several of our respondents make improvements to the place they sleep and treat it as though it were their home (by cordoning it off and furnishing it with objects).

- R (46, m, homeless for four years) is an example: "*When I'm not sleeping on the boat, I'm sleeping at the Hotel Intercontinental. There's a kind of viaduct there. In the František district **there's a kind of marble seating area, and below it you can stretch out**. You're protected from the rain and there's warm air blowing on you.*"
- Z (41, m, homeless for six years): "*Right now I'm sleeping outside. In Řepy, **beneath the entry doors to a building**, on my own.*"
- M (55, m, homeless for 17 years): "*The last two years I've been outside the whole time. I used to spend the night at **George of Poděbrady Square, where you get the warm air from the metro**. But they turfed me out of there.*"
- D (40, m, homeless for 19 years) is not particular about where he sleeps: "*I used to sleep behind the toilets at **Vltavská metro station**. We used to sleep here by the water when the temperatures were minus 20. But we survived and we even had a cat. And the woman who was here a moment ago works in the public toilets, so she sometimes allows us to sleep there.*"

Other respondents preferred calmer places, surrounded by nature or at least separated from the city bustle.

- B (51, m, homeless for 20 years): "*I sleep in Kyje. It's covered by a kind of bridge, it doesn't rain on you, and it's quiet. I'm there alone, thank god. Nobody bothers me so it's the ideal place. The police probably know of me. I arrive at night and then leave at six in the morning.*"

Illus. 9. Sleeping in the park (photo Martin Pokora).

Illus. 10. Sleeping outside with better quality gear (photo Martin Pokora).

Illus. 11. Sleeping in the street (photo Martin Pokora).

- Z (42, m, homeless for 11 years): "*I sleep wherever I can. I have two favourite places. One is in a kind of tiny little housing estate. Not on a bench, I don't sleep on benches. **I lie beneath a tree and place my bag under my head**. At least there's quiet. I sleep outside even during the winter.*"

Not every location is suitable for sleeping and **there is always the threat that people sleeping rough will be robbed** or injured in some way.

- More experienced homeless people know that certain Prague parks are dangerous in this respect. Z (42, m, homeless for 11 years) confirms this: "*Charles Square is not a good place to sleep. They'd steal the nose from between your eyes there.*"
- P (50, m, homeless for 12 years): "*I live in a tent because most of the time I'm on my own. Sometimes I can't sleep or I wake up and I can't get back to sleep. **When you're on your own you have to be watchful the whole night long**.*"
- S (52, m, homeless for 17 years) also finds it necessary to attend to his own safety: "*I travel as much as possible. I sleep outside. I have a tent and sleeping bag, and so **I always go somewhere I can't be seen**, but where I can see the road.*"
- Even animals can represent a threat. Z (47, m, homeless for 20 years) says: "*I've spent the last 20 years homeless, alternating between hostel, street and so on. I lived in a tent and also in a tree, because **there were wild boar in the area and they were forever bothering me. Once they attacked me**, and I climbed a tree. I put a couple of poles across the branches and laid a mattress on top.*"

Winter is difficult for people sleeping rough. Our respondents regard it as one of the most unpleasant experiences they have to come to terms with while living on the street.
- M (40, m, homeless for seven years) is not fussy about where he sleeps but doesn't like the winter: "*At the moment I'm sleeping outside. I don't have anything, not even a sleeping bag or blanket. Nothing. **As soon as I lie down I fall asleep. But in the morning I'm shivering**, around four, half past five and I'm cold. Today for example I slept at the National Theatre. There are these concrete blocks, and that's what I slept on.*"
- R (49, m, homeless for 20 years): "*I used to sleep below a bridge at Černý Most under the tube. I don't have good memories of that period. I sank as low as I could go. **I spent some time sleeping by the River Vltava and that was the coldest I ever got**.*"

SUMMARY

Sleeping rough affords our respondents a greater degree of freedom and independence. They do not have to abide by any rules or spend time with a group of people who may be unacceptable to them for some reason. They choose different places to sleep. Some opt for nature and a peaceful environment, whereas some prefer a busier location. A disadvantage of this method of survival is the greater risk of being robbed or suffering other injury. Winter is a big problem. Despite this, sleeping rough is something many people opt for, especially younger homeless people.

5.2 SLEEPING IN NON-RESIDENTIAL PREMISES AND SQUATS

Our respondents spend their nights in many different non-residential spaces. This is an option chosen by 16% of middle-aged homeless people. (According to our questionnaire, 12% of homeless people spend the night in non-residential premises.) The corridors and cellars of buildings serve as emergency lodgings, especially in winter, because they are warm. The people we spoke to also use garages, garden huts, public toilets, airport halls, and of course stations, where there is often neither warmth nor tranquillity to be found. A person found sleeping in such places can be moved on not only by the police, but by tram drivers and the occupants of the buildings to which they manage to gain access.

- R (40, m, homeless for five years): "*A friend of mine suggested building entrances and said that there are these **little nooks where the electricity and gas meters** are to be found. So I stayed in them a few times.*"
- V (38, m, homeless for 13 years): "*When it was cold then the **first building entrance, which I opened with a card**. Either that or I had a shed somewhere, a squat, whatever.*"
- M (54, m, homeless for nine years): "***I've slept on a bench at Main Station**, because I didn't know where I was supposed to go. I liked it at that station.*" O (53, m, homeless for 20 years) has also slept at a station: "*I slept at **Main Station on a bench**. I've slept everywhere conceivable.*"
- V (46, m, homeless for three years): "*I slept at the airport when I didn't have the money for a shelter.*"
- S (52, m, homeless for 17 years): "***Right now I'm sleeping on the night lines**, on buses and trams. Or if I've got a few crowns, I'll sit in KFC. I buy a set menu and if they're open nonstop, the time passes quickly. I know it's stupid, but what can I say?*"
- D (48, m, homeless for five years): "*For about a year we slept in a garage in Chuchle. It wasn't up to much. It had **lice and it was cold and dirty**.*"

Some homeless people sleep in a squat, a deserted, sometimes dilapidated, building or hut that is not intended for accommodation. This is only a provisional solution and may not be comfortable. Squats tend to be cold, and there is no running water, electricity or privacy. Living in a squat is the preferred option of young people but is not so attractive for older people. Many of the latter may have lived in a squat in the past but no longer have any interest in group accommodation.

- C (47, m, homeless for 23 years). "*I lived in a squat for a while. But I didn't like it. I need my privacy, peace and quiet.*"
- People can feel at risk in a squat. M (37, m, homeless for five years) says: "*We began to live in a squat, but then it was subject to an arson attack. We were in Řepy in a **hut and someone threw a Molotov cocktail** at it.*"

Problems can arise with cohabitees, though this tends not to happen as often as in a reception centre.

- R (48, m, homeless for seven years) has no problems with his fellow squatters: "*I've never slept in a reception centre because there are too many people. **Right now I'm living in a squat**. It's fine. We have sleeping bags and blankets and **when someone arrives and stays here then we let them sleep**.*"

- On the other hand, V (46, m, homeless for seven years) feels that it is important to restrict the number of cohabitees: "***We slept in a hut**. There were three of us, **which is a manageable number**. As soon as there are more, everything falls apart.*"

- E (46, f, homeless for 11 years) had problems: "*I'm living here right now, in this squat. **It's a little hut made of pallets**... When my friend died, it was passed on to me. For two months I had a friend staying, and now it's been four months and **he doesn't want to leave and on top of that he's threatening me**.*"

- P (45, f, homeless for eight years) also had problems: "*I used to live with a friend **in a kind of garden hut**. I lived there for quite some time, three years maybe, but **then we had an argument** and she chucked us out... It happened to be a really freezing cold November and we had nowhere to go. So for two days we walked the streets and slept by garbage bins.*"

- J (50, f, homeless for more than 20 years) would be frightened of being on her own in a hut: "*I lived in a squat, a kind of rundown hut. I mostly lived with my partners. **Once time I lived on my own**, for a couple of weeks maybe, **but I was scared**. I used to walk around Prague from morning till evening and from evening to morning. A barrel of fun it decidedly wasn't and I wouldn't wish it on anyone.*"

Illus. 12. A more stable dwelling place in the countryside that has been fitted out by its inhabitants (photo Martin Pokora).

SUMMARY

Homeless people sleep in various different non-residential premises, where the only advantage is that they do not have to pay. However, such places are often cold and dirty, and their occupants may find themselves being moved on or attacked. Sleeping on night trams and buses is also not safe. It can also

Illus. 13. A dwelling place tends to be fitted out mainly for sleeping (photo Martin Pokora).

Illus. 14. Even a dwelling place beneath a bridge can have a personal touch (photo Martin Pokora).

be a risky business living in allotment huts and squats, which can be visited by people who represent a threat. Since the occupants of such places are not their owners, defending them is difficult. Women typically do not live alone, but with a partner or group of other homeless people. Young people prefer living in a group, sometimes a large group. Middle-aged homeless people tend to set the limit at five, and in practice two or three.

Illus. 15. Sometimes an entire residence can spring up beneath a bridge (photo Martin Pokora).

Illus. 16. Another furnished dwelling place beneath a bridge (photo Martin Pokora).

5.3 SLEEPING AT THE APARTMENT OF A FRIEND OR RELATIVE

It is relatively rare for a person who has been homeless for a longer period of time **to sleep in someone else's apartment**. We found only two percent of our middle-aged respondents did so. In the case of men this usually involves moving into a woman's apartment and living there until they are thrown out, often for drinking.

- L (38, m, homeless for 21 years): "*I lived illegally in an apartment. I've never had my own apartment ever, I have simply moved from one to the next. **Maybe I got off with a girl and moved in with her**. I didn't see myself as being homeless. I got off with a woman then stayed in her apartment for a couple of days, a week, whatever.*"
- P (50, m, homeless for 12 years): "*For a while I lived in a cellar, then in a tent. And then I met a girl in Nusle and **I lived in her apartment for close on a year**. Like a jerk I refurbished the whole place and then they put me in prison. When I got out, she'd already found herself another bloke.*"
- Sleeping in someone else's apartment does not last long in the case of women too. K (37, f, homeless for ten years): "***Me and my new boyfriend lived with my father***. *We were together for over seven years, but then one day my boyfriend knocked my father about a bit. He didn't mean to, but my father deserved it because he was a real alcoholic.*" Living with family or friends tends to be a temporary solution. The main problem appears to be that homeless people have no desire to contribute to the overheads and can be conflictual and aggressive.

5.4 SLEEPING IN RECEPTION CENTRES

Homeless people often resort to reception centres, especially in winter, though not without reservation.[5] About one fifth (22%) of our middle-aged respondents occasionally sleep in a reception centre. Kuchařová et al. (2015) found that it was mostly people aged 35–54 with a basic education and no job that availed themselves of this possibility. A reception centre is a short-term solution in a crisis situation. A person may only stay overnight and must respect certain rules, something that many homeless people find difficult. Moreover, they often do not have the money to pay for a reception centre, which is alien territory where they have no sense of belonging and sometimes feel unsafe. Such establishments differ in terms of value for money. They are far from ideal, though they do allow people facing a crisis to sleep in a warm and relatively tranquil environment. J (39, f, homeless for nine years) has this to say about reception centres: "*If you've*

---

5 Reception centres for the homeless are run by non-profit organisations or the church. They are only for sleeping in, and a person cannot remain in them during the day. There is a vessel anchored in the River Vltava in Prague that serves as a reception centre.

spent the whole day outside in the freezing cold, then what else can you do if you're home-less? You don't have money, but at least you've got something."

Reception centres represent an emergency solution to an unfolding crisis and **homeless people are in the main happy to have a place to sleep.**

- I (41, m, homeless for only a year) is glad to have the opportunity to sleep in a reception centre: *"It's not so bad at the Salvation Army. Nothing bothers me there, I'm not a demanding kind of person. **I like the fact you've got somewhere to lay your head**. I'm able to pay for it from my benefits."*
- H (40, f, homeless for nine years) rates reception centres positively: *"For a while I dossed on the boat [Hermes]. Things were pretty good there because I found myself amongst other women. You can wash, drink hot tea, make yourself a sand-wich... **I liked it. Having slept on trams or walked the street all night, it was wonderful**."*
- L (50, m, homeless for one year) received assistance from a reception centre, though he has reservations: *"I see them positively in that **you can relax** and they can be accessed by anyone. But they should be better fitted out and the **staff should be more willing and the other people should be nicer to each other**."*

Individual reception centres are assessed differently depending on price, how they are fitted out, and how they operate.

- J (50, m, homeless for two years): *"I slept on the Hermes and it was a disaster. But then I was allocated a smaller room and there were only three of us, and that was fine. Then they transferred me to **Na Slupi** [run by Naděje], **which was perfect**."*
- Š (46, m, homeless for four years) sees differences between individual recep-tion centres: *"We slept in V in reception centres run by the Salvation Army. **The Salvation Army runs the best centres**. You have showers, you receive soup for din-ner, bread, and it all costs CZK 30 [USD 1.3]."*
- J (45, m, homeless for six years) has similar feelings: *"I've got no complaints regarding the Salvation Army. **They have their rules and they observe them** and I'm glad about that, because there are some characters there who would go mad oth-erwise."*

The presence of other people in reception centres bothers many of our respon-dents. When such establishments are assessed negatively it tends to be for the **poor hygiene** of those using them and the risk of lice.

- A (47, m, homeless for 20 years): *"I spent one night in a Salvation Army shelter and wild horses wouldn't drag me back there. **The people don't ever wash and have lice**."*
- J (52, m, homeless for 15 years) feels similarly: *"**I don't use reception centres because they're full of lice**."*
- I (40, m, homeless for only a year): *"Hermes is all right for a night, it's not so bad. **If they could just sort out the hygiene** of some of the people there..."*

- M (54, m, homeless for nine years): "*I guess it's ok here, **though the people are pretty gross**. Some seem to have no idea of basic hygiene. **They're filthy and smell**, and some of them drink. They arrive here already drunk.*"

Another problem is the fact that **the reception centres become crowded** and that many of those occupying them are problematic characters.
- H (50, m, homeless for 20 years) hates the sheer numbers of people: "*Reception centres... I've only ever experienced the Vackov centre in winter. I can tolerate a lot, I'm not a spoilt little brat, but... **It's horrible, 20 blokes packed into one room**. I guess it's better than a kick in the nuts.*"
- P (50, m, homeless for 12 years) feels similarly: "*I've slept in a reception centre twice. Twice I've slept on the boat* [Hermes] *and both times I absolutely fucking hated it. I've also slept here at the Michelská heating plant. I spent three days and it was bloody horrible. **Before I got to the centre there was this massive crush**. You couldn't even get to the bathroom.*"
- J (51, m, homeless for seven years): "***It would be bearable if it weren't for the people**. But I don't pay any attention. I'm used to them from prison.*"
- F (40, m, homeless for ten years): "*I don't spend time in reception centres. **I hate having masses of people around me**. Idiots what's more, and idiots I don't know. No fucking way.*"

Sometimes it is not so much the number of people and their hygiene that is a problem, but **the way they behave**. This is enough to put some people off visiting reception centres.
- S (52, m, homeless for 17 years): "*I've experienced shelters and all I can say is, never again. **It's the people that bother me**. I'd rather travel the streets by tram and enjoy some peace and quiet rather than listen to endless rows.*"
- V (51, m, homeless for 10 years) tells a similar story: "*Lots of them are problematic and I simply don't need that in my life. **Junkies, alcoholics, criminals**... not my cup of tea. Next to me there's a alcoholic granddad who has no control over his bladder and pisses all over us at the entrance.*"
- H (50, m, homeless for 20 years): "***It's the people that bother me in shelters** and the fucking mess they make.*"
- J (39, f, homeless for nine years): "*It's really hardcore at these reception centres. There are people who want to sleep, and people who don't want to sleep but simply **fight and talk bullshit** so that no one else can sleep... **It's the behaviour of these people** I mind, and the fact it's not exactly the most fragrant environment in the world.*"

Some of our respondents are afraid of being robbed by the other homeless people in a reception centre.
- R (46, m, homeless for four years): "*I sleep on the Hermes when I can, i.e. when I have some cash, or at the Salvation Army in Holešovice. I've never had a problem*

on the Hermes. But it's a different story at the Salvation Army. **You use your bag as a pillow and in the morning you discover that half your things have disappeared**. Hermes is cheaper and more young people go there. It tends to be people around 45 who opt for the Salvation Army."

- Č (42, m, homeless for five years): "*I don't use reception centres because I have a telephone and the **last thing I need is for someone to steal it from me**.*"
- D (48, f, homeless for five years): "*I slept in a reception centre once. I had all the money I own in my bra. **I slept on my rucksack in which I had a tablet and other expensive things, which is why I was so frightened**.*" Bad experiences with other homeless people leads to greater caution, even though someone sleeping rough can be robbed anywhere, and not only in a reception centre.

The routine and rules of a reception centre can present a problem.

Some people are not used to getting up early and have difficulties with the **enforced early rising** of reception centres and the **restrictions on movement**. A person is usually allowed to be present in a reception centre from 7pm to 7am. They must not leave their personal belongings in the centre and have no way of knowing whether there will be a bed free for them the next day. Each centre has its own rules. Some erect minimal barriers and are open only in winter. They are also free, e.g. Michle and Vackov.

- P (50, m, homeless for 12 years): "***I like peace and quiet. I don't like arriving, having to sleep and having to leave at seven**. If I have nothing else on, I like to sleep in to eleven o'clock for instance.*"
- M (51, m, homeless for one year) is another who does not like the operating hours: "*I'd hit rock bottom when I slept at the reception centre. But it didn't really help me much. **They kick you out at half past six and at half past seven in the evening there's a queue**. I had found work that ended at half past two, so I had to wander the streets until eight o'clock.*"
- P (37, m, homeless for 15 years): "*I used to visit the Hermes frequently when it still belonged to Naděje. I've been to the Vackov centre a couple of times. **The problem is that no sooner have you fallen asleep than they're waking you up**. Since I'm used to getting up around nine or ten o'clock, this early rising was a killer.*" It is clear from their stories that our respondents do not have a standard daily routine and are not used to getting up early. The reception centres do not and cannot respect this fact.

The price of a reception centre is also important to homeless people.

- K (42, m, homeless for two years): "*The St. Theresa centre is the best, though it's also the most expensive at CZK 40 [USD 1.8]. I mean, **who'd want to pay that for a night's sleep when you could buy two cartons of wine?**"
- Some reception centres are free of charge and demand for their services is high. M (40, m, homeless for seven years): "*If I've earned a bit of money, then*

*I'll sleep at the Salvation Army shelter. If I'm skint, then I'll go to **Michle or Vackov where it's free**."*

The ban on alcohol and being intoxicated in a reception centre is another problem for many homeless people.

- M (40, m, homeless for seven years) is not always able to control his consumption: *"I sometimes sleep at the Salvation Army. **But I'm not allowed to drink**, and so I sleep there for a few nights then I manage to do a bit of casual work. But then **something goes off in my head and I start drinking again**."*
- People who behave aggressively are also prevented from entering a reception centre. L (38, m, homeless for 21 years): *"I'm banned from the charities. **You go to a charity and someone gets on your tits**... that happened to me at the Salvation Army, and now I'm banned from going there."*

SUMMARY

Homeless people avail themselves of the services of reception centres often, especially during the winter months. Though they are pleased they have somewhere to sleep, they are critical of the establishments. They are irritated by the fact that they are not permitted to be present during daytime hours and have to comply with rules. This attitude to the rules is relative: many of our respondents are aware that an establishment must apply at least some rules, because otherwise the atmosphere would be intolerable. They often express reservations regarding the people at reception centres. They do not like the way that large numbers gather in a small space, and they are put off by the standards of hygiene and behaviour of some people. There is also a significant risk of being robbed. Despite these reservations, reception centres are important means of survival for homeless people, especially during the winter, when sleeping rough would be excessively dangerous.

5.5 SLEEPING IN SHELTERS

Shelters provide accommodation to homeless people for a designated period of time.[6] They aim to help their users to become independent and assist with their reintegration into mainstream society by means of social work provided on a

---

6 Shelters are for the temporary accommodation of people in a crisis situation, though it would appear that they are often the only form of accommodation a homeless person is capable of using. The maximum length of time a person may stay in a shelter is one year. However, during this period most people are incapable of finding alternative accommodation or a job, and so return to the street or search for another shelter. The situation then repeats itself after a year.

one-to-one basis. They offer a higher standard of comfort than reception centres and offer their clients time to look for work and more stable accommodation. Our questionnaire revealed that 27%–28% of homeless people availed themselves of the services of shelters (Marek, 2017; Csémy, 2018).

However, adaptation to life in a shelter is not always easy, especially in the case of the chronically homeless. The necessity to respect set rules is often stressful, especially for people who have been living on the street for a long time and have lost the habit of abiding by any rules whatsoever. Such individuals have problems accepting many different forms of restriction. They may also find it difficult living in proximity with other homeless people, in this case their cohabitees. They are not used to adapting to anyone else's needs. Some of our respondents, e.g. G (50, m, homeless for ten years), do not regard life in a shelter as offering any specific benefits: *"For five years I slept under a tree... now I'm here and **I don't see any great difference**, except that there's a fridge here, I have a few items of my own and it doesn't rain on me."* This approach is not typical, and most homeless people rate shelters positively.

Notwithstanding their reservations, **most of our respondents are pleased to have the opportunity to live in a shelter**.

- P (47, m, homeless for seven years): *"**I'm simply grateful I've got a roof over my head**. This shelter helps people who want to help themselves. The advantage is it's cheaper than a commercial shelter."*
- M (51, m, homeless for one year): *"I wouldn't want to live here until retirement age. **But I'm glad I can spend at least some time here**. I don't want to grow mouldy and be a bother forever. But **all things considered it's a good thing**. I don't have any problem being here."*
- P (45, f, homeless for eight years): *"I've been living here for two months. **To be honest, I like it here**, because it's warm, you've got a bed, somewhere to rest your head, and you don't have to do battle with the cold and dirt and smell... It's amazing."*

Some of our respondents appreciate not only the possibility of living in a shelter, but the assistance provided by the social workers.

- M (43, f, homeless for eight years): *"This is my second year in a shelter. I'm not complaining. Everyone else moans about the services and I tell them, fine, it's not home, it's not your own. But it is a miracle for people like me and **I'm super grateful to be here**. I have spent time at the Šromovka shelter, but I was in a bad way psychologically. The social workers saved my life. I can't be anywhere else, it makes me turn to drink. I love it here. But soon I have to leave and I'm already stressed out about it. **I'm really scared of leaving, I'm simply not prepared**. People help you here. It's different to being in a hostel, where everybody pisses you off. You live your own life here, nobody is interested in you. You simply pay for accommodation and that's that."*

- M (40, f, homeless for 25 years): "*This is my first shelter. I opted for it after coming out of prison.* **What's great here is that the social workers really try to help people**. *Any time of day you can go to them and ask them to explain how to apply for things with the authorities. You won't get that at a hostel.*"

However, certain individuals can experience problems with their cohabitees in shelters. This is the most common reservation they have regarding this type of facility.

- V (38, m, homeless for 13 years) has no problems of this kind and is used to living with other people in prison: "*I've been in this shelter for three years. I have nowhere else to go. I get on with everyone.* **When you've spent as many years in prison as I have, people don't bother you**."
- M (40, f, homeless for 25 years): "*There are five of us here.* **I don't get on with all of them**, *but I'm used to that from prison. If I have nothing to say to someone, I simply ignore them.*
- D (39, m, homeless for four years): "*Almost on day one I found myself in a conflict with the guy I share a room with. But that was the first time. I've already lived in this shelter and met some fantastic people.* **I don't have any problem with them**, *on the contrary I get on really well with them.*"

Other clients find their cohabitees less acceptable. This often applies to people who have been on the street for only a short time and are encountering the problematic aspects of homeless people's behaviour for the first time.

- M (51, m, homeless for one year): "**I never for a moment dreamt I'd find myself in this situation with these people**. *I've never met this kind of person before, I have always lived amongst completely normal people.*"
- M (50, f, homeless for one year) also has problems with her cohabitees: "*It has a pretty bad psychological effect on me.* **These women are so strange**. *I'm glad to have a roof over my head and they have just extended my contract. But it makes me feel nervous with* **everyone gossiping about everyone else**. *I'm worried about how things will progress, because the people here aren't upfront, they're kind of weird.*"
- M (45, f, homeless for one year): "*I found myself in a refuge amongst other homeless women.* **It was a shock**, *because I was placed with someone with schizophrenia. But I didn't know that. She saw ghosts and god knows what, and suspected me of communicating with spirits.* **She would nip outside and then return in a real state**, *and I started to be a bit afraid of her.*"

Our respondents have similar problems with their cohabitees in shelters as they do in reception centres. Some people are lax in respect of bodily hygiene, others suffer mental health issues or are aggressive, while others are addicts. Meanwhile there is the ever-present risk of being robbed.

- V (46, m, homeless for three years): "*There's a guy in our room. Now I know he can't help it, but he has a urine drainage bag and sleeps with it. The smell pervades* *the entire room, **it stinks like an ape house**. And yet he's never satisfied. It's a problem."*

- D (37, m, homeless for nine years): "***There are people here who bring bedbugs off the street**, because they've been scavenging in bins and bringing stuff back. So the building is full of bugs. These people are sick or have lice or something, and they bring it here.*"
- H (50, m, homeless for 20 years) also believes that his cohabitees complicate life: "*It depends who you're living with. **If you're with a junkie who makes a right fucking mess, then it gets on your tits**.*"
- It is problems of this nature that have led Z (51, m, homeless for 10 years) to prefer hostels: "*Right now I'm here* [in a shelter], *because it didn't work out with the commercial hostel. To be honest I don't use these institutions much. **I don't want to live with eight pissheads**. I want a bit of peace and quiet. **I don't want forever to be checking my possessions**, having to carry money with me when I go to the shower or to the toilet.*"

Problems with cohabitees can arise when not all clients observe the rules of a shelter. Individual clients have different opinions regarding the necessity to abide by these rules:

Some recognise that such rules as essential if the shelter is going to function properly.

- V (45, f, homeless for seven years): "***I'm ok with the rules**. I mean, they do what they have to do if you're going to get better. What really gets on my tits are the people. They're always complaining. They're always moaning, but that's all they do. They don't actually do anything, they just sit around moaning.*"
- J (50, m, homeless for two years): "*It's not easy, but it's manageable. **There have to be rules**. In fact, I'd tighten up the rules on drugs and booze.*"

However, some of our respondents feel ambivalent about the rules applied in shelters. For instance P (37, m, homeless for four years): "*It's fucking horrible to be honest, **it's like being in prison**. I was looking forward to there being two-man rooms, but here we're sleeping eight to a room, which is like it is in prison. Then at ten it's lights out, though it's true that you can go out, in that sense you're freer. I arrived with every intention of avoiding a collective, but that's what this place basically is. A lot of the clients have been inside, I've met a lot of them in prison. I started to feel that I'd been sent back to prison, the only difference being this is a slightly better wing. **I lack privacy**, there is no fucking privacy. You can't drink, which for me isn't a problem. But a bloke who worked all week long and on Friday went for a beer was chucked out. I mean, it's great, **as a starting point it's great**. I don't want to be critical, but **it's really only the beginning**. The services they offer aren't bad, but the sense of collective here is not ideal. I understand the ban on alcohol because you can't have people drinking themselves stupid. But they might just occasionally turn a blind eye. It's the supervision that bothers me, though on the other hand **there have to be rules. If there weren't, it would be anarchy**.*"

Other occupants **resent having to abide by rules**. This is something they are not used to and they have no desire to submit to orders and prohibitions.

- D (37, m, homeless for nine years): "*Here's the thing. I'm glad it's clean and that I can take a bath every day, wash my clothes, use the kitchen, washing machine, etc. But I wouldn't stay here forever, and I'll tell you why. **It's a kind of bullying, you have no freedom. I hate the rules** and having to fulfil certain duties.*"
- J (44, m, homeless for nine years) felt so strongly that he left: "*I don't like the system. I lived in a shelter for two months and then I left. **I hate the fact you always have to abide by some rule or another.***"
- P (52, m, homeless for two years) is more concerned by the **behaviour of the staff during supervision**: "*The behaviour of the staff is sometimes a bit weird. I understand they have to be strict, but sometimes it's on the boundary of rudeness. I'm thinking in particular of the **body-searches they conduct**.*" P has a university education and has not been homeless for very long. He is not used to the no-nonsense approach of the staff, which is necessary when working with homeless people.

One of the rules applied in shelters is a ban on the consumption of alcohol and drugs. Our respondents had mixed feelings in this respect. Some deem it an advantage, because it prevents them from becoming dependent again, while others resent the restriction it places on them.

- D (37, m, homeless for nine years) appreciates the ban on alcohol: "*I have experience with commercial hostels and with the labourers that live in them and I know I would start drinking again. So the ban on alcohol in shelters helps me. I don't drink. The same goes for fighting. There is a risk of me finding myself back on the street. I'd say yes to a glass and then next day wouldn't go to work.*"
- K (48, m, homeless for five years) is of the same opinion: "*It's quite simple. There is a system in operation. **If they made an exception for me, then you can guess what would happen next**.*" This is the second time that K has been in a shelter: "*I was in a shelter three years ago. I lasted for six months and then they chucked me out because I was drinking. Right now I'm making an effort.*"
- M (40, f, homeless for 25 years) accepts the ban on alcohol: "***It's ok by me that you can't drink alcohol here** and that drugs aren't allowed, because otherwise things would end in disaster.*"
- H (40, f, homeless for nine years) feels similarly: "*It's safe here. **I like the fact that you can't drink or take drugs**. I like the fact that this shelter is a kind of safe space.*"

Some of our respondents would prefer to live in a commercial hostel without rules, but do not have the money. [7]

---

7 Commercial hostels offer accommodation for a fee. Socially disadvantaged people can receive a contribution towards this fee known as a "housing allowance", and many of them choose to avail themselves of this possibility.

- Z (51, m, homeless for ten years): "*I would pay to live in a **hostel, where I didn't have to listen to anyone telling me** I can do this, I can't do that. That's what really gets on my tits.*"
- S (52, m, homeless for 17 years) feels similarly: "***You're freer in a hostel**. You arrive, unlock the door, take a bath, eat, lie down, and you don't have to report anything to anyone.*" Both men have a problem with the ban on alcohol in shelters.

Many of our older respondents do not resent the restrictions placed on life in a shelter. They are simply pleased not to be sleeping rough. (64% of those using the services of the B. Bureš Centre of Social Services (CSSP) in Prague were older than 50.)

- O (53, m, homeless for 20 years): "*Services like a shelter are **to get people off the street and help them get their lives together**, sort out social security, get things in order, relax. The good thing is that you no longer prowl the streets like an animal, but you have a place to stay. I'm here for the third time. I don't have any problem. I don't argue or get into fights. I've lived my life on the street. I used to sleep under a bridge, and then I asked the social services if I could come here. I told them that I no longer enjoyed sleeping rough. **I don't get up to anything stupid, I don't drink or do drugs**, so everything's cool. I like the hostel, I like the fact there's a system. I don't want to die like a rat in a hole, I want to relax like a normal bloke.*"
- L (52, m, homeless for two years) feels similarly: "*They arranged a shelter for me. I stuck it out for four months, because that's the maximum there. Then I did the rounds of other shelters and cooperated with the social workers. **I wasn't involved in any offences or alcohol** or anything like that. Basically, you simply have to observe the rules.*"

SUMMARY

Both the short and long-term homeless avail themselves of the services of shelters. Most appreciate what is on offer and understand that it is aimed at helping them. However, some of our respondents had reservations, especially as regards having to live with people who get on their nerves. This usually involves the same problems as in reception centres, namely, that they do not want to share their accommodation with people who do not observe bodily hygiene and/or are aggressive and conflictual. There is also the ever-present threat of theft. Some of our respondents resent the rules that must be obeyed in a shelter, especially the ban on alcohol and drugs. On the other hand, they recognise that these rules are essential and that without them the problems involved in cohabiting with people who are very often somewhat unconventional would be greater. People who do not respect the rules are asked to leave the shelter, and this functions as a warning not only to them, but to those around them.

Experienced social workers point to the fact that a substantial proportion of the occupants of shelters have lived for a long time on the street and that the damage wrought to their personalities may be so great that full social rehabilitation is unlikely. Such people are restricted by their current possibilities and have no great motivation to change. Shelters offer their services both to people who have never learned how to live independently or have lost the skills and habits that they used to have, and people for whom, for financial reasons (debt, a lack of qualifications and insufficient motivation to look for work), shelters are one of the few options they can allow themselves. For some chronically homeless people, who are familiar with the rules that must be observed, a shelter is their end destination. There is a risk of their becoming dependent on the shelter and the way of life associated with it. This type of accommodation represents the highest possible standard they are capable of attaining. (The reason tends to be their inability to work, whether this be for health or social reasons.) It has been shown that 43% of people live in shelters on a long-term basis, while 34.4% are on at least their third shelter and simply move from one to the next (Marek, 2017). Other researchers, e.g. Busch-Geertsema and Sahlin (2007), have posited the possibility of a dependence on this type of facility being established. Ciapessoni (2016) believes that the possibilities made available in such facilities do not facilitate the transition from street to independent accommodation, but can, on the contrary, cultivate a certain form of institutionalisation. (Similar dependencies can be created by long-term stints in prison.)

6. HOW OUR RESPONDENTS SUPPORT THEMSELVES

In addition to somewhere to spend the night, a homeless person needs food and clothing. They acquire these items by various means. Charities provide them, and they can also be found in bins or amongst goods that have been thrown out. Homeless people may beg, steal or borrow. The means of livelihood and survival they choose depend on their age, the length of time they have spent on the street, and socio-cultural conditions.

There are no significant differences in the way that young and old homeless people search for sources of livelihood. The only exception to this would the willingness of younger people (aged 37–46) to work at least sporadically (chi-square = 4.58, df = 1, p = 0.039). Younger people are also more active in other spheres, salvaging and scavenging items from containers and skips. Older people are more passive and rely more on charities.

The length of time a person has spent on the street impacts on their preferences regarding sources of livelihood, as is clear in the graph above. Basically, the longer a person is on the street, the less they use legal means. People who have been living on the street for ten years and more often beg and collect items

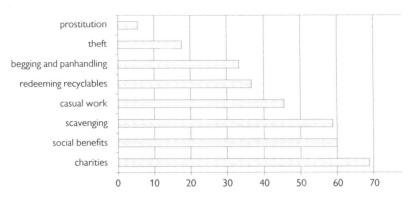

Graph 24. The preferences shown by older homeless people regarding their means of subsistence (shown in relative frequency).

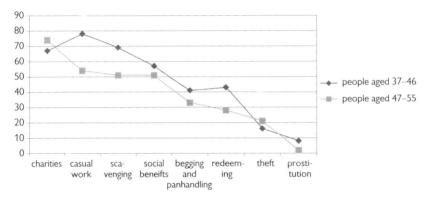

Graph 25. Differences in the means of subsistence by age (shown in relative frequency).

they can monetise (by redeeming recyclables), but also steal, i.e. they are more independent but engage in activities that are socially unacceptable. The difference between both groups is significant only in respect of the frequency of begging (chi-square = 4.8, df = 1, p = 0.039) and collecting (chi-square = 4.5, df = 1, p = 0.040), symptomatic more of chronic homelessness. This means that **people who have been living for a longer period of time on the street gradually lose their inhibitions** and more and more often resort to begging, something they would have found unacceptable upon first becoming homeless. The difference in the frequency of theft between both groups is not significant (chi-square = 1.9, df = 1), though the chronically homeless have fewer qualms in this respect.

6.1 CHARITIES

Charities offer homeless people everything they need to satisfy their basic material needs, namely food, clothes, hygiene, and assistance in dealing with the

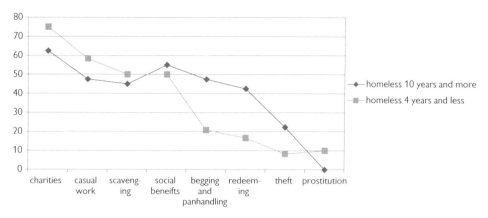

Graph 26. The means of subsistence of older people who have been on the street for different periods of time (shown in percentages).

authorities. Sixty-nine percent of middle-aged homeless people avail themselves of the services of charities. Those who do not may not wish to be put in the position of supplicant or may not wish to associate with other homeless people, who would remind them of their own social disaffiliation. (People living in shelters are forbidden from using the services of charities.)

Charities are the most common source of livelihood. They are easily accessed and socially acceptable. If a person can receive food from a charity, they do not have to beg, steal or scavenge, and their social benefits last longer.

- I (40, m, homeless for two years) uses charities: "*I visit centres. **It means I don't have to beg**. During the day I receive soup from the Salvation Army and I don't have to rummage through garbage bins.*"
- A (47, m, homeless for 20 years): "***I've never stolen anything in my life**, and I've never begged either. **I come here to Naděje for food**.*"
- H (50, m, homeless for 20 years): "*I receive food here at Naděje… It keeps me going until my next benefits come through. I've always bought my own clothes and the Salvation Army distribute pretty good stuff.*"

Charities provide hot food to their clients, something that is otherwise difficult to come by on the street.

- P (37, f, homeless for 15 years): "*We survived by collecting paper, but mostly we would go to Naděje or the Salvation Army. We did the rounds of the charities. They had soup, and on Saturday and Sunday we would most often go to the sisters* [nuns of the Order of St. Vincent], *because we knew that **they had hot soup**.*"
- J (52, m, homeless for five years): "*I go for breakfast and then to Bulhar* [a drop-in centre run by Naděje] *or visit the mobile soup kitchen, **so that at least once a day I have a hot meal**.*"

- H (40, f, homeless for nine years): "*I used to visit Naděje, **I just went to get free food**. I always went to **the Salvation Army for soup** and suchlike. A person will never die of hunger in Prague.*"

Charities help homeless people maintain an acceptable level of hygiene. They offer them washing facilities and clean clothes. This is important for those who wish to maintain some degree of self-esteem.
- Č (42, m, homeless for five years): "*I go to Naděje and **eat the food they offer, take a shower and pick out some clothes**. I have no other way of eating and washing.*"
- R (46, m, homeless for four years): "*The Salvation Army is a big help. I can eat some soup, relax, chat, **take a shower, shave, and pick out some clothes when I need to**.*"
- J (52, m, homeless for five years): "*I travel to Řepy for clean things like bed linen, tee-shirts, trousers whatever. There are nuns there, it's next to a church… so **I had clean clothes. I don't want to walk around filthy and smelling**.*"

How homeless people rate the services provided by charities
Charities provide different forms of assistance to homeless people, who pick and choose which services they wish to receive. Most are appreciative and **well aware that, without this support, life on the street would be a far tougher prospect**.
- J (51, m, homeless for one year): "*__I wouldn't be here if it weren't for the charities__.*"
- Z (47, m, homeless for twenty years): "*At the age of 27 I visited Naděje. I would often contact Naděje or the Salvation Army because I had spent whatever money I had earned on drugs and booze. I needed food and clothes. I didn't have the money for a dormitory, so I lived in shelters. **I'm really grateful for the way they've helped me**.*"
- V (38, m, homeless for 13 years): "*I used to visit the Salvation Army for soup and clothes. I reckon that **without them I would have been completely fucked**. I was a fool for not going there earlier. But the truth is that I didn't know that this kind of thing existed. It is definitely valuable.*"
- D (39, m, homeless for four years): "*If organisations like this, which distribute food, soup, clothes and stuff, didn't exist, **I believe that these people wouldn't last long**. They have no interest in work, no interest in anything whatsoever.*"

The fact that they can obtain everything they need to survive **leads some people to conclude that the comprehensive services provided by charities deprive people of the motivation to find work and accommodation**. They are convinced that the availability of these services means people remain for longer on the street because they can survive without any great effort. They become used to receiving food and clothing and have no reason to look for work.

- M (51, m, homeless for only a year): "*It occurs to me that this assistance might be counterproductive, that people are spoiled.* **Naturally they get used to receiving everything** *and no longer make any real effort.*"
- S (51, m, homeless for 14 years) agrees: "*I mean, why would a person look for work? Here they can eat and then go and beg for booze.*"
- J (50, m, homeless for two years): "**Most people here take advantage of the services without being deserving of them**... *They simply take the piss. You can fit yourself out in some clothes, take what you need, then sell it and buy a carton of wine.*"

The paradoxical impact of charities, which can contribute to a person remaining on the street and reinforce their passivity, is drawn attention to by Ravenhill (2014). Well-intentioned services can on the one hand save many homeless people from further harm. However, they can also consolidate the feeling that survival is relatively easy with the help of charities and that there is therefore no reason to look for work. It should nevertheless be pointed out that, without the assistance of charities, many people would resort to theft and begging more often.

L (38, m, homeless for 17 years) believes that charities should provide only temporary assistance: "*There's a good and a bad side to charities...* **They really pull out all the stops for people** *and these people should understand that. They say to themselves, well there's Naděje, I can eat there and pick out some clothes. But this isn't true. Naděje might also one day say, listen, you've been here a long time. You've got a month to find work and then you're out.* **Naděje needs to be a bit more cruel to be kind**."

Some of our respondents believe that charities help people claw their way off the street, though they concede that the effectiveness of such assistance also depends on the motivation of the individual.
- D (39, m, homeless for four years): "*At least here people have a roof over their heads and there are social workers* **who can offer them a different kind of assistance**. *The main thing is that a person must want to be helped.*"
- K (48, m, homeless for five years) believes that it is a good thing when the employees of charities oblige their clients to take responsibility for at least something in their lives: "*There is no doubt this service offers a lot and encourages people to look after themselves. If someone's a layabout and couldn't give a fuck about anything, then it's good when the* **charity forces them to take care of at least something in their lives**."
- J (50, m, homeless for two years) is very appreciative of people who are prepared to work with the homeless: "**The very fact that these social workers are prepared to work with us** *is admirable.*"

Some of our respondents took the opposite view. For instance, F (40, m, homeless for ten years) believes the assistance provided by charities is annoying, because he has no desire to change anything: "*I can't help feeling that these social workers sometimes come up with ideas that are completely useless for people living on the street...*" Some of our respondents believe the help provided by social workers in charities is useless, because it takes the form only of recommendations or at most support. These services usually require cooperation on the part of their users, but some of our respondents have no desire to expend energy on something that will only benefit them sometime in the future. This may well be because a sense of powerlessness and a feeling they cannot change anything has become ingrained. Working with homeless people who are often unwilling to accept any responsibility for themselves and who are forever in breach of the rules is very demanding and can be demotivating for social workers (Ravenhill, 2014).

Several of our respondents grumble that not everything is all sunshine and roses at the charities. There are various reasons why they might feel critical. Several have become so accustomed to these services that **they feel any restrictions as an imposition**. R (48, m, homeless for seven years) is convinced that the Salvation Army has reduced the level of its services: "*I spend most of my time here at the Sally Army. But they've gone and fucked it up. **They no longer make breakfast in the morning**. Basically they do bugger all, they just make soup. Instead of Monday, Wednesday and Friday, now **it's just on Tuesday**, because there's nothing there, they've given it all to refugees. Maybe they're receiving less in the way of grants or something.*" In fact the food was limited by the capacity of the facility. Refugees played no part in this.

Most of the reservations expressed by our respondents did not relate so much to the services provided but more to other clients and their behaviour. They resent those **clients of charities who are dirty, drunk or aggressive**, even though they themselves are no paragons of virtue.
- R (40, m, homeless for five years): "*I went to the Sally Army but **I didn't like the people, the clients**. Most were criminals and I didn't want anything to do with them.*"
- P (52, m, homeless for only two years): "*It annoyed me and I really had to stop myself from lashing out, when **someone who's been on the street for 20 years thinks that he has a greater right to what the charity is offering** than those who have been homeless six months. Let's be honest, he didn't have to be homeless for 20 years.*"

Some of our respondents do not avail themselves of the services of charities for a variety of reasons. They are ashamed of asking for favours and dislike the subordinate status of supplicant or the necessity to stand in a queue. These tend to be men who are alcoholics or drug addicts.
- F (40, m, homeless for ten years) is of this opinion: "***I'd rather go hungry than set foot in a charity**. The rest of them use the mobile soup kitchen. Me, I'd rather go*

hungry than stand in line and beg for a few drops of soup that someone's offering for free."

- Z (42, m, homeless for 11 years): "*I can't stand waiting in line for soup at these charities. I'm fully capable of making my own soup, and don't need to stand like a dickhead in a queue for bananas or whatever."*
- Z (51, m, homeless for ten years): "*I don't much like going to charities. It's a case of do this, don't do that. You no longer have the opportunity to decide for yourself."*

SUMMARY

For most of our respondents, charity services are very important. They provide assistance in many spheres so that people on the street do not have to beg, steal or scavenge. They also offer showers and clothes. Some of our respondents are convinced that they would not survive on the street without charities. On the other hand, the sheer accessibility of charities can establish a dependency, with a person no longer able to look after themselves. The reservations our respondents had related mostly to the behaviour of other homeless people. A third of people living on the street do not avail themselves of the services of charities, usually because they don't like the rules imposed on them and are unwilling to accept the role of supplicant. Sixty percent of young homeless people living on the streets of Prague availed themselves of the services provided by charities, which is comparable with the figures in other countries with different social and cultural conditions. For instance, 63% of the Australian homeless visit charities, while in Great Britain this figure rises to 80% (Booth, 2005; McDonagh, 2011; Vágnerová, Csémy, Marek, 2013).

6.2 SOCIAL BENEFITS

Sixty percent of middle-aged homeless people receive some form of social benefit. (Our questionnaire revealed the same results, with 61% of respondents receiving a social benefit, 38% emergency financial assistance [*dávka v hmotné nouzi* – the translation given on the website of the Ministry of Labour and Social Affairs is "assistance in material need" – tr.] and 23% a pension, either old-age or disability.)[8] **Emergency financial assistance is the commonest form of assistance** and often linked with top-up housing benefit. The money does not last long, since it is a relatively small amount and its recipients have no money man-

---

8 Homeless people are entitled to receive emergency financial assistance. This support is conditional upon their not having any other income and being able to apply for it at the relevant office (often with the help of a social worker). One advantage of this system, apart from the cash itself, is that health insurance payments do not mount up but are paid by the state.

agement skills. Furthermore, they are under pressure from those around them, who wish to take advantage of them. Some homeless people do not even receive emergency financial assistance, usually because they incapable of applying for it.

Emergency financial assistance helps homeless people survive.
- J (41, m, homeless for nine years): *"I've been signing on for a year. I receive emergency financial assistance. **If I didn't, I wouldn't survive**."*
- Other respondents are grateful for the way such assistance prevents unnecessary problems: P (40, m, homeless for 20 years): *"I sign on because they offer financial assistance with accommodation and living expenses. It's not enough of course, but **it's a lot better than finding yourself in dodgy situations** where you start operating outside the law."*

However, our respondents also say that the **emergency financial assistance they receive is not enough**.
- L (50, m, homeless for only a year): *"I receive emergency financial assistance. I've been receiving it for a while, **but you can't really call it earning a proper living**."*
- J (50, m, homeless for two years) feels the same: *"I've been receiving these benefits since 2015, but they're not enough. Occasionally I earn a bit on the side just to make ends meet."*

Many of our respondents have no clue as to how to manage their finances. They either want to spend everything immediately, or they are targeted by those around them, who sense an opportunity.
- J (51, m, homeless for a year): *"Suddenly you receive CZK 3,400 [USD 148]. **Three days later and it's all gone**. I didn't used to know how to manage money, but now I've learned."*
- H (50, m, homeless for 20 years): *"**You look forward to receiving your emergency financial assistance**, then for ten days you have a whale of a time, and then it's back to visiting soup kitchens. It's not ideal."*
- R (48, m, homeless for seven years) also finds it difficult to make ends meet, since he has to cater for the needs of others: *"**Social benefit only lasts me about three days**. The longest it ever lasted was ten days, because the other blokes know when I receive it and **all of them come and borrow from me** and I'll get through some of it myself."*
- J (50, f, homeless for more than 20 years) suffers the same problem: *"I've been signing on for about two years. The **emergency financial assistance I receive doesn't last long, because everyone wants a bite of the cherry**, and food costs a bit too."*
- Z (49, f, homeless for 15 years) prefers to spend the money she receives immediately so that no one else can take it: *"I receive a pension of CZK 7,500 [USD 325]. How long does it last? That's a good question. About three hours. I spend*

*it on the things I need, such as hygiene, shoes, clothes and suchlike. **I spend it quickly so that no one steals it from me**. That happens a lot."*

Some of our respondents are unable so much as to apply for emergency financial assistance or even find their way to the relevant office. They cite many different reasons, though these mostly involve rationalising their laziness and a reluctance to actually do anything.

The employment office is far away and they don't fancy making the trip.[9]
- J (45, m, homeless for six years): *"I received emergency financial assistance for years, but then I gave up visiting the employment office. **I have no desire to go back to Ostrava**."*
- K (42, m, homeless for two years): *"I used to sign on when they called. They didn't used to offer me work because there wasn't any. I received CZK 3,400 [USD 148]. I no longer receive it, firstly because **I'd have to sort it all out in Moravia**, and also because I owe back payments of alimony, so they'd only give me CZK 2,200 [USD 95]."*
- J (39, m, homeless for five years): *"I've been to the employment office twice. What can I say? **I got bored so I didn't return**."*
- M (38, m, homeless for two years): *"I could sort it out if I made an effort, but **I can't be bothered to go there**."*

They forget that they should go to the employment office, just as they forget other duties they have.
- L (52, m, homeless for two years): *"To begin with I went to the employment office and received some benefit or other. Now I don't receive anything, because I lost my job and **forgot to visit the office on the right day and they stopped my benefits**."*
- F (40, m, homeless for 10 years) has the same problem: *"Right now I'm registered at the employment office. I've been registered several times, but **they always cross me off because I forget to go or I don't have time**. I don't think the system is very well set up."*

They do not have the money to make the trip and do not look for another way of getting there.
- I (40, m, homeless for one year): *"I could have gone to the employment office, but recently **I've had no money for the trip**. I preferred to travel to Prague in order to find work."*
- D (39, m, homeless for four year): *"I registered at the office in L. The problem was I had a problem getting there. **I didn't have any money for the trip**, and because I didn't turn up, **they struck me off the register**."*
- P (37, f, homeless for 15 years): *"Right now I'm not signing on, though I plan to visit the employment office. I went there when I was homeless and registered. But most*

---

9 After signing on at the employment office, a client can be transferred to the office at the place where they live. However, most homeless people are unaware of this.

*of the time I earned a living or **I didn't have the money to travel there**. They cut my benefits twice, and the third time they didn't manage it because I told them to piss off because I was going to receive maternity benefit."*

Many of our respondents are unable to negotiate dealings with the authorities, be this because they are of low intelligence or alcoholics or drug addicts, and so do not even apply for benefits. Sometimes they do not wish to communicate with officials and complete forms containing personal questions.

- V (42, m, homeless for 21 years) only ever received a basic education and **has problems completing a form**: *"I went to the employment office once and I simply didn't like it. **They give you a form as long as your arm, and I'm not a form kinda guy**."*
- J (48, m, homeless for 17 years): *"I've been sorting out my benefit for six months, but **I'm not capable of filling out the form**."*
- D (48, m, homeless for five years): *"**I enjoyed alcohol to such an extent that I wasn't even capable of going to the employment office and sorting things out**, and they're not too keen when you turn up in that kind of state. I had the DTs, and if I went there sober I was shaking so much I wasn't able to sign the form. And if I managed to get myself together, they'd always find some obstacle or other."*
- J (45, f, homeless for 20 years) did not apply for emergency financial assistance for a long time because of her alcoholism and drug addiction: *"I'm finally registered at the employment office. After 12 years I'm receiving emergency financial assistance. **It wasn't possible before now because I was an alcoholic and a junkie**. When you booze and shoot up, you have no interest in organisational matters. Well, that's what experience has taught me at any rate."*
- Z (47, m, homeless for 20 years) does not visit the employment office because **he is ashamed of his appearance**: *"I've visited the employment office two or three times. One time I was registered for about six months and received benefits. The first time I went **I was ashamed to be amongst other people**. I knew that I smelt and that I was filthy. On the other hand, when I saw the others, I lost my temper."* It was the other applicants and how they were neatly dressed and appeared to be in no need of support that angered Z.

Some homeless people need help when dealing with the authorities. This may involve the reimbursement of travel expenses or being accompanied to the appropriate office.

- D (40, m, homeless for 19 years) is one such: *"I've been on benefits and they've told me I have to organise emergency financial assistance. **An outreach worker will come with me and arrange things**, otherwise I don't know how I'd cope."*
- P (50, m, homeless for 12 years) is also dependant on assistance: *"**I'm trying to sort things out with the employment office with the help of Naděje**. I have no way of getting there and right now I have no time. I have to make a little money."*

Some do not have social benefits because they became argumentative at the employment office.

- M (51, m, homeless for one year): "*The employment office is useless. **I got into an argument** and they cancelled the contract with me. So that was that, and I didn't return. I'm trying to sort things out for myself.*"

- J (52, m, homeless for 15 years): "*I'm not registered at the employment office. They threw me out. **They've banned me and now I have nothing**. They've literally banned me. There was a young girl… I should have grabbed her and told her to fuck off. I'd tear a strip off her, a stupid young girl. Why should I make a dick of myself? Better to maintain my dignity, innit?*" J is an alcoholic, and this may be the cause of his problematic behaviour.

- P (45, f, homeless for eight years) has also had problems with the employees of the employment office: "*I've been registered at the job centre for two years. But for a long time I didn't set foot in the place. I told them everything and **they were like, really arrogant. So I lost my temper and left**. Eventually I got registered. They said I had to tell them how I made a living and I told them I redeem empty bottles. They asked how much I made a day and I said CZK 50* [USD 2]. *As a result they subtracted that from my CZK 3,000. You know what, I said, every gypsy receives money and here you are deducting money from me from my life minimum because I collect bottles.*" The employee was at fault in this case, since only legal income can be deducted from a client's benefit.

Many of our respondents visit the employment office because **they are pleased that it will pay their health insurance and keep their debts from accruing.**

- Č (42, m, homeless for five years): "*I'm registered at the employment office it goes without saying, **so that they pay my health insurance** and so I don't incur yet more debt. There are not many such offers out there. The big problem is my criminal record, because everyone wants someone with a clean record. I receive emergency financial assistance.*"

- P (52, m, homeless for two years): "*Right now I'm not registered at the employment office. I was receiving emergency financial assistance and I've applied for invalidity benefit. The only thing the employment office is good for is **ensuring you don't fall into arrears with your health insurance**.*"

SUMMARY

Two thirds of our respondents receive social benefits, usually in the form of emergency financial assistance. This money is important, because it enables them to survive. However, it does not cover all of their needs, especially if they drink and smoke. Moreover, most of them have no idea how to manage money, either because they wish to enjoy life a bit and make up for their material frustration, or because other homeless people take money from them.

Some of them do not receive social benefits. This may be because they do not meet the official requirements, are unable to visit the appropriate office, are incapable of completing a form, or argue with the office employees. In such cases it is very useful to have a social worker accompany them to the employment office. Simply being registered at the employment office helps them in that their health insurance is paid and they do not incur further debts. Only 5% of young homeless people receive benefits: the rest do not apply for or receive them. That 5% began to avail themselves of the option later on, usually after serving a prison sentence and looking for a legal way of making money (Vágnerová, Csémy, Marek, 2013).

6.3 CASUAL (CASH-IN-HAND) WORK

The job opportunities and work morale of homeless people are even more limited than before they found themselves living on the street. Over the years they lose whatever work habits and professional skills they had to begin with. They become used to a life without any demands and are often dependent on alcohol or drugs. Many of them are repeat offenders and have a criminal record, and this reduces still further the likelihood of their finding work. Most have debts they are unable to repay, and as a result their motivation drops still further. In the unlikely event of their finding a job, workplace conflict and poor employee morale mean they often then lose it. Nevertheless, despite all of these complicating factors, just under half of our respondents (46%) report that they occasionally find temporary cash-in-hand work on the black market. According to our questionnaire, 36% of homeless people find themselves in this situation. As regards young people the figure is far lower, with only 25% reporting that they sometimes work, mostly without a contract (Vágnerová, Csémy, Marek, 2013).

Most of our respondents say that it is hard for a homeless person to find work, and that as they get older and their problems accumulate, this situation gets worse and worse. Another reason they find it difficult to find work is that **few of them have any qualifications**. This is true, for instance, of S (52, m, homeless for 17 years): "*Finding work is a real problem, and it doesn't get any better. **If you've got no training, then you've got no chance**. I can't even remember when I last had a job. It was years back, though I can't remember how many.*"

Having a criminal record is a major disadvantage when looking for work. Employers are not too keen on taking on someone who has spent time in prison.
- R (49, m, homeless for 20 years): "*I've been selling* Nový Prostor [the street newspaper, equivalent to *The Big Issue*] *for about ten months. Before that I used to work in a DHL warehouse. I was there for a year before they realised **I had a criminal record**.*"

- J (50, m, homeless for two years): "*I've applied for a few jobs, but **they always want a clean criminal record**, and when I tell them I've been convicted 14 times their faces drop. So you have to find casual work, cash-in-hand. These days nobody will give you a contract. The most you can hope for is an agreement to perform a job* [dohoda o provedení práce – an arrangement under Czech law], *just in case there's an inspection…*"
- M (40, f, homeless for 25 years) also has a criminal record: "*Even when I was in prison I was determined to find work. It makes me angry that things aren't organised in such a way that they find work for when you come out of prison. Rubikon is an agency that sends me here and there, **but nobody wants me when they see my criminal record**.*"

Some of our respondents find work but are unable to keep it. A common problem amongst the homeless is an inability to comply with rules, discharge their work duties, and respect their superiors. One reason they lose their job is **conflictual behaviour in the workplace**, which may often be associated with alcohol abuse.
- S (52, f, homeless for 17 years) is an alcoholic who lost her job because of conflicts with her managers: "*I began selling* Nový Prostor *here in Prague, but then I got into a quarrel with D. **I told the entire management to fuck off.** I just snapped, I don't know why. I was already pissed off and then I told them to fuck off. **I wasn't selling many copies, I was pissed off** and not thinking straight. They were constantly in a hurry and wanted everything done as quickly as possible. So by now I was beside myself with rage and started cursing. On the other hand,* Nový Prostor *helped me through the worst times, the biggest pile of shit I've ever been in.*"
- M (55, m, homeless for 20 years) is an alcoholic who had no respect for his superiors: "*I had no problem with the work as such. I did everything they asked of me. But **I had problems with the boss.** I refused to do something and gave him a piece of my mind and he told me not to bother turning up the next day.*"
- K (42, m, homeless for two years) does not abuse alcohol or drugs but had a bad relationship with his superiors and quit his job: "*I became bankrupt while living in Moravia and was unemployed for a year and a half. Then I worked in a pub on Charles Square. But the pub went bust owing me CZK 50,000* [USD 2,000]. *Then I worked in a pub in Březiněves, but the lads running it had to shut it down because the landlord kept raising the rent. Then I worked at Edimax. I quit there **because the boss was shit,** and rather than punch him in the face and be sent to prison, **I thought it politic to leave.** Right now I wash dishes in O2 Arena whenever they call me up.*"
- L (38, m, homeless for 21 years) **found himself in conflict with his colleagues**: "*When I came out of prison I found a job as a garbageman with Prague city council. I was sacked after two years because **I threw a dustbin at some prick and walked off.**"* L suffers impaired intelligence linked with personality defect, and this probably played a role.

- K (37, f, homeless for ten years) consumes alcohol and drugs: "*I was working cash-in-hand on building sites. But then it ended because **I had a run-in with someone**.*"

Another reason homeless people lose their jobs is because they can be **unreliable and display poor employee morale**, and these qualities are often related to the consumption of alcohol or drugs. For people who are alcoholics or drug addicts, payday is the trigger for massive consumption followed inevitably by absenteeism.

- H (50, m, homeless for 20 years): "*I worked as a doorman at ABL. I lasted about a year and a half. Before that I was with Rieger Security for a year. Then I spent two months on the street and then found work in Pilsen, where I worked for three years. Things seemed to be going well, they liked me, I liked them, and **then suddenly I didn't turn up for two days because I was drunk, and they fired me**.*"
- J (41, m, homeless for nine years) is an alcoholic: "*I'd work for a bit but then it would end. They'd take me on, but only for a short time, **because I'd not turn up for work because I overslept, whatever**.*"
- T (39, m, homeless for six years) says that unreliability is a common problem amongst the homeless: "***They're unreliable**. They try something, maybe receive payment upfront for two days, **get drunk, and then don't turn up for work for the next three days**. Then they wonder why no one wants to hire them.*"

Employee theft can often lead to dismissal.
- J (45, m, homeless for six years) is a repeat offender: "*I worked for Billa* [an Austrian supermarket chain that operates throughout Central, Eastern and South-eastern Europe], *because they weren't bothered that I had a criminal record. But in 2015 **they fired me for theft**. They didn't want to give me any money, so I took it from the cash register. That was my biggest mistake, that's what I'm most sorry about.*"
- M (54, m, homeless for 20 years) repeatedly lost his job because of theft: "*I've done some stupid things in my time. I've taken things, **stolen things**. The last straw came when I broke into the office. They fired me after that.*"

Inflated ideas of the wages they should receive can also be a problem.
- V (51, m, homeless for ten years): "*After two years I was back on my feet. Mainly thanks to Mr Pěnkav* [Pavel Pěnkav, probation officer for Prague 1], *who really helped me. I started doing casual jobs. Then I found a proper job as garbageman and I worked hard. But I left **because I'm not going to work for someone who doesn't pay a proper wage**. The pay was pitiful, only half a proper wage. Right now I'm signing on. I feel depressed to be honest. I'm no longer a spring chicken and finding work is going to be difficult.*" The question arises as to whether this was the fault of the employer or whether V simply did not work hard enough to merit a full wage.

- Z (51, m, homeless for ten years): "*I found some casual work as a cleaner for Billa and Albert. **But the money was rubbish**. I mean, I could stock shelves or unload goods for Kaufland.*" Z is hardly in a position to choose since he has a criminal record.
- M (54, m, homeless for 20 years): "*To begin with I was in a shelter in Liberec and they gave me a job sorting out the clothes. I was there for six months and **then it started to grate on me**. I didn't enjoy it because I was only being given a hundred crowns. After they had deducted money for accommodation and food **it left me with a hundred crowns** [USD 4] **pocket money**.*" M was unable to understand that he should pay for his accommodation and food.

Some of our respondents are simply incapable of persisting at anything for long.
- L (52, m, homeless for two years) has problems holding down a job: "*For the last ten years things have gone from bad to worse. I did casual jobs, everything you can think of. Right now I've been unemployed for three months. Last year I was a security guard, but relationships were toxic, so we reached mutual agreement on an end to the job. The fact is that **patience isn't my strong point**. I like change, so the impulse to move on came from my side too.*"
- P (47, m, homeless for seven years) is incapable of remaining for long in a job: "*I worked in a graveyard in Ďáblice. I was happy there, but I received an offer to work with some Ukrainians for more money, and like a dickhead I handed in my notice. Things started to drag on and I've basically fucked everything up, if you'll pardon my French. I've had all sorts of jobs but **I've never stayed in any of them for long. I've got something of a sloppy attitude to life**.*"

Alcohol or drug addiction can lead not only to job loss (usually caused by unreliability and poor employee morale), but negatively impact a person's motivation to work.
- R (46, m, homeless for four years): "*I found some casual work shelf-stocking, cleaning ventilation systems, that kind of thing. And then **suddenly along comes alcohol and that's that, I'm back on the rollercoaster**. I was absent from work and they fired me.*"
- M (40, m, homeless for seven years): "*Right now I'm doing casual work via the Salvation Army. The problem is that every morning I have to take a breathalyser because you can't arrive drunk. **I don't mind admitting that my main problem is with alcohol**.*"
- D (48, m, homeless for five years) is an alcoholic who has lost the motivation to work: "*I don't know what kind of job I could do. I can't imagine what I would do. I'm no longer physically strong enough, I have high blood pressure and something of a dicky ticker. Everything kind of collapsed around me and **I gave up looking for a job to be honest**. Sometimes I felt like I was just going to drink myself to death.*"

- Z (42, m, homeless for 11 years) is an alcoholic: "*I used to work from time to time, but* **now I can't be bothered**. *I believe the technical term is: Fuckus Offus!… I sold* Nový Prostor *for a while, but it didn't go well, I'm not a fucking newsboy.*"

Drug addiction is an even greater barrier. Drug addicts have no motivation to work and make no effort to find and hold onto a job.
- M (48, m, homeless for 20 years) is a drug addict who considers work too great a burden: "*I'm registered at the employment office at present as looking for work. In the past I did bits and pieces. But* **it would always confuse me**, *work is too much of a psychological burden.*"
- J (39, m, homeless for five years): "*I made a bit of cash by going through skips and bins. I made good money that way.* **But then I stopped. I didn't enjoy it any longer.**"

The state of health of some of our respondents was also a factor, especially in the case of the older ones. People who have had an accident, stroke or other chronic illness do not have a good chance of finding a job and are not entitled to a pension, because they have not paid into the system.
- E (53, m, in his first year of homelessness): "*I lost my job and then found another. But then I discovered it was all too much for me and* **that was when I had my first stroke**. *After that I never found another job.*"
- Z (51, m, homeless for ten years) is a similar case. "*At one time things were going well and I was making a living doing casual work. But then I started to have health problems.* **I have poor motor skills.** *Stairs cause me problems, going up and down a ladder would too. So right now I'm doing nothing. Maybe I could be a road sweeper.*"

An important factor behind the reluctance of homeless people to work involves debts, which most people living on the street have and which are often so large that they cannot be paid off. **The threat of execution proceedings is extremely demotivating** and leads many to give priority to work without a contract or to no work at all.
- J (50, m, homeless for two years) is a repeat offender who does not want work because of execution proceedings: "*I don't even want to find work, because if I started a job, they'd take 40% of my wages and I wouldn't even have the money to pay for a shelter. The worst thing is that I'm not even interested in work. I enjoyed it for a time, before I'd incurred debts.*"
- D (37, m, homeless for nine years) also has debts: "*I'm registered at the employment office, but* **I work on the black market because otherwise I wouldn't earn a thing.** *My debts mean that I simply can't have a normal job. I mean, I could, but I wouldn't be able to support a family. I do casual work and* **I'm afraid that if they took part of my wages from me in execution proceedings,** *my relationship wouldn't survive. I wouldn't be able to pay the rent, my partner would split up with*

me, I wouldn't have money for food, and I'd end up on the street again and start boozing. That's the problem in a nutshell."

- V (51, m, homeless for ten years) finds himself in the same situation. "***I'd quite like a proper job***, *except I have a huge problem. It's not that I'm unfit for work, but **I have execution proceedings hanging over my head***. *I haven't really paid much attention to it. I know that I'm bankrupt and that you have to work for a certain period of time, and that's why I don't go looking for a normal job.*"
- D (39, m, homeless for four years): "*Casual work suits me better. They pay you every day. I have debts incurred on an apartment, so **it makes no sense for me to get a proper job**.*"

Yet another problem is the knowledge that, if they earn money, they lose their social benefits, which is demotivating. H (50, m, homeless for 20 years) sums it up thus: "*I could look for work, except that **if you find a job and you receive emergency financial assistance, then they subtract part of it***. *If I earned say CZK 6,000 [USD 260], they would take away my housing benefit.*"

Cash-in-hand work without a contract suits many of our respondents, though it too has its downsides. The work tends to be poorly paid and sometimes they receive nothing at all. Despite this they accept such work because they like the fact of receiving cash that nobody can take away from them.

- P (50, m, homeless for 12 years): "*I used to walk the streets collecting bottles. I met a lad who offered me work, and I accepted. **I worked for about a month but didn't receive a cent***. *So I simply gave it up.*"
- Č (42, m, homeless for five years) works without a contract: "*After I came out of prison I worked on the black market. **A few times they simply didn't pay me what I was owed**.*"
- Š (46, f, homeless for four years) has a similar experience: "*We found work with J. **We worked for one guy who simply didn't pay us***. *Prior to that I had been a cleaner in Bohnice, after which I went to work for the guy who didn't pay us. That was on the black market. I never saw any agreement on the performance of a job.*"
- K (37, f, homeless for ten years) tells a similar story: "*I used to work cash-in-hand on building sites. It doesn't matter on construction sites whether you smell or if you're filthy. **But then they didn't pay us so we left**.*"

SUMMARY

Finding work is difficult for most homeless people, especially if they do not possess the requisite qualifications or have a criminal record. Because of this, only jobs for which no qualifications are needed are available to them, and these tend to be badly paid. As a consequence, it makes no sense for them to work. They would lose their social benefits and would be no better off than if they did nothing. If they do find work, they often lose it very quickly, usually because of unreliability and poor employee morale. Conflictual behaviour on the workplace and theft are also reasons why their employment contracts are terminated. Several of our respondents admitted that they have no real desire to work. It is clear that long-term homelessness, coupled with excessive consumption of alcohol or drugs, leads to a decline in whatever work and social habits our respondents may have possessed in the first place. Debt and the threat of execution proceedings are also demotivating factors. As a result, the people we spoke to prefer cash-in-hand jobs, with all the attendant risks, namely that the wages are often unpaid.

6.4 BEGGING AND PANHANDLING

A third of our respondents (33%) admitted to begging as a source of livelihood. The real figure could be higher, since some people are reluctant to admit to begging because they see it as shameful. To begin with a person feels embarrassed to be begging. However, they gradually get used to it. For certain people begging and panhandling are a standard means of subsistence, while for others they are activities to be practised only in an emergency or when their inhibitions have been reduced by alcohol. Homeless people do not consider all forms of begging to be equally degrading. Simple panhandling, in which a person appeals to passersby to give them something, is relatively acceptable for most of them, while begging on one's knees is rejected outright as being undignified. V (38, m) distinguishes between begging and panhandling: "*Not begging exactly, but just sort of casually mentioning money... yeah, I've done that.*" In addition, begging is banned and several of the people we spoke to do not want to take the risk of being apprehended by the police.

The difference between people who are the passive recipients of another's munificence and those who are more active in eking out a living is manifest in the method of begging (Groot and Hodgetts, 2015). This method may be active to the point of being aggressive and involves an individual asking for money directly, or passive, in which case they simply wait and see whether a passerby will offer them something, or at the very most ask for assistance. If begging or panhandling is to be effective, the supplicant must attract the attention of a potential donor, and so they must strike up contact and provoke some kind of emotional reaction (be this compassion or disgust). Depending on how they do this, the potential donor may be amused, but equally may be confused, intimidated or prompted by guilt into offering the beggar something. Sometimes the donor offers something simply in order to get rid of the beggar. The style of begging is very important. A beggar may present themselves as a sad wretch deserving compassion, an entertainer, servant, storyteller or aggressor (Lankenau, 1999; Lee et al., 2003). Performing minor tasks, e.g. washing car windows, busking, blowing bubbles, or being a living statue may be more effective than merely passive begging, since in this case the beggar presents themself not simply as supplicant but as someone offering a service, even if the general public for the most part remains unimpressed. Someone who is successful at begging or panhandling may not only acquire means of sustenance, but may boost their self-confidence and improve their position within the homeless community (Baumohl, 2004).

Panhandling is a completely normal activity among the people we spoke to, especially those who have living on the street for a longer period of time. For the most part it involves cigarettes and small change.

- V (48, m, homeless for seven years): "*We sit here all day long, walk around and **ask for small change or cigarettes***."
- J (52, m, homeless for 15 years): "***If I don't have any cigarettes,*** *then I ask someone if they might give me one. I also ask for small change. But I don't steal.*"
- E (46, f, homeless for eleven years). "*I've always begged and still do. But I act decently. I stop and ask a passerby politely **if they might have some small change for a homeless person** and if they might help in some way. Sometimes I receive a telling off, in which case I still offer my thanks and apologies etc. Prostitution and begging are the most difficult things for me.*"

Some homeless people regard begging and panhandling as a form of work.

- D (37, m, homeless for ten years): "***I go to work every evening. I ask passersby for small change.*** *Excuse me, you wouldn't have to have some small change on you, would you? One time I made 3,000 crowns* [USD 130]. *I've been fined about 600 times for begging and I've collected other fines for drinking too.*"
- D (40, m, homeless for 19 years) is a drug addict who begs, despite having been fined many times. "*Since last August **I've been making a living through begging***. *I've been fined forty times. In all the bill comes to 65,000 crowns* [USD 2,825], *and they seriously think I'm going to pay them. They've banned me from Prague 7. So I'll pop over to Prague 6 and after six months I'll return. Begging's fine. On a weekend evening I'll make 700 crowns* [USD 30]. *I buy food at a Vietnamese shop from the money I make.*" As is clear from what D says, bans and fines do not always have the desired effect.
- M (37, m, homeless for five years) is an alcoholic: "*Yeah, I beg. **I'd rather beg for food than steal it.** And **I ask politely, greet people**, ask them for food and small change, anything that will help. At the beginning, before I had learned how to do it, it was unpleasant, I felt ashamed. I completely respect them when they turn me down. The thing that bugs me the most is when they look right through me as though I'm not there.*"
- J (50, f, homeless since she was young) occasionally begs but admits she is not very successful: "***Sometimes I beg*** *or rummage around in garbage bins. With begging it depends. If it were going well, I'd be in a hostel. I walk around Old Town Square, that's my patch.*"

Some of our respondents regard begging to be humiliating. However, as one of them says, **it is better than stealing and then being sent to prison**.

- R (40, m, homeless for six years): "*Panhandling? Well what do you think? **It's humiliating, but you need the money**. Sometimes I earn a 1,000 crowns* [USD 43], *sometimes only 50* [USD 2]. *It depends on who you meet. It's best in winter. I walk a lot around Holešovice or the centre, when there's a nonstop bar open or a shop. Mostly at night, because during the day people tend to be more closed off than at night. When they roll out of the pub they're feeling more magnanimous.*"
- Č (42, f, homeless for five years) feels that begging is unpleasant: "*I've tried it. **It's not particularly pleasant**, but sometimes people give you some change. It's unpleasant **but it's better than stealing and being sent to prison**.*"

Some of our respondents find it **easier to ask for money when they have reduced their inhibitions by means of alcohol**.

- M (40, m, homeless for seven years): "*I'm ashamed of begging and **usually I'm drunk when I do it**, otherwise I wouldn't do it.*"
- D (48, m, homeless for five years): "*It all started with me asking people for cigarettes. **Then you gain a bit in courage and start asking for change**. That's the lesson of financial straits.*"
- M (43, f, homeless for eight years): "*During the whole time I've been on the street I haven't stolen anything. I preferred to beg. I used to travel to the centre. Sometimes it paid off, sometimes not, depending on how much I'd had to drink. **When sober I was too embarrassed to ask for a cigarette**. Sometimes it worked, so that in four hours I could make 500 crowns* [USD 20]. *But I had to smarten myself up. There were negative reactions too, it goes without saying. I felt ashamed when someone told me to fuck off.*"

Some of our respondents feel that begging is a risky activity. It is banned and there is therefore the **threat of intervention by the police.**

- Č (42, m, homeless for five years): "*I didn't used to go down on my hands and knees to beg. I simply panhandled people. **I don't want to receive a fine for begging**.*"
- D (48, m, homeless for five years): "*I didn't go down on my hands and knees. **I was too afraid of the police**. Or V (46, m): "*I wouldn't risk begging. **The police arrive really quickly**.*"
- J (50, f, homeless since she was young) is also afraid of the police: "*I wouldn't go down on my hands and knees, because one time the police arrived and fined me and told me that **if they were to catch me again, I'd lose my emergency financial support**.*" This is in fact impossible. However, J believed what the police said and stopped begging.

Several of our respondents expect people to give them something out of compassion. However, they do not want to beg directly, and so **play an instrument**

or offer a counter-service. As they see it, this is not begging but offering a product for which they receive a remuneration. In this way they rationalise actions that they are ashamed of.

- R (49, m, homeless for 20 years): "*When I was living on the street I tried to sustain myself through begging. To* **begin with I knelt down, but then I got hold of a recorder***, using which I was able to make more money.*"
- D (37, m, homeless for nine years). "*I was never much of a beggar, I was too ashamed. I was convinced that, being a gypsy, no one would give me anything.* **I preferred to play the guitar***. Whenever I played, people would throw me either money or food.*"
- L (52, m, homeless for two years) believes selling the magazine *Nový Prostor* to be a form of begging: "*I started to enjoy selling* Nový Prostor *because it meant I was among people. To be honest,* **it's legalised begging***, but it has a kind of class and people are often sympathetic to the vendors.*"

Several of our respondents attempt to evoke compassion in passers-by by presenting themselves as wretched, helpless and neglected.

- B (52, m, homeless for 20 years): "*I go to specific places where people know me. When they see me,* **maybe they'll offer me something because I'm dirty** *and dishevelled. Or I ask if they wouldn't happen to have three crowns. I'll stand by Billa with a cup. And either someone gives me 20 crowns, say, or a luncheon voucher.*"
- J (40, f, homeless for 15 years) uses a passive strategy: "*Begging depends on where you do it and who you have watching you. I only used to beg for food and cigarettes, nothing more.* **I got down on my hands and knees and simply waited until someone gave me something.** *After 20 minutes I had 200 crowns* [USD 8.6] *and that was enough for food and cigarettes.*"

Illus. 17. Begging on Charles Bridge (photo Martin Pokora).

Illus. 18. Begging in a busy street (photo Martin Pokora).

However, even begging requires some skill and not every homeless person possesses it. This is especially the case if they are unable to accept rejection and react aggressively, as is the case with L (38, m, homeless for 21 years): "*I have never known how to beg. I've found myself in a situation in which I have not a single cent, and so I went up to someone and asked for a cigarette. He looked at me and asked if I had clean hands. I didn't grasp what he was driving at, and I started to wonder if he was simply going to spout some fucking crap at me, in which case I'd fucking nut him. In the end he gave me a cigarette. The way I see it, **I'd rather go to work than beg**.*" L has limited intellectual ability and it would appear from his behaviour that this is combined with personality disorder.

Illus. 19. Begging that provokes sympathy can be effective (photo Martin Pokora).

Some of our respondents will neither beg nor panhandle, either because they don't know how to or find it humiliating. In this respect neither age nor length of time spent living on the street is important.

- T (29, m, homeless for six years): "*No way I'd beg, **I'm simply not cut out for it**. I don't even ask for a cigarette. I'd rather find myself a discarded butt.*"
- J (45, f, homeless for 20 years). "***I wouldn't even ask for 3 crowns for a bread roll**. It just doesn't feel right. **I don't even know how.** I've tried it a few times, asked someone for the money for a bread roll, told them I'm hungry and homeless, and their response has been: so look for work! Three times they told me that and it really pissed me off. Begging is simply humiliating for me.*"
- B (51, m, homeless for 20 years): "***I'd rather go without food than get down on my hands and knees.** Begging in the street, asking for money... it's not for me. If I desperately needed to go to the toilet or I'd shit myself, then maybe...*"

Begging is deemed humiliating and unacceptable above all by people with a secondary school or even university education, who have enjoyed a more acceptable status at some time in the past.

- I (40, m, homeless for one year): "*I've never tried begging. I think it kinda represents the lowest you can sink.*"
- R (46, m, homeless for four years): "*Begging is not for me. **I have my pride, and getting down in the street on my hands and knees is one thing I'm never going to do.***"
- M (50, m, homeless for 20 years): "*I wouldn't rummage through bins and I wouldn't beg. **Anyone who still retains a shred of human dignity will refuse to beg**. If you beg, you're a broken person. There's basically life pre-begging and post-begging.*" M has a university education and his homelessness is related more to psychological issues.

SUMMARY

It is clear from what our respondents told us that begging and panhandling are relatively frequent ways of eking out a living for many homeless people, even though not all regard it as acceptable. Some admit that they cannot or do not want to beg. If they do take the plunge, they prefer to approach people in the street with a request for a cigarette or small change. They are aware that they may be rejected and this is not a pleasant thought. However, they consider this method more acceptable than stealing, which could have even more unpleasant consequences. Some reduce their inhibitions by drinking, because sober they feel too ashamed. Begging is often associated with alcoholism, since food can be obtained in other ways. The street is also home to latent begging in the form of busking, performing a living statue, or blowing elaborate bubbles. This is more acceptable because the money received can be regarded as remuneration for services provided. Few homeless people are prepared to beg in the position of kneeling supplicant. This is not only because they do not wish to express their social disaffiliation so explicitly, but also because it might attract unwelcome attention from the police. According to McDonagh (2011), 32% of homeless people in Britain engage in begging. Among young people, the number of those who regard begging to be an acceptable way of making a living or cadging a cigarette is roughly the same as that of middle-aged people. About 30% of young people beg. The difference is that many young people regard begging as less acceptable and more humiliating than theft (Vágnerová, Csémy, Marek, 2013).

6.5 SCAVENGING AND COLLECTING (REDEEMING RECYCLABLES)

Scavenging, variously known as bin diving or dumpster diving and involving the retrieval of items from garbage bins, is also confirmation of a person's low social status, in that they are satisfied by the very items that others have deemed garbage and thrown away. However, the scavenger does not need to be in contact with the person who threw the garbage away. A container can be rummaged around in at night, when there is no one around. Almost two thirds (59%) of our older respondents are content with rejected or discarded food or clothes, regardless of how long they have been homeless. The difference between short-term and chronic homelessness is more about how they feel about this form of sustenance. Some find scavenging in bins humiliating. However, most regard it as an available source of whatever they need, especially when in a crisis situation. They justify their decision by saying that the items they are scavenging are not bad things in themselves, but have simply been put aside because they are not needed. An acceptable variant is food, which shops throw away when it passes its sell-by date and which has not yet gone off.

Many of our respondents believe scavenging is a simple means of subsistence in the absence of money, and is better than begging or theft.
- V (46, m, homeless for three years): "*I find food in bins on Old Town Square. I rummage around and quite a few times people have given me food when they see me looking. Often they decide they don't like something just from the smell, and they give it to me.*"
- M (40, m, homeless for seven years): "*I scavenge for food. If someone throws something in a bin on Old Town Square, then I take it. I always manage to find something to eat.*"
- S (52, m, homeless for 17 years) stresses one must know the right places to scavenge: "*You'll always find some source of food. You won't die of hunger in Prague. I see people rummaging in bins and I tell them they have to use their brains, they have to find the places where food is likely to be thrown out.*"

Homeless people often avail themselves of **discarded food to be found behind supermarkets**.

- M (55, m, homeless for 17 years): "***If you could only see what Albert throws out.*** *Bread and pastries that can no longer be sold over the counter but are perfectly fine to eat are wrapped in bags. The best thing to do is look behind Albert in Vinohrady around 6 o'clock, because that's when they package what they can't sell and throw it away.*"

- J (45, f, homeless for 20 years): "*I buy food if I have work. Otherwise I take it from bins. If I haven't so much as a cent, I go to Odkolek* [a bakery], *climb over the fence or get the lads to, and* **take the bread rolls that can't be sold** *or might be a little over baked.*"

- R (48, m, homeless for seven years): "*We know some of the warehouse workers and* **they give us bread or salami or whatever is past its sell-by date**. *There's always bread left over in the shop and in the morning it's thrown in bags into a container. One time we were rummaging around and we found about twenty turkey breasts. We know the warehouse workers at Albert. The food is past its sell-by date but that doesn't matter because it's vacuum packed and there's nothing wrong with it.*"

- K (42, m, homeless for three years) has no doubts: "*You have to live on something and if you don't want to steal or beg, then you look behind a supermarket and* **take the stuff they've thrown out**."

Illus. 20. Scavenging in a frequented spot where almost anything may be unearthed (photo Martin Pokora).

Bins and containers contain not only food, but other items that can be used or sold, e.g. clothes, electronics and bottles.

- V (48, m, homeless for seven years) avails himself of this opportunity: "*We used to eke out a living by **travelling to the bins in Barrandov** [the famous film studios, hence costumes: tr.]. They washed and packed up the clothes and **we used to take them to second-hand shops**. There was loads of stuff you could sell, bottles and so on. Not any longer. How have things changed? You just won't find as many items. In the good old days anyone could make money in this way.*"
- J (39, m, homeless for five years) rummages through containers for something to sell: "*Some containers are better than others. If I need money, **I look for electronics, which sell well**.*"
- G (50, m, homeless for ten years): "*I do cash-in-hand jobs. **But if there's no work, then I rummage in containers. You'd be amazed at what people get rid of**. If I need clothes, I travel to the large containers in Řepy and fit myself out from top to bottom.*"

Scavenging is a popular way of obtaining food or clothes. However, our respondents are in two minds about it, regardless of how long they have been on the street. Many of them are aware that it is not exactly a standard means of subsistence, and some reject it as being humiliating.

- P (42, m, homeless for one year) is uneasy about taking food from bins: "*I visit the bins every day. **But there's nothing inherently virtuous about it**.*"
- S (52, m, homeless for 17 years) has similar misgivings: "***It's not a great feeling rummaging around bins**, even though I know they're full of food, and good food at that.*"
- V (51, m, homeless for ten years): "*I survive by scavenging. I rummage around garbage bins, containers, whatever. But now, when I say it out loud, **I realise just how far I've sunk**.*"
- J (48, m, homeless for 17 years) refuses to rummage through bins: "***I'd die of shame if I started searching through garbage bins**.*"

The collection, and sometimes theft, of raw materials, especially metals, **used to be a popular means of subsistence** for many homeless people. At present, its popularity is declining because of changes to the way payment is made for metal. In order to deter theft, recyclables can only be redeemed by means of a bank account. This form of payment is of no use to the homeless, since they do not have an account and do not want to wait for money.

- V (48, m, homeless for seven years) used to survive by selling metal: "***Iron used to sell well**. You could pinch some cable and melt off the rubber on the black, or collect copper. Some people used to frequent building sites, the tough guys would do the roofs. Take your pick. **It used to be far easier to earn money than it is these day**.*"

- Z (51, m, homeless for ten years): "*I used to be forever visiting the metal collection point. We used to have these large handcarts, the collection point wasn't far away, and **we'd earn good money**. We used to able to make 3,000 crowns* [USD 128] *in an afternoon.*"
- M (40, f, homeless for 25 years): "*Life on the street has changed beyond all recognition. It's difficult to make money. **We used to visit collection points, but now they've restricted that option**. They used to be full of homeless people who would spend all day collecting. These days it's complex. You spend all day going through garbage cans and then receive twenty crowns for the paper.*"
- J (45, f, homeless for 20 years): "*I used to collect brass and copper, and aluminium used to be good too. These days, forget it. **Collection has gone to the dogs**, everything has changed.*"
- F (40, m, homeless for ten years) agrees: "***These days nobody gives a toss.*** *What's the point of collecting cable, dragging it along somewhere, burning off the plastic, ending up filthy, and then waiting 14 days for the money? Everyone's given up on it.*"

These days homeless people are only able to earn a little on the side through returning **paper or bottles**. Summer festivals are a good source of returnable paper beer beakers.

- Z (42, m, homeless for eleven years) earns a living by collecting paper and bottles: "*I used to collect scrap iron until they introduced that stupid law on metals, saying you had to have a receipt. **These days I collect paper**, which is still being bought normally. The problem is that any number of people are doing the same thing, so you're happy if you find 10 kilos. Bottles too…in the summer **I collect bottles** because you can make money out of them too.*"
- Z (44, m, homeless for 15 years) collects bottles: "*Recently I went collecting in Brno. **You earn a few hundred crowns in a month**, but it's heavy work… **I collect bottles**, but only at certain times and in certain places.*"
- Z (49, f, homeless for 15 years) opts for paper: "***I have to be on the move, doing something, even if that means collecting paper***. *At least it's an activity that keeps my head above water and it's a way of passing the time. I earn around 80 crowns* [USD 3.4] *and that's enough for me. It's enough to pay for a bed, and then I buy some food and cigarette papers. I don't buy tobacco, I collect it.*"

SUMMARY

Rummaging through garbage bins is more acceptable than begging and is practised by most older people regardless of how long they have been on the street. Half of the young people we spoke to earned a living in this way (Vágnerová, Csémy, Marek, 2013). Many of our respondents are aware that it is not a common practice, but rationalise it as being better than stealing or begging. It is a means of livelihood that is socially stigmatised, but does not open them to prosecution. More acceptable is the consumption of food that has been discarded, since it is in perfectly good condition and would be acceptable to anyone, homeless or not. Our respondents are aware that not only food, but other items such as clothes or items that can be sold are to be found in dustbins. Many homeless people collect raw materials, though this is less easy these day because of the cash-free payment method in operation. People living on the street rarely have a bank account to which they could have money sent, and do not on the whole wish to wait for payment. As a consequence, the collection of paper and bottles, which are not subject to such limitations, is far more popular these days.

6.6 THEFT

Eighteen percent of our middle-aged respondents admit to having committed theft, though they justify their actions in different ways. Some steal because they are hungry, especially if they are new to the street and unaware that they can eat at a charity or find food in a container. Some continue to steal. A third of our respondents have been prosecuted for property crime, i.e. theft, often prior to finding themselves on the street.

Some of the people we spoke to admitted to stealing, but only when they were hungry and did not know that they could receive food at charities.

- L (52, m, homeless for two years): "***I stole something once**. It was the only time I've ever done something like that. **I was hungry** and I stole something from a shop… I felt really bad, but I said to myself that if I didn't do it, I'd die.*"
- M (45, f, in her first year of homelessness): "*I've never tried begging. But **I've often thought that I could pinch something from a supermarket**. Especially when I've been really hungry. Once I put some cheese slices in my rucksack. It was an odd feeling.*"
- R (48, m, homeless for seven years) used to steal when he first found himself on the street: "*At the start, when I had no money, I used to go to Albert in Kotva [a shopping centre]. It was winter, **so I used to pinch stuff**. I always had at least ten or twenty crowns [40–80 cents] from bottles I'd collected, so I had enough to pay for a few bread rolls, with a piece of cheese or salami slipped into my pocket. I'd pay for the rolls and then steal a bottle of vodka. That was the first year I was homeless, when I was simply walking around Prague. I had no idea where I could eat or how.*"
- R (40, m, homeless for six years) found himself in the same position: "*I started to steal because I ran out of money and **I had no idea that charities were running food banks**.*"

Some people continue to steal food, even though they are aware of the existence of charities and often avail themselves of their services.

- J (48, m, homeless for 17 years): "*If I'm feeling hungry, then I'll enter a shop and steal something to eat. I only steal when I'm hungry. Charities hand out food too, but not always. When you've run out of money altogether, then what are you supposed to do…?*"
- F (40, m, homeless for ten years): "*When I hit rock bottom, then I might steal five bread rolls from Penny* [a discount supermarket chain based in Germany], *or I'll buy five rolls and **steal a can or some salami**.*"
- Many of our respondents do not regard shoplifting to be as serious an offence as stealing from a specific individual. M (37, f, homeless for five years) explains it thus: "***Yeah, sometimes I steal it's true, but not from people***. *But from shops for sure. If I found myself with nothing, I'd steal. But I don't do it anymore, I don't like the feeling. I prefer to beg.*" Many young homeless people share this opinion.[10]
- On the other hand, P (45, f, homeless for eight years) would never steal from a shop: "*I used to steal things that were lying around. If it's not nailed to the floor, I nab it. But **I've never shoplifted**. I wouldn't know how.*"

Some of our respondents used to steal, but are now too afraid to do so. M (40, f, homeless for 25 years) explains: "*I used to steal, but only the odd piece of salami or whatever. Just sausages that you either bought or pinched. Clothes, too, which I used to pull off washing lines… But life on the street has changed beyond recognition. These days **it's difficult to walk into a shop and steal something, because the security guards will beat you up**. They don't give a fuck whether you're a woman or a man.*"

A willingness to steal increases under the influence of drink or drugs.

- P (47, m, homeless for seven years) admits this: "***I have stolen things occasionally, but only if I'd had something to drink***. *Even if I had money, I'd steal a biscuit or something.*"
- Z (47, m, homeless for 20 years): "***Whenever there's been nothing to eat, I've stolen things***. *I tend to steal on Saturdays and Sundays on Národní třída, **usually under the influence**… but it was a bit of fun. A few times I exchanged the chocolate I'd shoplifted for drugs.*"
- P (37, f, homeless for 15 years): "*From time to time I steal things, but **I always have to have had a drink** so as to gain some Dutch courage.*"

Some of our respondents admit they survive by stealing. These tend to be alcoholics or drug addicts and are often repeat offenders.

---

10 The young people we spoke to stole clothes or items from a drugstore, which they then sold in order to buy drugs.

- M (48, m, homeless for 20 years): "*Whenever I ran out of money,* **I got by through stealing***.*"
- V (38, m, homeless for 13 years) is a drug addict: "*You rummage through garbage bins, of course. But when it comes to food, I steal it...* **I've only ever stolen it***.*"
- M (38, m, homeless for two years) is also a drug addict: "*I visit charities for food, or I go to Albert.* **But I also steal things, yeah***.*" These people are used to stealing and do not feel motivated to stop.
- J (50, m, homeless for two years) has long been a thief, though he is not an alcoholic or drug addict. In his case stealing has become a habit: "*I spent the five years up to 2014 stealing, and I'm still at it. I was on benefits,* **but that didn't stop me stealing***.*" Before becoming homeless J was often in prison.
- **Some of our respondents steal only alcohol**, because they cannot get this from the charities. J (51, m, homeless for seven years) is an alcoholic and repeat offender: "**I'm not going to pretend that I don't occasionally steal a bottle of something***, because I do.*"

Some of our respondents refuse to steal and prefer to beg.
- M (40, m, homeless for seven years): "*I've never stolen anything.* **I prefer to beg. I'm not going to steal***, not even from shops.*"
- Č (42, m, homeless for five years): "**It's better to beg than to steal** *and then be locked up.*"
- M (43, f, homeless for eight years): "**I have never stolen anything. I prefer to beg for stuff.**"

SUMMARY

Theft as a means of livelihood or a way of acquiring the bare necessities is less common in middle-aged homeless people. One reason might be their experience of the criminal justice system, since many are repeat offenders. Another might be their appearance, which attracts attention and a watchful eye from security guards in shops. Some of our respondents admit they are afraid to steal. Another reason might be the desire for comfort and passivity characteristic of older people, for whom it is simpler to visit a charity or rummage through garbage. Within our group of young people theft was far more common. Two thirds of them admitted to it, and several felt justified in following that course of action (Vágnerová, Csémy, Marek, 2013).

Life on the street has considerable criminogenic potential, and some researchers regard theft to be one of the characteristic manifestations of homelessness. According to McDonagh (2011), 38% of British homeless people have experience of shoplifting. Almost half of our Prague-based middle-aged respondents admitted that they already had experience of stealing before becoming homeless, and so we may conclude that theft is not simply the consequence of a life on the street but of a different course of socialisation. In the case of these people, their parents and siblings were often also involved in crime, especially property crime, and so such behaviour did not strike them as being unacceptable.

6.7 PROSTITUTION

Within our middle-aged cohort, prostitution is relatively rare, especially in the case of men. An exception to this would be B (52, m, homeless for 20 years), who is a homosexual with only a basic education who will resort to prostitution if he has the chance: "*I used to live a normal life with a bloke here in Prague. He lived in V. I lived at his place and he supported me... I'm a kind of apartment-hopping homosexual, so a guy might invite me to sleep over at his for three days, or give me money, and I tell him I haven't got the money for food, I'm homeless.*"

Prostitution is not as rare in the case of women. Twenty percent of currently homeless women have resorted to it at some point in the past, sometimes even before finding themselves on the street. In the middle-aged cohort it is less frequent than in the group of young women, probably because many women found themselves homeless later.

- P (37, f, homeless for 15 years) resorted to prostitution when young: "**Yeah, I used to sell my body**. *But it was a kind of style. I had to hide myself away. So where is a girl supposed to hide? I hid in a nightclub. A group of people came after me because they were trying to sell me.*"
- E (46, f, homeless for 11 years): "*I was a hooker for a while*. *What happened was I found a guy that I thought was my boyfriend. But instead he pulled me into working on Perlová Street* [a street in Prague well known for its prostitutes]. *So I began life as a hooker, maybe two years... It's the only thing I don't want people to find out about me.*" Both women took up prostitution under the pressure of men, either their partners or a pimp.
- Sometimes the situation was inverted, as in the case of K (37, f, homeless for 10 years): "*I've had guys who simply had to put up with it when I said, 'listen pal, I'm off to make a bit of money, know what I mean?' Either they accepted it or they didn't. Then the lease came to an end or the bloke wasn't into it, even though at the start he had sat in the room next door listening while I turned tricks. That was the third one, the one I'm still with.*"

Not all homeless women have earned their living by prostitution. Some of them unequivocally refuse to do so, e.g. Z (49, f, homeless for 15 years): "*No. Anyone who says that to me, they get a slap in the face. I say to them, 'listen cunt, get this into your thick skull. **I may be walking the streets, but I'm not a streetwalker**. Now piss off.'*"

SUMMARY

Prostitution is not as common in older homeless people as it is in our younger cohort. Middle-aged women who have been living on the street for a longer period of time usually earn a living by other means. The decline in prostitution is also in part due to the fact that these older women are not as attractive to potential clients. A life on the street, often accompanied by alcoholism and drug abuse, is evident in their appearance. Homosexual prostitution is also more common amongst young people.

7. ALCOHOL CONSUMPTION ON THE STREET

Drinking to excess and an ensuing inability to work and maintain acceptable relationships with other people is often the reason a person finds themselves on the street. The changes that take place to a person under the influence of alcohol – unreliability, cantankerousness, the accumulation of debts, and sometimes aggression – lead not only to loss of work but loss of a home. Other researchers have reached the same conclusions (Mallet et al., 2005; Martijn and Sharp, 2006; Salomonsen-Sautel et al., 2008; Shelton et al., 2009).

Excessive alcohol consumption can be both the cause and effect of homelessness (Stergiopoulos and Herrmann, 2003; Caton et al., 2006; Didenko and Pankratz, 2007; McVicar, Moschion and van Ours, 2015). Alcohol abuse is usually present before a person becomes homeless: according to Clark et al. (2011) this is so in 80% of cases. However, it also a contributing factor to chronic homelessness, since people living on the street usually increase their consumption of alcohol (Caton et al., 2007, Clark et al., 2011). This increase in alcohol consumption is due to the fact that people are no longer prevented from drinking, but instead use alcohol to deal with the unpleasant feelings and stress of a homeless life.

Various studies have shown that **alcohol abuse is a problem for many homeless people** (Anderson and Christian, 2003; Caton et al., 2006; Didenko and

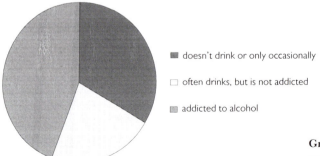

Graph 27. Alcohol consumption owned up to

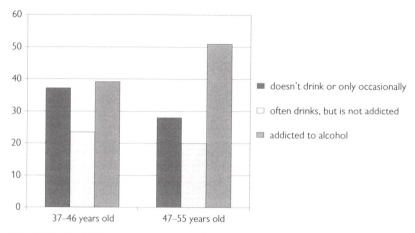

Graph 28. Alcohol consumption by age (shown in percentages)

Pankratz, 2007; Fazel et al., 2008). The homeless drink on average 2.5 times more alcohol than the majority population (Amato and MacDonald, 2015). According to Clark et al. (2011), 53% of homeless people drink to excess. Amato and MacDonald (2015) reached similar conclusions: in their case the figure was 50%. Brown et al. (2016) found that 47% of homeless people drank to excess. Dietz (2009) found that 51% of people aged 50 or over and 60% aged up to 50 had problems with alcohol. Koegel (2004) reports slightly higher values, with 58%–68% consuming alcohol to excess. Pillinger (2007) cites a figure of 61% and Zugazaga (2004) a figure of 68.5% of homeless people who drink to excess. Ball et al. (2005) concluded that the frequency rates vary between 30% and 60% depending on age.

Alcohol abuse is more frequent among older people, while drug abuse is typical of the younger generation. Research into young homeless people in Prague has shown that only 24% of people aged 19–26 drink to excess, while 61% take drugs (Vágnerová, Csémy, Marek, 2013). The opposite is true of middle-aged people (aged 37–54): 60% drink to excess and 20% take drugs. Alcohol abuse is more common amongst men (61%) than amongst women (44%).

As the graph makes clear, older people drink alcohol to excess and are addicted more often, even though the difference between both groups is not statistically significant.

Homeless people who drink to excess are usually aware that **it is a habit that causes problems that they would not otherwise have**. Over time they lose their work, family and accommodation. When asked why they drink so much, their answers vary. Some are the same replies given by alcoholics who are not homeless, but others are directly related to life on the street. People without a home are not subject to restrictions, and an alcohol addiction can develop more quickly (Vágnerová, Marek, Csémy, 2018):

I. An increase in alcohol consumption during time spent on the street has various causes

a) It can be a reaction to the stress that homeless people are exposed to and which they are unable to deal with. Alcohol offers relaxation, a temporary feeling of well-being, and eliminates unpleasant thoughts.

- D (48, m, homeless for five years): "*When I found myself living on the street, **I attempted to block everything out through alcohol** just to stop myself going mad.*"
- V (42, m, homeless for 21 years): "*I'm fully aware that alcohol is the pits, but I couldn't carry on without it. **You drink in order to forget everything.***"
- H (40, f, homeless for nine years) uses alcohol to improve her mood: "*I had problems and **I began to deal with them through alcohol**, because I have a history of addiction... I began to drink a lot, every day. A litre of wine a day is no problem. I drink in company or by myself. I experience psychological pain and feel that **I need to drink in order to feel better**.*" H's tendency to escape into alcohol most likely intensified her mental health issues.
- P (52, m, homeless for two years) does not drink: "*I don't need alcohol, but I understand that for some people **alcohol induces other thoughts or oblivion**, and in that way makes life on the streets bearable. It worries me that it can be any form of alcohol whatsoever and that people will reach for anything regardless of its quality.*" Homeless people do not have the money for better quality alcohol.

b) Excessive alcohol consumption is also related to **problems sleeping under poor conditions**.
- P (50, m, homeless for 12 years): "*I guess I can't cope psychologically. Also, **I sleep better after drinking**.*"
- S (51, m, homeless for 14 years): "*People on the street drink a hell of a lot because **you fall asleep more easily when you're drunk**. But it's still bad.*"

c) **Winter** can see an increase in alcohol consumption.
- This can be the reason why men drink who otherwise barely touch alcohol, e.g. L (52, m, homeless for two years): "*Yesterday **I drank a litre of wine because it was the only way of surviving the cold**. I don't feel a need to get drunk, but just to deal with the cold.*" L drinks out of a feeling of helplessness in a situation over which he has no control.
- Č (42, m, homeless for five years): "*I drink between five and six litres of wine, which is a fair amount. It begins when I wake up. **I start to drink because it's cold on the bench**.*"
- D (37, m, homeless for nine years): "*If you're sleeping rough, **you drink so as to ward off the cold**.*"

II. Alcohol consumption increases after a person becomes homeless

Some people begin to drink greater amounts of alcohol than they did before becoming homeless because they are no longer restricted by anything except money. They have no duties and no one reproaches them. The course of an alcohol addiction follows a particular trajectory. It leads to homelessness, and because a person in this situation has no need to control their intake, they drink more and more, often in the company of other homeless people who are also drinking. A community of drinkers is born, in which alcohol consumption becomes the norm and fills the day.

- J (51, m, homeless for seven years) began drinking after becoming homeless: "*When I became homeless, I lived in a garage in Michelská Street. I lived there for two years and it wasn't so bad. I was living on my own, which is perhaps why **I was completely drunk from morning to evening. I no longer had any brakes**... I had no money, so I drank cheap fruit wine, three or four bottles of the stuff every day. On top of that I wasn't eating. But when I was off my head I didn't care.*"
- D (48, m, homeless for five years) had no interest in the consequences of excessive drinking: "*When you're living rough **you don't give a fuck** whether you drink six litres of wine. There's nothing to stop you except a lack of money. I can't imagine life on the street without booze and fags.*"
- An awareness of his disaffiliation led R (49, m, homeless for 20 years) to drink more and more: "*I used to drink, but nowhere near so much. **The boozing really started when I became homeless**, and then **I was really letting rip**, maybe six cartons a day.*"
- D (37, m, homeless for nine years): "*When I became homeless I started to drink. I drank cartons of wine and I was a heavy drinker. **The problem with alcohol began on the street**. I used to make a living busking with a guitar. I made enough to buy food or else I'd piss it all away. **Mostly I'd piss it all away**.*"

III. Alcohol is related to life on the street

Boredom and the lack of any daily programme can provide a reason to drink.

- R (48, m, homeless for seven years): "*Of course you drink more when you're homeless. In the morning you don't want to get up. You have a bit of money and **you don't want to do anything so you buy a bottle**, find a place to sit and you're off. It's better to have a job.*"
- V (48, m, homeless for seven years) feels the same way: "*When you're living on the street you drink more and more. **It's boring, you've nothing to do**, nothing to occupy you.*"
- F (40, m, homeless for ten years): "*I sometimes drink out of sheer boredom.*"

Homeless people have no duties and no sense of direction, and so **they often drink all day long**, mostly in the company of other homeless people (Šupková,

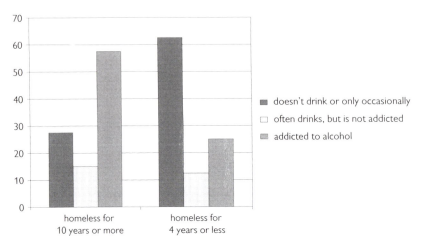

Graph 29. Alcohol consumption relates to length of time spent on the street (shown in percentages).

2008). People from mainstream society consume alcohol occasionally and cannot drink during the day. The lifestyle of a person living on the street increases the chances of their becoming an alcoholic.

- D (48, m, homeless for five years): "*I get hold of a bit of cash for alcohol by betting or collecting and **then I spend days drinking**, often with someone else.*"
- B (51, m, homeless for 20 years): "*I drink beer or wine. Drinking calms me down, so I buy a litre of wine and **spend the afternoon drinking it and then I buy some more**.*"
- R (40, m, homeless for five years): "*I drink a lot. I don't sit down of an evening and drink from time to time. **I drink all the time**. I like rum, that sort of thing, and some peace and quiet.*"

Some of our respondents drink only occasionally, but when they do they binge. This is known as gamma alcoholism, which means that when someone drinks, they are not capable of controlling the amount consumed.

- R (48, m, homeless for seven years) has problems with episodic (intermittent) drinking. The trigger for a bout of excessive drinking is receipt of his emergency financial assistance: "***I don't have to drink. But when I do, then I drink nonstop for two or three days**. That's where my problems lies. When the mood takes me I'm capable of drinking the whole night long, sleeping for a couple of hours, and then beginning again. Drink is dreadful, but when I'm on a roll, then nothing and no one can stop me.*"
- J (52, m, homeless for five years) is also incapable of regulating his intake: "*I like beer, but sometimes I go too far. The problem with me is that **I don't have to drink, but when I do, then I can't stop**.*"
- R (46, m, homeless for four years) is an episodic alcoholic: "***I can go for two months without a drink and then someone will shove something in my hand***

and I'm drunk for three days. Then you lose your job, you find casual work, and then you don't show up three or four times and they fire you."

Among people who have been homeless for ten years or more there are significantly more individuals who drink to excess than among those who have been living on the street for a maximum of four years (chi-square = 6.73, df = 2, p = 0.035). There is a feedback loop in operation between alcohol and homelessness. People who drink to excess are more likely to become homeless, and homelessness increases a person's tendency to drink.

IV. Long-term excessive alcohol consumption leads to various disorders

a) Under the influence of alcohol, **self-control is impaired**. Alcohol abuse leads to an increase in egocentric behaviour, a lack of consideration for other people, and often to a more generalised decline in social competencies. Inhibitions are reduced and alcoholics react disproportionately, inconsiderately and aggressively. The increase in aggression appears to be linked to a reduction in inhibitions and the irritability of the people we talked to.

- S (51, m, homeless for seven years) has a tendency to be aggressive: *"I resolved to give it up because I was horribly aggressive. With two litres of rum inside me I would have a go at several people at once. These days, when I want to drink, I go to the Prokop Valley and sit on my own, because I know what an idiot I am. I'm still really aggressive."*
- G (50, m, homeless for ten years) has a similar problem: *"**When I drink, I fuck things up big time**. I know it of myself, but after the second litre of wine there's nothing I can do about it, because a red mist descends. Everyone scarpers because I lay waste to everything."*
- J (45, f, homeless for 20 years): *"**I get aggressive when I'm drinking**. If I've drunk more than right now, say two litres."*

b) **Attention, memory and overall mental performance deteriorate** under the influence of alcohol. An alcoholic is incapable of processing all the necessary information, especially in the case of a more complex problem. Their thinking tends to be less critical and to display signs of perseveration and touchiness. Homeless people tend not to be concerned at this decline in cognitive functions.

- P (50, m, homeless for 12 years) has memory problems: *"I don't remember much anymore, but that's because recently I've been hitting the wine, and **if you're sleeping rough you tend not to notice**. Before finding this place I was drinking heavily."*
- R (40, m, homeless for five years): *"I drink all the time. I don't like the memory blackouts, so I try and remain compos mentis at least to some extent. **I hate not being able to remember what happened**."*

c) Emotional experience is also transformed under the influence of alcohol and **there is an increased tendency for dysphoria (dysphoric mood)**, anxiety and depression (Cox et al, 2001).

- Z (51, m, homeless for ten years) has phases of depression: "*I didn't use to have any problems and drink used to put me in a good mood. These days **I suffer from depression, but that's probably because I drink a lot**. I start in the morning, because otherwise I'm in a bad way, things don't feel right. I think it's the excessive consumption of alcohol. The fact is that one day the drink catches up on you, like when a bucket overflows.*"
- D (48, m, homeless for five years) also suffers from dysphoric mood: "*I like alcohol and I have a good time when drinking, **because when I'm sober I simply don't feel happy**.*" Both Z and D exhibit alcohol withdrawal symptoms.

d) Some of our respondents suffer from disorders related to long-term alcohol consumption. This mainly involves **alcohol withdrawal symptoms**, as a consequence of which they are unable to reduce their intake.

- M (40, m, homeless for seven years): "***You wake up in the morning and you feel awful. You need to get a grip on yourself, so you have some wine, and after that things are better***. *If you don't have anything to drink, you feel shit. I've never had the DTs and I don't ever want to. A few of my friends have and I've seen what it can do.*"
- D (48, m, homeless for five years): "*I've drunk so much that I've been unable to move. **I've experienced cold turkey**, I've trembled, I wasn't able to sign my own name. **I had to drink two litres of wine before things got better** and I stopped shaking and could function. Once I gave up for nine months. It was when I was still working and it was purgatory. You withdraw into yourself, nothing excites you and you don't feel like doing anything. Maybe I've destroyed my brain with alcohol.*"
- A (47, m, homeless for 20 years): "*I began drinking wine and I've never stopped. I also drink a lot of beer, 15 a day or thereabouts. Right now I drink 12 litres of wine a day. **Every morning I suffer withdrawal symptoms**. It takes a litre and a half before I'm ok.*" All of these men have been drinking since they were young.

Other have even more serious problems.

- D (40, m, homeless for 19 years) suffers from alcohol-induced epilepsy: "*Yeah, I drink. **I can't stop drinking because I'd have a fit**. The doctor told me to take things carefully, I can't cut it out altogether. Right now I drink about eight litres a day, and even so I occasionally have a fit.*"
- Z (47, m, homeless for 20 years) had more serious problems caused by alcohol: "***I've had the DTs three times. After the third I had mild Korsakoff syndrome**. If I'd carried on drinking, I wouldn't be here right now. I wasn't able to give up completely. I reckoned that if I had a beer from time to time it would be ok. I didn't realise that it simply didn't work that way. These days I know.*" Z began drinking

as an adolescent. He has undergone treatment several times without success. He has repeatedly attempted suicide. He has been diagnosed with personality disorder, an addiction to alcohol and other psychoactive substances, and a tendency to self-harm. He still drinks, though maintains he would like to give up.

- M (43, f, homeless for eight years): "*I'm an alcoholic and* **one day my body simply couldn't take it anymore**. *I was taken to hospital. I couldn't remain at the squat, I couldn't eat, I couldn't go to the toilet on my own,* **I couldn't walk, I couldn't do anything**. *When I look back I feel sick and I can't come to terms with the idea that I ended up in that state. Either I continue drinking and fall apart, or I stop drinking and begin life all over again.*"

V. Some homeless people manage to restrict their alcohol consumption

Half of those we questioned (55%) **said they no longer drank as much as in the past.** However, cutting down is a relative measure, and so the statement "I no longer drink" means something different than what it does to people who only drink occasionally. It can mean cutting down on spirits or reducing consumption from six litres to two, as is clear in the following examples. Dietz (2009) also notes a reduction in the quantity of alcohol consumed as homeless people get older (2009).

- V (51, m, homeless for ten years) has recently reduced his alcohol intake: "*These days I don't get drunk. But I have some wine from time to time. I don't go overboard.* **I keep things ticking over**, *about a litre of wine a day.*"
- S (52, m, homeless for 17 years): "*I used to drink, that's true. Wine, rum, vodka, 25 beers a day. I was drunk every day. But that's behind me.* **I'll have a beer, but otherwise I don't drink**."
- Sometimes a person will reduce their intake by only drinking occasionally. K (42, m, homeless for two years): "*I have a drink from time to time. On Tuesday I felt like one, so me and a friend had a bottle of vodka and four beers.* **I guess I drink about once a month**."

A **lack of money** is often a reason for reducing alcohol intake.

- Z (42, m, homeless for 11 years): "*I drink a fair amount. It depends on money.* **I drink when I can afford to**."
- V (46, m, homeless for three years): "*I have a problem with alcohol, especially* **if there is money to be had**. *Otherwise I kinda slowed down. I'd go for a beer or whatever, but in moderation.*"
- F (40, m, homeless for ten years): "*I drink beer. But if I'm stoned, I drink wine. I really know how to get absolutely plastered.* **It just depends on money**."
- P (42, m, homeless for one year) has things clear in his head: "**When I've got money, I get drunk**." P has repeatedly served time in prison.

Many of our respondents preferred to invest their money in something more useful. This is characteristic of those who are not alcoholics or had never previously drunk to excess.

- M (50, m, homeless for 20 years) prefers to buy food: "*If I don't have much money, then it's clear that **what I do have must be spent on food**. These days I drink less because I don't have as much money.*"
- M (55, m, homeless for 17 years): "*These days I'll not drink for three days and then have maybe two beers. That's only if I have the money, which I have to earn. **If I have money, I prefer to buy food**. I don't have a problem with booze, though I like a beer and if I have enough money then I'll have one.*"
- J (40, m, homeless for four years): "*I have a drink from time to time. I don't drink much, **I don't have much money**. And if I do have any, then **I mainly buy food and save for a dormitory**. So I drink two beers at most.*"

Having something meaningful to do in life can also cause people to reduce their alcohol intake. Take K (37, f, homeless for ten years): "*At the moment **I have a job, so I hardly ever drink**. I mean, I might have something, but in the past I used to drink three 2-litre cartons of wine a day, whereas these days I drink, say, one carton and that's enough. Sometimes I don't even drink that, because I have work to do and **no way am I going to sit on a bench with other people listening to endless bullshit**.*"

Health issues can lead a person to reduce their alcohol intake.

- J (51, m, homeless for one year) had a stroke that forced him to reduce his intake: "***I haven't had a drink** for the last year and a half, because suddenly **my organism gave up** and I spent ten months in a long-term care facility. I had a stroke and then I came here* [to a shelter]. *When I was in prison or hospital, I didn't need alcohol. But I reckon that **if I had remained on the street, I'd have started drinking again**.*"
- E (53, m, homeless for one year) does not drink for the same reason: "*When I was sleeping rough I drank a lot. It was completely out of control. Whereas **now I don't even think about it**.*" E has had a stroke that has caused him certain impairments. At present he is living in a shelter.

Some of our respondents reduced their alcohol intake for **fear that alcohol would exacerbate problems they already have**.

- Č (42, m, homeless for five years): "*You can't solve things with alcohol. It doesn't even help much when you're sleeping rough. If you simply sit all day long with a bottle of cheap plonk, you'll go nowhere fast… You soon learn that **it leads nowhere**, or rather that it helps you to forget. But otherwise it doesn't help. Having to have a drink the moment you wake up gets to be a drag. I'm not saying I don't drink a thing, but I've cut down. I have a drink from time to time, maybe once every couple of weeks. You have to deal with it if you want to survive, because **nobody's gonna give you so much as a crust if they smell alcohol on you**.*"

- M (55, m, homeless for 17 years) feels similarly: "*Alcohol in the case of a homeless person is the road to hell. You don't sort anything out by getting drunk and falling asleep on a park bench.* **You simply postpone things**, *because the next day nothing has changed.*"

The **devastating effects of alcohol on other homeless people** can persuade some people to reduce their intake.
- J (52, m, homeless for five years) is aware of the risks: "*I have a beer from time to time. But I limit myself. I don't drink regularly like some homeless people, cartons of wine every day. The next day I meet them,* **beaten up, out of it, sleeping on park benches covered in piss**. *There's a good number of them, and* **I don't want to end up like them**."
- P (47, m, homeless for seven years) is of the same opinion: "*I've seen people who've been totally destroyed by alcohol, people who sit on park benches drinking wine, filthy, smelly...* **That's a line in the sand I don't want to step over**." Some of our respondents, especially older men, attempt to reduce their intake so as not to lose their place in a shelter, where drinking is not permitted.

Many of our respondents have undergone treatment for alcoholism that was not successful. They lacked motivation and a willingness to accept restrictions.
- L (50, m, homeless for one year): "*I was in rehab for three months with Dr. Nešpor and I realised that* **no doctor on earth can help you**, *you simply have to deal with it on your own.*"
- O (53, m, homeless for 20 years): "*I received psychiatric treatment in Kosmonosy and Beřkovice for alcohol and drugs.* **But it didn't help me**."
- Z (42, m, homeless for eleven years): "*I spent some time in a psychiatric hospital in Dobřany because of alcohol, but* **they didn't cure me**. *I'm trying to ensure I don't end up in a drunk tank on a permanent basis. My stepmother said that if I didn't want to sleep under a bridge, then I had to seek treatment. But they didn't cure me.*" Some of our respondents appear to believe that everything should be sorted out by someone else.

Treatment for alcoholism failed in the case of women too.
- M (37, f, homeless for five years): "*I was in rehab when I was still at home, seven years ago. It didn't help. I completed the treatment and immediately treated myself to a shot.*" M had previously taken drugs before moving onto alcohol.
- D (48, f, homeless for five years) has been in and out of rehab: "*I first went into rehab aged 40. It helped me for about a year and half, but then I started drinking again. I still hadn't really grasped that I was an alcoholic with a problem. Then, when I was 41, I went back to rehab. That was the first time I had ever been to Červený Dvůr* [a psychiatric hospital in Chvalšiny, a village in South Bohemia]. *I was scheduled for four months, but I extended it by a month because I was afraid to leave.* **By then I had realised that I was an alcoholic** *and that it wasn't about not being*

*able to drink **but about not wanting to drink**, that alcohol had already wreaked enough damage... Yeah, of course, I'm homeless, a homeless alcoholic, I've worked all of that through.*" D has unfortunately started to drink again, and because she broke the rules of the shelter she had been in, she was excluded. Her daughter also lives on the street and is a drug addict.

Prison can sometimes function as an effective drying out facility.
* This was so in the case of D (37, m, homeless for nine years): "*The last time I was in prison cured me of alcoholism. It saved me, and I no longer drink as much.*"
* A stint in prison also helped P (37, m, homeless for 15 years): "*We used to go from pub to pub drinking the whole time. I was drinking beer like it was water. Every day I was off my head. Every day I was drinking 15 to 20 beers with chasers... I needed something to break the routine, and then suddenly **I was sentenced to 28 months**. I no longer drink as much.*"

Dealing with alcoholism is difficult enough for anyone, but it is even more demanding for a homeless person. Their motivation to give up is not great since they have many other problems that take precedence (finding something to eat and a place to sleep). Cutting down is also difficult because most of the people around them are also drinking. Alcohol consumption is a way of spending free time and a means of maintaining social contact. Since the homeless rarely interact with anyone else, they remain under the influence of their own community. M (40, m, homeless for seven years) is aware of the negative influence of other homeless people drinking alcohol: "*I have loads of friends who drink. It's fucking shit. **I need to be in a community where no one drinks**. What happens is I give up and then I meet someone who invites me to have some wine. Because I'm a fucking dickhead I say yes. The next day I feel like shit, so I look for some more wine and thus it continues.*"

Alcohol abuse is one of the most important causes of homelessness and subsequently chronic homelessness. Those living on the street who are addicted to alcohol can be divided into two groups: individuals who began drinking in adolescence, usually because of peer pressure, and those who only began drinking to any great extent later as adults.

I. People who began drinking in adolescence. These tend to be individuals who grew up in a problematic family or an institution and have only a basic education. From the outset they had problems at work, lacked application, and were unable to hold a job down for long. Their problems with alcohol or drugs began early in life, and their relationships, such as they were, ended quickly. If they have children, they do not look after them. They show no restraint in respect of the law and frequently commit crimes. They ended up on the street around their thirties.
* Z (47, m, homeless for 20 years) is typical in this respect. His parents divorced when he was seven, because his father was an alcoholic and unfaithful.

Z remained with his mother, along with his two siblings. At school his behaviour was problematic and he belonged to a group of older boys, with whom he began drinking alcohol. He first got drunk aged 12. After completing basic school he began an apprenticeship but was expelled. He claims his problems arose because he had no father: "*I lacked a father. Everyone else but me had a father. I felt there was something missing in our family... Mum had to work in order to support us.*" After completing his national service, he found work on a building site, where he remained for two years. During that time his dependency on alcohol intensified. He first sought help from Naděje aged 27, because he had no money for food: though working, he had spent all his money on alcohol. He was living in Prague in a tent and going to work, but as he himself says: "*The money I earned was enough for booze and drugs but not for food.*" He repeatedly underwent treatment, but on the whole failed to see it through. He has no children. He has had girlfriends, but no relationship has ever lasted for long. He received a conditional sentence for conspiracy to commit burglary, and at his next appearance in court he was sentenced to 400 hours of community service, again for burglary. He has attempted to commit suicide on many occasions. He is dubious of the future, saying: "*I've attempted to sort things out on many occasions, but it only ever lasts a short while.*"

II. People who began to drink later. Such individuals tend to have had reasonably normal childhoods. They either completed an apprenticeship or completed secondary school and found a job. They started a family, but then, usually aged around 30, they began drinking to excess. As a result they lost their family and their work. They are in contact with their children and contribute at least partially to their upkeep. They are not involved in criminal activities. They usually found themselves homeless aged 35–40.

- R (46, m, homeless for four years) is a case in point. His parents were divorced, but his mother remarried and he enjoyed a good relationship with her new partner. His natural father was, in R's words, "*an alcoholic and aggressive with it*". He graduated from military high school and found a job. He got married at 21 and had two sons. He was expelled from the army in his thirties because he had begun to have problems with alcohol. He divorced and began a new relationship with a divorcee. The two relocated to S, where his new partner had a building she had inherited from her grandparents, and R found a job with Penny Market. He remained in the job for four years, but then began to drink. He repeatedly failed to turn up for work and was fired for absenteeism. He spent three months in rehab in Dobřany, after which he did not drink for 13 months. He was still living with his girlfriend, but began drinking again. He found himself on the street when his girlfriend, whom he had physically abused when drunk, ended the relationship. In R's words: "*After she ended the relationship, I held myself together for a time. I went to work, I found a dormitory to sleep in. I found casual work stacking shelves. And then suddenly there was alcohol and that was that."* Absenteeism cost R his job, after which he lost his place in the dormitory. He began sleeping rough. He has never been in prison. He is in contact with his sons over the internet. He alimony payments are small (CZK 1,000 or USD 42.6 per month), but he pays them. He does not have problems other than alcoholism. He became homeless aged 42.

SUMMARY

The numbers of middle-aged homeless people in Prague who drink to excess tallies with the figures from studies conducted in other countries. These findings are also the same with regard to an individual's life experience with alcohol. At least one parent is an alcoholic in the case of a third of our respondents with an alcohol problem. This figure is also backed up by foreign studies. For instance, McVicar et al. (2015) found that 28.5% of the fathers and 18% of the mothers of people living on the street who drink to excess were also addicts. People living on the street who drink to excess were heavy drinkers for several years prior to becoming homeless. Their alcohol abuse was not primarily triggered by the stresses of life on the street or an endeavour to fit in with those around them, as is so in the case of drug use. These findings tally with other studies too, e.g. Clark et al. (2011). North et al. (1998) confirmed that the first signs of excessive drinking appear on average 9.8 years prior to their becoming homeless. The same conclusions were reached by McVicar et al. (2015). This holds true even though alcohol consumption on the street tends to increase.

Homeless people drink more than they did before finding themselves on the street. They tend to stop regulating their alcohol intake, often because they are unable to. Unlike people in mainstream society, homeless people are open about their addiction, though like everyone they tend to search out the company of other drinkers. Many consume alcohol on an almost continuous basis, and have their first drink in the morning to combat the effects of withdrawal symptoms. It is clear that alcohol abuse increases the risk of chronic homelessness, since individuals are not motivated to change their behaviour. This also relates to their negative attitude to rehab and their unwillingness to accept any restrictions. Studies carried out in other countries have reached similar conclusions, e.g. Rosenbeck et al. (1998), Orwin et al. (1999) and Wenzel et al. (2001), who found that 15%–28% of homeless people seek treatment, but only a third of them see it through to the end. The same conclusions were reached by Collins et al. (2012) The chronically homeless are not motivated to seek treatment.

8. DRUG CONSUMPTION ON THE STREET

Drug taking and addiction is another reason why people become homeless and why this state can become chronic (McVicar, Moschion, van Ours, 2015). Drug abuse leads to homelessness earlier in life, which means that drugs represent a higher risk factor than alcohol (Johnson et al., 1997). Homeless people have problems with drugs far more often than members of majority society. Teesson et al. (2003) point out that the Australian homeless use drugs on average six times more often than the rest of the population. The figures relating to homeless drug users range widely between 25% and 75%, which is far higher than in the population at large (Zugazaga, 2004; Ball et al., 2005; Caton et al., 2006, 2007; Sadock a Sadock, 2007; Johnson and Chamberlain, 2008; Dietz, 2009; Amato and MacDonald, 2011). Bulíček (2005) reports that 80% of young Czech homeless people admit to experimenting with drugs, usually with pervitin. Johnson and Chamberlain (2008) found that 43% of the homeless use drugs, while Caton et al. (2006) reported a figure of 47%. Brown et al. (2016) found that 50%–70% of homeless people use drugs, and the frequency of drug uses increases during the time they remain on the street. Grenier et al. (2013) report that up to 83% of homeless people take drugs. (This difference may be the result of the way that data was collected. There are more drug users in large cities and among young people. A willingness to admit to using drugs also depends on the questioner and their relationship to the people being asked. For instance, those being questioned may be more open within the framework of certain services.) Life within the homeless community supports the tendency to use drugs, since they are readily to hand and there is no pressure on restricting their use (Johnson and Chamberlain, 2008; Stein et al., 2008; Rhoades et al., 2011).

The average age at which an alcoholic becomes homeless is 36.9 (SD = 7.37), whereas in the case of drug addicts this figure is far lower, on average 30.6 (SD = 5.44).

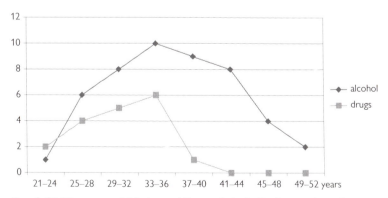

Graph 30. The age at which drug addicts and alcoholics became homeless (shown in absolute figures).

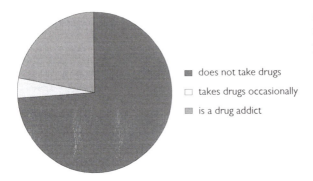

Graph 31. Level of drug use as reported by middle-aged homeless people

■ does not take drugs

☐ takes drugs occasionally

▨ is a drug addict

There are three stages in the process by which a drug user finds themselves homeless (Hartwell, 2003; Johnson et al., 2008; Keys, Mallet and Rosenthal, 2006). Firstly, there are problems at work. Drug users are unreliable and often absent to such an extent that they lose their job. Since drug taking is financially demanding, they soon run out of money. They borrow money, but do not return it, or begin to steal. As a consequence, they lose the support of their friends and family, who are no longer willing to assist a drug addict. They then enter the next phase, characterised by a transformation in their social network. They interact mainly with other people active in the drug world, either as consumers or dealers. The third phase is their descent into homelessness and the society of other homeless people who use drugs or drink alcohol.

Young people use drugs more often than older people, and drug users become homeless more quickly than those who have problems such as excessive alcohol consumption. Sixty percent of our younger cohort took drugs (Vágnerová, Csémy, Marek, 2013), while in the older cohort this figure was just under a quarter (22%). Older people tend to have a problem with alcohol rather than with drugs (Hecht and Coyle, 2001; Dietz, 2009). Of those who have been homeless for 10 years or more, 41% take drugs occasionally, while in the group of people who have been homeless for four years or less, this figure is only 8%. The difference between both groups is statistically important (chi-square = 7.18, df = 2, p = 0.024). In general we are justified in saying that **drug use leads** to homelessness faster than alcohol addiction, and also **increases the risk of chronic homelessness**.

People living on the street for ten years or more usually started taking drugs before becoming homeless when they were aged 15–25; only 20% began using drugs on the street. Johnson and Chamberlain (2008) came to a different conclusion, finding that only a third of homeless people who are dependent on drugs used them excessively prior to becoming homeless, while two thirds of them began using them only after becoming homeless. This difference is probably down to the fact that the study group comprised very young individuals: 60% were aged 18 or younger and had started sleeping rough for another reason. In their case, drug use was part of their socialisation within the homeless subculture.

Middle-aged people who have been living on the street for a long time, i.e. found themselves homeless at a younger age, use drugs significantly more often than those who have only been homeless for a short period of time, i.e. began sleeping rough later in life (chi-square = 6.74, df = 2, p = 0.034).

Drug use usually begins with experimentation carried out within a peer group, and this is true in the case of our respondents. As one of them says: "*I wanted to give it a go, I was curious.*" **Most of the people we talked to had tried drugs in their adolescence.**

- K (37, f, homeless for ten years): "*I was training as a shop assistant, but I didn't complete the course because **I began taking drugs and basically became a junkie while an apprentice**.*"
- G (50, m, homeless for ten years) was experimenting with drugs even earlier: "***I began taking drugs when I was 14**... then we burgled a drugstore.*"
- Z (47, m, homeless for 20 years): "***I began when I was 14** on prescription drugs, various combinations with beer. That was followed by toluene. I first overdosed on pervitin when I was 22.*"

Most of our respondents began taking drugs before becoming homeless.

- M (38, m, homeless for two years): "*As soon as you entered secondary school you began taking drugs. To begin with grass, then around the age of 18 I tried pervitin. I really got off on pervitin and things went downhill after that. **Drugs are the reason I'm homeless**. Once you start, you can't stop.*"
- J (39, m, homeless for five years): "***I had already begun taking drugs before I became homeless**. It began when me and my girlfriend split up.*"
- M (40, f, homeless for 25 years) was already on drugs prior to becoming homeless, though to begin with this was not her decision: "*They began giving me drugs in Aš. **To begin with I didn't know what they were giving me** and it was*

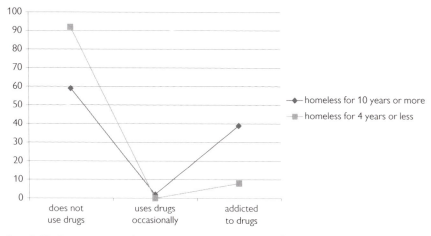

Graph 32. Drug use according to time spent on the street (shown in percentages)

*there that I actually began doing drugs. When I started sleeping rough, I took drugs with other homeless people. **I guess I tried just about everything on offer**, though it was pervitin that remained and it's pervitin's fault that I ended up in prison... When it became difficult to get hold of drugs, I started stealing from shops. I began with the DM drugstore, then grocers... I lived like that for almost two years. I was about thirty when they sent me to prison."*

Some of our respondents only began taking drugs after becoming homeless.
- D (40, m, homeless for 19 years): *"Yeah, there were drugs. Pervitin and grass. First of all grass and then pervitin. And still pervitin. I beg, so if I need money, I take some pervitin, because it makes me babble on even more. **I've been taking drugs since I became homeless.**"*
- J (45, f, homeless for 20 years): *"**I only began boozing and taking drugs when I started sleeping rough.** I took pervitin. I don't know why. Life passed by more quickly on drugs. When you take pervitin it all goes more quickly."*

Our respondents cited many reasons why they took drugs. For many it was a way of dealing with the anxiety they experienced at being homeless, or reducing their inhibitions in order that they be able to beg or steal.
- M (40, f, homeless for 25 years): *"On the street **I needed drugs in order to cope**, in order to be able to function at all."*
- Some people enjoy the stimulant effects of pervitin, which allows them to be more active. For instance, M (38, m, homeless for two years): *"**It gives me the energy to go out and earn some cash or steal from shops.**"*
- F (40, m): *"I took drugs because I enjoyed it and **I was more active**. You have more experiences on drugs and you do far more things."*
- J (39, m, homeless for five years) has different reasons for taking drugs: *"**I took drugs in order to forget** and in order to relax."* However, he himself admits drugs do not help much: *"... rather than helping, drugs actually make things worse."*

Opinions on drug use change the more time a person spends on the street. **At present, half of those (54%) who took drugs in the past say they have not reduced their intake, while the other half (46%) say they have.** They may have cut back because they no longer experience the same satisfaction, or because of some new impulse that makes abstinence more attractive.
- Some of our respondents gradually cut out drugs altogether, e.g. J (48, m, homeless for four years): *"I used to do drugs. I was on pervitin for a while, and then I stopped. About six months later I took it and then I thought, fuck this for a lark. I was kinda weak and **it no longer gave me any pleasure.**"*
- K (39, m, homeless for five years) tells a similar story: *"I took drugs for four years and then I thought, fuck it, **this is going precisely nowhere**... I actually lost relationships because of drugs."*

- M (49, m, homeless for twenty years) has cut down on drugs: "*Basically, I haven't taken drugs since about 2008. Twice I've relapsed, but only for a short time, and it was only thanks to my dog that I didn't end up in prison like before.* **This dog was the motivation I needed to detox.**" M has a relationship with drugs stretching back years. He began experimenting with different substances aged 14. He did not have a normal childhood. He grew up with his paternal grandmother, because his father was in prison and his mother abandoned the family. His grandmother was unable to cope, and he spent the rest of his childhood in different institutions. As an adult he attempted to track down his mother, but she was not interested. The only stable emotional attachment he has in his life is with his dog.

There are many reasons why people reduce their consumption of drugs. As well as a simple aversion, a **lack of funds** is the main reason.
- H (50, m, homeless for 20 years): "***I don't do drugs any more. I haven't got the money*** *and they don't do anything for me. At the start it's kinda nice, but that's all.*"
- F (40, m, homeless for ten years) feels the same way: "*I don't shoot up any more. I took drugs for the ten years I was on the street. There was a time me and my girlfriend were doing fucking shitloads of drugs. That's actually why we split up, cos I* **no longer wanted to take drugs**. *I had stopped stealing and because of that I stopped taking drugs.* **Pervitin is expensive, mate.** *I still buy grass, which also eats into the cash, but I buy it regularly.*" As we see, F has stopped taking pervitin but replaced it with marijuana.

Other people have moved over from pervitin to marijuana, e.g. R (40, m, homeless for five years): "*I used to do pervitin, but that was 12 years ago... I stopped because I wasn't enjoying it.* **I might smoke a spliff, but the hard drugs are too fucking heavy.**"

Marijuana is not deemed a drug by most homeless people, e.g. C (47, m, homeless for 23 years): "***I don't think of marijuana as a drug***. *I smoke three joints a week, maybe a month.*" Z (42, m, homeless for 11 years) feels the same: "*I like a joint occasionally. Recently I haven't been feeling that great and I'm glad I've got the grass.* **I smoke a joint and I feel good.**" Z also consumes alcohol.

P (45, f, homeless for eight years) is looking for a substitute for pervitin: "*It's an ongoing battle and it has been the whole of my life.* **I no longer do drugs,** *I can't afford to be high. It may not be visible, but that's the way it is. Right now* **I'm trying to find something to replace it,** *but I don't know what. I don't want to sleep rough, so I have to somehow carry on.*"

Some of our respondents **switch between drugs and alcohol**. The tendency to rotate psychoactive substances is also mentioned by Ravenhill (2014).

- Z (47, m, homeless for 20 years) moved over from massive alcohol consumption to drug use: "*I seriously reckon that drugs saved my life, though obviously they took a lot out of me too.* **If I hadn't made the acquaintance of drugs, I would have remained with alcohol** *and I wouldn't be here to tell the tale today. Yeah, the drugs created huge problems in my life. I became addicted, and I guess I also lost family and lots of other things.*"
- The process was reversed in the case of M (43, f, homeless for eight years): "*I gave up drugs when I was sent to prison, and since then I don't even want to see them. I think* **I've probably replaced drugs with booze.**"
- K (37, f, homeless for ten years): "*I did drugs for a long time. But then I realised that was why I'd lost my children, my boyfriend, all because of being a junkie. I said enough is enough and I stopped. These days I might take drugs occasionally…* **I've moved over from drugs to alcohol,** *though that's possibly even more destructive. You replace one with the other, one addiction for another.*"

A stint in prison is an effective way of breaking a drug addiction. Many drug users are forced to abstain while in prison, though upon being released often relapse fairly quickly, usually under the influence of other homeless people who still use drugs, but also because of their vulnerability and the easy availability of drugs (Rowland, 2011).
- Some of our respondents did not take up drugs again upon being released from prison, e.g. P (37, m, homeless for four years): "*I began taking heroin at the age of 16 or 17. They banged me up for six years and* **then for another four years**. *Since then I haven't taken drugs and don't even want to. I broke my ties with the past and my addiction to opioids. I thought a lot about it and I was worried about beginning normal life again from square one, because I knew I had nowhere to go, no money, and no work.*" P is not taking drugs at present. He is living in a shelter, where he is not exposed to a high level of risk. He has broken off contact with his former acquaintances, who live on the street and take drugs.
- J (39, m, homeless for five years): "*I'm a recovering drug addict.* **I haven't taken drugs for about ten years, since being released from prison.**" P was already an adult and living on the street when he began taking drugs. His main problem is that he is a repeat offender.
- M (40, f, homeless for 25 years): "**I stopped taking drugs in prison** *and right now I'm really making an effort, because my family have given me a last chance. Here I don't need drugs. When I was sleeping rough I did, but here, when you actually have something to live for, it's not necessary.*" M is living in a shelter.

More than half of those who took drugs continue to take them. **In several cases a long-term addiction to pervitin has led to substance-induced (toxic) psychosis**.
- This is so in the case of H (50, m, homeless for 20 years): "*When I took up pervitin again,* **I started hearing voices**. *They told me that* **I must listen to them**

and that they would turn me into an agent. If I reached for a bottle of alcohol, they would reprimand me. 'You fucking shithead,' they'd say. I didn't know what was causing the voices, and then during psychiatric treatment they told me the voices were in my head and that it was my fault. Have you any idea how mad you get when someone tries to blame you and you don't know who to turn to? These psychotic episodes kept repeating."

- P (40, m, homeless for 20 years) has experienced toxic psychosis several times: "*I've taken marijuana and heroin, soft and hard drugs... but my drug of choice is pervitin, that's what I'm addicted to. And then a voice began in my head... **There was a voice in my head that created a story.***"

- D (37, m, homeless for ten years) suffered toxic psychosis as a result of pervitin abuse: "*I would have conversations in my head with heaven, my friends, dead people... **I saw Jesus's head while in Ruzyně prison. I also saw the devil...** He has horns. I named him Edward. None of my friends sleep so I talk to them. I thought I was having hallucinations. But when I was on Charles Square, I was suddenly convinced. There was the Archangel Gabriel. Everyone was competing with each other as to who would be the first to welcome me and show me what God looked like. When I came out of prison I still had the visions on Charles Square. I realise some people will call me mad, but I'm not.*" Our respondents possess different levels of understanding of the causes and significance of these hallucinations. D lived on the streets for ten years and was drinking to excess towards the end. This year he died due to complications caused by his addiction.

Many of our respondents have undergone treatment for drug use, often repeatedly. However, it has rarely helped them, and if so, then only temporarily. If they return to the street, they are more than likely to begin taking drugs again.

- P (40, m, homeless for 20 years): "*I kept hearing voices in my head. I underwent psychiatric treatment and was sent to the therapeutic community in Němčice. I managed to stick it out until phase 2, i.e. seven months. Well **of course I fell back into drugs and started doing them again**, and lo and behold I'm back on the street.*"

- M (49, m, homeless for 20 years): "*I've been in rehab maybe five times. **It hasn't helped me even once**. I was in a community, but I'm not one for that kind of thing. There's too many people.*"

- P (45, f, homeless for eight years): "*It's been a battle ever since I was 19. I spent time in Bohnice and completed the therapy, but the longest I've ever gone without drugs was six years after the community in Němčice. When I was 22 I overdosed and ended up in Bohnice, where I lasted three months. Then **I managed to stay off the drugs for a month or so, and then I started up again**.*"

For many homeless people a strict regime of treatment is unacceptable, since they are unable to accept the slightest restrictions.

- Z (47, m, homeless for 20 years): "*I've done the whole rehab thing from start to finish three times. The first time ended after two hours. I couldn't agree to the condi-*

*tions, because **the moment you sign some scrap of paper, you lose your freedom**, and I wasn't ready to do that. These days I have a better understanding of things and kinda appreciate that you have to give up some degree of freedom in order to get it back over time. I've had treatment maybe 30 times. I was desperate and I knew that happiness didn't reside in drugs or booze, but I was caught in the current..."*

- Many of our respondents are dissatisfied with their situation but are unable to pluck up the courage to make any sweeping changes. Some refuse treatment, e.g. M (38, m, homeless for two years): *"They offered me treatment, but I said no. **If I'm to give up, I have to give up on my own**. I reckon I'd manage, sure. A girlfriend would be nice, someone to help me pull myself out of this shit."* The "treatment" provided by girlfriends tends to be ineffective, because male drug addicts usually find a partner with the same problems they have. However, they view the assistance of someone close to them to be more acceptable than impersonal institutional treatment, which they associate with restrictions on their freedom and which often does not have the desired effect.

The case history of V (38, m, homeless for 13 years) serves as an illustration. V spent most of his childhood feeling ok, as he puts it, in a functional family. His parents were divorced when he was 13, and V remained with his father. The building they were living in belonged to his father, and so his mother moved in with her boyfriend. V did not want to visit her. He trained as a chef/waiter and found a job, even though he had by then begun taking drugs. Over to V: *"I began taking drugs when I was 18 or 19. Drugs were everywhere at college, and then one day I decided I wanted to give it a go. That, unfortunately, was that. I began with pervitin, but after only six months I was on heroin. When I had money I was capable of taking huge amounts."* In order to have the money for drugs he began to steal and ended up in prison. Upon his release, he moved in with his mother, because his father had by then sold their house. However, he did not stop taking drugs: *"I managed not to take anything for a year, but then I started again. So I said to my mum, 'listen, I'm acting stupid, it's better if I move out'. So I moved into a dormitory."* After this V was either on the streets or in prison. In all he was in prison eight times over a period of ten years. He has not stolen anything since his last stint inside, but he continues to live on the street. He moves between dormitories, shelters and sleeping rough, depending on how much money he has. Three months after being released from prison he started on a course of methadone, and since then he has not taken any other drugs. He has been repeatedly in rehab, but without success. As V himself says: *"I've sat with a psychologist loads of times. I've also spent time in clinics, though I haven't completed a single course of treatment. I've only ever managed a week up to three months. Then for a while I've done without drugs, but then I've started again."* However, his treatment did have a positive effect, in that V began to grasp the impact his addiction was having on his loved ones. *"Yeah, it was beneficial in a way. I began to realise what I was doing to people, to my mum, my grandmum, my sister... It was like the first time that I had really begun to understand that I was hurting them.*" V has a good relationship with his mother and sister and does not want to exploit them.

Whenever he can find casual employment, V works. He is registered at the job centre, but is unable to find a proper job because of debts he is unable to pay off. Some of these are fines imposed for criminal activities, and so he is unable to declare himself bankrupt. His criminal record is also an impediment to finding work. He has had girlfriends, but only for short periods of time broken by his stints in prison. His girlfriends have tended to be drug addicts too. At present he has a girlfriend who, like him, is on methadone. He does not have children, and though he would like a family some day, he himself says: "*I don't have either the money or the stable environment… I've been fucking things up for twenty years*". It is difficult to anticipate how he will manage to sort out the accumulated problems he has.

SUMMARY

Drug use is a less frequent cause of homelessness in the case of older people than younger people. This is probably because older people found themselves on the street at a time when drugs were not as readily available as they are now. If they use drugs, they usually began experimenting in adolescence in their peer group. This means that they were already taking drugs before becoming homeless. They are less likely to have started taking drugs after becoming homeless. They often take pervitin and develop a dependency relatively quickly. When asked to explain why they take the drug, they point to its effect as a stimulant.

During the course of their life on the street, their opinion of drug use often changes. About half of former users still take drugs, but the other half have cut down. As well as sheer disinclination, lack of funds plays a part in this decision. Some of our respondents switched from pervitin to marijuana, which they do not regard as a drug. We also often find a switchover from drugs to alcohol, and vice versa. Drugs cause these people many problems, including toxic psychosis. Drug rehabilitation programmes tend to be unsuccessful and are often repeated. The problem is that homeless people are reluctant to submit to a strict routine and are unable to accept even mild restrictions on their behaviour. When treatment is successful, its effects tend to be short-term, and its recipient often begins taking drugs again. Sometimes a stint in prison proves more successful than rehabilitation in weaning an individual off drugs.

9. PSYCHOLOGICAL PROBLEMS

Many studies show that **mental health issues and disorders increase the risk of a person becoming homeless**. This is often because they are unable to cope with the demands of ordinary life, are more vulnerable, and are incapable of withstanding even low-level stress. The frequency of mental health issues and personality disorders is higher amongst street people than in the population at large. Shelton et al. (2009) report that the occurrence of these problems is three to four times higher amongst the homeless. Psychological problems may sometimes develop only after a person has become homeless, probably as a consequence of stress or the excessive consumption of psychoactive substances (Early, 2005). Excessive drug use or alcohol consumption plays a significant part in the development of psychiatric disorders. Especially noted has been the influence of smoking marijuana on the development of schizophrenia.

Researchers have found that 25%–45% percent of homeless people have psychological problems or some kind of mental health issue or personality defect (Sullivan et al., 2000; Breakey, 2004; Caton et al., 2006; Štěchová, 2008; Shelton et al., 2009; Johnson and Chamberlain, 2011). Sullivan et al. (2000) reports a figure of 20%–25%. These figures are confirmed by the American National Institute of Mental Health (NIMH), which reports that 20%–25% of homeless people suffer a mental health issue (National Coalition for the Homeless, 2009). Brown et al. (2016) come to the same conclusion, citing a figure of 25%. Pillinger (2007) claims the figure is 33%. Research carried out by Johnson and Chamberlain (2011) shows that 31% of homeless people suffer psychiatric disorders, 15% having suffered them prior to becoming homeless and 16% only developing them later, probably as the consequence of a homeless lifestyle that includes drug use and alcohol abuse. Psychiatric problems prior to becoming homeless were more likely to have been had by people older than 25. The difference in the conclusions reached by different researchers is probably explained by the particular group of homeless people forming the basis of their study. Goering et al. (2002) found that up to 69% of the chronic homeless suffered psychiatric disorders. Different results may ensue from the different criteria used by individual researchers when assessing the psychological state of their subjects.

The psychiatric problem most often suffered by people living on the street is depression. This claim is backed up by many researchers, e.g. Johnson and Chamberlain (2011). According to Shelton et al. (2009), 26% of homeless people suffered depression and 16% had thoughts of suicide. Similar results were reported by Garibaldi et al. (2005), whose study showed that 35%–40% percent of street people suffered depression. According to Brown et al. (2016), 38% suffered depression. Rhoades et al. (2011) report that 46% of homeless people suffered depression. According to Goering et al. (2002) this figure is even higher on 50%. McDonagh (2011) even reports that the majority of people living on the street (79%) are at increased threat of anxiety or depression. Loneliness and social exclusion, or the loss of family, are key factors in the increase in rates of depression. Ravenhill (2014) shows that higher levels of depression increase the likelihood of a person becoming homeless, while homelessness contributes to increased depression. Depression is both the cause and effect of homelessness.

People who suffer depression or anxiety are prone to using drugs or alcohol as a means of eliminating unpleasant feelings. Regardless of the different results of different researchers, there is no doubt that homeless people suffer anxiety and bouts of depression more often than members of the population at large. We are often talking about a **dual diagnosis**, in which depression is combined with alcohol or drug abuse (Rhoades et al., 2011).

People living on the street have far more experience of traumatisation, often repeated, than members of the population at large, and therefore display several symptoms of post-traumatic stress disorder (PTSD). This applies to 10%–35% of young homeless people (Vágnerová, Csémy, Marek, 2013). This most often involved excessive irritability, avoidant personality disorder (less often), and emotional numbness. Post-traumatic stress disorder usually occurs in combination with other psychiatric problems, above all with depression or anxiety disorder, but also with the excessive use of psychoactive substances.

Homelessness is not the cause of any serious mental illnesses, be this schizophrenia, schizoaffective disorder or bipolar disorder, even though homeless people may suffer these disorders. It is more that the problems linked with such disorders, especially an inability to meet the demands of everyday life, increase the risk of someone becoming homeless, especially if such a person lacks the necessary social infrastructure (Buckner, 2004).

Given the accentuation of undesirable personality traits amongst many homeless people, especially men, a higher frequency of personality disorder is likely. Such individuals are more prevalent in our cohort than in the population at large, above all because they are not able or willing to accept restrictions and comply with rules. People with personality disorder often consume drugs or alcohol (Ball et al., 2005).

Graph 33. The frequency of psychological problems among older homeless people (shown in percentages)

Thirty-eight percent of older homeless people suffer longer-term psychiatric problems, women slightly more often than men. **Depressive episodes** are experienced by 22% of our respondents, i.e. more than half of those people who have psychiatric disorders. The answers given to our questionnaire showed that 19% believed they suffered depressive episodes and 25% anxiety disorder. Twelve percent have suicidal tendencies, and several have actually attempted to commit suicide. Depressive episodes **are often linked with excessive drinking or drug use**, whether this be a consequence of addiction or the need to block out unpleasant feelings.

- D (37, m, homeless for nine years) suffers depressive episodes: "*You lie awake at night thinking about things and you get depressed. On the one hand you like the street. You can booze to your heart's content, you feel good, you scrounge this or that... But then you picture how you look to others as you walk along the street... You've nothing to eat, you're filthy, you look through the window of a house in which there's a happy family, who can return home whenever they want... yeah, I get depressed.*"
- F (40, m, homeless for ten years) consumes drugs and alcohol: "*Sometimes you get depressed and self-pitying and you wonder how you could have fucked things up so badly and how you didn't have to.*"
- L (50, m, homeless for one year): "*I've suffered depression the whole of my life, every autumn. I'll be honest with you, sometimes you feeling like throwing yourself off a bridge. You've had enough, you're tired, you haven't slept for several days, maybe you haven't eaten, you're constantly being moved on, you don't know what to do... it's hardly surprising you get depressed.*"

D (48, m, homeless for five years) suffers depression. His mother was an alcoholic who also probably suffered depression, since she attempted to commit suicide. His grandmother was diagnosed with bipolar disorder and was treated in psychiatric hospital. D is fully aware of the connections: "*Maybe I inherited this tendency to depression. I was nervous the whole day long at work, and every little thing would cause me stress. And so booze helped relax me, at least for a while. Right now I'm taking pills. I'm trying to sort things out, whereas in the past I just used to think, fuck it.*" It is clear from what D says that the consumption of alcohol might be both the cause of his depression and a reaction to his depressive episodes. At present he is living in a shelter. A lack of activity may be contributing to his difficulties. While he was sleeping rough, he was able to block out feeling of emptiness with alcohol. In the shelter he is forbidden from drinking.

The causes of depressive episodes can be more complex, as in the case of J (48, m, homeless for 17 years), who is HIV positive and also takes drugs: "*I've come to terms with the HIV, but I still suffer depression. Homelessness is particularly bad for me. My girlfriend died. We had lived together for twelve years and when she died I fell apart. I basically began taking drugs in order to cope. But then I ended up in Bohnice, and several times I wanted to commit suicide. I don't know where the depression comes from. In my case it seems linked to the fact that I'm on my own, I don't have a partner, I don't have anyone. You think about things and once again you're plunged into depression and you wonder whether it's worth carrying on, because there's no pleasure in anything."* J takes drugs in order to block out unpleasant feelings.

Depressive episodes are not always linked with drugs and alcohol. **They may arise from the very nature of a homeless existence**, or may be a reaction to an unmanageable situation and life on the street.

- M (45, m, homeless for five years): *"My nerves are shot to pieces. I have no money, **everything is fucked**, I lost my daughter, my mum died... When you start thinking about everything, you realise that it's all a heap of shit."*
- T (39, m, homeless for six years) suffers depression as a result of being unable to cope with stress: *"For a long time I couldn't find work, and it was just at that moment they deregistered me from the job centre. I had psychological problems and ended up spending a month in Kosmonosy* [a psychiatric clinic]. ***I was completely depressed and wanted to throw myself under a train."***
- J (51, m, homeless for one year): *"**I see a psychiatrist at Naděje. When things are really bad and I'm really depressed** he gives me pills. I have phases during which I have to take pills in order to pull myself together."* None of the above respondents are dependent on alcohol or drugs.

Depression can result from having spent time in prison, though this can also act simply as a trigger. This was so in the case of V (51, m, homeless for ten years), a repeat offender who is not dependent on alcohol or drugs: *"While in prison I saw a psychiatrist. Actually leaving prison actually made me depressed... **I've been depressed for about a month**. I've been sleeping at the Salvation Army and no longer care about anything."* V suffers from depression at present even though he is not in prison.

E (53, m, homeless for one year) suffers episodic depression that might be related to a stroke that has reduced his abilities: *"I've been treated twice, the second time in Bohnice. **I had depression and anxiety** because I'm always on my own. That was when I was sleeping rough. Then I was hospitalised and I take pills. I still get depressed. I hate the mornings, they're the worst. I'm full of **dark thoughts about the future**."* E is aware that he is unable to look after himself.

Some people may have a predisposition to **depression that is manifest prior to their becoming homeless** and may indeed be one of its causes.

- L (52, m, homeless for two years): *"I have psychological problems. **I have suicidal tendencies**. Ever since my problems began around ten years ago when I lost my job, it occurs to me that I could end it all. **It's the feeling of hopelessness**, the feeling there's no way out of this situation. When you're in this state of mind and you're sleeping rough, you have all sorts of feelings like this."*

- M (50, m, homeless for 20 years) sees no point to living. He does not drink or take drugs, but suffers personality disorder and has spent most of his homeless life living in the woods: "*I have no reason to live. I'm dead, certainly as far as social life is concerned. Yeah, of course a psychologist or psychiatrist would come up with some diagnosis or other, but frankly I don't give a fuck what people with a roof over their heads think. I've got my reasons.*"

Our respondents often have suicidal tendencies and these again may be associated with drug use or alcohol abuse, as well as a more general despair at the state of their lives. Twelve percent of homeless people speak of wanting to kill themselves, which is far more than in the population at large, where the figure is usually around one percent. Shelton et al. (2009) bear these claims out and report that 16% of homeless people display suicidal tendencies. Baker (2001 in Ravenhill, 2014) reports that 25% of homeless people will attempt suicide, while McDonagh (2011) cites as many as 38%.

- Z (47, m, homeless for 20 years) is dependent on alcohol and drugs: "*A few times I've wanted to kill myself. One time I was found on the Nusle Bridge* [often referred to as 'suicide bridge']. *I've also self-harmed.*"
- M (43, f, homeless for eight years): "*I slit my wrists and they took me off to a nuthouse. I have psychological problems and I can't cope with them. I hate myself. I had them when I gave up drinking. I hate myself, I'm aggressive even to myself. I think about it, but I reckon it started on the street. I needed meds for anxiety. I was afraid I'd deal with the stress by resorting to drink.*" M's suicidal tendencies may also be related to drug use and alcohol consumption.
- O (53, m, homeless for twenty years): "*I wanted to throw myself under a tram. The police caught me and took me to Beřkovice* [a psychiatric hospital]. *I just don't like living, like when I'm on the street with no money. I don't like life and I don't like people, I just feel bitter. On top of that I drank and did drugs because I'm a twat. I didn't want to carry on because I had no one, nothing, I just didn't care. I self-harmed while in prison in Bory, I was completely fed up so I cut myself. I was afraid of prison and it was never-ending. I didn't want to live and there was no pleasure in life… I didn't want to be amongst the dickheads there.*" As we see, many people experience a feeling of hopelessness at the thought of a wasted life, and are pessimistic regarding the future. Suicide is a way of escaping a situation that causes them nothing but dissatisfaction and which they have no idea how to resolve.

Some of our older respondents had been diagnosed with **more serious mental health problems that had been a contributory factor in their homelessness.** These people (7% of the study group) suffered schizophrenia, schizoaffective disorder, and bipolar affective disorder. Our questionnaire revealed that 9% of homeless people suffer schizophrenia. This applied more to young people than to middle-aged people.

- M (45, f, homeless for one year): "*I have depression for sure. It's related to being homeless. But I have had anxiety and am afraid of groups. I used to receive invalidity pension, and when I came out of Bohnice I was at home on sick leave. They diagnosed me with* **schizoaffective disorder**." M lives in a shelter and receives invalidity benefit. A problematic partnership was another factor in her becoming homeless.
- P (52, m, homeless for two years) suffers bipolar disorder: "*In 2014 I ended up in a psychiatric clinic because I was depressed. Ever since then I've been attending on an out-patient basis.* **I guess psychiatry helped me in a way by keeping my manic depression at a level I could cope with**. *During the manic phase it was no problem to throw tens of thousands* [of crowns] *at anything and anyone, anywhere, anytime. If something caught my eye, I bought it, no questions asked. At that time I wasn't sleeping rough and had some money.*"
- D (48, f, homeless for five years): "*I have been receiving invalidity benefits since 2009. I have* **bipolar disorder** *and I also suffer attacks of agoraphobia. My spine is injured and I have several other problems.* **Several times I've tried to kill myself** *with pills and booze. Twice I slashed my wrists and twice I overdosed, so four times in all, maybe five. I was depressed. I have problems with meds, I refuse to take them. The first time was when I was 28 and still married.*" D drinks to excess and this intensifies her problems. She has just been excluded from a shelter for non-compliance with the rules.

Anxiety disorder can be a contributory factor in a person's becoming homeless. M (50, f, homeless for eight years): "*I have spent time in Bohnice on a number of occasions. I'd spend six months at home and then three months in Bohnice, three months at home and three months in Bohnice. I couldn't leave the house, I couldn't even do the shopping. I can't go anywhere on my own. I have to take a Neurol in order to walk out of the front door. I am aware of everything on an intellectual level, but if I am outside and on my own or don't have Neurol, I freeze. If I decided to go somewhere and didn't have Neurol, I'd panic.* **I have panic disorder**. *Panic is the pits.* **I once tried to commit suicide**. *I took five packets of Neurol and washed them down with a litre of vodka, and in that state I cut my wrists. That was after I lost the building.*" Her psychological problems probably contributed to M's descent into homelessness, since they prevented her from resolving problems relating to her financial situation and relationship. In addition, during a critical period she was drinking to excess. At present she is living in a shelter, where she has no difficulties.

Psychiatric disorders do not necessarily have to relate to the stresses and strains of life on the street, though they may have contributed to a person becoming homeless. This is confirmed by the fact that such disorders are suffered to the same extent by people living on the street for ten and more years as those who have been homeless for four years maximum (chi square = 0.04). People who have been homeless for a long time do not have significantly worse

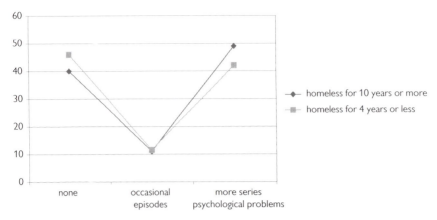

Graph 34. The frequency of psychological problems suffered by our cohort depending on the duration of their homelessness (shown in percentages)

mental health problems than those who have been on the street for a shorter time.

A good illustration is to be found in the case study of H (40, f, homeless for nine years), who receives a small invalidity benefit for psychiatric indications. H found herself sleeping rough prior to her mental health issues presenting. Her parents did not have a good relationship. Her father had schizophrenia and did not behave well. He would break things in the home and threaten to commit suicide. Her mother, too, ended up in a psychiatric ward. H has one younger brother who does not have problems of this kind. H studied at secondary school and entered university. However, she did not complete her studies. She experienced a high level of stress, which she attempted to combat through alcohol. She was still living at home, her mother died, and she found herself on her own with her father, who threw her out of the house after one particular argument. She travelled to Prague and found employment, but was unable to hold down her job and found herself sleeping rough. Her relationships have been short in duration, and after getting pregnant, she gave up her baby for adoption. At the age of 35 she suffered a psychiatric disorder that she describes as follows: "*I had always suffered delusions. For instance, I became convinced I was going to kill little babies and that I would be shot.* **I tried to jump under a car** *and they sent me to Bohnice. I thought it was all one huge mistake, but after they had put me on pills I began to realise that I really had gone mad. The diagnosis was* **acute psychotic disorder.** *It's like anxiety is a burden I carry.*" At present H does not drink alcohol. She visits a psychotherapist and moves between shelters. She is registered at the employment office and has a small disability benefit. However, because in recent years she has not been in regular employment, she receives no unemployment benefit. Her sole income is emergency financial assistance.

SUMMARY

More than a third of our respondents suffered serious psychological problems, and this figure is borne out by other studies. There is no doubt that people sleeping rough suffer these problems more frequently than members of mainstream society. If a person lacks any kind of supportive environment, mental health issues and disorders can lead to homelessness or at least be a contributory factor. This is usually because such people are unable to deal with the demands that life makes upon them and opt for ineffective solutions to problems arising. There is a complex relationship between these disorders and homelessness. People who suffer psychiatric problems often use drugs or drink to excess, because they wish to alleviate their suffering. However, this in turn contributes to a deterioration of their situation and overall condition. Sullivan et al. (2000) have shown that homeless people with mental health issues use drugs or drink to excess more frequently than those without such issues. Fifty-two percent of our respondents who had psychological problems drank to excess or used drugs. However, people with no psychological problems resorted to alcohol or drugs just as frequently.

Homeless people most commonly suffer depressive episodes, with 22% of our respondents reporting such episodes. Their depression can be congenital (the parents or grandparents also experienced depression), or can be a reaction to their conviction that life lacks meaning and to the stress of life on the street. Alcohol or drug abuse does not always provoke depression, but may be a contributory factor and can intensify symptoms. Given the numbers of people experiencing depression, it comes as no surprise to find higher numbers of people with suicidal tendencies or with attempts at suicide in their past. Though more serious mental illnesses are less common amongst homeless people, their number is higher than in the population at large.

10. CRIMINAL ACTIVITY

Criminal activity is more common amongst the homeless than the general population. Life on the street increases the risk of crime (usually property crime) being committed. This is because a person may find themselves in a crisis situation, may have less self-control, and may be under the influence of drugs or alcohol. Furthermore, in the homeless community such conduct is common and there is no risk of attracting the censure of others. Criminal activities may also have roots stretching back to the family and peer group (Štěchová, 2009). Homeless people are often undeterred by the thought of punishment, since in prison they have everything they lack on the street. For many of them, alternating between life on the street and in prison is the norm (Mabhala et al., 2016). People who have been in prison often find themselves sleeping rough upon

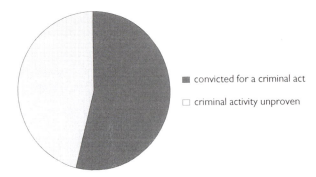

■ convicted for a criminal act

☐ criminal activity unproven

Graph 35. Criminal activities among older homeless people

being released, because during the course of their sentence they lose whatever accommodation and stable environment they previously had, and upon being released have nowhere to return to. A longer period of time spent in prison can rupture relationships and result in a person being excluded from the family community. According to Caton et al. (2005), 13% of homeless people find themselves sleeping rough upon being released from prison.

The results of various studies show that at least 30%–60% of homeless people have spent time in prison (Fischer, 2008; Caton et al., 2005, 2006; Brown et al., 2016). Shelton et al. (2009) found that 29% of their cohort had been in prison, and this figure was 37% according to Rhoades et al. (2011). Goering et al. (2002) came to the same conclusion, reporting a figure of 38%. Štěchová (2009) cites a figure of 40%, McDonagh (2011) cites 45%. Caton et al. (2005) found 59% of their cohort had been in prison, as did Brown et al. (2016). Our findings tally with those of foreign studies: 54% of our cohort of older homeless people in Prague had been in prison at least once, usually for property crime. Our questionnaire yielded similar results: 37% of those living on the street at been in prison at least once. (In the group of young homeless people the figures were almost identical, with 50% having committed at least one criminal act.) Zugazaga (2004) reported higher figures amongst homeless men, with 82% having committed a criminal act, while 25% of Irish prisoners were homeless people, most of them repeat offenders.

Criminal activities perpetrated by people living on the street tend to increase because of a reduction in the influence of mainstream society, a deterioration in living conditions, and low levels of self-control that were often a contributory factor leading to homelessness. This lack of self-control is manifest in many areas. Such individuals will be unable to hold down a job, unable to refuse drugs and alcohol, and unable to deal with the demands of family life and respect the needs of other people. This in turn leads to social disaffiliation and finally to homelessness, where no demands are made any longer. An inability to regulate one's own behaviour reinforces a tendency to commit criminal acts, since the perpetrator is more interested in the immediate satisfaction of their needs than the potential consequences. This is another area in which a focus on the present is characteristic of the homeless. Most tend to react impulsively, without reflecting upon the consequences of their behaviour. They are willing to take risks and to act without thinking, yet possess low frustration tolerance for any restrictions or postponement of their own satisfaction. These people do not plan criminal acts, but tend to act impulsively (Baron 2003).

Our respondents commit various different criminal acts, though the most common is theft or burglary. Most of those convicted for theft **steal repeatedly**, and in this way attempt to meet their immediate needs.

- J (50, m, homeless for two years): "*When I came out of the children's home, **they put me straight in prison for theft**. I became a criminal. **I've spent 12 or 13 years in prison**. The last time I was in for four years.*"
- M (49, m, homeless or in prison for 20 years): "*I've been in prison thirteen times, which altogether comes to 12 or 13 years. From 1989 to 2008 **I was constantly in and out of prison for theft**, and when I wasn't in prison I was on the street.*"
- B (52, m, homeless for 20 years) is a repeat offender: "*I was in prison in Ostrov nad Ohří and then I moved to Prague. That time I was only in for six months, for petty crime, burglary, something like that. I stayed out for two years, and then I was sent back to prison. That was in Prague and the sentence was for burning cable. **I tend to be in and out of prison**.*" M comes from a highly problematic family. He spent part of his childhood in an institution and has never enjoyed a stable, supportive environment.

Many homeless people began stealing early in life, and upon being released from prison commit further crimes. Crime becomes the norm, with all its attendant consequences, of which homelessness is only one. Such people have a tendency to act impulsively and not to reflect upon the possible consequences of their behaviour.

- J (48, m, homeless for 17 years) committed his first criminal acts as an adolescent: "***They put me in prison for theft when I was 18**, but after a year and a half I received an amnesty. I used to burgle shops. Of course, I learned the tricks of the trade while inside, and then I began to burgle apartments.*"
- V (48, m, homeless for seven years): "*Me and my friends used to pinch fruit and veg, or we'd nick crates of empty bottles. But we were caught and convicted and **they sent me to a young offenders' institution in L. After that it became a routine, from prison to prison**. After the first time inside I found a job. But they didn't pay you upfront, so I burgled a pub. They caught me and sentenced me to three years. When I came out I behaved myself for a while and I worked for Metrostav* [the largest Czech construction company]. *I got out of that in 1988 and they banged me up until 1991. I'm not a particularly skilful thief, more like a dickhead who gets drunk and gets caught.*" V is an alcoholic and this reduces his self-control.

- J (45, m, homeless for six years) began his criminal career early in life: *"The first time they banged me up for 14 months. I got two years, but they released me on probation. **It was curiosity that made me start**. I came out of the army and my younger brother was already involved in criminal activities, and I wanted to know what it was like. I stole a cassette recorder, and **after that things took off. Three months later and I was back inside for the same crime,** always for burglary and stealing cars. When they chucked me out of Billa one time saying I'd stolen money, I returned later and took 37,000 crowns* [USD 1,500] *from the cash till. My feeling was that if they were going to punish me, it might as well be for something worthwhile."* J admits to having stolen from his parents.

Fraud is another crime commonly committed by homeless people. It would appear that they do not reflect upon the future consequences of their actions, but only upon the immediate benefits. It may well be that the future is of no concern to them.

- J (45, f, homeless for 20 years): *"**I was in prison for five and a half months for defrauding** Eurotel. I bought a telephone at a reduced price and sold it on after a year. I was meant to make the repayments, but didn't."*
- E (46, f, homeless for 11 years): *"**I committed fraud**. I took out a loan for a notebook. Then I offered it to the homeless: buy this and get x amount of money. But I never repaid the loan and ended up serving time for fraud."*
- P (37, f, homeless for 15 years): *"I was sent to prison for non-payment of maintenance and for **fraud. I was what is known as a straw man**. I was sent down for a year and a half, which became 28 months cos I already had a suspended sentence hanging over my head."*

Failure to pay alimony is often the reason homeless people end up in prison. This was so in the case of 17% of those of our respondents who had spent time in prison. The commonest reason homeless people do not pay alimony is that, living on the street, they do not work and have no money for maintenance. In addition, they make no attempt to resolve this situation.

- S (51, m, homeless for 14 years): *"I ended up in prison for non-payment of alimony. They gave me six months. It was winter and **I had no work and I simply didn't have the wherewithal**."*
- R (49, m, homeless for 20 years): *"In 2005 I was sent to prison for non-payment of alimony. I couldn't find any work and I already had a criminal record, including suspended sentences, and that was enough. The suspended sentences were for the non-payment of alimony."*
- P (37, f, homeless for 15 years): *"I was supposed to pay maintenance, but **I didn't because I didn't have any money**."*

Homeless people are not so much given to planning criminal acts as being incapable of controlling their conduct. They tend to be unrestrained in all respects, even as regards alcohol and drugs. This was so in the case of Č (42, m, homeless for five years): "*A few years ago I was in prison. **I had stolen things and been involved in brawls. Nothing had been planned**, everything was spur of the moment, but because there had been several such incidents they added up.*" Č drinks to excess. He is aware that he has problems but makes no attempt to resolve them.

Alcohol and criminal activities go hand-in-hand in the case of the homeless. Alcohol abuse is an important factor that both contributes to a person's descent into homelessness and increases the risk of their committing criminal activities. Our respondents are unwilling and often unable to work. They have no money to buy drugs and alcohol, so they steal it. In addition, alcohol reduces their inhibitions and increases aggression, and criminal acts committed under its influence are more ruthless and involve more serious consequences.

- B (52, m, homeless for 20 years): "*I was sent down for three years. **I mugged someone. I got drunk and barely knew what I was doing**.*"
- J (52, m, homeless for five years): "*I've spent time in prison. The longest period was six years in Rýnovice. **I got that for mugging someone. I got drunk and attacked some bloke**. I used to drink like a fucking fiend in those days.*"
- Z (51, m, homeless for 10 years): "*At the end of national service I was sent to prison. Then there was another stint of two and a half years and yet another of one and a half years. And then there were two conditional sentences. I was involved in a **brawl** and in **breach of the peace**. **Alcohol usually played a part**. If I'd known then what I know now, I wouldn't have got involved. I would have thought things through. But at that time **I wasn't really thinking** and suddenly it was too late.*" All the men involved were alcoholics, and one of them admitted that he never gave a thought to the consequences of his actions. These days they are more willing to admit that they should not have acted as they did and that it was ultimately to their own disadvantage.

Drugs also play a part in the criminal activity committed by homeless people. Their aim is to acquire the funds to buy more drugs, though the criminal activity itself is often committed under the influence of drugs and does not therefore have to have an unambiguous objective. Many of our respondents now realise they lost out because of drugs and the criminal activities committed because of them, and regret having been under their influence.

- P (37, m, homeless for four years) has been in and out of prison for theft: "*Six months ago I got out of prison. I'd been inside for stealing cars... **it was like a merry-go-round, heroin, theft, prison, heroin, theft, prison...** The last time I was in prison I started to look anew at my values. Suddenly you realise that you've lost everything you loved and the only people you have left are those in it for the drugs. It's not especially pleasant talking about it. For instance, stealing cars was like a hobby, except this hobby has cost me my life.*" P simply got a kick out of stealing. As he himself says, "*I used to get off on it*".

- V (38, m, homeless for 13 years): "*Yeah, **I used to steal things so as to have money for drugs**. To begin with it was enough to work as a waiter. But then that changed and I began to steal. And then it became a case of prison, then three to six months outside, then prison, and so on and so on. Up until the age of 35 that was my life. I spent around ten years in prison, usually for theft, shoplifting... I'd steal everything, from booze to chocolate to soap. Anything I could sell.*" V is a classic case of someone who stole in order to sate his addiction.
- M (43, f, homeless for eight years) was convicted for drug dealing: "*I was sent down in 1997 and released in 2001. I'd got to know an Arab through drugs. We got married and he used to deal. To begin with I didn't know, but then I tried it for myself and that's how things remained. So **I was sent to prison for distributing drugs**. I was sentenced to three and a half years.*" M was to have problems not only with drugs, but also with alcohol.

Although the majority of our respondents who commit crime drink to excess or take drugs, there is no clear relationship between the abuse of psychoactive substances and criminality. Even homeless people who do not consume drugs or alcohol to excess can be involved in criminal activities.

Criminal activity is one of the most important predictors of chronic homelessness. Seventy-two percent of people who have been homeless for ten years or more have committed a crime, while this figure is only 42% in the case of people who have been homeless for four years or less. This difference is statistically significant, chi-square = 7.03, df = 1, p = 0.005. The crimes committed are mostly property related: violent crime is not as common. This means that criminality and time spent in prison leads not only to homelessness, but is an important contributory factor in chronic homelessness, which in turn increases the risk of criminal conduct. J (48, m, homeless for 17 years): "***Homelessness drives you back into crime, because if you have nothing, then you steal.*** *What other choice do you*

Graph 36. The frequency of older homeless people addicted to alcohol or drugs (shown in percentages).

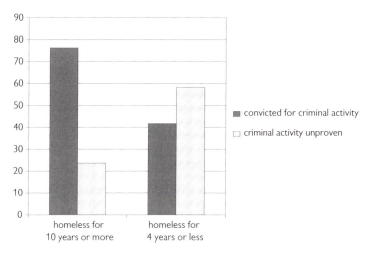

Graph 37. Criminal activities of older people depending on duration of homelessness (shown in percentages)

have if you can't find a job? You sign on at an agency, you can't find work, you're hungry and you want to eat, so where do you go?" This tendency to justify crime by appealing to material destitution and a lack of employment opportunities is shared by many homeless people.

People who have been living on the street for ten years or more usually began (in 64% of cases) a life of crime prior to becoming homeless, when they were aged 18–25. Only 36% committed their first crime while living on the street. People who have been living for a maximum of four years on the street also began a life of crime prior to becoming homeless (87.5%), with only 12.5% committing their first crime upon becoming homeless. Similar findings are reported by Fischer et al. (2008), who claim that **such people have an increased tendency to engage in criminal behaviour even prior to becoming homeless**. Homelessness is thus both a cause and effect of criminal activity (Rowland, 2011). However, in this respect the behaviour of men and women differs. Prior to becoming homeless, 88% of men had already been involved in criminality and only 12% began subsequently. In contrast, the majority of women (80%) began to engage in criminal activity only after becoming homeless. We cannot therefore fully accept the opinion of Shelton et al. (2009) that criminal conduct is an effect of homelessness rather than its cause.

There are many reasons why people who are released from prison can easily become homeless. If a person adapts to life in prison, a necessity in the case of longer-term sentences, he or she will adopt forms of social interaction and survival strategies other than those needed for life in mainstream society. As a consequence, they are unable to adapt to the very different demands made on them by mainstream society upon their release. Furthermore, they tend to lose contact with people they knew on the outside. Upon being released they find themselves socially isolated and have to deal with this situation as best they can. They end up sleeping rough, often in the company of former cellmates.

The criminal activities committed by homeless women differ from those committed by men. They have different causes and more often take place in a group or under the influence of another person, usually a boyfriend.

- E (43, f, homeless for eleven years) was part of a gang: "*I was handed down a suspended sentence of a year and half for **acting as lookout while they committed burglary**.*"
- Z (49, f, homeless for 15 years): "*They banged me up for stealing redeemables. My job was to look after the security dogs. But it wasn't my plan. I fell in with some gypsies who knew I had a way with dogs, **so I was useful to them**.*" It is safer for women to be part of a group, and this entails acceptance of the group's way of life, including criminality.
- A partner is very often the initiator of criminal activities. This was so in the case of M (40, f, homeless for 20 years), who was taught how to steal by her boyfriend: "*The first time I went to prison it was for six months. I'd been dating a guy who taught me to steal from DM drugstores. We'd walk into the shop together and **he showed me how I was to put things in my bag**. We'd sell the stolen goods to taxi drivers and the Vietnamese. I split up with that guy and began a relationship with another, and that was a big mistake, because he used to steal from apartments, cellars, cars, whatever. We found a squat. He said he'd find us some money and I told him that if it involved risk, then I was coming with him. In the end I was on vacation* [i.e. in prison] *four times. At present I'm on the outside.*" M regards theft to be a natural part of a homeless life.

Some of our respondents, having spent some time on the street, managed to stop stealing, as indeed they were able to limit their drinking or drug use. This may be down to increased passivity and a tendency to rely on charities, or a reluctance to spend more time in prison. Sometimes they cannot even say exactly what made them give up their criminal activities. This is so in the case of F (40, m, homeless for ten years): "*I used to steal things. When I was 19 they locked me up for five years. After that I continued to steal. **I've been on the street since I gave all that up, which is ten years or so**. I don't know why I gave it up, I just don't enjoy it anymore. I used to steal because I got a kick out of it and I had money in my pocket. And then one day I decided to stop. I don't know why.*" Nevertheless, F admits that "*if the worst came to the worst, I'd steal food*". Cutting down on crime is perhaps related to the fact that F used to be a drug addict. Now he drinks alcohol, which is not as expensive.

Homeless people are mostly involved in property crime, for which 44% have been convicted. However, **sometimes there is a gradual increase in the seriousness of their criminal behaviour,** which can graduate from theft to violence.

- V (38, m, homeless for 13 years): "*One time I entered a shop and held the shop assistant hostage with a knife while a friend took whatever he could. **That counted as mugging. At that precise moment I didn't give a fuck.** I wouldn't have hurt the shopkeeper, it was just about restraining her.*" It is clear that, over time, the seriousness of V's crimes increased and his inhibitions were reduced under the pressure of withdrawal symptoms.
- D (37, m, homeless for nine years) is an alcoholic: "*I'd already been in prison in České Budějovice for property crime. I had stolen some money and **she said I had shoved her, so I was done for mugging**... I received four years for gross bodily harm, and after coming out of prison I simply headed for the street.*"

For some men, but less so for women, **criminal activity is linked with an inability to control aggression**, especially under the influence of alcohol or drugs. (Twenty percent of our respondents have been convicted of violent crime). Violent crime is commoner amongst younger people, especially men.
- O (53, m, homeless for 20 years): "*I've been in prison four or five times. In total I've been in prison seventeen and a half years. My first stint was in 1980. I was sentenced to three years, after which I spent some time outside. But then things went downhill. I was always stealing stuff or **telling someone to fuck off or punching them in the face**.*" O drinks and takes drugs.
- L (38, m, homeless for 21 years): "*Twice I was in prison in Oráčov, but only for a short time. I was given a few months for affray. **I've beaten up so many people I've lost count**. I promised my girlfriend I'd never get in a fight again, but it's impossible. She told me to cool it, to chill, not to notice... but it's impossible.*" L drinks to excess. His problems with aggression may also be related to personality disorder and a low IQ.

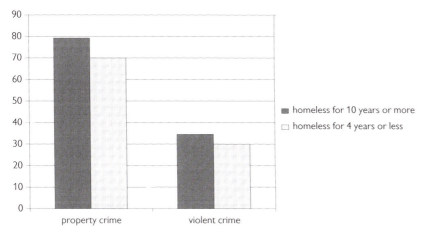

Graph 38. The crimes committed by older people depending on how long they have been homeless

- K (37, f, homeless for ten years): "*I was given a suspended sentence for actual bodily harm. **I kicked some bitch in the face when she was hooked up to tubes and she nearly died.**"* K drinks to excess and takes drugs. She has been on the receiving end of violence and as a child was subject to physical abuse by her father, an alcoholic.

Property crime is the commonest form of criminal behaviour amongst homeless people. It is independent of age and probably reflects the need to find new survival strategies. Violent crime depends on age. Young people are more aggressive than older people, who are often afraid of their younger counterparts. In general, commission of a crime depends on the degree of desocialisation given by the length of time spent on the street. Fisher et al. (2008) found that a willingness to commit property crime increased in parallel with the time spent on the street. As the following graph shows, these findings correspond to the results of our study.

The length of time spent on the street does not have any significant influence on what criminal activities a homeless person perpetrates (chi-square = 2.61).

10.1 WHAT OUR RESPONDENTS THINK ABOUT LIFE IN PRISON

More than half of our respondents have served time at least once. This is commonplace amongst homeless people and they are not ostracised for it by those around them, which means they may evaluate it differently. **They have different opinions regarding time spent in prison. Some complained** and found prison life stressful, in which case they did not want to return.
- R (49, m, homeless for 20 years): "***Prison was tough psychologically.*** *You're not free to do as you please or to have a good time. Being on the street is ten times better than being in prison.*"
- J (50, f, homeless for 20 years): "***Mentally it's tough****. You're not used to it and so you're not prepared for it. When you're in a confined environment you feel fucking awful.*" J is less a repeat offender than someone who simply cannot cope with life.

Other people deal more easily with prison, though regard it as time wasted.
- S (51, m, homeless for 14 years): "*I can't say I'm proud of having been in prison. It was comfortable, **I had no problems, but it wasn't good**, and I wouldn't recommend it to anyone. It's a waste of time.*"
- Z (49, f, homeless for 15 years): "*Everything simply happens around you. When I find myself in that kind of situation, **I try to merge into the background**, I don't pay attention to people. I try to remain calm and not get worked up needlessly.*"

Some of our respondents actually quite like being in prison.

- J (45, f, homeless for 20 years): "*I was sent down for fraud. I don't know why, but **I quite liked being in prison**.*" J has got used to even worse conditions over the many years she has spent sleeping rough.
- P (37, m, homeless for four years). "***I don't have any bad memories of prison**... you have to think of it as an adventure and learn from it.*"
- P (42, m, homeless for one year): "***What's not to like?** Have I learned not to steal? I've never thought about it. Either I was in prison or I was on the outside.*"

Some of our respondents enjoy having everything done for them and not having to worry about things. Their daily routine in prison has a certain structure of the kind they themselves are incapable of creating.

- G (50, m, homeless for ten years): "*I'm not bothered. If it comes to it I'll break something, take something, and go straight to prison. **Three square meals a day, television, a gym**... what more could a guy ask for?*"
- F (43, m, homeless for five years): "***It's cool in prison**. I spent a very pleasant winter there and ate like a king.*"
- M (49, m, homeless for 20 years): "*It was, like, **I had security in prison, everything laid on**. Of course I wanted to leave, like everyone. But then I wanted to return, I was incapable of living a free life.*" Some of our respondents admit they are incapable of fending for themselves. They have spent several years in prison and have become used to having things decided for them. This is the phenomenon known as "prisonisation", i.e. the process of accepting the culture and social life of prison society. This in turn results in huge problems with adapting to normal life at the end of a sentence, and, as we see above, can entail problems adapting to street life.

Our respondents' opinions of prison life changed over time. Some of them found it more difficult to cope the older they got.

- V (48, m, homeless for seven years) is an alcoholic: "*The older you get, **the less pleasant prison becomes**. Previously people used to help each other out, even prisoners. These days prison are stuffed full of fucking junkies.*"
- V (38, m, homeless for 13 years) is a drug addict: "***I've been trying hard to stay out of prison**. Something snapped inside me and I said, no way. You'll never get the time you spent there back, that's one thing. The other thing is that you end up wasting time with people you don't want to be with.*"

For the sake of illustration we cite the life story of J (50, m), who has spent a large part of his life in prison. J grew up in a socially disadvantaged family as one of 12 children. "*My parents were old and not really up to looking after us... I was the youngest... I paid no attention to my parents and didn't listen to what they said. At the age of 12 or 13 I was placed in a children's home. I bunked off school, didn't listen to the teachers. They placed me in an institution until I was 18. At the age of 18 they released me and everyone thought it would be back to the family for me.*" Soon after rejoining his family, J was sentenced to a prison term for theft. However, after the amnesties of the 1990s he was released. "*Prison life had stressed me out and I had learned everything from the other cons. Prison turned me into a criminal. I worked for about a year in a factory, but then I got bored and left. I thought about how I might make money without having to work. And that's how I began to steal. I received another prison sentence, this time for a year. When I came out I found a job, but again it was only for a short time. Then they banged me up again. I've been in prison fourteen or fifteen times, each time for property crime.*" J did not receive nor did he apply for benefits. He survived through theft. In 2015 he became homeless and began to receive social security benefits. He lived in various different dormitories and shelters. He tried to find work, but his criminal record meant that no employer would look at him. His original partner left him, and though he began another relationship, his next partner left him too. He does not look after his children or pay maintenance. He is not dependent on alcohol or drugs. At present he is living in a shelter.

SUMMARY

Criminality is more prevalent in the homeless community than in the general population. It is one of the most significant contributory factors leading to homelessness and thence to chronic homelessness. People who repeatedly commit a crime will more easily find themselves on the street and are more likely to remain there. They have a greater tendency not to respect any rules, including laws, even prior to becoming homeless. Most of them began to steal very early in life and upon being released from prison carry on a life of crime. These crimes mostly involve theft and fraud. Most of our respondents stole repeatedly and many regard theft as a standard means of subsistence. Such crimes are not usually planned in advance but involve impulsive behaviour that the people concerned are unable or unwilling to correct. Homeless people are often convicted for non-payment of alimony due to a lack of funds.

The criminal activity of people on the street is influenced by their consumption of alcohol or drugs, either because of reduced inhibitions or the pressure caused by withdrawal symptoms. Violent crime forms a specific subcategory and is not as frequent amongst homeless people as property crime. Alcohol or drug abuse can play a part in such cases by changing the personality of long-term users and reducing their inhibitions. The criminality of homeless women follows a different trajectory to that of men, and the circumstances under which they commit a criminal act are also different. Women often only begin committing criminal activities upon becoming homeless, most under the influence of another person, be this their partner or a group of homeless people. Our respondents hold very different opinions regarding a stint in prison. Some found it to be highly constraining, while others were unconcerned or even appreciated the security afforded them, which they did not have on the street. These results tally with those of Rowland (2011), who found that homeless people did not regard prison as punishment, but as a relaxing break from life on the street.

11. WHAT OUR RESPONDENTS THINK ABOUT THEMSELVES AND THEIR TRANSFORMATION

An individual's self-concept (self-image) reflects what they think of themselves and what other people think of them. Becoming homeless involves a fundamental change to a person's life and social standing, and this impacts on self-image and the opinions of others. Homelessness involves loss, rejection and social isolation, and this provokes feelings of anxiety and depression. The knowledge that one has been rejected by others and the shame one feels is manifest in reduced self-respect and self-confidence. This feeling of worthlessness is intensified by signs of rejection, scorn, and even violence on the part of the majority. For mainstream society a homeless person is someone who has excluded themselves from society and is therefore not deserving of consideration (MacKenzie and Chamberlain, 1994). This distance from society reinforces a tendency to establish relationships with other homeless people. These can offer a sense of rootedness and support, however illusory (Williams and Stickley, 2010).

The transformation of the identity of someone living on the street depends on the level of identification with the homeless subculture and the people who are part of it. Usually it is people who became homeless while still young and have been living on the street for a considerable period of time who identify with this culture and its inhabitants. Contact only with members of the homeless community leads to a more rapid transformation in self-image. An awareness of membership of this social group tends to be nurtured on a feeling of sharing the same destiny and a sense of belonging with individuals who are living on the margins of society. The likelihood of a person identifying with homelessness is closely linked to the length of time spent on the street ($r = 0.60$) and with the number of friends they have who are also homeless ($r = 0.73$) (Osborne, 2002). If a person does not fully identify with the homeless community, they will attempt to highlight their difference from others, especially from the most conspicuously homeless, by making it clear that "I am not one of them". They will attempt to present themselves as best as possible within the homeless group, and will sometimes not even regard themselves to be genuinely homeless. Such individuals are often reluctant to admit that they live on the street even to their friends and family, but instead make out that they are working or living in a dormitory. The length of time spent on the street will influence the defence strategy chosen, i.e. whether an individual distances themselves from the homeless community or identifies with it (Snow and Anderson, 1993; Osborne, 2002).

The transformation of someone living on the street takes place in four stages (Farrington and Robinson, 1999; Boydell et al., 2000; Auerwald and Eyre, 2002; Vágnerová, Csémy, Marek, 2013; Ciapessoni, 2016):

- Phase 1 lasts approximately a year and can be described as a **period of initial orientation and familiarisation with a new lifestyle**. During this phase individuals place a great emphasis on their ability to survive, their self-sufficiency, and their ability to deal with the burdens they encounter on the street. Their self-image remains basically intact, since they are convinced that this is a temporary situation.

- Phase 2 involves a **gradual adaptation to life on the street** and can last approximately one year. People begin to come to terms with the specific nature of this new social context and lifestyle, and acquire the skills necessary for survival on the street. Habits are gradually formed that are useful on the street but that would complicate a return to mainstream society. During this stage, people become used to a life without any great demands, to focusing on the present and not giving thought to the future, and to postponing their return to mainstream society indefinitely. They are by now aware that life on the street is far from idyllic, that there are rivalries and an ongoing struggle for scarce resources, and that not even relationships with other homeless people are always problem-free. They are as yet unwilling to self-identity fully as a homeless person, but are aware that they have changed and adapted to life on the street: this is a cause of regret. Such a shift signals the conviction that there may be a positive aspect to this way of life.

- Phase 3 involves the **stabilisation of a homeless way of life, identification with the homeless community, and a transformation in self-concept**. Someone who self-profiles as homeless has less chance of escaping this lifestyle. An awareness of their membership of such a stigmatised group and the low social status ensuing therefrom is demoralising and means they no longer even attempt to return to mainstream society (Osborne, 2002; Rowland, 2011). The likelihood a person will self-profile as homeless increases with the length of time they spend living on the street, and is manifest in an increase in the number of friends they have who are also homeless. By this time most people are aware that they are homeless. They nevertheless continue to distance themselves from the most tragic cases, who provoke disgust by virtue of their appearance and behaviour. The transformation of self-concept is an important milestone. At this point most people lose control over their lives and are less and less likely to return to mainstream society. In general, the longer a person is on the street, the more they will change. They will become accustomed to living in a different way, lose whatever skills and habits they used to possess, become more and more influenced by drugs and alcohol, and may begin to commit crime and find themselves in prison. People who have been homeless for longer periods of time are aware that it is now extremely difficult for them to return to normal society.

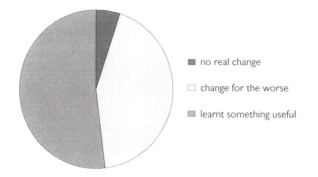

Graph 39. How older people think they have changed while homeless

- no real change

- change for the worse

- learnt something useful

- Phase 4 is characterised by **continuing desocialisation and personality disintegration**. This is exacerbated by excessive drinking or drug taking. This segment of the downward spiral usually takes place after four years on the street, though the speed at which the personality changes differs from individual to individual. People in this situation no longer seek to change their lives and have resigned themselves to never returning to majority society. They are aware that they have changed for the worse and that society has rejected and condemned them, but are indifferent to the fact. They have honed the competencies needed for survival on the street and no longer possess the skills required in normal society, and their outlook is dominated by the need not to have to address any fundamental issues.

The attempt to survive on the street and to adapt to existing conditions inevitably translates into the development of new habits and skills and the atrophy of those that had previously been possessed (Kidd and Davidson, 2007). An individual's new self-concept may reflect not only an awareness of their downward spiral and skills atrophy, but an appreciation of what they have learned on the street. Some people are simply pleased they were able to survive and deal with the problems thrown up by this way of life. They may have a tendency to interpret their homeless past as a period during which they worked on the development of their own abilities and personality, which in turn may serve to reinforce their self-concept. Their self-image now reflects how they feel amongst other homeless people and the extent to which they have discovered a meaning to this lifestyle during time spent on the street. The feeling of having survived what are sometimes traumatic experiences may provide this meaning. The transformation of identity is the outcome of the interaction of individual and social factors that a person processes in different ways.

If a person accepts homelessness as part of their identity and ceases to associate with people other than those who also live on the street, their way of thinking will change and they will better adapt to the conditions of street life. However, in turn this means that they will no longer feel the need to change their life and claw their way back off the street. Osborne (2002) reports that self-identifying as homeless is manifest in different ways, e.g. by reducing the need one has to fall back on the services of charities (r = 0.82), cutting back on efforts to get off the street (r = 0.60), and in an increase in self-confidence (r = 0.82) resulting from the feeling that one is capable of surviving on the street.

A change in self-concept can be manifest in the mere **admission that one is genuinely homeless** and the absence of any need to put a more attractive gloss on the situation. Someone living on the street gradually accepts themselves for who they are and stops trying to fool themselves into thinking that nothing has changed.

- Z (49, f, homeless for 15 years): *"When you find yourself in this situation, the first thing you have to do is **accept yourself**. Accept that you're fucked and that **you're homeless**. There's no point in lying, there's no point in saying things are fine when they're not, and you know it."*
- P (37, m, homeless for four years) has no illusions: *"**I'm homeless, that's all there is to it.**"* However, this raises the question of whether such people admit that they have changed, for better or for worse.

Only a few homeless people believe that they have remained unchanged after years spent on the street. Sometimes this is because they are in denial, other times because they have not been living long enough on the street for any fundamental change to their personality to have taken place.

- Z (52, m, homeless for ten years) exhibits signs of denial: *"**I get the feeling it hasn't changed me much** and that I could easily return to normal life and function. Perhaps I'm not exactly the same as I used to be, my nerves are a bit shot at. But if I were to return to normal life I reckon I'd adapt."* Z is an alcoholic with all that that entails, including personality change and a haemorrhage of competencies.
- J (50, m, homeless for two years) is a repeat offender whose opinion reflects the relatively short time he has been sleeping rough: *"**It hasn't changed me** for the simple reason that I said to myself that, having already endured so much in life, then this wasn't going to destroy me. So I set about finding somewhere to sleep, made sure I kept myself clean, etc."* It is possible that J's personality may already have undergone change during the course of his repeated stints in prison.

Most of our respondents come round to the idea that life on the street will leave its mark on a person, even though to begin with they were reluctant to concede this. They realise they have changed and in general evaluate this change negatively. They believe that **life on the street impacts a person negatively**, because they learn to do what they would not have done previously. They become resigned to their fate. A change for the worse can be manifest in different areas of life: their physical and mental resilience, abilities, appearance, and self-confidence. They compare themselves to the people they were before they became homeless and understand that they have changed for the worse, that they have lost not only their home and their place in society, but also many abilities.

- F (40, m, homeless for ten years): "*Undoubtedly it changes you. **You have to abandon a lot of the principles you used to have**, even as far as people are concerned, because on the street you have to mix with people you'd rather not be with. But you have no choice.*"
- R (40, m, homeless for five years): "***I do things I would never have done previously**. Things like rummaging through garbage, begging, that kind of thing.*"
- V (51, m, homeless for ten years): "*The street has influenced my behaviour for the worse. **I'm no longer the person I used to be**.*"
- M (43, f, homeless for eight years): "*When I ended up on the street I began to walk around filthy, not caring what I looked like. I had to get used to the fact that I was homeless. I didn't give a fuck about anything, just put it all out of my head. **I became resigned to everything**.*" The transformation of someone living on the street is not only an internal matter of behaviour, but affects the exterior too. Sometimes it even involves acquiring a new name or nickname.

A realisation of just how far one has fallen can appear very early on. At this point it serves as a warning that might contribute to a desire to effect change, even if this requires the necessary effort. Even people who have only been homeless a year are aware that they have changed.

- J (51, m, homeless for less than a year): "***I've lost all my self-confidence**. I'm completely confused, because I don't know what to do, where to go. I've lost everything, and now I'm waiting to see what happens.*"
- L (50, m, homeless for less than a year): "*The biggest change is the feeling of humiliation, the sense that **the street has pulled me down**.*"

Some of our respondents are concerned that things might get worse, and would like to maintain the traits and abilities they deem important. Take P (52, m, homeless for two years): "*I'm worried I'll sink lower and lower and simply give up. **I would at least like to retain some discernment and moral decency**.*" P has a university degree and has not been homeless long enough to have become fully resigned to his situation.

There are also people to be found who **view these developments in a positive light, as the manifestation of a personal transformation wrought by the experiences they have acquired on the street**. They are convinced that they have matured in some way. They compare how they were when they first became homeless with how they are now after their resocialisation, and are satisfied by the results.

- P (37, m, homeless for four years): "***I have grown up**, I've become a better person in terms of outlook. **In the past I saw everything as an adventure** and I never thought it possible that I'd sink so low.*"

- V (51, m, homeless for ten years): "***I think about things much more***. *I used to be kind of careless, not give a fuck. These days I think about things more.*"
- A person's experience of life on the street sometimes forces them to realise they must be more proactive if they want to achieve something. D (37, m, homeless for nine years) is a good example: "*To begin with all I thought about was booze. As time went by **I learned that, however I wanted to feel, it was up to me to sort it out***."

Some of our respondents feel that their **experience of life on the street and the people who live here has benefitted them**.
- L (50, m, homeless for one year) is especially appreciative of the fact that he now understands better the lives that homeless people lead: "*I think I've changed. **I understand far more the situation of people on the street because I've lived amongst them***."
- I (40, m, homeless for two years): "*I think this has been a positive experience because **I have learned that this world exists***."
- On the other hand P (45, f, homeless for eight years) has doubts as to just how beneficial the experience of being homeless has been: "*I've guess I've learned that I'm capable of surviving amongst them and I've maintained a degree of self-confidence. **But to argue that it's been worth it, that would be taking things a bit far***."

The experience of being homeless leads to greater mistrust of other people. This is probably due to the unpleasant experiences that most homeless people have had on the street. An awareness of threat that cannot be completely eradicated enters into their dealings with other people, both those from the homeless community and those from mainstream society.
- V (46, m, homeless for three years): "*I've learned to survive. I won't be duped so easily, **I'm no longer so credulous**. To be honest I'm probably too suspicious. Even my girlfriend says so.*"
- D (39, m, homeless for four years): "***I no longer trust people as before***. *I've closed myself off from others, which is perhaps not a good thing.*"
- J (39, f, episodically homeless): "***I reckon the street has opened my eyes to reality***. *People are cunts.*"
- M (54, m, homeless for nine years): "*Life on the street has changed me a lot. **I'm a hell of a lot more cautious** and make sure I'm not taken in.*"

H (40, f, homeless for nine years) believes that she has been changed most of all by the **behaviour of mainstream society**: "*I've changed a lot. I've had **some really bad experiences with people**. They cast really nasty looks at me if I fall asleep on the tram. It's only because I haven't been able to sleep during the night, but they look at me with contempt and **I end up hating the whole world**.*"

Many of our respondents are aware that **street life has rendered them tougher and more ruthless**. In order to survive they have had to change the way they behave.

- I (41, m, homeless for one year): "*If you were looking at the positive aspects, then **it has toughened me up, made me more resilient**, and this has allowed me to survive.*"
- P (52, m, homeless for two years): "*I reckon I've acquired a tough shell. I'm cruder, harder... I reckon you have to be prepared to fight.*"
- G (50, m, homeless for ten years): "*How has the street changed me? It's turned me into a wolf, that's how it's changed me. Whatever I want, I take, and **I don't give a fuck about anyone else**.*"
- K (37, f, homeless for ten years): "*It's changed me beyond recognition. **I've begun to be really nasty**. I used to be afraid of receiving a slap and now I'm happy to dole them out.*"
- D (48, f, homeless for five years): "*It's toughened me up. I don't tiptoe around people like a shrinking violet and **I don't let them take the piss out of me. Psychologically I am more resilient**.*"

Life on the street teaches people the value of things, including those things they used to take for granted, such as food and shelter. L (52, m, homeless for two years): "*I've changed in that **I appreciate everything now**.*" Z (47, m, homeless for 20 years) feels similarly: "*There is no doubt **I have begun to appreciate some things** I used to take for granted, e.g. the feeling of having a home.*" The difficulties associated with life on the street lead people to change many of their entrenched opinions and attitudes.

SUMMARY

The life of a homeless person is one of unleavened monotony, and as a result they have to give up many of the activities they used to pursue prior to finding themselves on the street. This then leads to the loss of certain abilities, skills and habits. They focus simply on satisfying their basic needs, and this in turn changes their outlook. Stress and a lack of material resources change the way they approach other people. Over time they lose habits they used to have (e.g. the maintenance of personal hygiene) and give up conforming to social rules. They gradually become desocialised (and in turn resocialised to a new environment), and a passive resistance is formed. These personality changes can lead to the development of an ability to deal with threats, and this results in a tougher and more ruthless approach to life. If a homeless person wants to survive life on the street, they cannot afford to be trusting, but must learn to anticipate potential dangers and defend themselves if necessary. Generalised mistrust and suspicion can become so ingrained that they will act in this way even in situations in which such conduct is counterproductive, e.g. when attempting to return to mainstream society.

Two thirds of our respondents admit that they have changed in some way, though do not always agree on the nature of such change. Our interviews showed that this awareness of change did not depend on how long a person had spent on the street. Some appreciate the experiences they have acquired, their ability to survive under such difficult conditions, and their capacity to estimate the dangers of being in contact with other homeless people. Likewise, they are aware of their own downward spiral. Even young people are aware of the changes they have undergone during their time on the street. Their daily confrontation with material want and discomfort means they appreciate more those things they had previously taken for granted. Young people, too, admit to having changed for the worse. They begin to realise they are no longer the people they used to be, and their self-confidence declines. Some young people, like their elders, are convinced that homelessness has taught them a useful lesson in life. For the most part this involves survival skills and the ability to look after themselves. In these respects the opinions of younger and older homeless people do not differ (Vágnerová, Csémy, Mare, 2013).

12. SUBJECTIVE REASONS FOR LONG-TERM HOMELESSNESS

Chronic homelessness is associated with a number of factors that prevent people from returning to society. These do not just include personality traits, a lack of abilities and skills, and adaptation to a simplified lifestyle, but also the persistence of an addiction to alcohol or drugs. Our respondents are also limited in terms of access to people from mainstream society who might support them. There is assistance available from institutions and non-profit organisations. However, this support is not provided on a personal and emotional level. Some of the people we spoke to did not avail themselves of the services of charities because this would mean compliance with rules, something that for them would be more demanding that simply surviving on the street. The assistance offered by friends and family also tends to come with conditions attached.

What is clear is that the same factors that drive a person onto the street also contribute to the process by which homelessness becomes chronic. This is due to the persistence of risky habits and behaviours and the disappearance of any constructive qualities a person might have possessed in the first place. Homelessness requires different competencies, and long-term adaptation to a non-standard environment can act as a barrier to any return to mainstream society. Many years spent on the street results in diminished social contacts outside the homeless community. This means there is a lack of close friends or relatives who might support someone attempting to turn their life around.

Many homeless people would like to escape the street. They would like to live like other people, to have a job and a home, and perhaps even a family. Only some of them have become completely resigned to life on the street. However, they are often unable to exert the necessary effort and accept the necessary restrictions if they are to realise their plans. It became clear from our interviews that **they are not capable of planning** and acting with greater forethought. I (40, m, homeless for two years): "*I'm just about getting by. But the thought of setting myself an objective and achieving it… no way. **It's about getting through the day, day by day.** I can't say what I'm going to do tomorrow. Maybe some work will turn up, who knows? The aim is to live like a normal person. I just want to be a person again.*" This client knows what he needs, but has no concrete plan to achieve it and is not completely convinced that he wants to make the necessary changes to his life.

Most of our respondents have no plan. **Were they to have such a plan, they would be unable to carry it out**.
- P (50, m, homeless for twelve years): "*I can't seem to get myself together. Maybe I just don't have the right character. **I keep thinking I'll sort things out, but it never happens**.*"
- Z (47, m, homeless for 20 years): "*Of course I've tried to stand on my own two feet loads of times. **But it doesn't last long**. I'll be in the middle of making changes and suddenly something turns up and bang, I'm back where I started.*"

This inability to plan is manifest in a lack of money management skills. The majority of our respondents have debts that prevent them returning to society. Many of them admit to having difficulties managing their finances, and usually had these problems prior to finding themselves homeless.
- B (51, m, homeless for 20 years): "***If you gave me half a million today, I'd have got through it by tomorrow**. That's just the way things are unfortunately.*"
- Z (47, m) is no better: "***I've always frittered away money**. I can't seem to live with money, nobody taught me how.*"
- F (40, m): "*You could give me 100,000 crowns* [USD 4,275] *and it wouldn't make any difference to my life, because I have no sense of responsibility and **can't think ahead**. When you don't have a single cent to your name and you think, yeah, I'd like to head to a bar, buy a few shots, get wasted… and then you get hold of some cash, then you tend to make up for lost time and before you know it the money's gone.*"
  Homeless people tend to focus on the satisfaction of immediate desires and are unwilling or unable to reflect upon the consequences.

Just to compound matters, many of our respondents are irresponsible and lazy. This is another manifestation of their focus on the moment, regardless of the consequences. This is more a cause than an effect of their homelessness, though living on the street tends to reinforce such traits. The situation is made more complicated by heavy drinking or drug taking.

- B (51, m): "*Why haven't I found work? I suppose you might say I **couldn't be arsed**. I can't really say right now.*"
- Z (51, m, homeless for ten years): "***I didn't really try**. I didn't think I'd become homeless. It's only really sunk in over the last few years that I don't go to work and that I'm dependent on emergency financial assistance.*"
- P (47, m, homeless for seven years): "***I've always had something of a lax approach to life**. I've always thought things would turn out ok of their own accord and that I didn't have to interfere. But they didn't. It's a kind of arrogance that leads me to banish worries from my thoughts.*"
- D (48, m, homeless for five years): "***I've always been a lazy bastard. I'm not your responsible kind**. I don't know how often I've decided I can't even manage the petty things, normal things like personal hygiene. I'm lacking in motivation.*"
- R (46, m, homeless for four years): "*What keeps me here? I don't know. **My irresponsibility and laziness**. I could have kept off the street if four or five years ago I had said to myself that I'd get a job, pay of this debt... and then I wouldn't have been sent to prison. I say to myself, 'tomorrow you're going to the job centre...', and then tomorrow comes and I don't really feel like it because it's quite a distance to travel or perhaps I've had a drink.*"
- P (52, m, homeless for two years): "*I was convinced that within a year I'd be back on my feet and off the street. I was wrong. **I reckon it's a lack of willpower**. You'd think, he wants to get off the street, so he finds a job... But the fact is I didn't. I don't know... I'm not looking for excuses. Maybe there was the hope that something better would turn up, because that's how things were looking.*" The tendency to delay resolving anything and to wait passively for problems to sort themselves out contributes to chronic homelessness, as the time a person spends on the street stretches on interminably.

Our respondents' awareness of their inability to manage things is occasionally manifest in a desire that someone else would do it for them. They are waiting for an outside impulse that never comes. V (48, f, homeless for seven years): "*I reckon **I need someone who would take me off somewhere and say: 'right, now you do this, now you do that'**, like in prison. Here's some overalls, here you're going to weld, here you're going to do this, and you know that you're going to get a meal down you three times a day and once a month you're going to receive some pocket money. I'd spend some, pay off debts with the rest, and Bob's your uncle. **I'm incapable of looking after myself**, I seem to have to spend all day looking for the wherewithal to buy food, whereas what I really need is to be paid every two weeks.*" This approach, which is far from rare amongst our respondents, explains why some accept prison as a relatively tolerable solution to their situation.

Many of our respondents are aware that it was their own fault they became homeless and that **they should by rights do something to improve their situation**. However, they are unable to muster up the resolve.

- Z (51, m, homeless for ten years): "*There's no meaning in life simply plodding the streets. I rail against myself every day, I tell myself that **I have to sort things out on my own and not pass the buck**. Every day I say to myself, no one is going to do it for you.*" Thus far there has been no change to Z's behaviour, perhaps because he drinks to excess.
- P (47, m, homeless for seven years): "*I'm beginning to realise that you have to pull your finger out if you want to achieve something in life.*" Unfortunately P, too, has done nothing to change his life.

Heavy drinking and drug taking can be reasons why a person remains on the street.
- O (53, m, homeless for 20 years): "*For the most part **it didn't work out because of booze and drugs**. I'd meet a pal and have a drink with him and then be disinclined to move my arse anywhere.*"
- M (54, m, homeless for 20 years): "*It's like, you say to yourself, ok, I'll go and register at the job centre. **But then you have a drink and... need I say more?**"*

An addiction to alcohol or drugs is a contributory factor in people remaining homeless, **not only because they become resigned to just about anything, but because of the downward spiral** and skills atrophy it involves. People who have not been on the street for that long and do not themselves drink to excess or take drugs are the most convinced of this. Seeing homeless people around them who have been devastated by drugs or alcohol operates as a defence mechanism, as they persuade themselves that their own situation is not that bad.
- D (39, m, homeless for four years): "*Some people simply **do not want to return to a normal life**. Being homeless suits them. Loads of us have the chance, but they refuse it **because they are addicted to drugs or alcohol**. There's no point in their even trying. There is absolutely nothing you can do with such people.*"
- I (40, m, homeless for two years): "*I've come across **people who live on the street of their own volition**. They love it. People throw a handful of change their way and they go off and buy alcohol.*"
- L (52, m, homeless for two years) is convinced that alcohol plays a huge role in chronic homelessness. He himself does not drink heavily or take drugs. "*There are people on the street who simply want to loll around all day. **The only worry they have is where the next carton of wine is coming from**. They have no aims or ambitions and this way of life suits them.*" It is possible that life on the street does not suit these people quite to the extent that L claims, but that they are no longer capable of making any changes.

For whatever reason, **some of our respondents have become used to life on the street and do not want to change anything.**
- Z (41, m, homeless for six years): "*I've got used to this lifestyle. Somewhat reluctantly, it's true, but that's the way it is.*"

- V (42, m, homeless for 21 years): "*I've been homeless for twenty odd years. But I don't care. I'm sailing through life. **I'm used to life on the street and I have no need to go anywhere else.***"
- P (52, m, homeless for two years) is convinced that everyone ends up feeling the same way: "*I can't say for certain, but I reckon that **in the end the street swallows you up, whether you like or not**. Some more, some less… but everyone gives up the struggle to an extent.*"

The outcome of many years of homelessness, habituation to a simplified monotonous lifestyle, and an unwillingness to make any changes is a loss of motivation and a sense of fatalism. This can also be a form of what we call "learned helplessness".

- B (51, m, homeless for 20 years) has lost all motivation to change: "*I've given up trying. I belong here. I deal with today, sometimes tomorrow, and that's that. **I'm not going to change.***"
- Z (42, m, homeless for 11 years): "***I can't say I'm thrilled to be here, but what other option do I have?***" People who have been homeless for some time no longer make any effort to change, even though this lifestyle may not be to their liking.
- F (40, m, homeless for ten years) has an ambivalent approach: "***Sometimes I kinda like being amongst these people and sometimes it pisses me off.** I'm not completely satisfied, but I'm not going to complain. It's only one person's fault, and that's mine.*"

Some of our respondents are very willing to speak of **other people's lack of motivation**, even though they themselves suffer the same problem.

- Take V (46, f, homeless for seven years): "*They could sort themselves out, but they would have to want to sort themselves out. The problem is **these people are completely lacking in motivation**. They have no opinions, they're basically lacking in everything. The truth is they feel ok and they'll probably die on the street.*"
- D (48, f, homeless for five years) is convinced that homeless people, men especially, lack motivation: "*A **lot of the men here have simply given up** and have decided the street is the best place for them. **It's mostly women here** [in D's shelter], **and there is still the hope** that we might live a normal life.*" A feeling of hope has considerable motivational power.
- M (43, f, in her first year of homelessness) emphasises the importance of motivation: "***You have to really want to return to normal life.** Here* [in a shelter] *I'd say there's a few people that have no desire to work. They're lazy and would rather leech off the state. If you don't really want something, you'll never achieve.*" It can be assumed that M will manage to return to society.

Some of our respondents claim they enjoy life on the street and therefore see no reason to change anything. However, this can act as a defence mechanism:

better to maintain that homelessness suits them rather than admit to being unable to change matters.

- Z (44, m, homeless for 15 years): "*I'm used to this life. That's the first thing. And the second is that **I'm enjoying myself**, I find it an interesting lifestyle.*"
- B (51, m, homeless for 20 years): "*I reckon it suits me. In the morning I buy myself a newspaper, drink a coffee, read in the park… I get through the winter somehow and **it all seems to come together**. It's horrible to say so, but that's the way it is. It is one hundred percent my decision.*"
- M (40, f, homeless for 25 years): "*My family are forever giving me another chance. They simply don't understand that **I like sleeping rough**. I'm not saying it no longer suits me, just that I know I can't carry on forever like this.*" M has been homeless since she was 15 and basically knows no other life.

SUMMARY

From our interviews it would appear that the same personality traits that contributed to our respondents finding themselves homeless (e.g. an inability to plan, irresponsibility and indolence) also affect their future lives. Furthermore, habits that would under other circumstances be deemed unacceptable become entrenched during their lives on the street. As a consequence, they find it extremely difficult to change their lifestyle, because it would involve, at least initially, too many frustrating experiences. Our interviews with older homeless people revealed their focus on the present moment, their inability to plan ahead, and above all their inability to carry out any plan. Planning ahead is a problematic concept for homeless people, even if all it involves is a visit to the employment office. The same goes for money management. Many of them admit that they are irresponsible and that they make no attempt to resolve their problems. A lax approach to life, laziness and sloppiness does not make a return to mainstream society any easier. An awareness of their lack of life management skills is sometimes manifest in their desire to have someone else take over for them. Some of our respondents realise that they themselves are responsible for their social disaffiliation. (The answers to our questionnaire showed that 43% of the men and 48% of the women felt a sense of guilt.)

People who have been living on the street for a considerable length of time admit that they have become accustomed to this lifestyle and are not attempting to change it, regardless of whether the life of a homeless person is to their liking or not. A sense of fatalism is to be found in many older people we questioned, especially the men. A significant cause of chronic homelessness is drug use and alcohol abuse. The need for alcohol or drugs is often uppermost in the minds of our respondents, and they will subordinate all their activities to the satisfaction of this need. A return to ordinary life is unmanageable because it would have to be coupled with a reduction in the consumption of these substances.

Younger people have similar problems. They too are aware that a successful return to normal life depends mainly on an individual's willingness, will and perseverance. Some of them appreciate the assistance of a third party, or at least an impulse that would get them moving. They believe themselves incapable of managing such a burden on their own and would like someone to encourage them. Many of them admit that the main reason they remain homeless is their own inability and lack of effort, along perhaps with the sense that such effort lacks meaning. (A third of our cohort expressed this feeling.) They are aware that they are incapable of accepting restrictions and doing what is necessary, or, as the case may be, refraining from doing what may be undesirable in relation to their future life. They admit that they feel disinclined to resolve these problems, which is why they remain on the street, where they are not obliged to apply themselves to these issues (Vágnerová, Csémy, Marek, 2013).

It is clear that many older people lack the motivation to make fundamental changes to their lives. They have become accustomed to life on the street and do not want to change anything. Whether the reason for this be alcohol addiction, a lack of self-confidence, fatalism, or the loss of the abilities and skills that a return to mainstream society would require of them, they are unable to accept the necessary restraints and exert the effort necessary to achieve this goal. The basic conditions for survival are met, and in cases where they are not, it is difficult to encourage them to overcome their frustration and stress and to act in ways they are unused to. One resolution of their situation could be to hold out the possibility of a dignified life without any greater demands.

13. DEBT AS AN IMPORTANT BARRIER TO ANY RETURN TO MAINSTREAM SOCIETY

Debt is a major problem for most homeless people. Their debts arose as a consequence of a disinclination to fulfil duties, a focus on the present, and an inability to consider the possible impacts of their actions. Though this brought them temporary satisfaction, it greatly complicated their future. Often they did not understand the risk involved in taking out a loan and were unable to react in good time to difficulties with its repayment. Eighty-five percent of our respondents have debts involving execution (debt recovery) proceedings. (Our questionnaire yielded a figure of 75%.) These debts represent a particular obstacle in the way of a return to society, because if a person cannot pay off their debt and avert the threat of execution proceedings, they will not look for stable work. The threat of execution proceedings is the reason homeless people take cash-in-hand work and do not save money. Personal bankruptcy is generally not open to them and they have no other options.[11]

In general, **the longer someone has been living on the street, the more debt they have**.

- Sometimes this can involve sizeable sums, as in the case of L (38, m, homeless for 21 years): "***I have huge debts***. *I owe people millions*."
- J (50, f, homeless for more than 20 years): "***I have debts all over the place***. *Debts to the state it goes without saying, plus transport fines, health insurance, social insurance, various court cases… just about everything your typical homeless person can have. I don't know for sure how much I owe, but it's got to be around half a million or so* [USD 21,300]. *There are execution proceedings underway, but let's not even speak about them*."
- M (50, m, homeless for 20 years) used to be an entrepreneur and owes even more: "***For twenty years I haven't submitted any tax returns***, *though my business licence is still valid. To begin with I owed only 107,000 crowns* [USD 4,500], *but over twenty years the social and health contributions etc. have gone up. Right now **I reckon I owe several million crowns**.*" Our respondents often have little idea of how much they owe and make no attempt to resolve their debts. They continue to live on the street convinced that nothing can be done.

- insurance
- fines for travelling without a valid ticket
- failure to repay a loan
- damages ensuing from criminal activities and legal fees
- fines for misdemeanours
- non-payment of alimony

Graph 40. Causes of debt amongst middle-aged homeless people

More than half of these debts arose as a result of non-payment of health insurance and transport fines. Penalties for late repayments represents another

---

11   Homeless people in the Czech Republic tend to have large debts and find themselves threatened by execution proceedings. This makes them reluctant to become officially employed. The debts tend to comprise unpaid health insurance (including penalties), since this is obligatory in Czechia. They also have unpaid loans, damages arising from criminal activities, fines for offences and non-payment of maintenance for a dependent child, etc. The possibility of debt relief is linked with a duty to pay at least 30% of the debt for a period of five years, something that is usually impossible for a homeless person.

significant category. It would make sense to resolve these defaults by other means in order to avoid further, more serious problems.

The debts of the long-term homeless were incurred for various reasons, many after the debtor had actually become homeless.

1) Debts are a direct consequence of a marginalised life. They relate to non-payment of health insurance, penalties applied for travelling without a valid ticket, and other offences. Homeless people tend to be indifferent to everything that does not relate to their immediate survival. They usually do not have enough money to buy a travel ticket or pay their health insurance. (If they were registered at the employment office, they would not have to pay this insurance. However, they are often unaware of this fact or unwilling to travel to the relevant office.) Only later do they realise what a burden they have incurred as a consequence of their debts, and how this will affect their life.

- M (45, m, homeless for five years): "*Yeah, of course, **I owe back payments of health insurance** plus all the penalties. I incurred these debts earlier on **during a hectic period of my life. I'm shit at all of that, so suddenly the amount rose** and I have to pay a hundred thousand crowns* [USD 4,200], *which I don't have.*"
- R (46, m, homeless for four years) is in a similar position: "*I have debts **because I couldn't be fucked to go to social security** and sort out my benefits. On top of that there are four penalties totalling around sixty thousand crowns* [USD 2,500]."
- K (42, m, homeless for two years): "***I have a debt incurred for health insurance because I'm not with the employment office.** I owe for both health and social insurance.*"

Debts incurred through failure to buy a ticket when travelling on public transport are common in the homeless community. The amounts tend to vary depending on how often they are caught. Homeless people do not have the money to buy a ticket and many of them regard travelling for free as a matter of course.

- J (51, m, homeless for less than a year): "***I've been travelling without a ticket ever since becoming homeless.** I received an annual season ticket from the company I worked for and then sold it on… It's the kind of nutty thing I do.*"
- Z (49, f, homeless for 15 years): "*I have loads of debts. Most of them are fines for not having a valid travel ticket. Almost all of us are in the same situation. **I don't know a single homeless person who hasn't been fined.***"
- Sometimes a person is simply indifferent as to the consequences of their actions. Take D (37, m, homeless for nine years): "*I used to travel without a ticket, because **when you're sleeping rough you don't give a fuck if it ends up in execution proceedings**. I used to travel for free and throw any fines in the bin. Now they're driving me mad.*"

2) Debts and the ensuing execution proceedings can arise as a consequence of failure to repay loans from the period prior to becoming homeless. The approach taken by our respondents to loans and repayments indicates that they are very unfamiliar with this sphere. A combination of denial and failure to resolve these debts sees the situation spiralling out of control.

- V (46, m, homeless for three years): "*I have debts from the time I refurbished a house behind Říčany. I lost my job and things started mounting up. The big problem was **I didn't understand what was going on. Nobody gave me any advice and I simply carried on as best I could**. These debts have risen steeply while I've been homeless.*"
- G (60, m, homeless for ten years): "*I have debts of around two million crowns* [USD 85, 300]. ***I took out a loan and made three repayments so that it wasn't fraud, and then I had to leave the country***. *For four years I lived like a king. Now I've hardly a cent to my name.*" G's case is less about failure to understand and more about gaming the system.

The loans our respondents take out in order to resolve immediate financial problems **lead inexorably to even greater difficulties**.

- L (50, m, in his first year of homelessness): "***I took out loans during a three-year period without work.*** *I had no other resources whatsoever.*" L was unable to repay his loans, the default penalties rose, and he ended up in a worse situation than he had been in previously.
- M (54, m, homeless for nine years): "*Yeah, I have debts... **twice I took out a loan because of my little girl and little boy, so that they had some money**. I'm not yet in execution proceedings, but I will be because there's no way I can pay back the loan.*" M failed to take into account what problems non-payment of a debt might cause him.
- J (39, f, homeless for nine years): "*Of course I have debts. If you're sleeping rough, it's normal. Loans too. **I only started taking out loans when I met Hans** [J's boyfriend, also homeless], and that's how I got myself in this shit, if you'll pardon my French.*" J adopted a casual approach to loans she took out for the sake of her partner, because she knew that she would not be able to repay them.
- M (45, f, in her first year of homelessness) took out loans because of problems with her unemployed partner and in order to make life easier for her daughter: "***We were always taking out loans** and worked up a mountain of debt. I was forever getting into debt when Andrea was still living with us. **I wanted to offer her something**, because she was always going on about how we were white trash. I owe three hundred thousand crowns* [USD 12,800]. *"Right now I'm crossing the Rubicon as far as debts go.*" M was unable to repay her debts and as a consequence ended up on the streets.

Execution proceedings may also arise as a consequence of failure to repay a debt to relatives, who then refuse to forgive the debt.

- Z (44, m, homeless for fifteen years): "*I've faced execution proceedings since 2003. **I owed my sister about sixty thousand crowns** [USD 2,500] and I didn't* *make the maturity date.* **She sued for recovery** *and I only learned of the execution proceedings in Prague, by which time I was already a client of Naděje."*

- M (51, m, in his first year of homelessness): *"I owe my sister and* **she sued for recovery**... *When I sold the apartment I was supposed to give her half. In the end I only gave her six hundred thousand instead of six hundred and fifty thousand, because I deducted tax and the official estimate."* Neither Z nor M is able to make repayment, and the threat of execution proceedings makes it impossible for them to take on anything but casual work.

3) Some of our respondents have debts incurred due to non-payment of alimony. This affects mainly younger people that have problems with non-payment of maintenance. The offspring of older people are now adults and have been obliged to resolve such issues in the past. Non-payment of alimony is often linked to homelessness, since a person has no income and is unable to contribute to the upkeep of their children.

- S (51, m, homeless for 14 years): *"***I ended up in prison for non-payment of alimony.** *They gave me six months. Then it was winter and I had no work and so I had no money to pay alimony..."*
- M (45, f, in her first year of homelessness): *"***I was given a suspended sentence for non-payment of alimony.** *There's still a threat hanging over my head, because I was put on probation on the understanding that I pay everything. But I still owe about twenty thousand crowns* [USD 855]*, which I simply don't have."*

4) Our respondents also incur debts because of criminal activities. These debts include lawyers' fees, court proceedings, and compensation for damages.

- D (37, m, homeless for nine years): *"***I have nine hundred thousand crowns outstanding for court fees, lawyers, etc.** *They apply huge penalties and then the bailiffs add on their share. I regret the whole business."*
- P (37, m, homeless for four years) is a drug addict and has similar problems: *"The execution proceedings relate to criminal activities and involved* **compensation for damages caused**, *court fees, lawyers, the whole caboodle. Things got so out of*

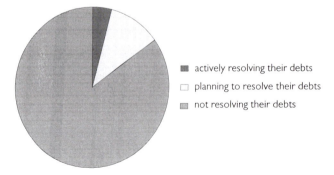

actively resolving their debts
planning to resolve their debts
not resolving their debts

Graph 41. The attitude of our older respondents to debt

hand we had to hand the house over to an agent. We still owe one hundred thousand crowns. When I was still staying at mum's, we paid off a sizeable chunk of the debt because my mum is loaded. Otherwise the debts would be seriously fucking mega." P still owes what his mother did not pay and is unable to resolve the situation.

The approach taken by our respondents to debt does not differ by age or length of time spent on the street. Only 15% of those we spoke to, mostly the younger cohort who have been homeless for a shorter period of time, are making any attempt to resolve their debt or at least thinking about it.

Debts represent an obstacle in the path of any return to mainstream society, because the moment a person finds a proper job, the bailiffs will move in and confiscate a significant proportion of their earnings. Consequently, they would rather not seek work.

- J (52, m, homeless for five years): "*If I were to work legally, under the terms of a contract* I'd lose almost everything because they would automatically deduct it."
- Z (44, m, homeless for 15 years): "*I'm putting off finding a job because of the execution proceedings.* I'm trying to save a bit. But I can't have an account, because then the executors would confiscate everything."
- J (50, m, homeless for two years): "*You think twice before taking a job paying twelve thousand, because they would take all you have.* Even if they took only four though, you'd be left with only eight thousand, which is what we get from the labour office."
- R (49, m, homeless for twenty years): "*If you're in debt, it's better to find cash-in-hand work. It's no problem getting off the street. The problems start* **when you've got debts and you discover there'll be nothing left and two months later you're back on the street**."
- M (43, f, homeless for eight years): "*If I find a job, I do it. But* **I'll be simply paying off debts for the rest of my life**. *There'll be nothing left for me. I might be left with six thousand* [USD 256] *and I'll spend the rest of my life in shelters or dormitories.*"

Despite the gravity of their situation, some of our respondents **are in fact attempting to repay their debts or at least thinking of ways how**. One option is to declare personal bankruptcy, but this is not always a realistic possibility.

- I (41, m, in his first year of homelessness) has opted for bankruptcy: "*I have debts, but* **I'm dealing with them through bankruptcy**. *I already have it approved.*"
- M (45, f, in her first year of homelessness): "*I've crossed the Rubicon and* **I'm declaring bankruptcy**. *I'm trying to get to grips with things.*"
- D (37, m, homeless for nine years) would like to resolve her situation in the same way but **does not meet the conditions attached**: "*In order to declare personal bankruptcy, you have to have an income and be in a full-time job. You have to be able to corroborate on paper that you are working, and right now I can't.*"

- M (43, f, homeless for eight years) is in a similar situation: "*I owe seventy thousand in health insurance, I have a debt dating back to when I was married, and I have received fines on public transport. **I'd like to declare bankruptcy**. But I can only do that if I have a job. I have a bit saved with my sister, so we'll see. What I want is to prevent other debts arising, so that I can finally live a little for the first time in five years.*"

For many people on the street, sorting out their debts is extremely difficult if not impossible, because they owe too much and do not have a job that would allow them to declare personal bankruptcy. **They become resigned to their predicament not changing in the slightest.** This feeling that there is nothing to be done means they remain on the street and the amounts they owe continue to increase.

- J (48, m, homeless for seventeen years) has given up any attempt to pay off his debts: "*I have no idea how many debts I have. I do know I have 17 execution orders hanging over my head… I did have a plan to resolve them, but **when I saw what it involved I decided against it**. It makes no sense.*"
- M (40, f, homeless for 25 years): "***I don't give a monkey's toss about my debts.*** *I owe money for health insurance, court fees, the prison service, public transport fines… All in all I owe at least half a million* [USD 21,000]."
- C (47, m, homeless for 23 years): "*The debts are a killer. Public transport fines, back payments of health and social security… **I'm completely beyond the reach of the system** and I don't expect to receive a pension. **I chose this life** and I don't expect anything from anyone. I simply know that one day I'll die surrounded by nature.*"

SUMMARY

Almost all our respondents are in debt. Most young homeless people (83%) have debts, even though they are not yet so astronomical as to be unmanageable (Vágnerová, Csémy, Marek, 2013). Some of these debts were incurred before they became homeless, while others arose later and in connection with a homeless lifestyle. The subsequent increase in the amount owed is both a consequence of their place on the margins of society and their unwillingness or inability to prevent this from happening, e.g. by registering at the employment office, which would at least ensure their health insurance is paid. The longer a person is on the street, the larger the sum they owe, especially if penalties are applied for non-payment of the original debt. If the level of debt rises to such an extent that it becomes impossible to repay, this will block any attempt at a return to normal life. The threat of execution proceedings sees people give up looking for a stable job, because they would be left with too little after deductions. The preference is therefore for cash-in-hand work, begging, scavenging and social benefits. The people we spoke to found themselves in an impossible situation: a declaration of personal bankruptcy is conditional upon an employ-ment contract they do not have and do not try to obtain because the executor would deduct a large part of their earnings. They see no other solution and are too passive to look for one. They remain on the street and the possibility of change recedes out of view.

Any assistance and support in resolving debts should be offered before the amount accumulates to an unrealistic level. If the debt has already become unmanageable and the standard solutions are no longer applicable, new ways should be found to resolve the situation. Consideration should be given as to whether the person in question still has a chance of a normal life, or whether they need simply the conditions for a dignified existence.

IV. IDEAS OF THE FUTURE

1. HOW OUR OLDER RESPONDENTS VIEW THEIR FUTURE PROSPECTS

People living on the street tend to focus on the here and now and do not give much thought to the direction their lives should take in the future. They are aware that it would be difficult to quit the street and that they would have to change their behaviour, learn how to function in society, find a job, and create or renew relationships with people who are not homeless. They are not sure they are capable of undertaking such deep-seated change and often do not want to. Their vision of the future is influenced by the degree to which they self-identify as homeless and the level of desocialisation they have attained, which in turn is related to the length of time they have been homeless. Adaptation to a homeless life is often accompanied by a reduction in efforts to change anything and an increase in indifference regarding negative outcomes.

When they turn their minds to the future and their own possibilities, our respondents display a range of feelings. These usually pertain to the spheres of accommodation, relationships and work (Ravenhill, 2014). Some people have a tendency to idealise things and are excessively optimistic, while others are fatalistic and pessimistic. Some focus only on the immediate future, and others on **desires that are not underpinned by any form of realistic plan** for their realisation. Some of our respondents would like to return to normal society, but have no idea how to.

- R (48, m, homeless for seven years) no longer wants to live on the street: "*If I can manage to hold a job down,* **I don't want to spend another day here**. *Everything is beginning to get on my nerves. You drink some wine, the verbal diarrhoea begins. Then suddenly there's no wine left and the arguments break out. It's no way to live. I don't know what the future holds, it's in the stars.* **For the moment I simply have to survive and then we'll see**." R has been drinking to excess for a long time and has difficulty managing his craving for alcohol.
- S (52, m, homeless for 17 years) would like to turn the clock back but has no idea how: "*I'd love to have some money and* **live a normal life** *like I did before I became homeless.*"
- B (52, m, homeless for 20 years) is a repeat offender: "*I'd like to be* **healthy and live a long life** *and I'd like some money, that goes without saying. I'd also like somewhere to live, because winter is on its way.*"

- E (53, m, homeless for one year) knows what he wants but has no idea as to how to achieve it: "*I'd like to find a partner and settle down. I'd like a job that pays me just enough so I don't feel hungry and don't end up experiencing what I have experienced here, i.e. being without food, being without anything, and having to rely on people around.*"

Many of our respondents expressed dissatisfaction, and it is very easy to believe that they genuinely would like to find work and have somewhere to live. However, **they tend to postpone achieving this goal indefinitely**. Take F (43, m, homeless for five years): "*I'd love to change things.* **Come spring I'd like to find a job.** *I still don't have one. The problem is I* **don't really want to work quite yet.**"

Some of our respondents expressed a **belief that their situation might change at some point in the future**. The hope that things might get better helps them survive.
- Z (47, m, homeless for 20 years): "*I feel sad when I look back on life. I look ahead at what awaits me, I look at what's behind me and around me, and I realise life sucks and I'm fucked.* **I believe there will come a moment when I start a job.**" Z has been drinking heavily since he was young. Later he took drugs.
- J (45, f, homeless for 20 years): "**I believe that things will get better.** *I'd love a place to live and to find a better job than the one I have at present, a job that pays more.*" J is addicted to drugs and alcohol and no longer has the job she refers to above.

Some of our respondents **do not believe they can ever return to society** and are not planning to. Not planning anything is an oft-resorted to strategy of the homeless and is derived from their experience of previous plans that were never realised.
- D (37, m, homeless for nine years): "*I tend to think that* **if I began doing something** *it would take forever,* **and before I had actually finished it I'd be back on the street.**"
- R (48, m, homeless for seven years) is sceptical: "**I no longer make any plans.** *Whatever I've planned for comes to naught.*"
- J (41, m, homeless for nine years): "*It's really difficult getting off the street. I'd love to find a flat, a nice woman, and live the quiet life. But I'm* **not planning anything quite yet.**"

Some of our respondents **are not even sure if they should attempt to return to society**. They are used to life on the street and feel no need to make changes.
- R (40, m, homeless for five years): "*I guess I really should sort out some accommodation above all, and then find a job. The thing is* **I'm not really sure I want to leave the street.** *I'm relatively satisfied, with the emphasis on relatively.*"
- D (40, m, homeless for 19 years): "**My future will be the same as my present: on the street.** *The street is our realm.* **I like it here.**" For the moment the homeless

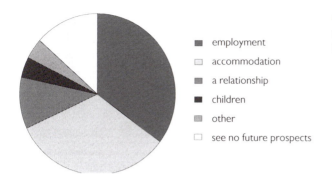

Graph 42. What our older respondents would like to have in the future

- employment
- accommodation
- a relationship
- children
- other
- see no future prospects

life suits D. He especially likes the fact that he is under no constraints, though he is not sure he will remain satisfied in the future, when health problems begin to take their toll.

Some of our respondents link their ideas of the future to a concrete plan. People who have been living on the street for a shorter period of time usually wish to return to normal life and **are often to be found wondering how to realise this ambition**. Most would like to find work and then sort out their accommodation.

- L (52, m, homeless for two years) thinks in more realistic terms than most of his peers: "*I would like to reapply for emergency financial assistance, so that at least I have a base… and **then I would find a proper job**. I'm trying to find a way out of this situation as quickly as possible and get a job and a wage. If I had a wage, then I'd sort out a roof over my head.*"
- L (50, m, homeless for one year): "***I'd like to find a job with a dormitory attached** and then dig myself out of this hole and live happily.*"
- M (45, f, homeless for one year) has found a job: "***I simply want to keep my job**. I've been working one day as a security guard on reception. So I'd like to keep this job and **save some money**. We need a normal life and then we're going to need an apartment of some kind.*" All of the above have debts that they are not including in their dream lives.

Many of our respondents are aware that it is difficult to return to work after a long layoff and so **want to ease the burden in some way**.

- P (45, f, homeless for eight years) used to be a drug addict and would like to adapt gradually: "*I really hope I find a job. Ideally I'd start with casual work, so **I could get used to getting up every morning**. Maybe three times a week… and then a roof over my head, maybe in a shared flat.*"
- It is even more difficult to begin working aged forty. J (40, f, homeless for 15 years): "*I need to find a job, except **who's going to employ me given I've never had a job in my life**. I guess one option would be invalidity benefit, though I don't know if I'd be eligible and I don't know how to set about applying for it.*" J does not have a realistic idea of her possibilities and has no work experience or skills.

She cannot receive invalidity benefit because she has not worked. She lacks professional qualifications and has only a basic education.

Ideas of the future include relationships with friends. Some of our respondents mention **sexual partnerships, though this is an area that men and women view differently**. Men would like to find a partner who would provide stability and look after them. However, it is not clear where they might find such a woman and whether she would have any interest in them.

- J (50, m, homeless for two years) has had a number of relationships with different women and would like to find a partner: "*I'd like to settle down and that's what I'm working on. I'd like to find a job, but that's not possible, so **I'd like to find a woman** who'd provide stability.*"
- K (42, m, homeless for two years) would like back everything he had before he became homeless, including a girlfriend: "*I don't want to be on the street. **I'd like to find a proper job and a girlfriend**. I'd like a roof over my head and money for food. I'd like to get back my old pub.*"
- D (37, m, homeless for ten years) has never had a stable relationship: "*What would help me? A woman. **A woman who'd look after me**.*" D died this year without achieving his ambition.

It is difficult to know what these men imagine a new relationship would bring them, whether emotional support, a life partner, or simply someone to look after them. Their previous life indicates that all these variants are possible.

For women, even though they are living on the street, **close relationships are more important** than they are for men. **A sexual partnership often figures in their plans for the future.** Many of them plan to share the future with a man who is also homeless, i.e. they assume they will remain with their current partner rather than finding someone new.

- V (46, f, homeless for seven years): "***My boyfriend and I would like to move into an apartment or at least a dormitory**. We simply want to escape from the street. My boyfriend is keen on the idea just as soon as we earn the money.*"
- D (48, f, homeless for five years): "*I receive benefit and I count on that. I am trying to save a bit so I can find accommodation. I'd like to be able to live at **Šromovka** [a shelter] **with my boyfriend** and maybe stay there for a year so as to scout out the lie of the land.*"
- J (50, f, homeless since her youth) wants a better relationship with her partner: "*I have a plan for the future. **I want us to be more understanding of each other**, to be a bit calmer, to agree on things, and trust each other, rather than constantly bickering over trivial matters. **I want us to find work**, some kind of casual work, so that we can start saving for a home.*" One cannot help but wonder whether J's partner is of the same opinion regarding their future together.

Some of our respondents would like to renew contact with the children they lost upon becoming homeless.

- Š (45, f, homeless for four years): "***I'd like my children*** *and a normal job. As I say, I need to find a proper job and then accommodation, and then most importantly of all my children.*" The children remained with their father, who has not supported Š's attempts at re-establishing contact.
- J (40, f, homeless for 15 years): "*I simply need to find some accommodation for me and my boyfriend and then* ***try to have at least my younger daughter live with us****.*" Both daughters are being looked after by their grandmother on J's side. The older of the two refuses to have any contact with her mother.
- K (37, f, homeless for 10 years): "***I hope to be able to see my children*** *and that they'll be able to visit me.*" K's children are looked after by her mother.

Few of the people we spoke to grasp that, in order to return to society, **they must first reduce their consumption of drugs or alcohol**.

- P (40, m, homeless for 20 years) is an exception: "***In the future I have to give up drugs****, spend a few months in Červený Dvůr* [a psychiatric hospital in Chvalšiny, South Bohemia] *and begin to live a normal life.*"
- M (40, m, homeless for seven years) is in a similar situation: "*I need to apply for an ID pass and* ***stop boozing****. In the future I need to find work, even if it's only casual. I need to sort out all my documents, find some gainful employment, and break all ties with these people* [other homeless people who drink]. ***I would really like to sort out my drinking****, because otherwise I have no idea how things will pan out.*" Both P and M are aware that drugs and/or alcohol are complicating their lives. However, it is far from clear that they will be able to at least reduce their consumption.

Several people we spoke to would like to resume a normal life but **want someone else to sort matters out for them**. They are incapable or unwilling to do anything themselves and rely on others. Waiting for Godot is a typical survival strategy deployed by homeless people.

- Z (42, m, homeless for 11 years): "*I'd love to escape this situation, but* ***only when someone offers me a chance****. I need proper accommodation. It's difficult to get up for work when you've been sleeping behind a tree or in a squat. I need an apartment and then I'd be happy to go to work. I'm not lazy.*" Z himself is not looking for work but is relying on someone else to find it for him.
- J (41, m, homeless for nine years): "*It would help me get my shit together if I could find someone.* ***Some generous minded soul who would represent stability****. I don't really try very hard, because after a while you simply wonder what the point is.*" J would like to find accommodation and stability, but admits that he is not being active in this regard.
- J (48, m, homeless for 17 years) would like the state to provide him with accommodation: "*I would be very grateful* ***if the fucking state could offer me a roof***

over my head where I could stay for longer than a year. Some kind of public housing. That would make me a happy man. I'd furnish it and live happily ever after." J too is not making any efforts to change his situation.

- J (52, m, homeless for 15 years) has an even greater need of assistance: "***I need someone to help me*** *find work and somewhere to live* [he last worked 15 years ago]. *I need someone to* ***find me a job***." This kind of approach is likely to see J remain on the street indefinitely.

People who have not been homeless for that long are quite clear in their minds that it is they who have to make the effort. Take Š (46, f, homeless for four years): "***You have to want it yourself and not wait for something to turn up.*** *When I see the booze and the plastic bottles of wine, I realise that these are people who don't really want to leave the street."*

Some of our respondents pay scant regard to the future. These are people who have usually been homeless for at least ten years or more and have adapted fully to this way of life. It is possible that they no longer have any idea of what else they would do.

- S (52, m, homeless for 17 years) is a case in point: "*I could be dead in two days' time.* ***No one can say what the future holds***."
- F (40, m, homeless for 10 years): "***I prefer not to think about it***. *I couldn't give a fuck when I die. Que fucking sera sera, if you'll pardon my Spanish."*
- G (50, m, homeless for ten years) expresses pessimism: "*My future is very simple.* ***I hope that I kick the bucket soon***. *I'm not afraid of death, I've seen too much of it."*
- Z (49, f, homeless for 15 years): "*Yeah, I often ask myself: what next? But I don't know... The future?* ***There is no future***."

SUMMARY

Homeless people have a variety of different ideas about the future. Some would like to live differently. They realise that they should find work and slowly organise some accommodation. Sometimes merely expressing a wish is as far as they get. Other times they are more realistic as to what they might achieve if they really put their minds to it. Generally speaking they know what they want but do nothing to achieve it or postpone taking any action. Some of our respondents expressed the wish that someone else organise everything for them and cajole them into going to work or find an apartment for them. Men and women have different ideas of the future. Women often include the re-establishment of relationships with loved ones, their partner or children in their plans. Men do not accord such importance to relationships. Inasmuch as they think about a partner, it is a carer that they really want. Ideas of the future differ depending on how long a person has been living on the street. In short, the longer someone has been homeless, the more they doubt they will begin a new life and very often give no thought to the future and do not make plans. The chronically homeless tend to be pessimistic and resigned to remaining so. As one of them told us: "*I've already lived through my future.*" They lack the motivation, self-confidence and competencies necessary if fundamental changes are to be made.

Our middle-aged respondents are more pessimistic and resigned than their younger counterparts, due to the length of time spent living on the street. Most young people (80%), whatever their doubts and their reluctance to undertake fundamental change, at least contemplate changing their lives. Almost half of them (40% of the entire cohort) actually managed to effect change. They found regular work and accommodation in a dormitory. However, many of them ended up returning to the street, usually because they were unable to hold down a job. As soon as they made any money, they stopped going to work and were given the sack (Vágnerová, Csémy, Marek, 2013; Vágnerová, Marek, Csémy, 2017).

2. THE MESSAGE OUR RESPONDENTS WOULD LIKE TO SEND TO ORDINARY PEOPLE

The attitude of homeless people to members of mainstream society varies. A common feeling is resentment at the way they are ignored, condemned, disrespected, or even subject to aggression. They take umbrage at being viewed as second-class citizens that must be avoided, and deem this an injustice. They believe that most people do not understand how easy it is to lose everything and to become homeless, and what life on the street is like. They sometimes feel that life has been unfair to them and resent the fact that better off people fail to understand this. **They would like to remind us that the life of a homeless person is very difficult**.

- L (38, m, homeless for 21 years): "*I just wish people could understand that life on the street is cruel. There's the cold and drugs, prostitution, alcohol, death... Hlavák [Hlavní nádraží or Main Station, a favourite hangout of the homeless] really does represent the terminal station.*"
- J (50, f, homeless for 20 years): "***It's a terrible life. It's a life without sense or meaning.***"

Our respondents recommend that anyone who does not understand how difficult life on the street can be **should give it a go**.

- M (45, f, in her first year of homelessness): "***They should give it go.*** *If they never try it, they'll never understand. This is something you have to experience to know what it's like.*"

- M (40, f, homeless for 25 years): "*These people who look down their noses at us, **they should give it a go sometime**. They should try living for just two days on the street, without money, without anything.*" Both women believe that people would have a different opinion were they to experience homelessness for themselves and realise just how difficult it is.

Despite these reservations, homeless people do not think badly of people living a normal life and would urge them to **make every effort not to end up homeless**. It is easy enough to find yourself on the street, but a lot more difficult to escape it.

- P (52, m) only became homeless in his fifties and preaches caution: "***Do anything and everything to avoid ending up on the street**. It is a lot tougher than it looks.*"
- J (50, f) is of the same opinion: "*Be grateful you have a roof over your head and make sure you pay the rent and go to work. In this way you'll live a normal life and **ensure you never become homeless**.*"
- L (38, m) stresses how easy it is to find oneself homeless: "*I just hope that people understand that the street is not something to be trifled with. **You can easily find yourself on the street**. One day you return home and you've lost your job. You have debts and your wife files for divorce. Next thing you know…*"
- L (50, m) is keen to point out how difficult it is to return to normal life: "*The best thing is to organise your life in such a way that you don't end up on the street. It's easy to find yourself on the street, **but a hell of a lot more difficult to drag yourself off it**.*" These messages for members of mainstream society tend to be warnings that reflect the messenger's own negative experience and which should therefore be taken seriously.

Our respondents **want those who are better off to stop judging them and to be more tolerant**. They need to realise that the same thing could happen to them.

- J (48, m): "*I would ask them **not to despise people who are homeless**, because they never know when it might happen to them.*"
- D (48, m) feels the same way: "***I don't like it when people who don't know me judge me**, because you never know how you might end up and how quickly you might find yourself homeless.*"

The people we spoke to would like others **not to lump them all together, because they are not all the same**. Homeless people are individuals who ended up on the street for all sorts of different reasons.

- V (48, m), who admits it was his own fault he ended up on the street, rejects any generalised condemnation of the homeless: "*The most important thing is that **people don't put us all in the same bag**, because it is not always a person's fault that they become homeless. In my case it was, because I acted like a fool.*"

- M (54, m): "***Please don't judge all homeless people by the same measure***, because we are not all the same. *There are both good and bad in our ranks.*"
- Some of our respondents realise that people often have reasons for their negative attitude: G (50, m): "*I'm not at all surprised they judge us. There's some bloke sitting in a station covered in piss and smelling up to two metres away. **The problem is they lump us all together. They need to show some tolerance**, because in a year or two it could be them sitting there. So don't spit at them, because they're people too. I know that they are sometimes filthy. But they simply can't help it.*" People should be more tolerant and learn to distinguish between individuals, because not all homeless people deserve condemnation.

SUMMARY

Experience has taught our respondents that it is easy to suddenly find oneself without a home and that it can happen to anyone. In this respect their opinion is as distorted as that of members of mainstream society, since most people attempt to avoid risks and to exert control over their lives. However the homeless rate their lives, they wish to remind people to make every effort to ensure they too do not end up on the street. Though some of the people we spoke to are aware that they can look somewhat off-putting, they would like others not to judge them and treat them with contempt, because they are not all the same. An inability or unwillingness to differentiate between individuals is common, and generalisations are usually made when evaluating the members of any group. However, these generalisations are hurtful for our respondents, who regard them as unwarranted. Greater tolerance on the part of those around them would help them retain a sense of self-respect, something which is always at threat on the street.

V. CONCLUSION

In order to assess the options open to a middle-aged homeless person, we need to know why they are in this situation and what the causes were of such a dramatic downward spiral. It is clear from our analyses of individual stories that a complex of interrelated problems is often involved that the individual in question is unable to cope with. They had no one who might help them, or they themselves refused to accept assistance because it came with strings attached (e.g. that they give up alcohol and find a job). The factors increasing the risk of social disaffiliation, including homelessness, can be categorised according to the point in time they began to impact the individual and their life trajectory, and whether they might act as triggers for other problems. As a person gets older, the causes of homelessness become more and more complex.

- A **primary risk factor** of fundamental significance is a **childhood spent in a dysfunctional family**. Parents and other relatives have a crucial influence on a child. These relationships are not always positive and the child may be neglected or subject to a poor upbringing. The negative influence of undesirable genetic predispositions acquired from problematic parents cannot be overlooked. A dysfunctional family reduces a child's chances from the very start of life, influences them by its attitude to upbringing and education, and provides a negative model of behaviour in respect of other people and lifestyles. The relationships in such families are often insufficiently warm. This impacts on a child's ability to form and sustain close relationships with other people later in life. The child learns that people cannot be trusted and that it is impossible to predict how they will behave. A lack of interest on the part of the parents results in a low level of education, a lack of any professional qualifications, and problematic behaviour. This then culminates in an inability to adapt to life in society.
- **People who have had a problematic childhood are often unable to deal with the transition from adolescence to adulthood.** When they begin to live an independent life, difficulties that arose previously are manifest in an inability to answer many demands made upon them and a failure to respect common standards. A poor education and a lack of professional qualifications reduces their chances of finding employment. They are often unable to work systematically and achieve financial independence. They survive by means of parasitism or criminal activity. They also experience problems in their private life, are unable to maintain a stable relationship, and have

difficulties creating and sustaining a family life and accepting the responsibilities of parenthood. They sometimes have no interest in a family life and the duties it involves. Hutson and Liddiard (1994) created a model of the slow descent to the street that takes the form of a descending spiral. Homelessness can operate as an escape into a social vacuum in which there are no duties or responsibilities, and can be seen as one of the manifestations of dysfunctional behaviour and the resolution of problems.

- **Homelessness is not always a consequence of disadvantages originating in childhood.** The problems that lead a person to live on the street can arise later in life. Some people only begin to experience difficulties in their working and private life as adults. This is sometimes because they do not experience success in their chosen field and are unable to deal with their role as employees, partners or parents. If they opt to cope with stress through the consumption of alcohol or drugs, these problems intensify. Failure to face up to these problems leads to the breakup of the family and the loss of employment and accommodation. The subsequent descent into homelessness is often the consequence of accumulated problems and an inability to resolve them.
- **Severe mental health issues**, which can appear at any point during adulthood, **can also contribute to social failure**. They restrict the ability of the sufferer to manage their own life, both in terms of financial independence and coexistence with the people around them. If they lack a stable family environment, the risk of social failure, including homelessness, increases. In this instance homelessness is the consequence of an inability to cope with an unfavourable situation.
- Social failure can also be caused by the **accumulation of negative events** such as mass redundancy, debt, divorce, or family breakup and the loss of accommodation ensuing therefrom. The risk of homelessness increases because of a **poor risk assessment of the situation and an inability to deal with it**. This includes an inability to seek out effective assistance and a tendency to resort to strategies that exacerbate the situation, e.g. by taking on more debt or escaping with the aid of alcohol.

We have shown that a descent into homelessness and an inability to escape it can take place in many ways. In this respect our older respondents can be divided into several subgroups:

- **People who had problems as far back as childhood**. They grew up in a problematic family or an institution and have only a rudimentary education. They failed to complete any professional training and are restricted by a lack of qualifications. From the start they had problems in employment, lacked application, and were unable to hold down a job. They soon began to have problems with alcohol or drugs, and their relationships (always supposing they had any) fell apart. If they had children, they neglected them, as they themselves had been neglected by their parents. They had destructive relationships with people close to them that might involve domestic violence or a partner addicted to alcohol or drugs. This group of people paid little heed to the law and were often involved in criminal activities, usually repeatedly. A criminal record made it even more difficult to find work and contributed to their social disaffiliation. Prior to becoming officially homeless they lived for a period of time in the position of someone who belongs nowhere and survives on a hand-to-mouth basis. They tended to fetch up as homeless in young adulthood aged around thirty. Such people account for 43% of the middle-aged people we spoke to.

- **People who began to have problems later in life**. They had a normal childhood, did an apprenticeship or completed secondary school and found work. They had a family, but gradually began to drink heavily, alternating partners and jobs. They were unable to cope with their situation and lost their family and their job. They usually found themselves on the street around the age of forty. This group is also quite large and accounts for 37% of the middle-aged people we spoke to. Their main problems are alcohol and debt.
- **People who suffer mental health issues** and were therefore unable to meet the ordinary demands of life, look after their children, and maintain a relationship, family and work. (Another risk factor involves being in a relationship with someone with mental health problems.) These problems can be combined with drug abuse or alcoholism. Depending on the course of their psychological disorders, their descent into homelessness can take place at any time during adulthood, usually between the ages of thirty and fifty. Mental health issues contributed to homelessness in the case of 8% of the people we spoke to.
- **People who became homeless as a consequence of miscalculation and an inability to cope with a particular life situation**, usually following divorce, loss of employment and accommodation, debt, or a deterioration of their state of health. Such people tend not to be addicted to alcohol and do not have a criminal past. They suffered problems that, though serious, are dealt with successfully by most other people. They usually find themselves sleeping rough later in life, aged between forty and fifty. Such people do not fit into the homeless community and tend to survive outside it. They have a better chance of returning to mainstream society. They benefit from the assistance provided by social workers because they have the requisite motivation and residual abilities, and their problems are for the most part manageable. Such people accounted for 12% of the middle-aged people we spoke to.

Many different researchers, e.g. Pillinger (2007) and Chamberlain and Johnson (2011), have investigated the causes of homelessness and analysed the factors leading to chronic homelessness. Our study of middle-aged homeless people is largely consistent with their findings. In general we can say that, the longer a person is homeless, the more they are at threat of other risks that arise during this time and can be deemed secondary. This would include the risk of social exclusion, the breakdown of relationships, and a lack of contact with people outside the homeless community. Homelessness also involves an increase in self-destructive habits, e.g. the lack of a daily routine, indolence and a growing inability to resolve any situation, increased antisocial behaviour, and often a growing addiction to alcohol or drugs.

Chronic homelessness is caused by the same factors that led to a person becoming homeless in the first place. Such individuals behave similarly to how they did previously. They drink, take drugs, steal, and are aggressive and unscrupulous. Their outlook and behaviour is distorted still further on the street and they become yet more egotistical and asocial. The way that people living on the street deal with problems is ineffective and focused mainly on satisfying their immediate needs and feelings. Their inability and reluctance to work increases and they experience skills atrophy. Not only comfort and laziness, but irresponsibility and an inability to manage money contribute to chronic homelessness. This is exacerbated by poor life strategies, such as the consumption of drugs and alcohol, and problematic behaviour, such as unscrupulousness and private microaggressions that would be highly problematic in the event of a return to normal life.

Our study of older homeless people shows that the habits and attitudes formed during a negative experience with parents during childhood have a major impact on whether a person remains homeless. A dysfunctional family can influence a child's personality to such an extent that they are unable to cope with the demands of society. They will be impeded by a low level of education and a lack of professional qualifications, as well as problematic behaviour. Such people are unable and unwilling to work and make a living in socially acceptable ways. This also represents a major obstacle to their returning to normal life. Another important factor that contributes to chronic homelessness is the inability of such people to maintain relationships with people close to them, be they siblings, partners or their own children. They behave in unacceptable ways to their partners and children, in much the same way as their parents behaved to them, and are therefore unable to maintain a stable environment that would help them return to mainstream society.

Chronic homelessness is subject to other factors, above all alcohol abuse and drug use. Regardless of a person's previous experiences, abilities and social skills, this can then lead both to homelessness and its chronic iteration. Criminal activity and its consequences in the form of prisonisation, i.e. the process of accepting the culture and social life of prison society and being excluded long-term from society, can have a similar influence. Under these circumstances relationships can easily break down, former contacts can be lost, and many abilities, skills and habits can atrophy. Severe psychiatric disorders and illnesses can also impact negatively, be this in the form of long-term hospitalisation or a loss of ability to manage the demands that life makes.

It becomes more difficult for a person to return to normal society the longer they live on the street and the more entrenched homeless habits and attitudes become, i.e. the greater is their overall disaffiliation. The way out of homelessness is a process that, in addition to motivation, requires a certain amount of time, because it does not only involve a change of accommodation and lifestyle, but a shift in an individual's psychological and emotional outlook (Ravenhill, 2014). A person must decide for themselves to leave the street and must have some idea of how to set about doing so. At the very least they must know where to seek help. A person's motivation to leave the street dwindles the longer they are homeless. Many chronically homeless people make no effort to change their life, often because they regard their situation to be irresolvable and do not believe they would succeed. They are convinced that they have no future. They have taught themselves to focus on the present and to survive on a day-to-day basis. Alternatively, they expect the problem to go away by itself and appear to be waiting for a miracle to take place. This passive resistance is sometimes related to their inability or unwillingness to request help and to accept such help as is offered. They display an excessive emphasis on independence combined with an entrenched distrust of people, especially members of mainstream society. Sometimes, on the contrary, they want help, but imagine it to take the form of an unconditional guarantee that they will receive everything they need without themselves having to lift a finger. Without the support of someone else, be this a professional or someone close to them, a return to society will be impossible or doomed to failure.

The length of time a person spends on the street is also linked to an increase in the problems that would arise were they to return to society. There is no doubt that the longer an individual is homeless, the more problems they will experience. Returning to society is not easy, and during the transitional period a person has to overcome many obstacles. One such obstacle is a feeling of loneliness, of not belonging, and of exclusion. They have made a break with the homeless community, and yet the society to which they are returning has not yet accepted them and they do not have any friends or acquaintances. They lack ordinary contacts, because those they used to have are gone and they have not yet managed to forge new ones. For this reason work is important, since it is not only a means of making a living, but a way of meeting new people.

A return to society is often accompanied by a culture shock ensuing from the sudden and dramatic change of lifestyle. This can be more powerful than the shock experienced upon first becoming homeless. People who have experienced homelessness often lack self-confidence, and are unsure as to whether they are up to dealing with a return to society. Ravenhill (2014) considers their fear of failure to be an important limiting factor. They often feel that they do not belong in majority society, and this is reflected in increased levels of anxiety. They are unable to navigate this new environment and do not know what is required of them and when, and how they should behave under particular circumstances in order to fit into society. They lack the requisite knowhow and social skills, all of which they did not need on the street. Another obstacle in the way of successful inclusion is a tendency to react in critical situations as they have been taught to react on the street: unscrupulously and antisocially. They may have difficulties in managing everyday activities such as doing the laundry, cooking, cleaning up after themselves, etc. They have no idea how to manage money, because they are used to living day to day. Their smooth integration into employment is hampered by skills atrophy, the absence of professional experience, and insufficient qualifications.

If someone who has been homeless is to return successfully to society, they must change their approach to life, their behaviour and the way they dress, and abandon many other habits acquired on the street. They must learn how to live in society and how to deal with problems arising. They must react differently to how they are used to reacting on the street, i.e. by turning their backs on difficult situations rather than resolving them. They need help and support, since they are unable to manage all of this on their own. Finding work and accommodation is important, but yet more important is managing the adaptation to a new lifestyle. For this reason they need support in other areas of life too.

APPENDIX

VI. THE FOLLOW-UP STORIES
OF YOUNG HOMELESS PEOPLE

1. INTRODUCTION

In the first stage of our research we investigated what changes had taken place in the lives of young homeless people two years on from the first interviews we conducted with them in 2010. Some of our respondents had found work and accommodation, others had returned home, and some had remained on the street. Two fifths (40%) of our respondents were no longer homeless and had found regular work and accommodation, usually in a dormitory. During this time some returned to the street. A third of the original cohort remained on the street and made no attempt to change their lives. We had no information regarding a fifth of our respondents and do not know where and in what fashion they are living. It is possible that some of them are no longer living on the street. Similar results were reported by Thompson et al. (2006) and Raleigh-DuRoff (2004): after a given period of time, 40% of young homeless people were still living on the street.

Six years on we again looked into where and how people who had been homeless were living. We were only able to obtain information on 50 of the original 90 individuals we questioned (of which 32 were men and 18 women). Our findings suggest only a relatively small change has taken place in the way

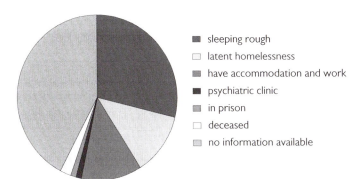

- sleeping rough
- latent homelessness
- have accommodation and work
- psychiatric clinic
- in prison
- deceased
- no information available

Graph 43. The current lifestyle of the young people we interviewed six years ago (shown in absolute figures)
NB: Latent homelessness means that an individual lives in a dormitory and has work, albeit often unstable. The relatively high frequency of people who are still homeless might be due to the fact that we have more information on them than on those who returned to society and are uncontactable.

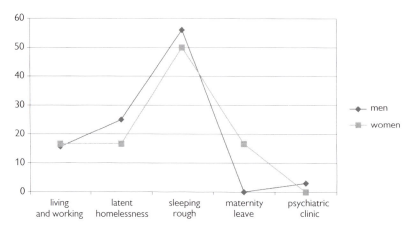

Graph 44. The current lifestyle of the young people we interviewed six years ago (shown in percentages)

these people live. Half of them, i.e. a third of the original group, are still living on the street. A quarter are latent homeless who have a job and live in a dormitory. A quarter have returned to society.

As we see in the graph, there is no significant difference between the relative frequency of men and women who manage to quit the street. To some extent the results are distorted by the group comprising homeless mothers, who receive various social benefits. The question remains as to whether these women will manage to look after themselves and their children after their maternity leave ends.

In order to understand better the life story of our respondents, we looked into **which factors impacted on whether they had remained on the street or re-entered society**. It turned out that the most significant influence in this respect was their experience of childhood. People whose parents had neglected them or who had ended up in institutional care were far more likely to remain on the street (r = 0.506). The following factors were also important, albeit to a slightly lesser extent: mental health issues (r = 0.386), drug use (r = 0.331), and behavioural problems originating in childhood (r = 0.295) that gradually led to criminal activity. Mental health issues and behavioural problems may be linked to negative experiences from childhood that impact the rest of an individual's life. Drugs will always have a desocialising effect regardless of the personality of the user and how they spent their childhood.

2. MORE DETAILED ANALYSIS OF CHANGES IN THE LIVES OF OUR YOUNG RESPONDENTS

The research also analysed the lives of 30 young people who had been living on the street six years previously (Vágnerová, Marek, Csémy, 2017). It was based on in-depth interviews that were held from January to June 2016. We used a partially structured interview, i.e. a predetermined range of topics and questions relating to the current life of the individual and their interpersonal relationships. When selecting the individual topics to be discussed we drew on data that we had received from the same respondents six years previously. The interview lasted on average between an hour and an hour and a half. With the consent of the participants it was recorded and then transcribed word for word. After identifying common themes, the testimony was divided into individual thematic areas and divided into subcategories on the basis of its content. Analytical induction, based on the principle of repetition and a constant comparative strategy (Osborn and Smith, 2008) was used to track down individual categories. Wherever necessary we also resorted to quantitative methods.

Our cohort comprised 30 people (19 men and 11 women) aged 25–32, who had previously lived on the street for at least one year. The individuals contacted were part of a group of 90 young homeless people analysed six years before, who had attended the drop-in charity Naděje in Prague. We managed to track them down via Facebook or their former acquaintances, i.e. we used the snowball method. Every single person contacted agreed to be interviewed, which may have something to do with their experience of the interviewer the first time round. Each person was given CZK 200 for the interview, and this may have motivated those who are still homeless. Since the cohort was a third of the size of the original group, the results may to a certain extent be skewed. For example, there may be a slightly higher frequency of the manifestly homeless and a lower number of latent homeless or people who have returned to society, live elsewhere, and are not in contact with their former acquaintances.

The aim of the research was to acquire information on the current lives of those we questioned and the relationships they had with those around them.

- **How they are living at present**, whether they have returned to society or are still living on the street or in a transitional state that might be deemed the partial abandonment of a homeless lifestyle. How they would evaluate their lives over the last five years. **Which factors led to their making it off the street** and which contributed to their remaining homeless. What kind of person managed to return to society and what kind of person remained on the street, i.e. which personality traits, opinions, attitudes and entrenched experiences had a positive impact and which a negative impact.
- **What kind of interpersonal relationships they have**, whether they are capable of maintaining a long-term relationships with someone. Whether their relationships with people over the last few years have changed and whether this has in any way affected their **motivation to change their lifestyle**. Good relationships with close friends can encourage a willingness to quit life on the street, whether this be thanks to the conviction that it makes good sense or the availability of the necessary support. It is highly likely that the

maintenance or restoration of relationships with friends will have a positive influence on an individual's maturity and insight into previous problems.

3. THE CURRENT LIFESTYLE OF OUR YOUNG RESPONDENTS

As regards current status and lifestyle, our cohort can be divided into three categories:

- **People who are working and living in an apartment**, be this their own, rented or with their parents or relatives. One of our former respondents (m) has his own apartment. One (f) returned home to her mother's, who is looking after the respondent's two children. Overall this subgroup represents a **third of our cohort**, with a preponderance of women (three men and three women have a job, and four women are on maternity leave). The number of young people who quit the street corresponds to other research findings (Levinson, 2004). A subgroup of this category comprises **mothers on maternity leave**.[12] These mums receive social benefits and either live with their partner in a rented apartment, on their own in an apartment paid for by a charity, or move between friends and relatives paying different rent. A (25, f) falls into this category: "*I live with my uncle, so soon I'll have to organise a shelter... I lived in an apartment in R. The social services paid half my rent, but then they stopped payment and I had to move because I owed CZK 5,000* [USD 212]... *Then me and a friend shared an apartment for a year or more... and then we moved into a dormitory.*" A question mark hangs over the fate of these women when their maternity leave comes to an end.

- **People who live in dormitories and shelters** and work, albeit under the terms of temporary contracts. This group comprises five people (four men and one woman), one sixth of the cohort. They do not have stable employment and are not attempting to find it because of the risk of execution proceedings. However, they recognise the need to work. They are no longer manifestly homeless and would like to quit the street definitively, but have thus far been unable to. They do not have the money to rent their own apartment, and some find it difficult to maintain their accommodation in a dormitory. Neither dormitory nor shelter is ideal for their needs and they are put off by the company they are surrounded by. T (26, m): "*As far as I'm concerned what would be ideal is a shelter specifically for people with jobs and not for those being paid by the social services to piss about doing fuck all. When you get in from work and see that they've just been lounging around in bed all day it gets on your nerves and saps your motivation to push things further.*"

---

12 Mothers on maternity leave receive social benefits conditional upon their looking after a child up to three years old.

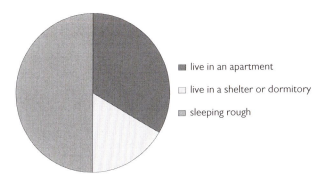

Graph 45. The current lifestyle of young people who were homeless six years ago

- **People still living on the street and sleeping in reception centres, on the Hermes boat, in non-residential premises, or outdoors**. During the course of the last five years, one third of this subgroup (five people) have lived in a dormitory, a shelter, or with relatives, but have not worked. Subsequently they have yet again found themselves on the street. Men predominate (eleven) over women (four). Some of our respondents prefer living in a squat or sleeping rough, because they do not want to be subordinate to anyone. These are mostly people who take drugs. If they work, then it is only sporadically on a cash-in-hand basis. Many of them are reliant on social benefits and charities, or resort to non-standard means of subsistence (panhandling and begging). They sometimes sleep on the Hermes or in reception centres, depending on the availability of beds (if they are not banned from the facility) and their own financial circumstances. Š (27, m) regards a reception centre to be an inexpensive solution to his situation, even though it does not offer him any privacy: *"The reception centre isn't that bad. I mean, beggars can't be choosers. I'm glad I've got somewhere to go where I can sleep, take a shower and have a square meal. That's basically all I need."* Similar feelings were expressed regarding reception centres by the cohort studied by M. Shier et al. (2010).

In terms of personal life story our cohort can be divided into five categories:
a) People who spent most of their childhood in a functional family that later split up. This breakup set off a chain reaction of other changes that provoked unfortunate outcomes. Conflict in their families led these people to the street, though they were able to return to society within a relatively short space of time. Such people do not need special support and assistance.
b) Women who found themselves homeless as a result of an unsuitable relationship or group of friends, tended to be in problematic partnerships, drank and took drugs. The birth of a child provided the impetus to change their lifestyle and was often accompanied by the breakdown of the relationship

with their partner, also homeless. These women need help and support, especially if such is not forthcoming from their family or new partner.

c) People who are disadvantaged in many ways (they grew up in an institution, have no stable family environment and no qualifications), but managed to reach an acceptable situation in life, usually with some assistance. However, they are unable to take the next step, that from casual work to stable employment and from a dormitory to their own apartment. They lack the support of a family, either because they have no family or because they have no close relationship with any of their relatives. They are able to work, even though they tend not to be systematic and are not always capable of holding down a job.

d) People who had a problematic childhood, have no stable environment, and lack the necessary habits and abilities. They have debts and a criminal record, often take drugs, and are not capable of pursuing any systematic activity. They need assistance. However, they are incapable of accessing the assistance on offer, especially if it comes with conditions attached, e.g. a ban on drugs or a duty to find work.

e) Drug addicts. What childhood they had and whether their family would support their return to society is no longer of any consequence, because without treatment no change to their situation is possible. Of paramount importance in the case of these people is the elimination of the addiction, something for which they do not always have the motivation. They would be assisted by a properly timed period of abstinence (rehab) and a stable environment.

4. FACTORS THAT INFLUENCED THE LIVES OF YOUNG PEOPLE

Our analysis of the interviews conducted shows that the **same factors that contributed to a person becoming homeless also impact on their subsequent lives**.

1. The family of origin

We anticipated that the experience gained in their family of origin would impact on the subsequent life of our respondents, and this assumption was confirmed. All of our respondents who are now working and have found accommodation grew up in a family that was functional until they were at least twelve years old. (One man lived in a functional adoptive family, and if his foster mother had not died would probably have not found himself living on the street.) The situation is more complex in the case of women on maternity leave. Two of our respondents had a functional family environment, and two spent their childhood in a problematic family but for the moment are looking after their children (or have just begun to look after them). The situation is different in the case of those who are still homeless. Their families were largely problematic (80% of cases). The parents did not look after their children or tyrannised them, with the result that many spent a sizable chunk of their childhood in institutions (27%) or foster families (13%). We may conclude from this that the **influence of a person's family of origin is manifest in their adult life**, e.g. in how they cope with the demands of life. Ongoing feelings of insecurity and entrenched defence mechanisms have a negative influence on the development of executive functions. This results in an inability to make and implement plans, insufficient self-control, and impulsive behaviour. Such people may also have inherited disadvantageous dispositions from their biological parents. One third of them have equally problematic siblings who have also lived or are living on the street. Moreover, it is clear that a relationship with a functional family could contribute to a return to society, and that the opposite holds true also. People whose relatives are also homeless have no reason to change their life.

2. Personality traits that influence a person's way of experiencing, reasoning and behaving

Certain personality traits can affect whether a person becomes and remains homeless. A comparison of the results of an EPQ/S completed by our group of young homeless people and a group of people close in age and studying at university (Koženỳ, 1999) showed that the homeless people attribute to themselves different personality traits than their mainstream contemporaries. People living on the street regard themselves as more social and open, but at the same time more emotionally unbalanced. They admit to having insufficient control over their feelings. They rated themselves as being less adaptable, and realised that they have a tendency to ignore social norms and to indulge in risky and sometimes asocial activities. A low lie scale score suggested a minimal attempt to present themselves in a better light, which can be interpreted as a manifestation of indifference regarding the opinions of other people and an unwillingness to submit to social expectations. A comparison of the results of the EPQ/S and our respondents' current lifestyle shows that people who are no longer homeless or who came close to quitting the street five years previously had a higher **social adaptability level** ($x = 2.87$, SD = 1.49) than those who remained homeless ($x = 6.21$, SD = 1.82, t = 5.23, df = 29, p = 0.05). In other categories the differences between both groups was relatively small. What this means is that a person's return to society can be influenced by certain personality traits.

3. Level of education and professional qualifications

Education does not play much of a role as regards whether or not a person escapes homelessness, since the majority of the group (84%) has no education. The initial work experience these people acquired prior to becoming homeless might have a certain significance. What we did discover was how important the **means of subsistence selected** while on the street was. The majority of people who later found stable employment and accommodation (70%) had already been working even when homeless. People who remained homeless had been less active five years previously, with only a fifth of them finding casual work. The commonest forms of livelihood amongst this group were theft (73%), use of charities (53%), and begging and scavenging (47%). This group adopted a more passive outlook and relied on others. (It should be pointed out that some of the people who no longer live on the street also stole and rummaged through garbage bins during this period of their life.) At present they are stealing far less frequently, since many of them are serving a suspended sentence and therefore prefer to beg.

At present, **those who are still on the street are surviving by means typical of the homeless**: by begging, scavenging, theft, and obtaining social benefits.

- M (25, m, homeless for six years) no longer steals: "*Yeah, **I used to steal**, but these days everything I would have stolen in the past I can find just lying around.*"
- M (28, m, homeless for six years) on the other hand…: "***I still steal** and finally I've got the social security on my case. Right now I'm waiting for my first payment. I've sorted out all the paperwork.*"
- S (27, f, homeless for six years): "***Right from the start I used to steal**. But I've had enough of all of that, I pushed the boat out too far and I was caught by security guards who locked me in a room… Stealing is no longer for me.*"
- P (27, m, homeless for seven years): "*I used to steal. I'd visit shops and businesses. I was caught a few times but never sentenced. **I still go begging**, but recently things have gone down the plughole. I walk around the area beneath the castle, and when the weather's nice it can be a lucrative gig.*"
- L (26, f, homeless for nine years): "***I've kept myself alive through begging for the last year and a half**. But then they banged me up and I was banned from Prague. My knees hurt, a couple of times I was kicked.*"
- O (30, m, homeless for six years): "*I go begging. I was once banned from Charles Bridge. **Most of us get down on our knees at some point**. How much do I make? Depends… it's good over bank holidays.*"

4. Inability and unwillingness to work

An inability and unwillingness to work systematically will often lead to home-lessness and will play a part in a person continuing to live this way of life. The chronically homeless have a **problem finding work as well as holding down a job**. This is often due to a lack of perseverance, an inability to keep to working hours, and workplace conflict. They quickly lose interest in the work and are fired or leave voluntarily.

- M (28, m): "*Yeah, I've found work a few times over the last five years. It's been on building sites and lasted a month. I left after a while. I don't know why. **I just don't*** *particularly like going every day to a job that's killing me. I need an afternoon or evening shift, I can't get up in the morning. I don't even want to learn how. I simply have no desire to get up at five in the morning and go to a factory.*" M does not have the necessary work habits. In addition he is a drug addict, a factor that severely restricts his activities.

- L (27, m) is a drug addict: "***I work on a casual basis***, *two or three times a week. I'll take anything that's going. I work on building sites, and if I'm feeling hungry then I'll stand at traffic lights and wash windscreens. I once worked at a solar power plant for about three months, but **after a while I got bored**.*"
- L (26, f) was fired from her job: "*I was working in Jihlava on a crate washing machine at Albert. I was there for nine months, but **they sacked me in December** for attacking a girl... she simply pissed me off. Something snapped inside me.*"

Many of our respondents have no desire to work because they are facing execution proceedings for the recovery of debt, and so a large part of their income would be deducted. This applies to M (29, m): "*From time to time I find work. But it's the same old thing, time and time again – is it worth going to work if you have no way of knowing if you're going to be paid for it. **If I found a job** paying CZK 18,000* [USD 765]*, they'd take it all and leave me with the existential minimum... To work an entire month for six thousand crowns is just fucking nuts.*"

Overall, a person's ability or willingness to work may be negatively influenced by personality traits (a tendency to provoke conflict, an inability to work in groups or respect authority, etc.), inadequate self-discipline (an inability to get up for work and respect working hours), and an inability to cope with stress. A person's willingness to work may be negatively impacted by unpaid debt and the threat of execution proceedings. Drug addiction is a significantly limiting factor.

5. Debts

Debt represents a real problem for a person attempting to return to normal society. Most of our respondents ignore debt for a long time, which means the amount owed gradually accrues to such an extent that it is unpayable practically speaking. Accepting responsibility for one's life means displaying a willingness to resolve this problem too, regardless of how unpleasant a prospect it may be. There is a difference between our two subgroups, not only in terms of the acceptance of responsibility for debt, but also for the level of debt and the extent to which it is repayable. Those of our respondents who managed to return to society were mostly on the street for only one year, and so their debts did not grow too much. **People who work and have accommodation are usually in the process of dealing with their debt** (70%).

- L (27, f): "*Yeah, I've got debts. I don't know how much I owe. I owe for health insurance, social insurance, fines from the police and public transport. I mean, that goes* *hand in hand with being homeless. **Right now I'm paying off two bailiffs**, and I can't take on more than that.*"

- K (29, f): "*Right now they're deducting the amount I owed from my wages… five thousand at least, depending on how much I make. **I've applied for bankruptcy**.*"

Even those who work and live in a dormitory or shelter **are trying to pay off their debts**.

- P (25, m) cancelled his debts by means of personal bankruptcy: "*When they calculated my debt during the court proceedings, I owed CZK 280,000 [USD 11,900]. The fines kept on mounting up on the execution orders, but **the fact I declared personal bankruptcy** meant they put a cap on the penalties.*"
- T (26, m): "***I'm trying to pay off at least part of the debt**. I don't have much choice with the bailiff breathing down my neck. What persuaded me to take this course of action? The fact that I don't want to remain homeless until god knows when, so there was nothing for it but to start re-integrating into normal life. If everything goes according to plan, then I'll declare bankruptcy in September.*"

Mothers on maternity leave do not repay their debts, because they have no funds.

- A (25, f): "*I started to make repayments, except then I found myself in a financial situation in which I could no longer carry on… I realise there are problems that have to be sorted out, but all that will have to wait until I start work. For the moment I'm not doing a thing because **there is no way I can make payments out of maternity benefit**.*"
- K (27, f) is completely resigned to being in debt: "*Yeah, **I've always got debts. I can barely make ends meet as it is**, so even though the lawyer from WfW [Women for Women] drew up a payments schedule for me, I'm ignoring it. If I had a permanent job I'd drag myself out of this situation, except I'd be left with precisely bugger all.*" As a result K remains in her existing situation regardless of whether resolving it will be even more difficult in the future.

Most people (70%) **living on the street do not give a thought to repaying their debts**.

- M (25, m) does not even know how much he owes and certainly has no idea how to deal with his debts: "*I'm not sure how much… around a million maybe. When I was eighteen I took out a loan of CZK 100,000 [USD 4,240], plus there's health insurance, social insurance, transport fines, credit… I have no idea how much it all comes to. The manager said something about insolvency, **except I don't know how to set about organising it**.*"
- M (28, m) believes that prison could help him: "*I've got these debts, so I really hope they bang me up for something soon. **I have debts… what more can I say?** And what's the point in going to work when you know you're gonna end up with bugger all? I want them to throw me in prison, because I'd stop taking drugs and get myself together.*"

- P (29, m, homeless for eleven years): "*I owe about six million.* ***I've resigned myself to being on emergency financial support for the rest of my life.*** *A friend of mine is a lawyer and he told me that if I work, they can deduct just about everything from my wages.*" Debts are enormously demoralising for people on the street. Paying them off means being incredibly frugal, and combined with the demands of work represents such a huge burden that many people are unable to accept it. Some have tried to find a solution, but without success. Personal bankruptcy is not an option for many, because they would have to pay off one third of the debt within three years, something they are unable to do.

6. Use of alcohol and drugs

Most of our younger respondents drink alcohol at least occasionally, and some often. However, six years previously only one man, who is still homeless, could have been considered an alcoholic. **There were no significant differences as regards drug use, especially marijuana**, which most of our cohort smoked occasionally. Only three individuals, pervitin users, could be deemed addicts at the time of our interviews. Over five years since the original interviews a change had taken place in this sphere too.

People who had quit the street had reduced or eliminated their alcohol intake and drug use (involving marihuana mostly).
- L (27, m) who has been working for several years and lives in his own apartment, stopped drinking: "*I kept away from drugs. I simply drank. I used to drink a hell of a lot. I reckon I was a borderline alcoholic. Firstly, I liked the taste, and secondly, it put me in a state in which I simply no longer cared about a thing.* ***But I've recovered and stopped drinking.*** *A young daughter was the impulse that made me give up.*"
- Z (32, f): "*I've been clean for three years. I basically stopped doing drugs when I got pregnant.*"
- K (29, f): "***I stopped doing drugs in prison.*** *It simply wasn't possible before, because I always had access to them. I used to take Subutex* [Buprenorphine] *and pervitin. The Subutex was the worst thing ever to happen to me. I was afraid of rehab, but when I started walking like a zombie, I began to look forward to the prospect of prison.*"

People who are still on the street are usually ongoing drug users. All that has changed is their preference for a certain type of psychoactive substance.
- K (27, m) switched from pervitin to Subutex: "***It was my ex-girlfriend that got me onto Subutex.*** *Before that I had taken pervitin, heroin, and I had smoked. Then I discovered I was addicted and things started to go downhill. I wanted to go into rehab.*" At present K is in prison.

- L (27, f, homeless for nine years): "*I took Subutex for maybe four years. Pervitin kills you, Subutex kills you, and booze kills you. These days I'm completely stoned all day, every day.*" L has had several stints in prison.
- Some of our respondents stopped using hard drugs (pervitin) and took up smoking marijuana instead. P (27, m): "*I managed to stop doing hard drugs and I'm pleased about that. These days I just smoke grass. For the moment I'm sticking to that, though I'm smoking more and more and acting like a twat. I wake up in the morning and I have to have a joint just to get going. I didn't used to smoke so much. I'm beginning to think that I'm addicted to grass. There are times when I genuinely have no control over it.*"

People who find themselves back on the street often return to drugs. M (28, f) is a case in point: "*When my baby was born, I gave up completely. I only started again when I became homeless, in order to get by on the street. But then I'll definitely give up again.*" Alcohol and drugs are ways of eliminating unpleasant feelings. They resolve the immediate situation while worsening prospects for the future. Drug addicts and alcoholics need treatment. The social services on their own cannot help, and the treatment of addictions does not fall under their purview. These people admit to having a drug problem and have already realised that drugs are the cause of many of their tribulations. They are aware that they are unable to resolve their addiction and are reconciled to it.

7. Criminal activity and early predictors of crime

Five years ago there was no difference between both groups as regards **the frequency of behavioural disorder or criminal offences committed**. At that time two individuals who now live normal lives and four individuals who are still homeless (two of whom were in prison at that time) had a suspended sentence for criminal acts and both now live normal lives. However, there was a difference in the severity of problematic behaviour during childhood. Half of the currently chronically homeless men had been placed in a youth detention centre as adolescents. None of those who returned to normal society had this experience, which might be explained by the fact that the group comprises mainly women.

Over the past five years, two people (one man and one woman) who are no longer homeless have served time in prison. **This proved to be the catalyst for them to change their lifestyle**. In their case a prison sentence served as a strong deterrent.
- J (33, m): "*I was inside for eight months. I was caught driving without a licence and sentenced to eight months. It brought order into my life and since then I've been living normally. It was my own stupidity. I was convinced I'd receive a suspended sentence. I was always pushing the boat out further and further.*"

- K (29, f): "*I was banged up for a year and a half for burglary. I was sentenced to three years and right now I've been seven months at home on probation. The worst thing about prison was the other people. Most of them were gypsies and they were forever popping pills and being aggressive and vile. **It was while I was inside that I realised I wanted to live a normal life**, find a job, be with the kids.*"

A stint in prison does not always serve as a deterrent, as we see in the case of L (26, f): "*I was inside for a year and a half. At least I got myself off Subutex. It was a fucking holiday inside, I don't know what all the fuss is about. **They look after you**, you have a shower every day, three meals a day.*" L spent a short time on the street before returning to prison.

For some homeless people theft is perfectly normal and part of their daily routine. M (28, m): "*There are no security guards in Albert from seven to half past eight, so you earn your keep then go for a coffee. **Each day is the same**. I get up, **go to the supermarket, steal something, sell it**, have something to eat, and I'm ready to face the day. There's maybe 200 crowns* [USD 8.5] *left over for me, plus minus. I'm lazy. I won't get out of bed for less than 1,000.*"

Others steal while under the influence of drugs, such as L (27, m): "*You know those shops in the centre? **Well occasionally, when I run out of money, I go there and steal things**. Recently I got totally shit-faced on pervitin… apparently I kicked open the doors and took a notebook that was lying on the floor. I don't remember a thing.*"

The frequency of property crime and violence increases the longer a person spends on the street. Some of our respondents had **problems with aggression**. These were mostly individuals addicted to drugs or alcohol. Their tendency to react unreasonably makes it difficult for them to return to society.

- M (25, m): "*I've been prosecuted for affray and gross bodily harm. I've been up before the magistrate's court twice for gross bodily harm. **I'm always getting into scraps**.*"
- N (27, m): "*About three years ago I received a suspended sentence. And then I was sent to prison because I was in breach of that sentence. **I punched some guy**. I didn't break anything, but it took him a long time to get off the ground. He was taken away by ambulance with a busted face and that was that.*"
- J (28, m) was given a suspended sentence for causing affray: "*I got five years suspended. **I got into some stupid fight or other**. I was completely off my face.*"

8. Degree of adaptation to a homeless lifestyle

The length of time spent on the street and an individual's adaptation to a homeless lifestyle is also important. The longer someone spends on the street, the more their habits and attitudes change, usually for the worse. It then becomes more difficult for such people to turn their life around. Most of our respondents who escaped the street were homeless for only one year on average. The only exception was one woman who spent seven years on the street. However, after serving a prison sentence she returned home to her mother and children and now has a job. Half of those who remain homeless six years on had already been living on the street for two or more years at the time of our first interviews. In other words, they had become accustomed to a homeless lifestyle and it is highly likely they will continue to live on the street.

9. The age at which a person becomes homeless

The age at which a person becomes homeless is also important. A certain degree of maturity and previous **experience of a normal way of life** can positively impact on their willingness and ability to quit the street. The people we interviewed who managed to quit the street were 24 on average when they became homeless, while those who are still homeless were on average only 21. They had not yet acquired the requisite habits and accepted the fact that an adult person has certain duties and responsibilities. Their time on the street had reshaped them, and this was an obstacle to a smooth return to normal life.

10. The significance of earlier hopes and plans

Our young respondents had often attempted to quit the street, not always successfully. This is borne out by the ideas they had of their future six years previously. The majority (70%), who returned to society, already had a **clear plan worked out**: they wanted to find work and accommodation, and this they did. Of the group that continues to live on the street at present, only one third had such plans. Half of this group had never given any thought to their future. Two people said they did not want to be sleeping rough, but did not further specify their hopes and were doing nothing to realise them.

4.1 A DESCRIPTION OF THE PEOPLE WHO REMAINED HOMELESS

Our analysis of the interviews conducted with the group of chronically homeless people who have been on the street for more than six years throws up several, probably generally valid, findings as to what kind of people these are and why they remain on the street or fall back repeatedly into episodic homelessness:

1) People who remain on the street focus on the present. They postpone unpleasant decisions and do not resolve their problems. They have taught themselves to survive on a day-to-day basis. They will always opt for the line of least resistance and will remain in their comfort zone, their defence against stress.

They do not pursue active life management, and inasmuch as they make plans, these tend simply to be merely declarations of intent that they are unable to fulfil. They do not have sufficiently developed volitional traits, they are unsystematic and lack tenacity, they lack discipline, and they are unable to accept so much as normal constraints. Their approach is passive: they are resigned to their situation and fatalistic in outlook. They admit to being lazy and comfortable as they are. They do not especially like street life, but are unable to do anything to improve their situation. Moreover, they do not believe that any positive outcomes would result were they to change. Their approach is the result of a combination of negative life experience and deleterious personality traits, and their adaptation to a homeless lifestyle and drug use spanning many years. This approach is clear in the following comments:

- O (28, m): "*I have no idea what I'm going to do. **I don't give it much thought**. Things'll work out somehow.*"
- M (28, m): "*I'm homeless because **I'm a lazy fucker**. I don't feel like making an effort. Why should I make an effort just for myself? It's comfortable here, **I'm too comfortable to do anything**. All I'm worried about is that feeling this comfortable I'll find myself in a situation in which I simply die on the street.*"
- P (27, m): "***I'm resigned to things**. Things just didn't work out for me.*"
- J (27, m): "***Perhaps this is how things are meant to be**. Perhaps this is where I was meant to end up. I'd like to change things, but who knows what karma has in store for me?*"

It would appear that these people are aware of their problems and inabilities and have become resigned to the situation. They are waiting for some spur from without that would transport them off the street, but are not themselves making any effort to resolve their situation.

2) They do not respect rules and do not fulfil their obligations. They are unwilling and mostly incapable of accepting responsibility. They cannot hold down a job because if they are not satisfied at work they will not comply with the daily routine but enter into workplace conflicts. As a result, either their employer gets rid of them or they quit their job. They cannot resist a more attractive offer. They have no money management skills and simply fritter away any money they make. Normal work does not satisfy them because it does not offer money immediately and they always have the feeling they are not being paid enough. They like the freedom that street life offers them.

- M (28, m): "***I just don't see the point in killing myself every day at work**. I don't get up in the morning and I don't want to learn how.*"
- L (27, m): "*One day I just realised that I wasn't enjoying work and I never returned. **It's simpler to live on the street than to go to work**.*"
- M (35, m): "*People go to work when they need money, and **when they've got some money then they don't go to work**.*"

- L (26, f): "***The moment I have money I spend it on fripperies*** *and then I'm back where I started.*"

Their problems adapting to normal life are tied up with their personality traits as well as to their lack of social skills, and this may be a consequence of their life experience. These people are unable to respect the ordinary demands that life makes and are unable to adapt to others and respect authority.

3) Unpaid debts and execution proceedings represent a huge burden that our respondents are unwilling and perhaps unable to accept. They are not motivated to work systematically because they know that they would have to pay off their debts from their wages, in which case they would be left with almost nothing. It is also possible that the risk of execution proceedings offers a way for them to rationalise their unwillingness to function systematically.

- M (28, m): "*I would find a job except that* **I don't want to have to pay off my debts**. *It means going to work with the prospect of earning absolutely fucking sod all.*"
- P (29, m): "***If I find a job, they'll deduct almost all of my wages.***"

4) Drugs and the destructive effects of an addiction on behaviour **are very often the reason a person cannot quit street life**.

- O (30, m): "*I hate it here but the drugs stop me doing anything about it. I've become very comfortable, though* **the drugs play a large part in that**. *You become a slave to the drugs.* **I hate being where I am, but I'm incapable of doing anything about it**. *I have no desire to do anything. I need to be locked up in prison, perhaps that would do me some good. I've become resigned to the fact that I'm here for good.*"
- P (27, m): "*I wake up in the morning and have to have a joint before I can do any-thing. And when it's time to go to work, I can't move because* **I'm totally fucking mashed**."

5) They would like someone to wave a magic wand over all their problems and cause them to disappear. They need someone who would lead them to safety, though it is by no means clear what they would be willing or able to contribute in the way of cooperation. They are clear as to what they don't want, but have very little idea of what they actually do want.

- P (27, m): "*I don't know.* **No way I'll manage it on my own**. *I need help.*"
- L (26, f): "*You have to want something. Right now I want something, but* **I need help**. *I need someone to kick me in the ass.*"

6) They are tied to the homeless community, and even though they are aware that it has a negative impact on them, outside of it they often no longer have any significant personal social links. **They do not trust members of mainstream society** and it is clear to them that they would not be accepted by them. There is a mutual lack of understanding, since each group has different experiences and is used to different modes of conduct. All of our respondents grew up in a very problematic family or an institution, and their parents were incapable of accepting responsibility even for their own lives.

- M (25, m): "*If I were in touch with a different sort of person* it might work out."
- S (32, f): "*I'm used to being amongst these people. **I need to get out of Prague in order to clear my head**.*"
- O (30, m): "***I'm kind of frightened of normal life**. I'm scared of going somewhere and people asking me what I do, etc. What should I tell them.*" O's worries are related to the ongoing stigma of being or of having been homeless. In order to quit the street, O would have to cut himself off entirely from the past, his relationships with other homeless people, and his experiences on the street.

Our respondents are not satisfied with street life but **are unable to do anything to improve their situation**.

- P (27, m, homeless for 19 years): "***I've been sleeping rough for eight years and I've had enough**. The cold, the frost, sleeping in reception centres... I mean, this is no way to lead your life. I was young and stupid, I thought I was cool, I thought that sleeping rough was a hoot. But that's all bullshit. It's a fucking nightmare.*"
- M (28, m, homeless for six years) is of the same opinion: "*What's so fucking great about sleeping rough? Bugger all. **You're the scum of society**, people look at you askance, for them you're either a criminal, an alcoholic or a junkie, and it's all your fault. Absolutely everything about being homeless gets on my tits.*"
- Z (32, f, homeless for nine years): "***Everything is fucking horrible**. Everyone judges you for having sunk so low. You no longer have the strength to do anything about it. The street is simply another name for hell.*"

4.2 A DESCRIPTION OF THE PEOPLE WHO RETURNED TO SOCIETY

Our analysis of the interviews we conducted with the group of people who no longer live on the street reveals several valid findings relating to their character and the difficulties they faced upon their return to normal society, i.e. what they believe is important if a person is to escape homelessness. These people had to resolve a host of problems. They had to stop drinking and taking drugs, find self-confidence within themselves and create a new daily routine, and in some cases re-establish relationships with their family (Johnson and Chamberlain, 2008). Most of these individuals had been homeless for two years at most. Their recommendations are as follows:

1) Reach a firm decision to resolve the situation and act. They had to accept responsibility, cope with unpleasant situations, and most importantly not give up. Those of our respondents who quit the street had to activate their will and maintain their motivation in the face of unpleasant feelings.

- Z (32, f, homeless for eight years): "*You have to find the strength inside you. **You have to really want** to get off the street and then just do it. If you give up, you're fucked.*"
- P (25, m, homeless for two years): "***The most difficult things was taking the first step***."
- V (32, f, homeless for two years): "*Don't look for excuses, **just start**. I suddenly realised I had spent too long on the street, but that is something you only become aware of when you're no longer homeless.*"
- J (33, m, homeless for two years): "*The whole time I was homeless I was waiting for something, for some opportunity or for something to change. But the truth is that every day offers such opportunities. **You simply have to grab them**.*"

2) Find a job and remain in it even though it might not be one hundred percent satisfying and can occasionally be unpleasant. Create a new daily routine and stick to it.
- T (26, m, homeless for two years): "*I have a job. **I'd prefer something else, but at least it's work**.*"
- L (27, m, homeless for two years): "*The most difficult thing is getting up in the morning and going to work. **You have to set up a routine**. I just keep saying that I have to get up and go to work, that I have no choice.*"

3) Rely on yourself and not expect someone else to resolve *your* problems. It is of course true that people with greater problems and fewer competencies will need assistance, and that without it they would not even be partially self-sufficient.
- T (26, m, homeless for two years): "*The social services can't help you any more than they already do. **It's now down to the will of the individual**. Either you want to get your ass off the street or you don't.*"
- J (28, f, homeless for two years): "*It's down to the individual and their will power and **whether or not they have a burning desire to drag themselves off the bottom**. I simply told myself I had to get up and pull myself together and lead a normal life.*"

4) Break ties with people who remain on the street and with the entire infrastructure that helps homeless people and paradoxically keeps them dependent on its services.
- T (30, m, homeless for two years): "*What really helped was relocating and **cutting all ties with people I'd known on the street**.*"
- K (29, f, homeless for seven years, during the whole of which time she took drugs): "*You need the **help of someone who's not on the street** and you have to be outside the range of the drug activity.*"
- T (26, m, homeless for two years): "***It was when I started to cut down on visits to the drop-in centre*** [Naděje] *that I began to realise I had to take myself in hand.*"

Some of our respondents were helped by an outside intervention, e.g. a stint in prison, **or an event of personal significance**, such as the birth of a child, that encouraged them to change their lifestyle. The mere realisation of the intolerable changes taking place within them, for instance when confronted by former acquaintances, was also enough to trigger change. However, achieving the desired change depended on the willingness of their family of origin to accept and assist them.

- K (29, f, homeless for seven years): "*It was while I was in prison that I realised that I was no longer living a normal life. If it hadn't been for prison, I would still be homeless and maybe even worse.*"
- J (33, m, homeless for two years): "*Prison brought order to my life.*"
- Z (32, f, homeless for eight years): "*I came to my senses when I realised I was pregnant and that I had to stop thinking only of myself.*"

SUMMARY

The lives of young homeless people, both past and present, displayed a certain dynamic. Their self-image (self-concept), needs and behaviour all changed. Most of them thought about quitting the street at least occasionally, but only some of them managed to. Others did nothing, usually because they were not sufficiently persistent and systematic. This latter group continues to believe that one day they will successfully return to mainstream society for good. Some of them have become resigned to their situation and realise that they are not capable of changing it. Sometimes they do not care and are indifferent to everything, including their own lives. Assistance for these people would consist solely in meeting their basic needs. As regards successfully quitting the street there are important skills, especially executive skills, that ensure self-management as well as sufficient self-confidence and determination. Support and assistance can also be important in a situation in which there has been an accretion of the burdens linked with a return to society. Since various factors contribute to a person becoming homeless and remaining so, these must be taken into consideration when a suitable form of help is being chosen.

5. THE INTERPERSONAL RELATIONSHIPS OF OUR YOUNG RESPONDENTS

Relationships with friends and relatives, especially if they are members of mainstream society, can be important for a homeless person. These relationships can help them in their efforts to return to mainstream society. This usually involves parents or siblings. Conversely, the relationships that were created while they were homeless, often sexual partnerships, may make leaving the street more difficult. The relationship a homeless person has with their children is a special case. For certain women the birth of a child provided the impetus necessary for them to change their lifestyle. Since all of these relationships are important, several of our questions were aimed at discovering our respondents' opinions of their parents, siblings, partners and children, as appropriate. The questions related to the following areas:

a) **How they rate their relationship with their parents**, i.e. their family of origin. Whether they are in contact with their parents and siblings and what their opinion is of the reasons behind improvements or breakdown in these relationships. Whether they have any insight into the causes of previous problems, whether they are capable of self-reflection and a recognition of their own culpability for the deterioration of these relationships, or whether they continue to feel hurt and incapable of owning up to their own mistakes.

b) **How they rate their partnerships up till now**, including relationships between people living on the street. Whether they have any insight into their own culpability in the breakdown of a relationship or are convinced it was their partner's fault.

c) **How important their child is** and whether it changed their life. How they understand parenthood and whether they are able to take responsibility for their offspring. Whether they are aware of their failure as parents and what conclusions they draw from this.

5.1 RELATIONSHIPS WITH PARENTS AND SIBLINGS

More than half of our cohort (N = 16) grew up in a dysfunctional family or in an institution. Eight of our respondents had such a problematic family that they were placed in institutional care. This means that more than half of our respondents lacked a stable family environment and the associated feelings of security and safety. Another five respondents lived with foster families. Only nine of our respondents, i.e. 30% of the group, lived within a functional family environment until the age of at least 12. Two thirds of the people who had a difficult childhood are still on the street, while the remaining third have managed to quit the street, even if only partially (they have a job and sleep at a dormitory).

Problematic family relationships and the lack of a stable environment **are often the reason a young person finds themselves sleeping rough**. Six years ago, half of our respondents were involved in conflictual situations with their parents and confessed to having bad relations with them. A third had reservations regarding their mother, and 40% found their father or stepfather intolerable. In certain cases the break with the parents had already taken place in childhood, especially in cases involving neglect or abuse. In other cases the breakdown in relations took place later, usually during adolescence. This was sometimes caused by the break-up of the family and the mother finding a new partner, or such problematic behaviour on the respondent's part that the family could not accept them.

At present, sixteen of our respondents (roughly half the group) say that **the relationship they have with their parents has improved.** (Six years ago one third of the group was in touch with their mother and just under a fifth with their father.) Most of our respondents spoke of losing what had previously been a hatred for real or perceived injustices. They now felt differently about their parents and were more accepting of their faults, and were even capable of acknowledging their own mistakes. This new perspective is a prerequisite for a return to mainstream society. An inability to forgive one's own misdemeanours is less common and was apparent in only four cases out of thirty, i.e. in 13% of cases. At present our respondents rate their relationships with their parents in various ways..

In particular, **people who no longer live on the street** (eight out of ten cases) were more successful in re-establishing contact with their parents and improving their relationship, a fact we may interpret as being part of their resocialisation. This does not mean that these relationships are ideal even now, but rather that they have been accepted for what they are.

- V (32, f, homeless for two years): "*I'm in contact with them by telephone. My mum is not the sort to display emotion. I'm in touch with my stepfather, whom I think of as my dad. He still drinks, but **I've learned to take him as he is.***"
- Sometimes contact is re-established with the parents only when our respondent has stopped living on the street and has found a job. Take J (28, f, homeless for two years): "***I got in touch only after I had moved off the street.** Before that I wasn't able to contact them because I knew they'd be disappointed. I've already visited them and things are ok.*" In J's case this involved a reconciliation with her adoptive parents.

Sometimes the birth of a child can lead to an attempt at reconciliation and the ironing out of relations within a family.

- K (29, f, homeless for seven years): "*I live with my mum now. **We only began to communicate after the birth of my little daughter.** Dad visits us once a month. Mum and dad are divorced but got back in contact because of my child.*"
- Z (32, f, homeless for eight years): "*Things got better with my family with the birth of my little girl, though otherwise it's just the same. Me and mum, we're constantly at each other's throats, though the situation is getting a bit better. **Both sides had to make an effort and own up to their mistakes.***"

Forgiveness of past injustices is not always easy, and despite the resumption of contact, some people find it hard to forget.

- Z (30, f) is reconciled with her parents, though the sense of grievance persists: "*I kept my distance because **I couldn't forgive them** for what they did to me.*

When someone hurts you, the experience remains with you. It was my mother who threw me out of the apartment, which is why I ended up as I did." Z's parents were in fact left with little choice in the matter, since their daughter, a drug addict, was the source of real difficulties.

- S (27, f, homeless for six years), whose ex-partner started going out with S's mother, feels similarly: "*My mum, sister and me, we get on ok, talk together. I visit them pretty often. **I've forgiven her, but I'll never forget**.*" Reconciliation is the first step towards a re-establishment of trust. However, this depends on both parties.

When a person has gained their own experience of life and greater maturity, they have an **overview of a situation and can understand their parents more and forgive them**.

- M (28, m, homeless for six years) is a case in point. Five years ago he forgave his mother, an alcoholic: "*I didn't speak to my mother for several years. It's because of her that I ended up like this. She was a drinker, she drank away the entire apartment. I couldn't get it out of my head for a long time, it made me sad. What happened, happened. My mum was largely to blame, but **at the end of the day she's my mum**... These days I look at it differently to how I used to and I see that **she wasn't entirely to blame**.*" M behaves as his mother used to. He does not look after his children and does not even pay maintenance.

A more mature opinion of the relationship they have with their parents is also manifest in a person's **willingness to accept a share of the blame for problems arising** (this applies to three of the eight people still on the street who grew up in a functioning family, either their own or adoptive).

- L (27, m, homeless for six years) grew up in a functional, adoptive family: "*I have a pretty good relationship with mum. She's even lent me her car. **I really disappointed my parents**. From the start they helped me out financially. I was forever lying to them, forever inventing stories. I was interested in money, to be frank, but I missed them.*" This represents a huge shift in L's opinions. When we spoke with him five years ago, he claimed to have no feelings for his parents. His problems and the relationship he has with his parents are caused by his drug addiction. At present he is in prison.

Some of our respondents, including those who have re-entered society and those who are still homeless, **would like to re-establish a relationship with their parents**, but the parents are not interested. This might be because the child disappointed them and they do not want new problems, or because they never had any interest in their offspring.

- T (30, m, spent two years on the street) attempted to make things up with his mother, but without success: "*I'm mainly in contact with my father. I last saw my mother a year ago. **I'd like to change the relationship I have with my mum**, but* *unfortunately the feeling is not mutual."* At present T has a job and is living in a rented flat.

- L (27, m, spent two years on the street) has tried in vain to establish contact with her adoptive father: *"I'm still not in contact with my father, **though I've been trying the whole time**. I've made loads of overtures, but there's been no response from him."* L's adoptive mother died and his adoptive father has no interest in him.

Sometimes a person's relationship with their parents does not improve even in adulthood, especially if the parents had no interest in the child (this was so in the case of half of those who remain to this day on the street).

- M (25, m, homeless for six years) grew up in a very problematic family: *"We're in contact via Facebook, but all that means is that **mum will occasionally write me something when she has to**, say for a birthday. Otherwise zilch. I had problems with both parents depending on which one I was living with. Dad drank and hit me, so I used to sleep round at the neighbour's. They're still the same. **Mum pretends to be pleased to see me** when I pop round. She says it's lovely to see me but as soon as I've closed the front door she's like, 'Oh, so you've come round here to eat again, have you?'"*

Many of our respondents who fetched up in a children's home or juvenile detention centre ask their parents why they didn't look after them. Their questions usually meet with little in the way of response. Bitterness and a sense of rejection remain with them, especially if neither of the parents has any interest in them even now. This is so in the case of J (27, m, homeless for six years): *"I tracked my father down using Facebook and we began to write to each other and meet up. It was a shock, to be honest. He had **never shown any interest in me, even when I was little**."*

Some of our respondents **have been unable to come to terms with a sense of grievance**, however justified or otherwise, even in adulthood.

- K (27, f, spent one year on the street) has no interest in contact with her mother, a drug addict: *"I don't talk to my mum at all. I don't know where she is, I haven't seen her for ages. It's not just because she's a junkie, it's also because of what she did. **She abandoned me and my brother** and told the court she had no interest in looking after two bastards. **I don't think of her has my mum any more**. Dad drank, but he only started when he found out that mum was a junkie. I tell everyone he failed as a father, but in the case of mum I can't for the life of me understand it."* Childhood left a negative mark on K, manifest both in her homelessness and problems she is having at present. Her version of events corresponds only partially to reality. Her mother initially left home because she was facing domestic violence. She only began to drink and take drugs upon becoming homeless.

- The relationship of another, 26-year-old female drug addict to her mother has only changed in that **it has shifted from hatred to ambivalence**. It includes reproaches and accusations on the one hand, and an openly expressed need for help on the other. This woman cannot forgive her mother for having found a new partner when she was still a child and not being willing to help her out even now: "*I don't speak to my mother. She's written a few letters and she visited me in prison in November, but that's all. She says I'm to get in touch as soon as I've found a job and somewhere to live. If I were a mum, I'd tell my child to come home. So often I've asked her to let me live with her and to help me. If mum said, yeah, she can live at home, then they'd have let me go. But she didn't, she said she wouldn't have me and that I could go to prison.*" This respondent's behaviour is so problematic that it is difficult to see her relationships with her mother improving. In addition to being a drug addict, it is very likely she suffers a personality disorder. She has been living on the street for nine years and at present is again in prison.

Some of our respondents have accepted **there will be no improvement in their relationship with their parents** and no longer make the effort.

- P (26, m, homeless for seven years) has made repeated attempts to contact his mother but has now given up: "*Nah, I'm not going try any longer. It's useless. I wrote to her on Facebook that I'm down and out in Prague, and she wrote back: 'you wanted to end up like this, so that's how you've ended up.' I realised she was kind of right, so I didn't get back in touch. I haven't seen her since I was twelve and in a children's home and then in a youth detention centre.*" Six years ago P's mother refused to meet him. It is clear that P has no stable environment anywhere and that this, along with this drug addiction, is the main reason he remains on the street.

- M (25, m, homeless for six years) has no interest in improving matters with his parents: "*I'm not even sorry they're not interested anymore. I've just accepted the idea.*"

Sometimes it is the parents who cannot forgive their own child.

- Š (27, m) was unable to cope with the arrival of his mother's new partner. He ended up fighting with the man and causing him bodily harm, something that did nothing to improve matters with his mother: "*I stood up for mum, because he came home completely pissed and slapped her. So I beat him up and was sent to prison for nine months. When I came out I was kind of expecting her to welcome me home and to tell him to fuck off, since I'd been the one to stick up for her. But no such luck. So in some way he had got inside her head. Because of him, my mum and me have no relationship whatsoever. We haven't spoken for two years.*" Š got in contact with his mother upon being released from prison, but their relationship did not improve. For whatever reasons his mother was not willing to leave her partner because of her son. Š works and alternates between sleeping rough and living in a dormitory.

Relationships with siblings are generally better and more balanced than relationships with parents, regardless of whether they are also homeless and have similar problems or live in mainstream society. Siblings are less frequently blamed for an unwillingness to offer sufficient support. At present, 60% of our respondents are in contact with their siblings. Six years ago this figure was only 15%.

The siblings of homeless people often have similar problems. This should not come as a surprise, since a dysfunctional family affects all the children equally badly.

- J (27, m, homeless for six years): "*I have a brother, but he's in prison right now. He and his girlfriend had a little girl and he stopped taking care of her and began to take drugs and steal. Mum had taken stealing since he was young, but nonetheless I was sad to see how my brother ended up.*"
- M (28, m, homeless for six years): "*My sister is at the shelter in Prachatice. She has her little girl with her. And my brother lives abroad and is unlikely to be coming back soon. He's in a shitload of trouble.*"

The relationship of homeless people to their siblings often depends on whether they feel that their brother or sister treats them badly.

- L (26, f) prefers her brother, who is also homeless: "*I don't speak to my sister but things are normal between me and my brother. My sister is a piece of shit. She accused me of stealing from her, that's the kind of person she is. She frittered away her money and then had to find a scapegoat. She's a really suspicious person and never made me feel at home in her place.*" L's brother recently died and L herself is back in prison.

People who are no longer living on the street enjoy good relations with those of their siblings who have never been homeless.

- L (28, m): " *I get on well with my sister. We write to each other, everything is fine, she has three small boys. She was the only one in the family to be worried about me.*"
- P (25, m): "*My sister now lives in Z and has a second child. She's fine and has work. Yeah, things are good between us.*"
- V (32, m) re-established contact with his brother upon quitting the street: "*Me and my brother began to write to each other and we've organised a visit.*"

SUMMARY

At present the people we spoke to are more interested in re-establishing contact with their parents than they were at the start of adulthood/end of adolescence. Above all, people who no longer live on the street have better relationships with their parents or have at least renewed contact. Their willingness is often related to the fact that they did not present themselves as homeless to their parents, and contacted them only when they had found work and accommodation. Reconciliation is sometimes related to the birth of a child. Renewed contact is not always accompanied by the complete forgiveness of past injustices, but is more the first step on the path to acquiring renewed trust. Our respondents now view their parents' behaviour with greater insight. They attempt to understand and sometimes to forgive. They are also able to admit their own guilt in respect of past or existing problems. Some attempt to improve their relationship with the parents even when this desire is not reciprocated. Becoming resigned to not renewing contact tends to be the result of repeated rebuffs on the part of the parents. In some families the relationships are as bad as they were years ago. Feelings of resentment and grievance can persist on both sides. They may relate to a mistrust engendered previously, to the current behaviour of the individuals involved, or to fear of ongoing problems.

The current relationships of past and present homeless people with their parents vary greatly and are not always dependent on their immediate situation. A sense of grievance may persist, both in people who no longer live on the street, as well as in those who have spent the last six years on the street. Many individuals, even if they are homeless, tend to forgive and forget the negative experiences of the past. Obviously, this cannot be expected in all cases. Generally speaking, if family relationships were good during childhood and adolescence, there is a greater chance of contact being re-established and support being offered. People who somehow manage to drag themselves off the street and take responsibility for their own lives tend to re-establish contact with their parents. They do not focus to the same extent on past injustices, and recognise their own part in the creation of problems in the past.

5.2 SEXUAL PARTNERSHIPS

Sexual partnerships are important for our young respondents and can form the basis of a future home. However, these can be problematic relationships that often become the source of other difficulties and even trauma. The character of these relationships is influenced by family experience, the personalities involved, and the abuse of drugs and alcohol. One of the conditions of successfully quitting the street is uncoupling oneself from the society and lifestyle of homeless people, and the same applies to partners (Vágnerová, Marek, Csémy, 2017).

People who have a job and accommodation have partners who are not and have never been homeless.
- L (27, m): "*I have accommodation and a job. **I married into it**. I got to know my wife through my father-in-law. One day he took her to the dormitory where I was staying and it all started there.*"

- V (32, f): "*I live with my boyfriend, nothing new there. We met at work. He comes from K, and travelled here to find work.*" A partnership with someone who is not homeless also provides support for the formation of a new social status and the creation of new social networks, which would not only involve homeless people.

If people who are no longer homeless do not have a relationship at present, they tend to claim that they would like one, but that **they are not prepared to accept just anyone**.
- J (33, m): "***I just want a nice, normal girl*** *that I feel attracted to and who gets on with my sister.*"
- T (26, m) would not want a homeless person as partner: "***I always look for a relationship amongst ordinary folk****, because it forces me to pull my socks up. Whenever I've had a girlfriend, I've had work.*" These two men are aware that a relationship with someone on the street could send them back into the gravitational pull of the homeless, and this is something they want to avoid.

Of the four women on maternity leave, two have partners (who were also homeless in the past) and two do not.
- Z (32, f) has a partner who used to be homeless: "*I'm fine. I have accommodation, a daughter, my feller has a job. Of course there's the odd crisis. In fact, there's been a few of them and he has moved out. But that's the same for everyone.* ***But we got over it, because of our little girl****. No way could I hand her over to a children's home.*"
- K (27, f) was abandoned by her partner: "*When I found out I was pregnant, I moved to his apartment in P. One day he came home from work and* ***told me to pack my things and leave****. He didn't say why.*" K spent her childhood in institutional care and does not have sufficient experience with functioning relationships.

The relationships initiated between people living on the street tend to be problematic, though they can also be quite long-term. Our respondents often took a casual approach towards relationships, which is fully in line with the approach they take to just about everything. For them, freedom and non-commitment are paramount.
- M (25, m), who takes drugs and does not worry his head over occasional misdemeanours, takes this approach to relationships: "***Right now I don't have a girlfriend****. I had one a while back. How long since we split up? I don't know, two or three weeks.* ***We were together almost two months****. She's not pregnant, that's someone else, someone I was with in N. I was there for four months. I don't know how things will work out. She has three kids already, though not with me. When we split up she said something about giving up the child for adoption.*" M grew up in a highly problematic family surrounded by domestic violence. His parents displayed

no interest in him and that remains the case today. It is difficult to imagine him being able to have a serious relationship with anyone.

Homeless women are often abused in various ways by partners who are also homeless. What this means is that intimate partner violence is not only a cause of homelessness but a regular aspect of street life (Nemiroff, 2010). Three out of four women who are currently homeless have experienced it.

- D (29, f), who was taken under the care of the Salvation Army, is an extreme case. The charity said that, at the time she came to them, she was suffering "severe pneumonia, a high temperature, bruises all over her body, four broken ribs and was malnourished. She had been the victim of two slave masters who had taken advantage of her inability to resist. As soon as something displeased them, **they kicked her and let her starve**. They kept her documents and forced her to do everything that made them a profit." D explained things. "*It was my ex, M. He would attack anyone, man or woman. At the start he wasn't like that, but then he changed.*" D is used to violence, and the same pattern appears to repeat itself again and again. Her ex-boyfriend (also homeless) says of her: "*She was here and was pimped out by one bloke, who **beat her up really badly**. She used to sell herself for 1,500 crowns* [USD 64] *and then he'd go and lose it all on vending machines. He'd give her just a hundred and beat her up.*"

- L (26, f) tells a similar story: "*I had relationships but they were always shit. I was in love with B to begin with, but that soon turned into hate. For two years he abused me. He even hit me in the head with a pickaxe, he stomped on my head and gave me concussion. Something would snap inside him and he would simply fly off the handle. You can't run away, because he'd find you and really kick the shit out of you. But then somehow I managed it. I don't know why I was ever with him. The fact is that when you're homeless **you don't want to be on your own**.*"

Homeless women beg, steal and prostitute themselves for their partners, who then abandon them, regardless of whether they may be expecting a child.

- M (28, f): "*My boyfriend left me when I was expecting P. He now works at Kolbenka* [a flea market] *and has no interest in his son whatsoever. At the time I was living on the Hermes and begging. At that time I could successfully make a thousand a day through begging. I was supporting the both of us. He was homeless, though now he has accommodation. He found another girl and has a child with her. I was sad when he left, but life goes on. Right now I'm single. I wish I could find a long-term boyfriend. I've always had bad luck with blokes. **Either they drink or do drugs or fuck around**. Me and guys, not the happiest of stories.*" Shortly after this interview M returned to the street and began a relationship with someone similar (who is at present in prison) and had a fourth child with him. According to social workers, she is not attracted to other types of men, and this situation is likely to be played out again and again.

The relationships of homeless men are no better, and the question arises as to whether they are capable or even interested. They tend to have relationships with women who are or have been homeless, and **alcohol and drugs play a large part in these affairs**. Physical aggression often contributes to the breakdown of these partnerships, something they usually regret and own up to.

- M (28, m) could not deal with the demands of cohabitation: "*I just had the one girlfriend. No way could I get her back, **I hurt her too much**. I did something she would never forgive me for, **I punched her**. She ended up with a broken temporal bone and a broken rib. I don't know why I did it, I just lost it... I met her in KFC on Ipák* [I. P. Pavlova metro station], *when she had been released from rehab in Bohnice. We got together and then we had a child. We took drugs and I used to steal from shops. For a year and a half it was fine and dandy.*" M grew up in a highly problematic family. He had no model to look to of a standard intimate relationship and probably had no idea how it should look. He lacks the necessary habits, is unaccustomed to working and accepting any responsibilities, and his behaviour is deteriorating under the influence of regular drug consumption.

- P (27, m), a drug addict, tells a similar story: "*I lived with S for a year or two. To begin with things were ok, but then I kind of lost it. **I punched her and I shouldn't have**. And it wasn't only her, it was her grandmother too. It was definitely a mistake to have split up with S.*" P, too, is sad that the relationship ended, but was unable to change his conduct.

The problematic nature of relationships between homeless people is linked to the fact that **many women are also drug addicts**.

- M (27, m) had a relationship with a woman who as a drug addict: "*With H it was what we call a methamphetamine love story. Our relationship was dependent on crystal meth. I was making money 20 hours a day so that we could buy drugs four times a day. It didn't stand much of a chance. It ended because **she's a whore, she hangs out with blokes for money and drugs**. I got nothing out of it, on the contrary it was costing me money. On the street the girls operate on a simple basis. If some geezer offers them drugs or money, then the girls throw their knickers at him.*" M also drinks to excess and takes drugs. His mother was an alcoholic.

- O (30, m) decided an acceptable girlfriend was not to be found on the street: "**The street is no place to go looking for an ordinary kind of girl**. *Everything is about drugs.*"

- J (27, m): "*I went out with one girl. But **when I found out she was a whore I left her**. I was actually living at her place at the time.*" These men themselves are far from being ideal partners. They drink to excess, take drugs, and are aggressive and unreliable.

The desire to find a suitable partner leads to the endless repetition of the same experience, often because the individual involved does not even know what a functioning partnership looks like and is unaware of how partners should behave towards each other.

- M (28, m): "***I'll never understand women.*** *I keep trying, another one pops up, after H yet another one. And you say to yourself, this time things'll be different, and all that happens is you end up spending money on her.*"
- P (27, m) has a string of problematic relationships to his name and yet has no idea what went wrong: "*I found myself a girlfriend and really love her. I would do anything for her. She was living on the street, I was too, and so I paid a visit to Mrs E [his probation officer] and within two days we were living in a dormitory. Recently we've been fighting like cat and dog because her ex appeared on the scene. He took her last two hundred crowns and travelled to Moravia. So we're arguing and M is fucked up and crying because we're splitting up and it's not worthwhile carrying on. I don't know if she'll stay with me or not, she's always in a bad mood or depressed. **I did everything I could** from my point of view. **I did everything I could think of.** She got food off me. Whatever she wanted, I'd buy. I don't know what to do.*" In the past it was P who tended to leave his partners, notwithstanding the fact they were expecting a child with him. P spent his childhood in institutional care with all the consequences ensuing therefrom, including insufficient experience of a functional relationship between his parents or grandparents.

The repeated failure of a relationship has led many homeless people, both men and women, to become resigned to never having a partnership. This was so in the case of 10 out of 14 people we spoke to, i.e. 70% of our respondents.

- P (27, m): "*Right now I don't have anyone and **don't want anyone. I don't ever want to be with anyone.** I want to be alone and die alone. Maybe it's the grass, maybe if I stopped smoking weed I'd find a normal women. But right now I don't want anyone.*"
- O (30, m): "***I've got a dog and that's enough for me.***"
- L (27, m): "*Right now I'm not seeing anyone **and I'm happy. I've got enough on my plate just looking after myself.** I had a girlfriend for a year or more. I don't really know why we split up. When I look back I don't think that any girl was worth it in the end.*"
- M (25, m): "*It used to be just **junkies and alcoholics.** Right now I don't have anyone. I was such a fool. I no longer trust women.*" All of these men are drug addicts who tend to hook up with women with the same problem. Under these circumstances it is difficult to imagine a relationship working out well.
- S (27, f) is a woman who has no wish to find a man because of her negative experiences: "***I don't want so much as to set eyes on a bloke. They're all just filthy pigs.** Pissed motherfuckers. All they want is money, money and weed. P was like that, which is why I ended it with him. Stoned the whole time. All he ever did was wander round all day with a joint in his hand. Nothing interested him, certainly not work.*" The truth is that S also behaved badly on occasion. Her ex-boyfriend

Š (27, m), also homeless, told us: *"After a while there was simply no understanding between us. She started sleeping with other blokes and fell in with a bad crowd."*

Not even a quitting the street for life in a dormitory is enough to save a partnership, especially when it involves people from the same social group. K (30, f) says: *"I've got a boyfriend at present. We've been together about six months. I tended to look at all blokes in the same light, because **they're all the same if you ask me**. I've always managed to fetch up with a complete fucking moron. All talk, no action. Worst thing is I reckon even this latest is the same."*

SUMMARY

The quality of relationship depended on both the individuals involved and how and where they lived. People who are no longer homeless often have partners who are not and have not been homeless, and their relationships are not tainted by alcohol, drugs and prostitution. If they do not yet have a relationship, they want to break away from the homeless community even at this level and find someone from mainstream society. Life on the street is not organised according to normal rules. There is a lack of empathy and regard for other people, including partners. Street relationships tend to be dramatic and generally unsatisfactory, especially if they are accompanied by drugs and alcohol. Homeless women are very often abused by their partners and end up begging, stealing and prostituting themselves for them. These negative experiences lead them to conclude that any relationship with such men must inevitably end badly and that it is therefore best not to have a partner. Homeless men often realise that they are hurting their partners but are unable to act differently. When they find another partner, the same experience is repeated, especially if the new partner is also a drug addict. In the end the men, too, decide that a normal woman is not to be found on the street. They become resigned to never having an intimate relationship. As in the case of the women, this is a reaction to the lack of satisfaction to be gained from relationships between homeless people. Our findings show that it is extremely difficult for a homeless person to create an acceptable, functioning relationship that could become the basis of a new home, with all the feelings of security and safety associated with it.

5.3 RELATIONSHIPS WITH CHILDREN

The birth of a child can be an important, life-changing catalyst, especially amongst women, even though this is not always the case. Six years ago most of the mothers we spoke to had given up their offspring or had released them into the care of relatives. Women in her late twenties and early thirties gradually underwent a change of approach to their own children and became interested in looking after them, even though they did not always completely fulfil their maternal role. At present some of the men we spoke to have children: this is true of half of the group (N = 15), though only seven of them look after the kids or at least contribute towards their upkeep.

Half of the mothers we spoke to had surrendered their parental rights. Some had offered up their children for adoption because **they did not feel capable of offering the requisite care**. Sometimes the women's relatives had assumed responsibility for the children and so it was still possible that they would not lose them.

- K (30, f) offered up her children for adoption: "*I used to want a family. These days I can't actually have a family. But at least I know that my children have a good life because they are in good families. **I know I wouldn't be able to cope**. I haven't seen any of them. I know where the last one lives. If they ever want to, they know where to find me. I won't interfere, I don't want to make things difficult, and **anyway I have nothing to offer**.*"
- K (29, f) is of a similar opinion: "*I gave birth to a little girl here in L. I was with her for a while in hospital and then I basically just went bonkers and fled to Prague. **We really wanted to raise her on our own, but suddenly we got kind of freaked out and decided against it**. When I gave birth a second time I simply figured I couldn't look after it. I was on the street and it was best to put it up for adoption. It found its way to my mum via the social services.*"

For Z (32, f) a child was a **catalyst for a fundamental change in life**: "*I think the turning point was realising that I was now responsible for another life and that I had to stop thinking only of myself. No way would I give up my little girl. She's a constant presence in my thoughts, she's my lifeline. That's when you realise **you have to be around for someone else***." Z quit the street, stopped taking drugs, and was reconciled with her family. At present she lives with her partner and looks after her child. When her maternity benefit ran out she returned to work and is in control of her life.

To begin with, motherhood was not that easy for many women, who were convinced that they would not be up to taking care of a child. However, **they gradually changed their mind and now wish they could look after their children**.

- K (29, f): "*Both kids are looked after by my mum, because they wouldn't give them to me. **I'd slap them if they were the slightest bit naughty**. I just wish I could get my act together and be capable of looking after my kids... We spoke about it the last time round. I simply lack a maternal instinct.*" K's desire to turn her life around and attempt to take on the role of mother was provoked by a stint in prison. Only the future will show whether she is successful.
- M (28, f), who found herself back on the street, wishes she could have her children back: "*For the last year the youngest one has been with my parents. But I want him back, I want him out of there. When I was looking for work, I didn't*

have anyone to babysit. I lived with him in different shelters for three years. **I would simply love to have the children back with me and to live a quiet life**. I didn't have it in me at the time." M abandoned her first three sons immediately after they were born. The boys are looked after by relatives. At present she lives with her fourth child in a dormitory. Her partner and the child's father is in prison.

Some women who used to be homeless look after their children, **though have problems raising them**.

- K (27, f): "*I wasn't in favour of kids and M was not planned. At present he attends kindergarten from Monday to Friday. I only have him over the weekend. He'll drive me to an early death, I swear, because **he has tantrums and doesn't listen** and makes a fuss and so on. I mean, **the kid just does whatever the fuck he wants**.*" K herself has no model to look to. Her own parents were incapable of looking after her. She has no support from her partner or any of her relatives. A question mark hangs over whether or not she will be able to raise her son.

Mothers who used to be homeless and are on maternity leave and looking after their children **often have problems with the fathers** (in seven out of nine cases). The fathers tend also to be homeless and show no interest in their offspring. They do not pay maintenance, usually because they have no jobs. They are irresponsible and unreliable, often because they take drugs. If they have new partners, they too tend to have been homeless in the past. It is clear that these women are still in contact with people they know from the street. A certain period of time passes before they create a new network of friends. This fact prevents them from finding a more promising partner.

- Much of the above applies to K (29, f): "*A year before I was sent to prison we lived together. Then we separated because **he had no interest in the children**. When my daughter was born I thought things might get better, but instead it drove us even further apart. **The only thing he was interested in was drugs**. When I asked him about the children he simply told me he didn't want to speak about them. And then one day he was violent with me and a line in the sand had been crossed.*" At present K is not in a serious relationship. She lives with her mother, who has looked after the children since they were born.
- A (25, f) tells a similar story, though her partner did make an effort to begin with: "*I had a different idea of things to him. To begin with things were okay between us. He stopped injecting, he stopped drugs altogether in fact. But then he replaced them with booze and weed, something I had been on for a while. **The drugs changed him and he was also really influenced by his friends**. So, for instance, he'd take the dog on a walk and then return five hours later totally off his head. And whenever he came home drunk, there was always a row. Yeah, he punched me, though the violence was on both sides.*" A's partner returned to the street, does not contribute to the children's upkeep and does not look after them.

In the case of men the birth of a child did not provide any incentive for life-style changes, or if so, then only short-term. Not one of the homeless men who are fathers that we spoke to look after the children, and none of them pay alimony. The main reason they fail in their parental duties is drug addiction and an inability to change their way of life.

- P (29, m): "*We got married because of P, my son, so that they wouldn't take him away from us. P was in Klokánek* [an organisation for children at risk] *and now S shares him with her grandmother. I see him once every six months. That's basically what the courts ordered. I was given a choice. Either he would call me dad and I'd have to pay, or he'd call me uncle and I don't pay a cent.* **I knew I wouldn't pay anything whatever** *and we'd just sit with the alcoholics, and I didn't want that. I had a chance but I fucked it up. It's not like I don't care. He's my flesh and blood after all.*" P spends a lot of time thinking about his own situation but displays no interest in his child. He himself grew up in a children's home and his mother still has no interest in him, even though he has often tried to re-establish contact.

Returning to society requires a willingness to accept responsibility for one's own child and sometimes the offspring of a new partner.

- L (27, m) formed an emotional bond with his stepdaughter. "*The little girl gave me the motivation I needed to stop drinking. She was four years old. We kind of hit it off and after six months she started calling me dad.* **We do her homework together and I take her to school.**"
- V (32, f), who used to be homeless, renewed contact with her children upon returning to mainstream society. Until then she had not looked after them or contributed to their upkeep: "*My younger son is in an educational care centre in P because he has ADHD. He's hyperactive and he suffers from personality disorder. The older is fine. He lives with his dad.* **I visit him** *and sometimes have him for the weekend. Plus* **I contribute to his upkeep.**"

Men who work and have found accommodation, if only in a dormitory, **are more responsible fathers than men sleeping rough**, probably because they are not addicted to drugs or alcohol. T (26, m) is more than happy to play an active role in caring for his son: "*Basically* **I don't have any problem participating in his upkeep**. *We were able to reach agreement on that, though I guess that, over time, things will get more demanding when* **he starts visiting me**. *I'm really going to have to do something about myself.*" The child's mother has never lived on the street and has a stable family environment.

SUMMARY

Becoming a mother has been the catalyst for change for several women, especially the older ones. However, initial plans to care for their child do not always work out. Some admit they were unable to cope with motherhood but would like to put their earlier failure to rights and begin to take responsibility for the child. Up till now they have relied on the support of relatives. Bringing up a child is a huge burden, even for women who are used to meeting different duties, and even more so for homeless women incapable of accepting even minimal restrictions and observing a daily routine. It is therefore understandable that childrearing is a challenge even for women who used to be homeless and who have custody of their child, especially if they lack the support of a partner or close relative. Their partner and the father of their child either abandoned them before the child was born or shortly after. This is usually because they were unable to give up drugs and alcohol and find a job. Though they may have made an effort to begin with, they were unable to continue occupying the role of father for long. At present these men do not look after their children or contribute to their maintenance. They are aware of not having been able to cope with parenthood and regret the fact. However, they are unable to rectify the situation. Resignation is the easiest solution in this case. The relationship they have with their offspring reflects their personal experience from childhood with their own parents, who represent the only model of parental behaviour they know. As a consequence, many of these men have no idea how a parent should act. People who quit the street are able and willing to accept responsibility, not only for themselves, but also for their children or those of their partner. It is clear from their behaviour that the process of desocialisation was not complete and they do indeed stand a chance of finding their feet in society. Such people tended to have lived at least until the age of twelve in a functional family and therefore have positive experiences and know how parents are supposed to behave with their children.

Overall we can say that this change of attitude on the part of our respondents towards their parents, as well as towards their partners and their role as parents, is part of a comprehensive transformation in the way they view their lives and in the motivation they have to act in a more responsible way. Quitting the street is associated with a tendency to mitigate former conflicts (at least with certain members of the family), to break away from the street community, and to find a partner who was never part of it. People gradually create a new social network that helps them overcome difficulties with resocialisation. Remedying earlier relationships or creating new ones is extremely important. The acceptance of responsibility for their own life, and perhaps that of a partner or child, is a prerequisite of success in respect of such a fundamental change of life as moving from the street back into mainstream society. It needs a willingness and readiness to deal with different stresses and to think beyond the satisfaction of merely immediate needs. Interpersonal relationships, especially the closest, indicate a degree of psychological balance and personal maturity. Close friends can offer support in stressful situations and offer meaning to an individual's life. The non-binding situational relationships of the street community are unable to fulfil such a function, because though they do not require much, in turn they do not offer much. If a person lacks stable and reliable relationships when quitting the street, it is difficult for them to cope with all the obstacles ensuing from acceptance of a new and more demanding lifestyle. In this respect it is necessary to support both the restoration of previous family relationships if there is at least a functional core to them, and the creation of new relationships with people who are not homeless.

VII. CAUSES, CONTEXTS AND PROSPECTS OF HOMELESSNESS

There are many reasons why a person ends up sleeping rough. They stretch back to different periods in a person's life, sometimes right to the start, and predetermine the entire trajectory of their destiny. Genetic disposition to a certain mode of behaviour and experience is also a salient factor. A person's development can also be influenced by environmental factors, especially those of early childhood. A dysfunctional family and the inability or unwillingness of parents to look after their offspring also has a negative impact, though does not necessarily have to influence all children in the same way. In such cases what is important is how a person handles negative inputs, and this is influenced by genetic predisposition. Above all they need an ability to manage stress and to cope with a lack of important stimuli (e.g. emotional). The psychological development of children from problematic families who, in addition, have an unfavourable genetic makeup, depends to a greater extent on external stimuli, which in these cases tends to be negative.

A lack of interest, rejection, or even beating and abuse, will prevent a child from establishing a strong bond with an adult and acquiring the necessary sense of security and safety that is regarded as an important condition of smooth personality development and socialisation. The long-term operation of a model of undesirable parental behaviour also plays a role, since to the children growing up in a dysfunctional family this model comes to be seen as standard, and later in life they will behave in the same way. The imitation of parents, whether this involve thoughtlessness, aggression, alcohol abuse or criminal activities, is one of the causes of adult failure in all spheres.

Parents who neglect their children often fail to support them in the sphere of education. The child then fails at primary school and is later incapable of completing vocational training. This is the case even when a child might otherwise possess real talent. As a result, there is an additional risk of poor work habits and a lack of qualifications. People with such a background have problems with self-assertion, cannot find work, and if they do find a job are incapable of holding it down.

Adolescence is associated with the need for independence and self-determination, i.e. with the development of one's own identity. Someone who does not have a stable family will search for a satisfactory means of acceptance and application elsewhere, using whatever means are at their disposal. Given the lack of a positive parental role model and the influence of the group, these alternative means will often be undesirable and laden with risk. In such cases the need for freedom and independence is not balanced by responsibility, since these individuals have a different experience. No one has ever behaved responsibly and thoughtfully to them. They are not used to respecting set rules and putting the satisfaction of their immediate needs to one side. These limitations mean they have no opportunity to assert themselves in a positive way, and so define themselves negatively, for instance by sleeping rough and gradually adopting the identity of someone excluded from society.

Their childhood will continue to impact them in adulthood, since many disadvantages lead to the creation of others. This is already happening in adolescence, when an individual is deciding on their future direction. If they reach a poor decision, this can have a huge influence on the rest of their life. Such decisions might include experimentation with drugs and criminal activities as part of a group. This can be a phase they go through and come out of, or it can be a lot more. Poor decisions can trigger social disaffiliation that becomes apparent later in life. Sometimes the main problem is the inability of young people to realise the impact their current decisions may have on their lives, for instance whether leaving home without alternative accommodation and a job will not lead to further problems.

The downward spiral that ends in homelessness can take different forms. At the end of adolescence there is often a desire to escape problems associated with relationships or unpleasant social pressures. These may be associated with the family, but also with the social vacuum that arises upon being expelled from school or fired from a job, or with an unwillingness to find employment. Young people who end up on the street are often searching for an identity, a satisfying lifestyle, and above all freedom. Becoming homeless can be an extreme form of adolescent moratorium, sometimes delayed. Establishing relationships with other homeless people and adapting to street life is another step in the process of gradual social disaffiliation.

Even in the period of adulthood, between the ages of thirty and forty, social disaffiliation may be linked with childhood experience and the impact it had on personality. However, it may also be the result of new problems that have nothing to do with early experiences. Sometimes the trigger is losing a job, something a particular individual may find impossible to deal with. It may also be related to an inability to come to terms with the breakup of a relationship and to resolve the problems arising, e.g. accommodation. If, on top of an unwillingness to grab life by the horns, a person has a problem with alcohol, the risk of becoming homeless increases. The most serious reason why an adult is unable to deal with such problems is an addiction to alcohol or drugs or a mental health disorder.

Adults who have lived a standard life for a certain period of time have nothing to gain by sleeping rough, but a lot to lose: their status in society, their former identity, and their friendships. They often react to such a situation in a way that exacerbates matters and ensures they remain on the street. In these cases, too, one can find connections between individual events that, taken individually, would have presented no real challenge, but that when added together prove fatal. For instance, if a man who moves into a dormitory after breaking up with his partner loses his job, he will lose the roof over his head. Under such circumstances the best thing he can do is look for another job and seek help from the job centre. If he puts off resolving his problem and begins to loiter and drink alcohol in the company of others in a similar position, his problems will simply get worse. The same chain of difficulties can arise when a person underestimates the level of their indebtedness and puts off resolving the situation, or elects to resolve it by taking on further loans.

Our interviews with homeless people reveal areas in which there is a real possibility of effective assistance. There is no doubt that the organisations at present helping homeless people are doing a great job. Without their help matters would be a lot worse. The problem is that in many cases their interventions are too late to be truly effective, or there is no interest in them. The process of social disaffiliation begins far earlier, and when it reaches the phase in which an individual is already on the margins of society, it is difficult to rectify. The prevention of social disaffiliation should begin far earlier, ideally in childhood. This is of course happening, and children from dysfunctional families are often placed elsewhere, where there are conditions in place offering them a better chance of standard development. Schools offer assistance to pupils who have behavioural problems and poor prospects. However, the situation is not always being managed as well as it might be.

Prompt assistance to people who have lost their jobs and accommodation is also of the essence. A limiting factor is that an adult cannot be forced to receive assistance, but must request it. One problem is that such people do not know where or how to set about requesting assistance. The fact that several of them are incapable of dealing with the authorities and completing forms is so limiting that they prefer to do nothing.

Very often a person becomes and remains homeless due to heavy drinking and drug use. Again, it is true that there is treatment already in place for both forms of addiction. However, the problem is a lack of motivation. Any genuine attempt to resolve the situation would involve increasing motivation and supporting the willingness of these people to accept the necessary restrictions that would lead to a positive change in their lives. Since the length of time spent living rough increases the risk of chronic homelessness, any remedial measures must be taken as soon as possible. Another task is deciding how to motivate people to opt for treatment. Our interviews with people who are no longer homeless to an extent offer an answer to this question. They show that the initial impulse to effect change can vary depending on what is personally important for the individual in question.

People who manage the return to normal society say that they had to force themselves to resolve their situation and that, most importantly, they had to make that crucial first move and not postpone their plans indefinitely. They had to break their ties to people who remained on the street. They had to rely on themselves and not expect others to solve their problems. As is clear, assistance in the form of active intervention on the part of a social worker who determines what a homeless person must do will very often not lead to the desired outcome. Unless the individual concerned is convinced that they must work for change, they remain in a passively resistant position and their lifestyle remains the same. It would be more effective to offer options in such a way that it is clear under what conditions a person could receive help. However, the final decision would be theirs.

A radical intervention in the life of a homeless person, such as time spent in prison, can also act as an effective catalyst for change. At the very least it means a person is taken away from the society of the homeless and prevented from continuing to pursue undesirable activities such as heavy drinking or drug taking. Under these circumstances a risky moment arrives when a person leaves prison. If they have nowhere to go, any chance of prison having a positive impact is lost.

Indebtedness and debt-recovery (execution) proceedings represent a highly demotivational factor in a homeless person's life. As soon as a person finds a job, the bailiff will deduct a significant portion of their earnings. As a consequence, many homeless people actively avoid looking for a proper job for this reason. At present there is no real solution to this problem. Again, the longer a person is homeless, the larger the debt and the greater the risk that they will remain on the street. For many, especially young, homeless people who would otherwise be able and often willing to work, some form of manageable debt relief would represent effective assistance. It could come with strings attached, so that a person would not be able to assume that, if they fail, they will receive another chance.

For the older, chronically homeless, who can no longer be expected to adopt a new approach to life, the solution to their situation may be to provide a life of dignity under conditions corresponding to the current level of shelters.

It is not that workers in the helping professions are doing their job badly, even if one might wish the effect to be more visible. The problem of homelessness is so difficult to resolve that without their efforts the lives of many sufferers would be even bleaker, and their chance of escaping street life even less. As a twenty-six-year old man who used to be homeless says: "*I very much doubt the social services could do more than they already do. This is more about a person's will. Either he or she wants to get off the street or they don't.*" Better results cannot be achieved without bilateral efforts. The fact that people living on the street *need* help does not necessarily mean that they *want* it and are willing to accept it. This is especially true if such help comes with conditions attached that they do not wish to conform to.

1. SOCIAL SERVICES FOR HOMELESS PEOPLE IN THE CZECH REPUBLIC

Overall, services for homeless people are included in the category of **social prevention services**. These are defined under the Social Services Act as follows: "*Social prevention services help prevent the exclusion of persons who would thus be at threat of a crisis in their social situation, life habits, and lifestyle leading to conflict with society, a socially disadvantageous environment, and a threat to rights and legitimate interests by the criminal activities of another natural person. The aim of social prevention services is to assist people overcome their unfavourable social situation and to protect society against the emergence and spread of undesirable social phenomena.*"

Services in this category are primarily aimed at **changing the client**. Services and assistance for homeless people are designed for motivated individuals, and are less effective when working with people who are not motivated or suffer substance use disorder or have mental health issues. A suitable client for these services is someone who wants to change and is capable of achieving this change in their behaviour. The problem is the homeless population has undergone change, and nowadays those who remain on the street tend to be those who are unable to achieve the desired changes under the present configuration of services.

1.1 STATE ASSISTANCE

A problem we have not yet touched on a relates to a person's **permanent residence and how this affects the local jurisdiction**. The authorities tend to close their eyes to the problem of "non-local" street people, which in the case of Prague means the majority of people in this situation. In order to register at their Labour Office, people must travel to their place of residence, even though the possibility of changing jurisdiction is enshrined in the law. From the perspective of the City of Prague, the solution to homelessness often involves concealment rather than eradication. The city councillors are dependent on the people who vote for them, and the voters are averse to having facilities targeting the homeless in their neighbourhood, since this would be an admission that their district has a very real problem. The issue of homelessness is peripheral to most people's interest and local councillors rarely address the social sphere. There is an attempt to economise in the social sector, and politicians are more interested in talking about people who, they claim, are abusing social benefits. At the same time, people who are not only unemployed but unemployable remain dependent on these benefits. **Homeless people often fall through the social safety net.**

Many problems arise due to misunderstandings on the part of both homeless people and individual civil servants. This is because local authority employees do not know how to communicate with a client who is behaving in a way they are not used to. Under the influence of their social disaffiliation and substance abuse, homeless people lose certain habits. For instance, they may be unable to keep to the timetable set by a civil servant. The authorities specify a particular time for a meeting, and **if a client misses the meeting, sanctions are applied**. This includes being struck off the register of persons looking for work, which then leads to a loss of income. For the homeless themselves, a visit to the local job centre can mean dealing with formalities that they do not understand and conditions they cannot meet. The sanctions intended to prevent the social security system being abused often fall most heavily on those who need help the most.

In general, homeless people do not have a good relationship with the authorities and are more inclined to trust social workers employed by charities. This is because civil servants **tend not to adapt their conduct to the individual needs of a client** and negotiate more readily with their escort. However, the escort is very restricted when dealing with the local authority, and it would be more appropriate to teach a homeless person how to cooperate with civil servants. The motivation of civil servants to reach agreement and assist homeless people differs considerably depending on the management of their particular department.

The system as it stands at present does not meet the needs of specific groups of homeless people. For instance, several of our respondents have a dual diagnosis and have deteriorated to such an extent that they need specialised social services. They need to be placed in a home catering for special needs. However, they have no automatic right to this nor the funds to pay for it themselves. In order to receive state aid, they have to undergo a series of interviews with the authorities that they often do not understand. They are unable to comprehend texts written in officialese, they are sometimes illiterate, and sometimes are unable to sign their own name. This may be because of poor eyesight or a deterioration in cognitive functions. Civil servants often refuse to speak with a client who is inebriated or unable to express what they need. **Civil servants do not understand such people and so refuse to process their claims**.

Homeless people have little motivation to avail themselves of the social services. **We would argue that establishing a relationship with a homeless person is the only way cooperation will be feasible**. Civil servants make no attempt whatsoever to strike up a closer, albeit professional relationship with homeless people. Civil servants are taught not to favour any single party and to comply with all the rules of the department they work for. The assistance provided by local authorities abides by the principle that a recipient must be deserving of a benefit, and this puts certain groups of the population at a disadvantage. Though this principle may be a safeguard against the abuse of the social security system, it can also be an obstacle to the acquisition of aid for certain clients. Homeless people are sensitive to their failings during negotiations at the local authorities. In addition, they are unaware of their rights and the duties of civil servants. This is yet another reason they have little confidence in the authorities.

At present, the solution to homelessness is based on **meeting basic needs, i.e. food, sleep and hygiene**. Once these are satisfied, a space is created for further work with the client within the framework of social work. This form of work dates back to the founding of the Salvation Army. The practice introduced by the founder of the organisation, William Booth, was based on the principle of the three S's: Soup, Soap and Salvation, the idea being that salvation cannot enter into the equation until a person is fed and washed. The question then becomes how we might help homeless people satisfy even higher needs than the basic. As far as the authorities are concerned, this mainly involves the provision of financial support for living costs and, where appropriate, housing benefit. **Other needs are difficult to meet without a good quality relationship being formed between a social worker and homeless client**. However, in practice it appears that political boxes are being ticked by the authorities rather than targeted assistance being provided. The blanket "education" of a client has been shown to be ineffective. This attempt was manifest, for instance, in an instruction issued to provide part of emergency financial assistance in the form of luncheon vouchers. Assistance cannot be compelled, it can only be offered. In contrast, an offer of employment opportunities can have a positive impact on a client and indeed on society as a whole. However, these offers are few and far between or are not tailored to the needs of homeless people.

1.2 OUTREACH PROGRAMMES

Outreach programmes are one of the few services that have homeless people as their target group. The overriding prerequisite for the success of an outreach programme is trust. However, this is not always a simple matter, for the reasons outlined above. Outreach workers are not always trained in dealing and working with different groups of the homeless. It would therefore be a good idea to establish a **multidisciplinary outreach team** that would include a nurse, social worker, therapist or psychiatrist, and an addiction specialist. The team would work with people who are hard to convince of the utility of visiting a certain facility, and could do a lot of work in the field. It has been shown that the cooperation of **peer workers**, i.e. homeless people who have already gained trust in aid organisations and now wish to help others, offers support in persuading people to visit a low-threshold treatment centre. In order to gain trust, outreach programmes must be combined with the services of a low-threshold treatment centre or the operations of an outreach worker trained in dealing with a certain type of homeless person (e.g. young people).

A major problem for outreach workers is that services are set up for a certain type of homeless person, above all people who are self-sufficient and motivated to change their risky lifestyle. However, experience with working with the homeless and our research outcomes show that **many people living on the street do**

not want or are unable to change their lives under the current conditions. For instance, it would be necessary to create separate facilities for alcoholics and people with a dual diagnosis. Most existing facilities have limits on the utilisation of services by homeless people who are under the influence of alcohol. **The limit on milligrams of alcohol in the blood** for entry into a facility is more a safety measure rather than an attempt to "educate" people. Homeless alcoholics do not use these services and the mortality rate is high. Such facilities would have to be connected to addictology services. In addition to addictions, chronic diseases of all kinds are a problem (35% of our older respondents suffer a chronic illness). Neglect of one's state of health is a consequence of a homeless person's lifestyle, which often leads to a fatal deterioration in health. It has been shown that the **separation of social and health services** is not a good idea, since poor health often worsens the social situation of sufferers. Homeless people with a chronic disease are not necessarily at risk of dying, but can be if they receive no treatment over the long term. For ill people life on the street can be devastating even if hospitalisation is not immediately called for. In view of this it would be advisable to establish a facility that would look after chronically ill homeless people. Up until now this role has been performed by shelters. Similar facilities are needed for people with chronic psychiatric conditions who are homeless.

Outreach workers possess the most up-to-date information on the group being monitored, since other services are used by only certain groups of homeless people. However, **outreach workers depend on other social services** and encounter the barrier of local jurisdiction both at hospitals and local authorities. It is they who might provide the impetus to different facilities to expand their offer and target the neediest homeless people.

1.3 LOW-THRESHOLD DROP-IN CENTRES

A low-threshold drop-in centre is an out-patient social service whose target group is homeless people. It is open during the day, while a reception centre is only open at night and does not allow for all-day accommodation. Even though the connecting up of these services is a logical step, whenever this is accomplished it provokes a negative reaction in the neighbourhood. Homeless people spend almost 24 hours a day there, which can lead to what is known as NIMBY syndrome, i.e. Not In My Back Yard, a source of threat in the eyes of some members of the general public. The original idea was that such facilities would be created near the places where the target group congregated. However, the current political representation, under public pressure, often pushes these services beyond the boundaries of the city centre to its peripheries. It is therefore often necessary to work with people living in outlying areas.

According to the register of social service providers there are 62 low-threshold treatment centres in the Czech Republic. These facilities have been created for the most typical age group of homeless people, namely the middle-aged. **Few low-threshold treatment centres are equipped to react to the specific needs of younger or older homeless people**. Because of this, visiting a low-threshold centre is an unpleasant experience for many individuals, especially because several are overcrowded during winter. Prague has two large centres, Naděje and the Salvation Army, which are visited by up to 200 people a day. These centres serve only for the distribution of food and the provision of sanitary facilities. There is no interest in the provision of specialist social counselling. This may be because the service is conditional upon the creation of trust in the social worker, which is less easy to generate in such large facilities.

Experience has shown that conflicts often arise between young and old homeless people. The young have different needs from the old. **They prefer a communitarian lifestyle and need to share their experiences with their peers.** They lead a different lifestyle, have different values, and behave differently, all of which can irritate an older person. For instance, the young will often accuse older people of poor hygiene, while the older people accuse the young of using drugs and being involved in criminal activity. The Prague centre Naděje is the only low-threshold drop-in centre that deals with younger people. It was here that data was collected for the study of young homeless people between 2010 and 2012 (Vágnerová, Csémy Marek 2012). Professionals experienced in working with homeless people believe that **young and old should be separated**. Where there is no specialist day centre, young people avail themselves of the services of contact centres, whose target group are people using non-alcoholic addictive substances.

The problems of people visiting low-threshold drop-in centres are complex and cannot be resolved here. **This is why social workers should have a wide network of contacts to different specialists** who could assist them. Leisure activities and joint games would appear to be an appropriate way of acquiring a client's trust. The greater involvement of the clergy in the running of centres and the provision of spiritual activities would also be a good idea.

1.4 RESIDENTIAL SERVICES

Residential services represent another variant of social services. One such is the offer of a shelter, the purpose of which is to provide accommodation *"to persons in an unfavourable social situation ensuing from the loss of housing"*. The law lays a duty upon a shelter to resolve all of the problems of a homeless individual within one year. After one year the idea is that the client moves into commercial housing or avails themselves of another service. At present, social services are based on the **Housing Ready System**, which is based on several interconnected forms of accommodation. However, these **interlinked accommodation services are unavailable**, either because of limited capacity or because the services that are available have other target groups and cannot be accessed by the homeless. Like other prevention services, a shelter is time-limited. A social worker has the task of "doing something with the client" in order that they acquire the competencies that will allow them to find and retain accommodation. The Housing Ready programme is based on merit, i.e. after accreditation on a lower level of accommodation people have the option of moving up a level (Marek, Strnad, Hotovcová 2012). A system of housing is currently being trialled in several cities based on the **Housing First principle**. This system rejects the premise that a person must deserve accommodation and that the bigger the effort they make, the greater their chance of finding accommodation. And so homeless people would not be obliged to undergo services in which they must adapt to collective cohabitation and experience a certain self-reliance. They would instead be given an apartment and would have individual support options open to them. Their task would not be to deserve accommodation, but to hold onto it.

At present shelters are often stand-ins for old-age people's homes and long-term health care institutions. In 2006, when the Social Services Act was drafted, the unemployment rate was higher than it is now and destined to rise still further due to the economic crisis of 2008. The Social Security Act therefore anticipated that many of the people who would be using their shelters would be the short-term homeless and capable of re-entering society within one year. However, there are now fewer and fewer clients who are fit for work and manage to find employment and some form of housing within a year. People in shelters often feel they are in the best place they could be. Either they have health problems and are not fit for work, in which case their re-inclusion in society is unrealistic, or they are so indebted that they lack the motivation to change anything and are grateful for whatever housing they are offered. A shelter is associated in the minds of users of all generations with boredom and insufficient stimulation. Personal hygiene, which can take a person sleeping rough an entire morning to sort out, takes a matter of minutes in a shelter. A user has no idea what to do with their free time. Most people receive some form of housing benefit and cannot or do not want to work for the reasons mentioned above. Emptiness and boredom lead to a further decline in skills and the growing conviction that a better life is beyond reach. A client either becomes dependent on a shelter or leaves it as soon as it has served its purpose (e.g. warm accommodation during the winter months). **It is becoming clear that the clients of shelters need therapy** and not simply professional social counselling. This is one of the basic services provided by shelters and is rarely offered.

The utilisation of accommodation services by middle-aged homeless people is sometimes called "**shelter tourism**", i.e. the constant movement of people from one shelter to another or between commercial dormitories and shelters. This phenomenon is caused by how the term "**temporary accommodation**" is interpreted. The provision of individual services is usually restricted to one year. Some shelters have an even shorter time limit. If a client fails to find accommodation in another related facility or on the open property market, he or she moves to a different shelter. The social work being carried out in their previous shelter is discontinued and begins all over again from the start in the new shelter.

In the case of senior citizens, the commonest problem is a **reduction in self-sufficiency**. Many clients of shelters really need care services rather than social prevention. These forms of accommodation facility often require a self-sufficiency that older homeless people lack. People in wheelchairs or suffering incontinence can have problems. In the first case the source of such problems are **physical barriers**, while in the second case having to wear diapers is a cause of **social stigma**, which in a shelter can trigger conflicts with cohabitees. Since the average age of the clients of one large shelter is 52 (Marek 2017), we are safe in assuming that the population using this service is clearly getting older.

If shelters could accept only clients who belong to their target group, there would be sufficient free capacity. However, people who are not self-sufficient have nowhere to go. **A shelter should operate as a "diagnostic service"**. During the course of a person's stay their needs would be ascertained and they would subsequently be sent to a facility specialising in the requisite type of service. They should be taught how to perform routine activities that would allow them to live independently. However, the outcomes of such attempts are unsatisfactory. This is due to a lack of employees and insufficient expertise. In practice a social worker carries out the requisite activity on behalf of the client, because it is simpler and takes less time. There are no follow-up, specialised services that would enquire more deeply into the specific problems of clients. Not every homeless person can be re-integrated into society, and in such cases the only realistic form of assistance is care. What is perhaps required is a "sheltered refuge" for people with reduced self-sufficiency. Such a facility would be staffed by people specialised in working with people with mental health issues, psychological problems, chronic alcoholics, and drug addicts.

BIBLIOGRAPHY

Amato, F., MacDonald, J. (2011): Examining risk factors for homeless men: Gender role conflict, help-seeking behaviors, substance abuse and violence. *Journal of Men's Studies*, 19, 227-235.

Anderson, I., Christian, J. (2003): Causes of homelessness in the UK: Dynamic analysis. *Journal of Community and Applied Social Psychology*, 13, 105–118.

Auerswald, C.L., Eyre, S.L. (2002): Youth homelessness in San Francisco: A life cycle approach. *Social Science and Medicine*, 54, 1497–1512.

Ball, S.A., Cobb-Richardson, P. Connolly, A.J. et al. (2005): Substance abuse and personality disorders in homeless drop-in center clients: symptom severity and psychotherapy retention in a randomized clinical trial. *Comprehensive Psychiatry*, 46, 371–379.

Baron, S.W. (2003): Self-control, social consequences, and criminal behavior: Street youth and the general theory of crime. *Journal of Research in Crime and Delinquency*, 40, 403–425.

Bassuk, E.L., Buckner, J.C., Weinreb, L.F. et al. (1997): Homelessness in female-headed families: Childhood and adult risk and protective factors. *American Journal of Public Health*, 87, 241–248.

Baumohl, J. (2004): Panhandling. In D. Levinson (ed.): *Encyclopedia of Homelessness*. London – Thousand Oaks, Sage.

Bearsley-Smith, C.A., Bond, L.M., Littlefield, L., Thomas, L.R. (2008): The psychosocial profile of adolescent risk of homelessness. *European Child and Adolescent Psychiatry*, 17, 226–234.

Booth, S. (2005): Eating rough: food sources and acquisition practices of homeless young peoples in Adelaide, South Australia. *Public Health Nutrition*, 9, 212–218.

Boydell, K.M., Goering, P., Morrell-Bellai, T.L. (2000): Narratives of identity: Representation of self in people who are homeless. *Qualitative Health Research*, 10, 26–38.

Breakey, W.R. (2004): Mental illness and health. In: D. Levinson (ed.): *Encyclopedia of Homelessness*. London – Thousand Oaks, Sage.

Brown, R.T., Goodman, D., Tieu, L., Ponath, C., Kushel, M. (2016): Pathways to homelessness among older homeless adults: Results from the HOPE HOME study. *PLoS One* 11 (5).

Buckner, J.C. (2004): Psychiatric epidemiology. In: D. Levinson (ed.): *Encyclopedia of Homelessness*. London – Thousand Oaks, Sage.

Bulíček, J. (2005): *Bezdomovectví a závislosti*. Závěrečná zpráva CTV. Ostrava, Filozofická fakulta Ostravské university v Ostravě.

Busch-Geertsema, V., Sahlin, I. (2007): The role of hostels and temporary accommodation. *European Journal of Homelessness*, 1, 67–93.

Caton, C.L., Dominguez, B., Schanzer, B. et al. (2005): Risk factors for long-term homelessness: Findings from a longitudinal study of first-time homeless single adults. *American Journal of Public Health*, 95, 1753–1759.

Caton, C.L., Dominguez, B., Schanzer, B. et al. (2006): Risk factors for long-term homelessness: Findings from a longitudinal study of first-time homeless single adults. *American Journal of Public Health*, 95, 1753–1759.

Caton, L.M., Wilkins, C., Anderson, J. (2007): *People who experience long-term homelessness: Characteristics and interventions.* National Symposium on Homelessness Research.

Cauce, A.M., Paradise, M., Ginzler, J.A. et al. (2000): The characteristics and mental health of homelessness adolescents: Age and gender differences. *Journal of Emotional and Behavioural Disorders*, 8, 230–239.

Chamberlain, C., MacKenzie, D. (1994): Temporal dimensions of youth homelessness. *Australian Journal of Social Issuess.*

Chamberlain, C., Johnson, G. (2011): Pathways into adult homelessness. *Journal of Sociology,* 49, 60–77.

Ciapessoni, F. (2016): Homelessness in Uruguay: A trajectories approach. *European Journal of Homelessness*, 10, 113–130.

Clark, C., Young, S., Barrett, B. (2011): *A transactional model of homelessness and alcoholism?* Developing solutions for complex problems. Louis de la Parte Florida Mental Health Institute, 11/15.

Coates, R.C. (1990): *A street is not a home: Solving America's Homeless Dilemma.* New York – Buffalo, Prometheus Books.

Collins, S.E., Malone, D.K., Larimer, M.E. (2012): Motivation to change and treatment attendance as predictors of alcohol-use outcomes among project-based Housing First residents. *Addictive Behaviours*, 17, 911–919.

Coward-Bucher, C.E. (2008): Toward a needs-based typology of homeless youth. *Journal of Adolescent Health*, 42, 549–554.

Cox, W.M., Yeates, G.N., Gilligan, P.A., Hosler, S.G. (2001): Individual differences. In: Heather, N., Peters, T., Stockwell, T. (eds.): *Alcohol dependence and problems.* Chichester – New York, J. Wiley.

Crane, M., Warnes, A. (2005): Responding to the needs of older homeless people: The effectiveness and limitations of British Services. *Innovation*, 18, 137–152.

Csémy, L., Vágnerová, M., Marek, J. (2011): Duševní poruchy mezi mladými bezdomovci. *Psychiatrie*, 15, 86–92, 2011.

Csémy L. (2018): *Bezdomovectví ve středním věku: analýza kvantitativních dat.* Konference o lidech bez domova. Praha, 30.–31.5. 2018.

Culhane, D.P., Metraux, S., Byrne, T. et al. (2013): The age structure of contemporary homelessness: Evidence and implications for public policy. *Analyses of Social Issues and Policy,* 13.

Daňková H. (2018): *Shrnutí dílčích výsledků šetření lidí bez domova v Praze a v Plzni metodou Respondent Driven Sampling (RDS)*; Konference o lidech bez domova. Praha, 30.–31.5. 2018.

Davies, C. (2010): *Experiences of homelessness: An interpretative phenomenological analysis.* London, Brunel University.

deWall, N.C., Baumeister, R. F. (2006): Alone but feeling no pain: Effects of social exclusion on physical pain, tolerance and pain thresholds, affective forecasting and interpersonal empathy. *Journal of Personality and Social Psychology*, 91, 1–15.

deWall, N.C., Maner, J.K., Rouby, D.A. (2009): Social exclusion and early-stage interpersonal perception: Selective attention to signs of acceptance. *Journal of Personality and Social Psychology*, 96, 729–749, 2009.

Didenko, E., Pankratz, N. (2007): Substance use. Pathways to homelessness? Or a way of adapting to street life? *Visions: BC´s Mental Health and Addictions Journal*, 4, 9–10.

Dietz, T.L. (2009): Drug and alcohol use among homeless older adults. *Journal of Applied Gerontology,* 28,235–255.

Early, D.W. (2005): An empirical investigation of the determinants of street homelessness. *Journal of Housing Economics,* 14, 27–47.

Farrington, A., Robinson, W.P. (1999): Homelessness and strategies of identity maintenance: A participant observation study. *Journal of Community and Applied Social Psychology*, 9, 179–194.

Fazel, S., Khosla, V., Doll, H., Geddes, J. (2008): The prevalence of mental disorders among the homeless in western countries: Systematic review and meta-regression analysis. *PLoS Medicine*, 5.

Fergusson, K.M. (2009): Exploring family environment characteristics and multiple abuse experiences among homeless youth. *Journal of Interpersonal Violence*, 24, 1875–1891.

Fertig, A.R., Reingold, D.A. (2008): Homelessness among at-risk families with children in twenty American cities. *Social Service Review*, 82, 485–510.

Fischer, P.J. (2004): Criminal activity and policing. In: D. Levinson (ed.): *Encyclopedia of Homelessness.* Sage, Thousand Oaks, London.

Fischer, S.N., Shinn, M., Shrout, P., Tsemberis, S. (2008): Homelessness, mental illness, and criminal activity: Examining patterns over time. *American Journal of Community Psychology*, 42, 251–265.

Garibaldi, B., Conde-Martel, A., O´Toole, T.P. (2005): Self-reported comorbidities, perceived needs, and sources for usual care for older and younger homeless adults. *Journal of General Internal Medicine*, 20, 726–730.

Goering, P., Tolomiczenko, G., Sheldon, T., Boydell, K., Wasylenki, D. (2002): Characteristics of persons who are homeless for the first time. *Psychiatric Services*, 53, 1472–1474.

Grenier, A., Barken, R., Sussman, T., Rothwell, D., Lavoie, J.P. (2013): *A Report on Aging and Homelessness.* SSHRS project, Gilbrea Centre for studies in Aging.

Groot, S., Hodgetts, D. (2015): The infamy of begging: A case-based approach to street homelessness and radical commerce. *Qualitative Research in Psychology*, 12, 349–366.

Hartwell, S. (2003): Deviance over the life course: The case of homeless substance abusers. *Substance Use and Misuse*, 38, 475–502.

Hecht, L., Coyle, B. (2001): Elderly homeless: A comparison of older and younger adult emergency shelter seekers in Bakersfield. *American Behavioural Scientist*, 45, 66–79.

Hodgetts, D., Hodgetts, A., Radley, A. (2006): Life in the shadow of the media: Imaging street homelessness in London. *European Journal of Cultural Studies*, 9, 497–516.

Holton, V. (2011): Distinguishing between homeless and unstably housed men on risk factors for homelessness. Virginia Commonwealth University, *VCU Scholars Compass*.

Hradecký, I. a kol. (2012): *Souhrnný materiál pro tvorbu koncepce práce s bezdomovci v ČR na období do roku 2020*. Praha, Ministerstvo práce a sociálních věcí.

Hradecký, I. (2015): *Co znamená pro společnost bezdomovectví?* Konsensuální konference o bezdomovectví v České repulice. Praha, Ministerstvo práce a sociálních věcí.

Huey, L. (2012): *Invisible victims: Homelessness and the growing security gap*. Toronto, University of Toronto Press.

Hutson, S., Liddiard, M. (1994): *Youth Homelessness. The Construction of a Social Issue*. London, Macmillan.

Janebová, R. (1999): Proces vzniku a stadia bezdomovectví. *Sociální práce*, 4, 27–28.

Johnson, T.P., Freels, S.A., Parsons, J.A. et al. (1997): Substance abuse and homelessness: social selection or social adaptation. *Addiction*, 92, 437–445.

Johnson, G., Chamberlain, C. (2008): From youth to adult homelessness. *Australian Journal of Social Issues*, 43, 563–582.

Johnson, G., Chamberlain, C. (2008): Homelessness and substance abuse: Which comes first? *Australian Social Work*, 61, 342–356.

Johnson, G., Gronda, H., Coutts, S. (2008): *On the outside: Pathways in and out of homelessness*. Melbourne, Australian Scholarly Press.

Johnson, G., Chamberlain, C. (2011): Are the homeless mentally ill? *American Journal of Social Issues*, 45, 29–48.

Kanioková M., Ripka Š., Snopek J. (2016): Ukončování bytové nouze a jednotlivců – východiska zahraniční praxe doporučení a strategie. *Platforma pro sociální bydlení*, Brno.

Keys, D., Mallett, S., Rosenthal, D. (2006): Giving up on drugs: Homeless young people and self-reported problematic drug use. *Contemporary Drug Problems*, 33, 63–98.

Kidd, S.A., Davidson, L. (2007): You have to adapt because you have no other choice: The stories of strength and resilience of 208 homeless youth in New York City and Toronto. *Journal of Community Psychology*, 35, 219–238.

Kidd, S., Shahar, G. (2008): Resilience in homeless youth: The key role of self-esteem. *American Journal of Orthopsychiatry,* 78, 163–172.

Kinsela, C. (2012): Re-locating fear on the streets: Homelessness, victimisation and fear of crime. *European Journal of Homelessness*, 6, 121–126.

Koegel, P. (2004): Homelessness. In: D. Levinson (ed.): *Encyclopedia of Homelessness*. Sage.

Koegel, P. (2004): Causes of homelessness: overview. In: D. Levinson (ed.): *Encyclopedia of Homelessness*. Sage.

Kožený, J. (1999): Odhad EPQ/A skórů na podkladě krátké verze WPQ/S. *Československá Psychologie*, 43, 14–19.

Kuchařová, V., Barvíková, J., Peychlová, K., Höhne, S. (2015): *Vyhodnocení dostupných výzkumů a dat o bezdomovectví v ČR a návrhy postupů průběžného získávání klíčových dat*. VÚPSV, Praha.

Kuchařová, V., Janurová, K. (2016): *Velikost a struktura skupin osob bez domova a osob vyloučených z bydlení*. VÚPSV, Praha.

Lankenau, S.E. (1999): Panhandling repertoires and routines for overcoming the person treatment. *Deviant Behaviour: An Interdisciplinary Journal*, 20, 183–206.

Lee, B.A., Farrell, C. R. (2003): Buddy, can you spare a dime? Homelessness, panhandling, and the public. *Urban Affairs Review*, 38, 299–324.

Leufgen, J., Snow, D.A. (2004): Survival strategies. In: D. Levinson (ed.): *Encyclopedia of Homelessness*. London – Thousand Oaks, Sage.

Levinson, D. (ed.) (2004): *Encyclopedia of Homelessness*. London – Thousand Oaks, Sage.

Mabhala, M.A., Ellahi, B., Massey, A., Kingston, P. (2016): Understanding the determinants of homelessness through examining the life stories of homeless people and those who work with them: A qualitative research protocol. *Diversity and Equality in Health and Care*, 13, 284–289.

MacKenzie, D., Chamberlain, C. (2003): *Homeless careers pathways in and out of homelessness*. A report from the counting the homeless 2001.

Mallett, S., Rosenthal, D., Myers, P. et al. (2004): Practising homelessness: a typology approach to young people's daily routines. *Journal of Adolescence*, 27, 337–349.

Mallett, S., Rosenthahl, D., Keays, D. (2005): Young people, drug use and family conflict: Pathways into homelessness. *Journal of Adolescence*, 28, 185–199.

Mallett, S., Rosenthal, D., Keys, D. (2006): Young people, drug use and family conflict: Pathways into homelessness. *Journal of Adolescence*, 28, 185–199.

Mallett, S., Rosenthal, D., Keys, D., Averill, R. (2010): *Moving out, moving on*. London – New York, Routledge.

Mental illness and homelessness (2009), National Coalition for the Homeless, Washington.

Marek J.: *Psychosociální bariéry v reintegraci bezdomovců* (2010). Praha, bakalářská práce, Husitská teologická fakulta Universita Karlova.

Marek, J., Strnad, A., Hotovcová, L. (2012): *Bezdomovectví v kontextu ambulantních sociálních služeb*. Praha, Portál

Marek, J.: *Analýza klientely azylového domu Centra sociálních služb B. Bureše v Praze* (2017), unpublished.

Marek J.: *Jak mladí bezdomovci zvládají vstup do dospělého života?* (2018); Konference o lidech bez domova. Praha, 30.–31.5. 2018.

Marek, J., Skopová, M. (2018): Workshop – *Aplikace výsledků výzkumu v rámci praxe pobytových služeb. Konference o lidech bez domova*. Praha, 30.–31.5. 2018.

Martijn, C., Sharpe, L. (2006): Pathways to youth homelessness. *Social Science and Medicine*, 62, 1–12.

McDonagh, T. (2011): *Tackling homelessness and exclusion*: Understanding complex lives. Joseph Rowntree foundation, UK.

McDonald, L., Degal, J., Cleghorn, L. (2007): Living on the margins. Older homeless adults in Toronto. *Journal of Gerontological Social Work,* 49, 19–46.

McVicar, D., Moschion, J., van Ours, J.C. (2015): From substance use to homelessness or vice versa? *Social Science and Medicine*, 136–137, 89–98.

Mohr, P. (2016): Šílenství, psychóza a schizofrenie: rozštěpená mysl, nebo porucha integrace? In: Horáček, J., Kesner, L., Höschl, C., Španiel, F. et al.: *Mozek a jeho člověk, mysl a její nemoc*. Praha, Galén.

Muňoz, M., Vázquez, C., Bermejo, M., Vázquez, J.J. (1999): Stressful life events among homeless people: Quantita, types, timing and perceived causality. *Journal of Community Psychology*, 27, 73–87.

Neale, J., Brown, C. (2016): We are always in some form of contact: friendships among homeless drug and alcohol users living in hostels. *Health and Social Care in the Community*, 24, 557–566.

Nemiroff, R. (2010): *Beyond rehousing: Community integration of women who have experienced homelessness*. University of Ottawa, Faculty of social sciences.

Newburn, T., Rock, P. (2005): *Living in fear: Violence and Victimisation in the lives of single homeless people*. London, Crisis.

Noom, M.J., de Winter, M., Korf, D. (2008): The care system for homeless youth in the Netherlands: Perceptions of youngsters through a peer research approach. *Adolescence*, 43, 303–316.

North, C.S., Polio, D.E., Smith, E.M., Spitznagel, E.L. (1998): Correlates of early onset and chronicity of homelessness in a large urban homeless population. *Journal of Nervous and Mental Disease,* 186, 393–400.

Orwin R.G., Garrison-Mogren, P., Jacobs, M.I., Sonnfeld, L.J. (1999): Retention of homeless clients in substance abuse treatment. Finding from the National Institute on Alcohol Abuse and Alcoholism Cooperative Agreement Program. *Journal of Substance Abuse Treatment*, 17, 45–66.

Osborn, M., Smith, J.A. (2008): Interpretative phenomenological analysis. In: J.A. Smith (ed.): *Qualitative Psychology: A practical guide to method*. London, Sage.

Osborne, R.E. (2002): I may be homeless, but I'm not helpless: The costs and benefits of identifying with homelessness. *Self and Identity*, 1, 43–52.

Panadero, S., Guillén, A.I., Vázquez, J.J. (2015): Report on the street: Overall happiness among homeless people in Madrid. *American Journal of Orthopsychiatry*, 85, 326–330.

Pěnkava, P. (2010): Výchovně vzdělávací prvek v sociální práci s cílovou skupinou osob bez přístřeší. Rigorózní práce, Praha, Univerzita Karlova.

Pěnkava, P. (2015): *Zaměstnávání lidí bez domova*. Konsensuální konference o bezdomovectví v České repulice. Praha, Ministerstvo práce a sociálních věcí.

Pěnkava, P. (2018): *Senioři. Sociální aspekty stárnutí u osob bez domova*. Konference o lidech bez domova. Praha, 30.–31.5. 2018.

Pěnkava, P., Schneiderová, J. (2018): Workshop – *Aplikace výsledků výzkumu v rámci praxe pomoci úřadům*. Konference o lidech bez domova. Praha, 30.–31.5. 2018.

Pickett, C.L., Gardner, W.L., Knowles, M. (2004): Getting a cue. The need to belong and enhanced sensitivity to social cues. *Personality and Social Psychology*, 30, 1095–1107.

Pillinger, J. (2007): *Homeless pathways*. Focus, Ireland.

Prudký, L. (2015): *Humanistický a otevřený přístup jako jediný pramen řešení bezdomovectví*. Konsensuální konference o bezdomovectví v České repulice. Praha, Ministerstvo práce a sociálních věcí.

Raleigh-DuRoff, C. (2004): Factors that influence homeless adolescent to leave or stay living on the street. *Child and Adolescent Social Work Journal*, 21, 561–572.

Rank, M.R., Williams, J.H. (2010): A life course approach to understanding poverty among older American adults. *Families in Society*, 9, 337–341.

Ravenhill, M.H. (2014): *The culture of homelessness: An ethnographic study*. London, School of Economics.

Renedo, A., Jovchelovitch, S. (2007): Expert knowledge, cognitive polyphasia and health: representations of homelessness among professionals working in the voluntary sector in London. *Journal of Health Psychology*, 12, 779–785.

Rhoades, H., Wenzel, S.L., Golinelli, D., Tucker, J.S. et al. (2011): The social context of homeless men´s substence use. *Drug and Alcohol Dependence,* 118, 320–325.

Robert, M., Pauzé. R., Fournier, I. (2005): Factors associated with homeless of adolescents under supervision of the youth protection system. *Journal of Adolescence*, 28, 213–230.

Rokach, A. (1998): Private lives in public places: Loneliness of the homeless. *Social Indicators Research*, 72, 99–114.

Rosenbeck, M.M., Morrisey, J., Lam, J. et al. (1998): Service system integration access and housing outcomes in a program for homeless persons with severe mental illness. *American Journal of Public Health*, 88, 1610–1615.

Rowland, L. (2011): *Looking through the eyes of a homeless prisoner, exploring homeless offender´s perspective on their transition from custody to community*. Dublin, Institute of Technology.

Sadock, B.J., Sadock, V.A. (2007): *Synopsis of psychiatry: Behavioural sciences/clinical psychiatry* (10. ed.). Philadelphia, Lippincott, Williams and Wilkins.

Salomonsen-Sautel, S., Van Leeuwen, J.M., Gilroy, C. et al. (2008): Correlates of substance use among homeless youths in eight cities. *American Journal of Addictions*, 17, 224–234.

Sanders, B., Brown, B. (2015): *I was all on my own: experiences of loneliness and isolation amongst homeless people*. London, Crisis.

Shelton, K.H., Taylor, P.J., Bonner, A., van den Bree, M. (2009): Risk factors of homelessness: Evidence from a population based study. *Psychiatric Services*, 60, 465–472.

Shier, M.I, Jones, M.E., Graham, J.R. (2010): Perspectives of employed people experiencing homelessness of self and being homeless: Challenging socially constructed perception and stereotypes. *Journal of Sociology and Social Welfare*, 37, 13–37.

Snow, D.A., Anderson, L. (1993): *A study of homeless street people*. Los Angeles, University of California Press.

Stein, J.A., Dixon, E.L., Nyamathi, A. M. (2008): Effects of psychosocial and situational variables on substance abuse among homeless adults. *Psychology of Addict Behaviour*, 22, 410–416.

Stergiopoulos, V., Herrmann, N. (2003): Old and homeless: A review and survey of older adults who use shelters in a Urban setting. *Canadian Journal of Psychiatry*, 48, 374–380.

Strnad A., Strnadová P. (2018): Workshop – *Aplikace výsledků výzkumu v rámci praxe terénních programů*. Konference o lidech bez domova. Praha, 30.–31.5. 2018.

Sullivan, G., Burnam, A., Koegel, P. (2000): Pathways to homelessness among the mentally ill. *Social Psychiatry and Psychiatric Epidemiology*, 35, 444–450.

Štěchová, M., Luptáková, M., Kopoldová, B. (2008): *Bezdomovectví a bezdomovci z pohledu kriminologie*. Praha, IKSP.

Štěchová, M. (2009): Bezdomovci a vybrané sociálně patologické jevy. *Kriminalistika*, 4, 265–277.

Štěpánová H., Vondruška O. (2018): Workshop – *Aplikace výsledků výzkumu v rámci praxe nízkoprahových denních center*. Konference o lidech bez domova. Praha, 30.–31.5. 2018.

Šupková, D. (2008): Závislost jako jeden z aspektů života bezdomovců. *Adiktologie*, 8, 44–51.

Teesson, M., Hodder, T., Buhrich, N. (2003): Alcohol and other drug use disorders among homeless people in Australia. *Substance Use and Misuse*, 38, 463–474.

Thompson, A.J., Maccio, E.M., Desselle, S.K., Zittel-Palamara, K. (2007): Predictors of posttraumatic symptoms among runaway youth utilizing two service sectors. *Journal of Traumatic Stress*, 20, 553–563.

Tually, S., Faulkner, D., Cutler, C., Slatter, M. (2008): *Women, domestic and family violence and homelessness*. Flinders University.

Twenge, J.M., Baumeister, R.F., DeWall, N. et al. (2007): Social exclusion decreases prosocial behaviour. *Journal o Personality and Social Psychology*, 92, 56–66.

Tyler, K.A. (2006): A qualitative study of early family histories and transitions of homeless youth. *Journal of Interpersonal Violence*, 21, 1385–1393.

Vágnerová, M., Csémy, L., Marek, J. (2012): Osobnost mladých bezdomovců. *Psychiatrie*, 16, 9–14.

Vágnerová, M., Csémy, L., Marek, J. (2013): *Bezdomovectví jako alternativní existence mladých lidí*. Praha, Karolinum.

Vágnerová, M. (2014): *Současná psychopatologie pro pomáhající profese*. Praha, Portál.

Vágnerová, M., Marek, J., Csémy, L. (2017): Mezilidské vztahy mladých bezdomovců a jejich vliv na další život. *Psychiatrie*, 21, 66–71.

Vágnerová, M., Marek, J., Csémy, L. (2017): Osobnostní faktory ovlivňující setrvání v bezdomovectví u mladých lidí. *Sociální práce*, 17, 41–54.

Vágnerová, M., Marek, J., Csémy, L. (2018): Narativní analýza role alkoholu v životních příbězích bezdomovců-mužů. *Česká a slovenská psychiatrie*, 114, 2, 53–59.

Vágnerová M. (2018): *Jací jsou lidé bez domova ve středním věku*. Konference o lidech bez domova. Praha, 30.–31.5. 2018.

Van den Bree, M., Shelton, K., Bonner, A. et al. (2009): A longitudinal population-based study of factors in adolescence predicting homelessness in young adulthood. *Journal of Adolescence Health*, 45, 571–578.

Votta, E., Manion, I. (2003): Factors in the psychological adjustment of homeless adolescent males: The role of coping style. *Child and Adolescent Psychiatry*, 42, 778–785.

Wenzel, S.L., Burmam, M.A., Koegel, P. et al. (2001): Access to inpatient or residential substance abuse treatment among homeless adults with alcohol or other drug use disorder. *Medical Care*, 39, 1158–1169.

Whitbeck, L.B. (2009): *Mental health and emerging adulthood among homeless young people.* New York – Hove, Psychology Press.

Williams, S., Stickley, T. (2010): Stories from the streets: people's experiences of homelessness. *Journal of Psychiatry and Mental Health Nursery*, 18, 432–439.

Wong, Y.I., Pilliavin, I. (1997): A dynamic analysis of homeless-domicile transitions. *Social Problems*, 44, 408–423.

Wong, Y.I., Pilliavin, I. (2001): Stressors, resources, and distress among homeless persons: A longitudinal analysis. *Social Sciences and Medicine*, 52, 1029–1042.

Zákon č. 108/2006 Sb. o sociálních službách.

Zugazaga, C. (2004): Stressful life event experiences of homeless adults: A comparison of single men, single women, and women with children. *Journal of Community Psychology*, 32, 643–654.

Marie Vágnerová / Jakub Marek / Ladislav Csémy

HOMELESSNESS AMONG
OLDER ADULTS IN PRAGUE

CAUSES, CONTEXTS AND PROSPECTS

Published by Charles University, Karolinum Press
Ovocný trh 560/5, 116 36 Prague 1, Czech Republic
www.karolinum.cz
Prague 2020
English translation by Phil Jones
Copyedited by Martin Janeček
Cover by Anna Issa Šotolová, layout by Jan Šerých
Documentary photo by Martin Pokora
Typesetting and print by Karolinum Press
First English edition

ISBN 978-80-246-4525-4
ISBN 978-80-246-4526-1 (pdf)